Gospel Origins
& Christian
Beginnings

FORUM
FASCICLES

PUBLISHED VOLUMES

1. *Gospel Origins and Christian Beginnings,* edited by James E. Goehring, Charles W. Hedrick, and Jack T. Sanders, with Hans Dieter Betz

2. *Gnosticism and the Early Christian World,* edited by James E. Goehring, Charles W. Hedrick, and Jack T. Sanders, with Hans Dieter Betz

GOSPEL ORIGINS & CHRISTIAN BEGINNINGS

IN HONOR OF JAMES M. ROBINSON

EDITED BY
JAMES E. GOEHRING
CHARLES W. HEDRICK
JACK T. SANDERS
WITH HANS DIETER BETZ

SONOMA, CALIFORNIA
POLEBRIDGE PRESS
1990

Design & composition: Polebridge Press, Sonoma, California
Cover: Helen Melnis Cherullo
Printing & binding: McNaughton & Gunn, Inc., Saline, Michigan
Display & text type: Plantin

Library of Congress Cataloging-in-Publication Data
Gospel origins and Christian beginnings : in honor of James M.
   Robinson / edited by James E. Goehring [et al.].
      p. cm. — (Forum fascicles)
   Includes bibliographical references.
   ISBN 0-944344-15-1 : $29.95
    1. Bible. N.T. Gospels—Criticism, interpretation, etc.
   2. Jesus Christ—History of doctrines—Early church, ca. 30–600.
   3. Bible. N.T. Epistles of Paul—Criticism, interpretation, etc.
   4. Christianity—Origin. 5. Robinson, James McConkey, 1924–   .
   I. Goehring, James E., 1950–   . II. Robinson, James McConkey,
   1924–   . III. Series.
   BS2555.2.G615   1990
   226'.06–dc20   89–77964
                                          CIP

Printed in the United States of America

Contents

Contributors

Harold W. Attridge is Professor of Theology at the University of Notre Dame, Notre Dame, IN.

Hans Dieter Betz is Professor of New Testament in the University of Chicago Divinity School and in the Department of New Testament and Early Christian Literature of the Division of the Humanities at the University of Chicago, Chicago, IL.

Kathleen E. Corley is Instructor of Religious Studies at Sioux Falls College, Sioux Falls, SD.

Stephen Emmel is a Ph.D. candidate at Yale University, New Haven, CT.

Thomas W. Gillespie is President of the Princeton Theological Seminary, Princeton, NJ.

James E. Goehring is Assistant Professor of Religion at Mary Washington College, Fredericksburg, VA.

Charles W. Hedrick is Professor of Religious Studies at Southwest Missouri State University, Springfield, MO.

Arland D. Jacobson is Director of the CHARIS Ecumenical Center at Concordia College, Moorhead, MN.

Karen L. King is Assistant Professor of Religious Studies at Occidental College, Los Angeles, CA.

John S. Kloppenborg is Associate Professor of Theology at the University of St. Michael's College, Toronto, Ont.

Helmut Koester is John H. Morrison Professor of New Testament Studies and Winn Professor of Ecclesiastical History at the Harvard Divinity School, Cambridge, MA.

Burton L. Mack is Professor of Religion at the Claremont Graduate School and Professor of New Testament at the School of Theology at Claremont, Claremont, CA.

Luther H. Martin is Professor of Religion at the University of Vermont, Burlington, VT.

Marvin W. Meyer is Associate Professor of Religion at Chapman College, Orange, CA.

Douglas M. Parrott is Professor of Religious Studies at the University of California, Riverside, in Riverside, CA.

Birger A. Pearson is Professor of Religious Studies at the University of California, Santa Barbara, in Santa Barbara, CA.

Petr Pokorný is Professor of New Testament in the Comenius Faculty of Protestant Theology, Prague, Czechoslovakia.

Gesine Robinson is a graduate student at the University of California, Riverside, in Riverside, CA, where she also teaches German.

Jack T. Sanders is Professor of Religious Studies at the University of Oregon, Eugene, OR.

John H. Sieber is Professor of Religion at Luther College, Decorah, IA.

Kathleen O'Brien Wicker is Professor of Religion at the Claremont Graduate School and at Scripps College, Claremont, CA.

Vincent L. Wimbush is Associate Professor of Religion at the Claremont Graduate School and Associate Professor of New Testament at the School of Theology at Claremont, Claremont, CA.

Antoinette Clark Wire is Professor of New Testament at the San Francisco Theological Seminary, San Anselmo, CA.

Frederik W. Wisse is Professor of New Testament, Faculty of Religious Studies, at McGill University, Montreal, Qué.

Greetings to the Honoré

James M. Robinson, most esteemed mentor and colleague:

With these volumes a group of your former students, Claremont colleagues, and other professional associates wish to honor you on the occasion of your sixty-fifth birthday, on 30 June 1989. From the days when you decided to stay at Claremont (instead of going elsewhere) and "build a program," through your long and thorough and so very productive labor on the Nag Hammadi Library, to your return to your even earlier interest in the Jesus tradition, you have helped and inspired us all. What you have been able to accomplish, by unflagging zeal and diplomatic negotiation, makes a fine study in the "art of the impossible." Your example, your enthusiasm, and your encouragement have helped all of us to make our own ways forward in the study of antiquity and Christianity. We are grateful to you for your creative leadership in international scholarship in our discipline. It is our expectation that your unflagging energy, meticulous scholarship, and steady pursuit of knowledge will continue to provide you—and through you us—with new insights in the years ahead.

Organization of this work began with a broad focus; potential contributors were asked to write on some "enduring problem" in the study of antiquity and Christianity. The results are, we think, indicative of the range of your interests. Burton Mack, Dieter Betz, John Kloppenborg, and Helmut Koester have taken up desiderata in the pursuit of the wily Q. Mack pursues further a theme with which he has been concerned recently, that of Jesus the sage revealed behind the sayings tradition. Betz reviews the history of scholarship on the Sermon on the Mount/Sermon on the Plain and determines that Matthew and Luke had access to separate Q traditions. Kloppenborg looks at the theory that Q presented a radicalized interpretation of Torah and decides that such was not the case for the earliest, formative stage of Q; the "nomocentric" stage of Q comes, rather, near the end of Q's evolution. Koester investigates the relation of Q to other sayings traditions contained in the Gospel of Thomas and in 1 Corinthians and finds the relationship to be complex. Koester's essay is followed by a contribution from John Sieber, who also takes up the relation of Thomas to the canonical gospels and drives home the point that Thomas is not dependent on the canonical gospels, but preserves an independent sayings tradition.

Charles W. Hedrick, Marvin Meyer, Petr Pokorný, and Douglas Parrott address a variety of further issues in the study of the gospels. Hedrick applies literary criticism to the gospel of John and finds that one need not resort to the theory of a redactor to explain the frequent corrective asides that occur in that gospel. Meyer finds traits of the Secret Gospel of Mark that, together with hints in canonical Mark and Lazarus and the beloved disciple in John, may point to an early aretalogical witness tradition. Pokorný sees in Luke-Acts a social programme of shared possessions based on Luke's theology of the presence of Christ in the congregation. Parrott asks why early Christianity developed the doctrine that the Holy Spirit could only be bestowed after Jesus' departure from earth, and what the early effects of that doctrine were. He concludes that while both John the Baptist and Jesus probably did bestow the Spirit on their followers, the later church found it necessary to emphasize the uniqueness of Jesus and thus to move the time of the Spirit to the time after Jesus.

Antoinette Wire, Thomas Gillespie, and Frederik Wisse take up important issues in the letters of Paul. Both Wire and Gillespie focus their attention on the prophets in 1 Corinthians, where Wire sees that Paul's attempt to keep women in a subordinate position in Corinth is part and parcel of his attempt to control charismatic phenomena, and where Gillespie shows that the Pauline concept of the bestowal of wisdom in chap. 2 is integrally related to Paul's views about prophecy in chaps. 12–14. Wisse takes a hard look at the way in which scholars find editorial interpolations in Paul's letters and decides that such findings are normally not adequately justified.

Karen King, Luther Martin, Gesine Robinson, Jack Sanders, and Birger Pearson deal in one way or another with the Coptic Gnostic Library (aside from the gospel issues related to the Gospel of Thomas). King analyzes in detail the spectrum of use of female imagery in the *Hypostasis of the Archons*. She shows that the ambiguity of female existence lent its imagery to gnostic interpretations of the human situation. Martin applies sociological perspectives to the *Apocalypse of Adam* and determines that the mythical genealogy of the gnostic work is an attempt to provide a kinship framework for the gnostic community's self-understanding. (Thus in King's essay we have an example of insight proceeding from social situation to myth, in Martin's essay an example of movement in the opposite direction.) Robinson pursues further her earlier study of the *Trimorphic Protennoia,* here in the context of a discussion with recent treatments of that work, and proposes that both the gnostic text and the prologue of the Gospel of John derive from the same gnosticized wisdom tradition. Sanders applies observations regarding the *Trimorphic Protennoia* to his earlier study of the New Testament christological hymns and finds that all, along with the Odes of Solomon, share the same gnosticized wisdom matrix. He then employs models from modern evolutionary theory to try to explain the developmental relationships that he has described. Pearson puts canonical 2 Peter, an anti-gnostic work, together with the gnostic Apocalypse of Peter and determines that, curiously enough, the gnostic author of the Apocalypse of Peter has used 2 Peter as a source, misappropriating some of its language to reverse its original intent.

Arland Jacobson looks at the wisdom tradition from a cultural-anthropological perspective and proposes that the biblical proverbial tradition, before it became fixed as collections of bits of didactic advice, served to control potentially hostile situations by attempting to bring about agreement with seemingly arcane tradition. Vincent Wimbush examines the ideal of moderation in ancient Greece and ascertains that it was a cultivated, aristocratic, male virtue that also had to do with control, either of the household or of the state.

Harold Attridge and Kathleen Wicker take up the relation of paganism to Christianity. Attridge finds that the heart of the Christian myth of Christ's descent into hell is an appropriation of the Herakles myth of liberating death's captives; and Wicker makes a comparison between Christians and Neoplatonists in the matter of sexual abstinence and the association of the sexes and shows that Neoplatonist leaders seemed to have more confidence in—and perhaps concern for—unmarried women under their spiritual care than did contemporary Christian leaders.

James Goehring and Stephen Emmel, finally, investigate early Christian Egypt. Goehring shows that the early monks who went into the wilderness could not have survived had they not maintained regular commercial and social contacts with the society that they had ostensibly left; and Emmel engages in academic detective work to piece together what can be known of the manuscript library of a later Egyptian Christian monastery.

We hope that these essays will provide you with a few hours of contented reading. Further, we also hope that they will serve to focus scholarly discussion on a few thorny topics, and that they will help both to clarify some of the currents issues in the study of antiquity and Christianity and to exemplify how those issues need to be addressed. We take this opportunity to thank Rod Parrott for supplying the ancient literature indices and Stephen J. Patterson for writing the biographical sketch.

Alles für die Wissenschaft!

The Editors
James E. Goehring
Charles W. Hedrick
Jack T. Sanders

James M. Robinson following the advice in the Greek inscription above him: "Search the Scriptures" (Photograph by Arthur Dubinsky)

James M. Robinson

A BIBLIOGRAPHY

Prepared by Kathleen E. Corley

Books Edited

The Later Heidegger and Theology. New Frontiers in Theology: Discussions among German and American Theologians, Vol. 1. Eds. James M. Robinson and John B. Cobb, Jr. New York, Evanston, and London: Harper and Row, 1963. Reprint edition. Westport, CT: Greenwood Press, 1979.

"The German Discussion of the Later Heidegger." In *The Later Heidegger and Theology*, pp. 3–76.

Der spätere Heidegger und die Theologie. Neuland in der Theologie: Ein Gespräch zwischen amerikanischen und europäischen Theologen, Vol. 1. Eds. James M. Robinson and John B. Cobb, Jr. Trans. Eberhard Fincke. Zürich and Stuttgart: Zwingli, 1965.

"Die deutsche Auseinandersetzung mit dem spateren Heidegger." In *Der spätere Heidegger und die Theologie*, pp. 15–93.

The New Hermeneutic. New Frontiers in Theology: Discussions among Continental and American Theologians, Vol. 2. Edited by James M. Robinson and John B. Cobb, Jr. New York, Evanston, and London: Harper and Row, 1964.

"Hermeneutic since Barth." In *The New Hermeneutic*, pp. 1–77. Abridged Korean translation: "Hermeneutics since Barth." Trans. Yong Ok Kim. *Theology and Modern Times* 2 (1966): 184–222. Italian translation: "L'ermeneutica da Karl Barth ai giorni nostri." Trans. Giovanni Torti. In *La nuova ermeneutica*, pp. 7–98. Ed. Antonio Ornella. Biblioteca di cultura religiosa. Brescia: Paideia, 1967.

Die neue Hermeneutik. Neuland in der Theologie: Ein Gespräch zwischen amerikanischen und europäischen Theologen, Vol. 2. Eds. James M. Robinson and John B. Cobb, Jr. Trans. Eberhard Fincke. Zürich and Stuttgart: Zwingli, 1965.

"Hermeneutik seit Karl Barth." In *Die neue Hermeneutik*, pp. 13–108.

Theology as History. New Frontiers in Theology: Discussions among Continental and American Theologians, Vol. 3. Eds. James M. Robinson and John B. Cobb, Jr. New York, Evanston, and London: Harper and Row, 1967.

"Revelation as Word and as History." In *Theology as History*, pp. 1–100.

Theologie als Geschichte. Neuland in der Theologie: Ein Gespräch zwischen amerikanischen und europäischen Theologen, Vol. 3. Eds. James M. Robinson and John B. Cobb, Jr. Trans. Eberhard Fincke. Zürich and Stuttgart: Zwingli, 1967.

"Offenbarung als Wort und als Geschichte." In *Theologie als Geschichte*, pp. 11–134.

The Beginnings of Dialectic Theology, Vol. 1. Ed. James M. Robinson. Richmond, VA: John Knox, 1968.

"Introduction." To *The Beginnings of Dialectic Theology*, 9–30; "Die ersten heterodoxen Barthianer." In *Die Theologie zwischen Gestern und Morgen: Interpretationen und Anfragen zum Werk Karl Barths*, pp. 3–37. Eds. Wilhelm Dantine and Kurt Lüthi. Trans. Karlhermann Bergner. Munich: Christian Kaiser, 1968.

Trajectories through Early Christianity. Eds. Helmut Koester and James M. Robinson. Philadelphia: Fortress Press, 1971; paperback edition, 1979.

"The Dismantling and Reassembling of the Categories of New Testament Scholarship," pp. 1–19; "Kergyma and History in the New Testament," pp. 20–70; "LOGOI SOPHON: On the Gattung of Q," pp. 71–113; "The Johannine Trajectory," pp. 232–268. Pages 1–16 were published in revised form as "The Dismantling and Reassembling of the Categories of New Testament Scholarship." *Interpretation* 25 (January 1971): 63–77. Pages 235–38, 242–52 were republished in revised form as "The Miracles Source of John." *Journal of the American Academy of Religion* 39 (September 1971): 339–48. Japanese translation by Hisao Kayama. Tokyo: Shinkyo Shuppansha Pub. Co., 1975.

Entwicklungslinien durch die Welt des frühen Christentums, by Helmut Koester and James M. Robinson. Tübingen: J.C.B. Mohr (Paul Siebeck), 1971.

"Demontage und neuer Aufbau der Kategorien neutestamentlicher Wissenschaft," pp. 1–19; "Kerygma und Geschichte im Neuen Testament," pp. 20–66; "LOGOI SOPHON–Zur Gattung der Spruchquelle Q," pp. 67–106; "Die johanneische Entwicklungslinie," pp. 216–50.

The Future of Our Religious Past: Essays in Honour of Rudolf Bultmann. London: SCM; Evanston, New York and London: Harper and Row, 1971.

"Preface," pp. i–iii; "Introduction," pp. 1–5 *Religion and the Humanizing of Man: Plenary Addresses, International Congress of Learned Societies in the Field of Religion*. Ed. James M. Robinson. The Council on the Study of Religion, 1972; 2d ed., 1973.

The Facsimile Edition of the Nag Hammadi Codices. Eds. James M. Robinson, et al. E.J. Brill, 1972–1984.

Introduction, 1984. "Acknowledgements," pp. xv–xix. Arabic trans. Victor Girgis, pp. xiv–xviii. "Introduction," pp. 1–102; "Addenda et Corrigenda" (with Stephen Emmel), pp. 103–33.

Codex I, 1977. "Preface," pp. vii, ix, xi, xiii, xv, xvii, xix, xxi, xxiii, xxv, xxvii, xxix, xxxi. Arabic trans. Victor Girgis, pp. vi, viii, x, xii, xiv, xvi, xviii, xx, xxii, xxiv, xxvi.

Codex II, 1974. "Preface," pp. vii, ix, xi, xiii, xv, xvii, xix. Arabic trans. Victor Girgis, pp. vi, viii, x, xii, xiv, xvi.

Codex III, 1976. "Preface," pp. vii, ix, xi, xiii, xv, xvii, xix. Arabic trans. Victor Girgis, pp. vi, viii, x, xii, xiv, xvi, xviii, xx.

Codex IV, 1975. "Preface," pp. vii, ix, xi,xiii, xv. Arabic trans. Victor Girgis, pp. vi, viii, x, xii, xiv, xvi.

Codex V, 1974. "Preface," pp. vii, ix, xi, xiii, xv. Arabic trans. Victor Girgis, pp. vi, viii, x, xii, xiv, xvi.

Codex VI, 1972. "Preface," pp. vii, ix, xi. Arabic trans. Victor Girgis, pp. vi, viii, x.

Codex VII, 1972. "Preface," pp. vii, ix, xi, xiii. Arabic trans. Victor Girgis, pp. vi, viii, x, xii.

Codex VIII, 1976. "Preface," pp. vii, ix, xi, xiii, xv, xvii, xix, xxi. Arabic trans. Victor Girgis, pp. vi, viii, x, xii, xiv, xvi, xviii, xx, xxii, xxiv.

Codices IX and X, 1977. "Preface," pp. vii, ix, xi, xiii, xv, xvii, xix, xxi, xxiii, xxv, xxvii. Arabic trans. Victor Girgis, pp. vi, viii, x, xii, xiv, xvi, xviii. xviii.

Codex XI, XII and XIII, 1973. "Preface," pp. vii, ix, xi, xiii, xv, xvii, xviii. Arabic trans. Victor Girgis, pp. vi, viii, x, xii, xiv, xvi.

Cartonnage, 1979. "Preface," pp. vii, ix, xi, xiii, xv, xvii, xix, xxi, xxiii. Arabic trans. Victor Girgis, pp. vi, viii, x, xii, xiv.

Nag Hammadi Library in English. Translated by members of the Coptic Gnostic Library Project of the Institute for Antiquity and Christianity, James M. Robinson, Director. Leiden: E.J. Brill, 1977, paperback edition 1984; San Francisco: Harper & Row, 1977, paperback edition 1981. Pp. 1–25. 3d rev. ed. 1988.

"Introduction," pp. 1–25; 3d ed., pp. 1–26.

"The Three Steles of Seth (VII, 5)." Introduction and trans., pp. 362–67; 3d ed., pp. 396–401.

The Chester Beatty Codex Ac 1390: Mathematical School Exercises in Greek and John 10:7–13:38 in Subachmimic. Eds. William Brashear, Wolf-Peter Funk, James M. Robinson and Richard Smith. Chester Beatty Monographs No. 13. Leuven and Paris: Peeters, in the press.

"Acknowledgements," and "Introduction."

Books

Das Problem des Heiligen Geistes bei Wilhelm Herrmann. Marburg an der Lahn: Karl Gleiser Inhaber der R. Friedrichs Universitäts-Buchdruckerei, 1952.

The Problem of History in Mark. Studies in Biblical Theology, Vol. 21. London: SCM, 1957; Naperville, IL: Alec R. Allenson, 1957; reimpressions, London: SCM, 1962, 1968, 1971. Reprinted in *The Problem of History in Mark and other Marcan Studies*, pp. 54–143. Philadelphia: Fortress Press, 1982.

Das Geschichtsverständnis des Markus-Evangeliums. Trans. Karlfried Fröhlich. Abhandlungen zur Theologie des Alten und Neuen Testaments, Vol. 30. Zürich: Zwingli-Verlag, 1956. Reprint of Chapter 4, "Geschichte seit dem Jahr 30 n. Chr. im Markus-Evangelium." In *Das Markus-Evangelium*, Darmstadt: Wissenschaftliche Buchgesellschaft, 1979.

A New Quest of the Historical Jesus. Studies in Biblical Theology, Vol. 25. London: SCM, 1959; Naperville, IL: Alec R. Allenson, 1959; reimpressions, London: SCM, 1961, 1963, 1965, 1968; London: Lewis Reprints, 1970; Missoula, MT: Scholars Press, 1979, with a new "Foreword to the Reprint," pp. 6–8. Reprinted in *A New Quest of the Historical Jesus and Other Essays*, pp. 9–125. Philadelphia: Fortress Press, 1983. Enlarged German edition, *Kerygma und historischer Jesus.* Trans. Heinz-Dieter Knigge. Zürich and Stuttgart: Zwingli, 1960; 2d rev. enlarged German ed., 1967. French trans. 1st German ed., *Le kerygme de l'église et le Jésus de l'histoire.* Trans. Etienne de Peyer. Nouvelle série théologique, Vol. 11. Geneva: Labor et Fides, 1961. Revision of pp. 149–74 of the first German edition appeared as "The Formal Structure of Jesus' Message." In *Current Issues in New Testament Interpretation: Essays in Honor of Otto A. Piper*, pp. 91–110, 273–84. Edited by William Klassen and Graydon F. Snyder. New York: Harper and Brothers, 1962. Slightly revised reprint in *A New Quest of the Historical Jesus and Other Essays*, pp. 126–52. Philadelphia: Fortress Press, 1983. Excerpt from pp. 58–82 of the 2d German ed. published in Korean with the title "The Debate Between Bultmann and His Pupils." Translated by Kyung Yun Chun. *Theological Studies* (Seoul) 9 (1965): 176–98. Reprint of "A New Concept of History and the Self," pp. 66–72 of the English ed. In *In Search of the Historical Jesus*, pp. 153–58. Ed. Harvey K. McArthur. New York: Charles Scribner's Sons, 1969.

Articles

"A Spy's Eye View of Our Church." *The Presbyterian Outlook* 127 (December 3, 1945): 7.

"The Witness of Paul: Christ the Lord." In *Who Say Ye That I Am? Six Theses on the Deity of Christ*, pp. 131–45. Ed. William Childs Robinson. Grand Rapids, MI: William B. Eerdmans, 1949.

"Jesus' Understanding of History." *The Journal of Bible and Religion* 23 (January 1955): 17–24.

"The Academic Roots of Dialectic Theology." The Emory University *Quarterly* 11 (March 1955): 41–51.

"Mark's Understanding of History." *Scottish Journal of Theology* 9 (December 1956): 393–409.

"The Historical Jesus and the Church's Kerygma." *Religion in Life* 26 (Winter 1956–57): 40–49.

"A Formal Analysis of Col. 1,15–20." *Journal of Biblical Literature* 76 (December 1957): 270–287.

"The Quest of the Historical Jesus Today." *Theology Today* 15 (July 1958): 183–97.

"The Radicality of Christianity," *Religion in Life* 28 (Summer 1959): 406–12. Republished in condensed form with the title "The Radicality of the Ministry." *Perspective: Southern California School of Theology Bulletin* 2 (January 1959): 3.

"New Testament Faith Today." *The Journal of Bible and Religion* 27 (July 1959): 233–42.

"The Biblical View of the World: A Theological Evaluation." *Encounter* 20 (Fall 1959): 470–83.

"The Bible Today; 2. The Historical Question: New Testament Scholars Engage in a New Quest for the Historical Jesus." *The Christian Century* 76 (October 21, 1959): 1207–10. Slightly revised and reprinted as "The Historical Question." In *New Directions in Biblical Thought*, pp. 73–94. Ed. Martin E. Marty. Reflection Book. New York: Association Press, 1960.

"Basic Shifts in German Theology." *Interpretation* 16 (January 1962): 76–97.

"The Historicality of Biblical Language." In *The Old Testament and Christian Faith*, pp. 124–58. Ed. Bernhard W. Anderson. New York, Evanston and London: Harper and Row, 1963; paperback ed., New York: Herder and Herder, 1969. German trans. "Heilsgeschichte und Lichtungsgeschichte." Translated by Werner Krämer. *Evangelische Theologie* 22 (March 1962): 113–41.

"The Sacraments in Corinth." *Journal of the Interseminary Movement of the Southwest* (1962): 19–32.

"The Recent Debate on the 'New Quest.'" *The Journal of Bible and Religion* 30 (July 1962): 198–208. Slightly revised reprint in *A New Quest of the Historical Jesus and Other Essays*, pp. 153–71.

"Ascension." In *The Interpreter's Dictionary of the Bible*. Vol. 1, pp. 245–47. Ed. George Arthur Buttrick, et al. New York and Nashville: Abingdon, 1962.

"Descent into Hades." In *The Interpreter's Dictionary of the Bible*, Vol. 1, pp. 826–28. Ed. George Arthur Buttrick, et al. New York and Nashville: Abingdon, 1962.

"New Birth." In *The Interpreter's Dictionary of the Bible*, Vol. 3, p. 543. Ed. George Arthur Buttrick, et al. New York and Nashville: Abingdon, 1962.

"New Man." In *The Interpreter's Dictionary of the Bible*, Vol. 3, p. 543. Ed. George Arthur Buttrick, et al. New York and Nashville: Abingdon, 1962.

"Quick, Quicken." In *The Interpreter's Dictionary of the Bible*, Vol. 3, p. 975. Ed. George Arthur Buttrick, et al. New York and Nashville: Abingdon, 1962.

"Regeneration." In *The Interpreter's Dictionary of the Bible*, Vol. 4, pp. 24–29. Ed. George Arthur Buttrick, et al. New York and Nashville: Abingdon, 1962.

"Restoration." In *The Interpreter's Dictionary of the Bible*, Vol. 4, pp. 38–39. Ed. George Arthur Buttrick, et al. New York and Nashville: Abingdon, 1962.

"Geburt Jesu." In *Biblisch-Historisches Handwörterbuch*, Vol. 1, p. 528. Ed. Bo Reicke and Leonhard Rost. Göttingen: Vandenhoeck und Ruprecht, 1962.

"Preaching." In *Dictionary of the Bible*, pp. 789–91. Ed. James Hastings; rev. ed., Eds. Frederick C. Grant and H. H. Rowley. New York: Charles Scribner's Sons, 1963.

"Theology as Translation." *Theology Today* 20 (January 1964): 518–27.

"Interpretation of Scripture in Biblical Studies Today." In *Ecumenical Dialogue at Harvard: The Roman Catholic-Protestant Colloquium,* pp. 91–109. Ed. Samuel H. Miller and G. Ernest Wright. Cambridge, MA: Belknap Press of Harvard University Press, 1964.

"LOGOI SOPHON: Zur Gattung der Spruchquelle Q." In *Zeit und Geschichte: Dankesgabe an Rudolf Bultmann zum 80. Geburtstag,* pp. 77–96. Ed. Erich Dinkler. Tübingen: J.C.B. Mohr (Paul Siebeck), 1964. Rev. enlarged English version "LOGOI SOPHON: On the Gattung of Q," in *Trajectories through Early Christianity,* pp. 71–113, in the German ed., pp. 67–106. The enlarged English version is also reprinted in *The Future of Our Religious Past: Essays in Honour of Rudolf Bultmann,* pp. 84–130.

"Heilsgeschichte." In *Biblisch-Historisches Handwörterbuch,* Vol. 2, pp. 685–86. Ed. Bo Reicke and Leonhard Rost. Göttingen: Vandenhoeck and Ruprecht, 1964.

"Krippe." In *Biblisch-Historisches Handwörterbuch,* Vol. 2, p. 1014. Edited by Bo Reicke and Leonhard Rost. Göttingen: Vandenhoeck und Ruprecht, 1964.

"Liturgie: 3. NT." In *Biblisch-Historisches Handwörterbuch,* Vol. 2, p. 1099. Ed. Bo Reicke and Leonhard Rost. Göttingen: Vandenhoeck und Ruprecht, 1964.

"Die Hodajot-Formel in Gebet und Hymnus des Frühchristentums." In *Apophoreta: Festschrift für Ernst Haenchen,* pp. 194–235. *Zeitschrift für die neutestamentliche Wissenschaft.* Beiheft 30. Trans. Gustav-Alfred Picard, ed. Walter Eltester. Berlin: Alfred Töpelmann, 1964.

"Scripture and Theological Method: A Protestant Study in *Sensus Plenior.*" *Catholic Biblical Quarterly* 27 (January 1965): 6–27.

"The Problem of History in Mark, Reconsidered." *The Union Seminary Quarterly Review* 20 (January 1965): 131–47.

"The Pre-History of Demythologization." *Interpretation* 20 (January 1966): 65–77. German trans. "Einleitung," *Augustin und das paulinische Freiheitsproblem: Eine philosophische Studie zum pelagianischen Streit,* by Hans Jonas, pp. 11–22. Forschungen zur Religion und Literatur des Alten und Neuen Testaments, Vol. 44. Edited by Rudolf Bultmann. 2d ed. Göttingen: Vandenhoeck und Ruprecht, 1965.

"What is the New Hermeneutic?" *The Center* 6 (Spring 1965): 1–11.

"Braaten's Polemic: A Reply." *Theology Today* 22 (July 1965): 277–82.

"For Theology and the Church." In *The Bultmann School of Biblical Interpretation: New Directions?* pp. 1–19. *Journal for Theology and the Church,* Vol. 1. Ed. Robert Funk in association with Gerhard Ebeling. Tübingen: J.C.B. Mohr (Paul Siebeck), 1965; New York: Harper and Row, 1965.

"A Critical Inquiry into the Scriptural Bases of Confessional Hermeneutics." *Journal of Ecumenical Studies* 3 (Winter 1966): 36–56. Reprinted in *Encounter* 28 (Winter 1967): 17–34. "New Hermeneutics and Ecumenics." Korean trans. Kyung Yun Chun. *Christian Thought* (Seoul) (October 1965): 64–73.

"Kerygma and History in the New Testament." In *The Bible and Modern Scholarship*, pp. 114–50. Ed. J. Philip Hyatt. New York and Nashville: Abingdon Press, 1965. German trans.: "Kerygma und Geschichte im Neuen Testament." Trans. Ernst Eberhard Fincke. *Zeitschrift für Theologie und Kirche* 62 (December 1965): 294–337. Rev. version in *Trajectories through Early Christianity*, pp. 20–70; in the German ed., pp. 20–66.

"Introduction to *The Quest of the Historical Jesus*, by Albert Schweitzer, pp. xi–xxxiii. New York: Macmillan, 1968; nine reprint editions through 1975. Slightly rev. reprint in *A New Quest of the Historical Jesus and Other Essays*, pp. 172–95. German trans. "Einführung," *Die Geschichte der Leben-Jesu-Forschung*, by Albert Schweitzer, pp. 7–24. Taschenbuch-Ausgabe. Munich and Hamburg: Siebenstern Taschenbuch, 1966.

"Hermeneutical Theology." *The Christian Century* 83 (4 May 1966): 579–82. Reprinted in *Frontline Theology*, pp. 61–68. Ed. Dean Peerman. Richmond, VA: John Knox Press, 1967. German trans.: "Hermeneutische Theologie." In *Theologie im Umbruch: Der Beitrag Amerikas zur gegenwärtigen Theologie*, pp. 64–71. Munich: Christian Kaiser, 1968.

"The Coptic Gnostic Library Today." *New Testament Studies* 14 (April 1968): 356–401. Reprint ed., Claremont, CA: The Institute for Antiquity and Christianity, 1970. Second reprint, Occasional Papers 1. Claremont, CA: The Institute for Antiquity and Christianity, 1972.

"L'herméneutique du kerygme en tant que herméneutique de la liberté chrétienne." In *L'ermeneutica della liberta religiosa*, pp. 325–34. Ed. Enrico Castelli. Archivio di Filosofia. Rome: Instituto di Studi Filosofici; Padova: Cedam—Casa editrice Dott. Antonio Milani, 1968. In *L'herméneutique de la liberté religieuse. Actes du Colloque organisé par le Centre international d'études humanistes et par l'Institut d'études philosophiques de Rome, Rome, 7–12 janvier 1968*, pp. 325–34. Ed. Enrico Castelli. Paris: Aubier, Editions Montaigne, 1968. German trans.: "Hermeneutik des Kergyma als Hermeneutik der christlichen Freiheit." In *Religion und Freiheit: Zur Hermeneutik der religiösen Freiheit*, pp. 174–80. Ed. Franz Theunis; trans. Marianne Mühlenberg. Theologische Forschung 52. *Kergyma und Mythos* VI-5. Hamburg-Bergstedt: Herbert Reich Evangelischer Verlag, 1974.

"World in Modern Theology and in New Testament Theology." In *Soli Deo Gloria: New Testament Studies in Honor of William Childs Robinson*, pp. 88–110, 149–51. Ed. J. McDowell Richards. Richmond, VA: John Knox, 1968.

"Jesus' Parables as God Happening." In *Jesus and the Historian: Written in Honor of Ernest Cadman Colwell*, pp. 134–50. Ed. F. Thomas Trotter. Philadelphia: Westminster, 1968. Slightly rev. reprint in *A New Quest of the Historical Jesus and Other Essays*, pp. 196–210. Abridgement supplemented with discussion published in *Parable, Myth and Language*, pp. 45–62. Ed. Tony Stoneburner. Cambridge, MA: The Church Society for College Work, 1968. French trans.: "Les paraboles comme avènement de Dieu." In *Parole et avènement de Dieu*, pp. 33–49. Trans. Madame P. Vignaux. "Débat avec J. M. Robinson," pp. 51–62. Le point théologique 3. Paris: Beauchesne, 1972.

"The Institute for Antiquity and Christianity." *New Testament Studies* 16 (January 1970): 178–95. Reprint ed., Claremont, CA: The Institute for Antiquity and Christianity, 1970.

"Language in a New World." In *Projections: Shaping an American Theology for the Future*, pp. 154–65. Eds. Thomas F. O'Meara and Donald M. Weisser. Garden City, NY: Doubleday, 1970.

"The Hermeneutic of Hope." *Continuum* 7 (Winter 1970): 525–34.

"On the *Gattung* of Mark (and John)." In *Jesus and Man's Hope*, Vol. 1, pp. 99–129. Eds. David G. Buttrick and John M. Bald. A Perspective Book. Pittsburgh: Pittsburgh Theological Seminary, 1970. Slightly rev. reprint in *The Problem of History in Mark and other Marcan Essays*, pp. 11–39.

"The Coptic Gnostic Library." *Novum Testamentum* 12 (April 1970): 81–85. Reprinted in *Essays on the Coptic Gnostic Library: An off-print from Novum Testamentum XII,2*, pp. 81–85. Leiden: E.J. Brill, 1970.

The Facsimile Edition of the Nag Hammadi Codices: Introduction. Leiden: E.J. Brill, 1972. Reprinted as Occasional Paper no. 4 of the Institute for Antiquity and Christianity, 1972. 19 pp.

"The International Committee for the Nag Hammadi Codices: A Progress Report." *New Testament Studies* 18 (April 1972): 236–42.

"Inside the Front Cover of Codex VI." In *Essays on the Nag Hammadi Texts in Honour of Alexander Böhlig*, pp. 74–87. Edited by Martin Krause. Nag Hammadi Studies 3. Leiden: E.J. Brill, 1972.

"Die Zukunft der neutestamentlichen Theologie." In *Neues Testament und christliche Existenz: Festschrift für Herbert Braun zum 70. Geburtstag am 4. Mai 1973*, pp. 387–400. Eds. Hans Dieter Betz and Luise Schottroff. Tübingen: J.C.B. Mohr (Paul Siebeck), 1973. English trans. James M. Robinson: "The Future of New Testament Theology." *Religious Studies Review* 2 (January 1976): 17–23. Reprinted in *Hermeneutics and the Worldliness of Faith: A Festschrift in Memory of Carl Michalson*. Eds. Charles Courtney, Olin M. Ivey and Gordon E. Michalson. *The Drew Gateway* 45 (1974–75 [1977]): 175–87. Reprinted in *Studia Evangelica*, 7. Ed. Elizabeth A. Livingstone. Texte und Untersuchungen, 126. Berlin: Akademie Verlag, 1982. Pp. 415–25.

"The Literary Composition of Mark." In *L'évangile selon Marc: Tradition et rédaction*, pp. 11–19. Ed. M. Sabbe. Bibliotheca Ephemeridum Theologicarum Lovaniensium 34. Gembloux: Duculot and Leuven University Press, 1974. Nouvelle édition augmentée, pp. 11–19. Additional Note, pp. 19–20. Leuven: University Press and Uitgeverij Peeters, 1988.

"Interim Collations in Codex II and the Gospel of Thomas." In *Mélanges d'histoire des religions offerts à Henri-Charles Puech*, pp. 379–92. Paris: Presses universitaires de France, 1974.

"Nineteenth Century Theology as Heritage and Fate." *The Drew Gateway* 44 (Winter/Spring 1974): 54–71.

"Jesus as Sophos and Sophia: Wisdom Traditions and the Gospels." In *Aspects of Wisdom in Judaism and Early Christianity*, pp. 1–16. Ed. Robert L. Wilken. University of Notre Dame Center for the Study of Judaism and Christianity in Antiquity 1. Notre Dame and London: University of Notre Dame Press, 1975.

"The Internal Word in History." In *No Famine in the Land: Studies in Honor of John L. McKenzie*, pp. 293–98. Eds. James W. Flanagan and Anita W. Robinson. Missoula, MT: Scholars Press, 1975.

"The Construction of the Nag Hammadi Codices." In *Essays on the Nag Hammadi Texts in Honour of Pahor Labib*, pp. 170–90. Ed. Martin Krause. Nag Hammadi Studies 6. Leiden: E.J. Brill, 1975.

"On the Codicology of the Nag Hammadi Codices." In *Les textes de Nag Hammadi: Colloque du Centre d'histoire des religions (Strasbourg, 23–25 octobre 1974)*, pp. 15–31. Ed. Jacques-E. Ménard. Nag Hammadi Studies 7. Leiden: E.J. Brill, 1975.

"The First Season of the Nag Hammadi Excavation 27 November–19 December 1975." American Research Center in Egypt. *Newsletter*, no. 96 (Spring 1976): 18–24. Rev. and reprinted in *Göttingen Miszellen* 22 (1976 [1977]): 71–79.

The Nag Hammadi Codices: A General Introduction to the Nature and Significance of the Coptic Gnostic Codices from Nag Hammadi. Claremont, CA: The Institute for Antiquity and Christianity, 1974; 2d rev. ed., 1977. 18 pp.

"The Jung Codex: The Rise and Fall of a Monopoly." *Religious Studies Review* 3 (January 1977): 17–30.

"The Second Season of the Nag Hammadi Excavation, 22 November–29 December 1976," by James M. Robinson and Bastiaan van Elderen. American Research Center in Egypt. *Newsletter*, nos. 99–100 (Winter/Spring 1977): 36–54. Reprinted in *Göttingen Miszellen* 24 (1977): 57–73.

"The Three Steles of Seth and the Gnostics of Plotinus." In *Proceedings of the International Colloquium on Gnosticism (Stockholm August 20–25 1973)*, pp. 132–42. Stockholm: Almqvist and Wiksell International; Leiden: E.J. Brill, 1977.

"Gnosticism and the New Testament." In *Gnosis, Festschrift für Hans Jonas*, pp. 125–43. Ed. Barbara Aland. Göttingen: Vandenhoeck und Ruprecht, 1978. Slightly revised reprint of the Marcan part in *The Problem of History in Mark and other Marcan Essays*, pp. 40–53.

"The First International Congress of Coptology." American Research Center in Egypt. *Newsletter* 106 (Fall 1978 [1979]): 24–40. Reprinted in *Bulletin* of the Société d'archéologie copte 23 (1981): 281–98. Abridged Italian trans. by Tito Orlandi.

"Il I Congresso Internazionale di studi copti (Cairo 8–18 dicembre 1976)." *Rivista di Storia e Letteratura Religiose* 14 (1978): 337–40. Abridged French trans. "Le premier congrès international de coptologie." *Le monde copte* 6 (Second Quarter 1979): 28–30.

"The Future of Papyrus Codicology." In *The Future of Coptic Studies*, pp. 23–70. Ed. R. McL. Wilson. Coptic Studies 1. Leiden: E.J. Brill, 1978 (1979).

"Codicological Analysis of Nag Hammadi Codices V and VI and Papyrus Berolinensis 8502." In *Nag Hammadi Codices V,2–5 and VI with Papyrus Berolinensis 8502,1 and 4*, pp. 9–45. Ed. Douglas M. Parrott. Nag Hammadi Studies 11. The Coptic Gnostic Library. Leiden: E.J. Brill, 1979.

"The Discovery of the Nag Hammadi Codices." *Biblical Archeologist* 42 (Fall 1979): 206–24. Unabridged with footnotes as "From the Cliff to Cairo: The Story of the Discoverers and the Middlemen of the Nag Hammadi Codices," *Colloque international sur les textes de Nag Hammadi (Québec, 22–25 août 1978)* (Bibliothèque copte de Nag Hammadi, Section "Etudes" 1; Québec: Les presses de l'Université Laval, and Louvain: Peeters, 1981 [1982]), pp. 21–58.

"Getting the Nag Hammadi Library into English." *Biblical Archeologist* 42 (Fall 1979): 239–48.

"Sethians and Johannine Thought: The *Trimorphic Protennoia* and the Prologue of the Gospel of John." In *The Rediscovery of Gnosticism: Proceedings of the International Conference on Gnosticism at Yale, New Haven, Connecticut, March 28–31, 1978*, Vol. 2 *Sethian Gnosticism*, pp. 643–62, "Discussion," pp. 662–70, "Concluding Discussion," pp. 671–85. Ed. Bentley Layton. Studies in the History of Religions 41 (Supplements to *Numen*). Leiden: E.J. Brill, 1981.

"Jesus from Easter to Valentinus (or to the Apostles' Creed)." *Journal of Biblical Literature* 101 (March 1982): 5–37.

"Early Collections of Jesus' Sayings." *Logia: Les Paroles de Jésus–The Sayings of Jesus*, pp. 389–94. Ed. Joël Delobel. Bibliotheca Ephemeridum Theologicarum Lovaniensium, 59. Leuven: Peeters and Leuven University Press, 1982 (1983).

"The Nag Hammadi Library and the Study of the New Testament." *The New Testament and Gnosis: Essays in honour of Robert McL. Wilson*, pp. 1–18. Eds. A. H. B. Logan and A. M. J. Wedderburn. Edinburgh: T. & T. Clark, 1983.

"The Discovering and Marketing of Coptic Manuscripts: The Nag Hammadi Codices and the Bodmer Papyri," *Sundries in honour of Torgny Säve-Söderbergh* (Acta Universitatis Uppsaliensis: *Boreas: Uppsala Studies in Ancient Mediterranean and Near Eastern Civilizations 13*, 1984). Pp. 97–114. Reprinted in *The Roots of Egyptian Christianity*, pp. 1–25. Eds. Birger A. Pearson and James E. Goehring. Studies in Antiquity and Christianity. Philadelphia: Fortress Press, 1986.

"The Sayings of Jesus: Q." *The Drew Gateway*, 54:1 (Fall 1983 [1985]): 26–38.

"Judaism, Hellenism, Christianity: Jesus' Followers in Galilee until 70 C.E." In *Ebraismo Ellenismo Christianesimo*, pp. 241–50. Ed. Vittorio Mathieu. Archivio di Filosofia, directed by Marco M. Olivetti, 53 (1985),1. Padova: Cedam, 1985.

"How My Mind Has Changed (or Remained the Same)." *Society of Biblical Literature 1985 Seminar Papers* 24. Ed. Kent Harold Richards. Atlanta, GA: Scholars Press, 1985. Pp. 481–504.

"Bultmann and Time: Ecstasies of his Temporality." *Bultmann, Retrospect and Prospect: The Centenary Symposium at Wellesley*, pp. 17–34. Ed. Edward C. Hobbs. Harvard Theological Studies 35. Philadelphia: Fortress Press, 1985.

"The Gospels as Narrative." *The Bible and the Narrative Tradition*, pp. 97–112. Edited by Frank McConnell. New York and Oxford: Oxford University Press, 1986.

"On Bridging the Gulf from Q to *The Gospel of Thomas* (or *vice versa*)." *Nag Hammadi, Gnosticism and Early Christianity*, pp. 127–75. Eds. Charles W. Hedrick and Robert Hodgson, Jr. Peabody, MA: Hendrickson Publishers, 1986.

"Chester Beatty Accession Number 1499: A Preliminary Codicological Analysis." With Alfons Wouters. *Miscel-lania Papirologica Ramon Roca-Puig en el seu vui-tante aniversari*, pp. 297–306. Ed. Sebastia Janeras. Barcelona: Fundacio Salvador Vives Casajuana, 1987.

"Acts." *The Literary Guide to the Bible*, pp. 467–78. Eds. Robert Alter and Frank Kermode. Cambridge: Harvard University, and London: Collins, 1987.

"Very Goddess and Very Man: Jesus' Better Self." *Encountering Jesus: a debate on Christology*, pp. 111–22. Ed. Stephen T. Davis. Atlanta, GA: John Knox, 1988. Rev. and reprinted in *Images of the Feminine in Gnosticism*, pp. 113–27. Ed. Karen King. Studies in Antiquity and Christianity. Philadelphia: Fortress Press, 1988.

"Critique" [to the essays by John H.Hick, Stephen T. Davis, Rebecca D. Pentz and John B.Cobb, Jr.]. *Encountering Jesus: a debate on Christology*, pp. 25–27; 59–61; 99–101; 164–67. Ed. Stephen T. Davis. Atlanta, GA: John Knox, 1988.

"Response" [to the Critiques by John B. Cobb, Jr., Stephen T. Davis, John H. Hick and Rebecca D. Pentz]. *Encountering Jesus: a debate on Christology,* pp. 132–40. Ed. Stephen T. Davis. Atlanta, GA: John Knox, 1988.

"Religious Studies as Humanizing Studies." *The Santa Barbara Colloquy: Religion Within the Limits of Reason Alone. Soundings* 71.2–3 (1988). Pp. 207–19.

"The Pachomian Monastic Library at the Chester Beatty Library and the Bibliothèque Bodmer," *Manuscripts of the Middle East* 5 (1990), in the press.

"The First Christian Monastic Library." *The Third International Congress of Coptic Studies (Warsaw, 20–25 August 1984)*. Warsaw: Academy of Sciences, in the press.

Reviews

Review of *The Mission and Achievement of Jesus: An Examination of the Presuppositions of New Testament Theology*, by Reginald H. Fuller. *Theology Today* 12 (July 1955): 273–76.

Review of *Oral Tradition*, by Eduard Nielsen; *The Mission and Achievement of Jesus*, by Reginald H. Fuller; *Life in Christ*, by Théo Preiss; and *Studies in the Book of Lamentations*, by Norman K. Gottwald. Studies in Biblical Theology, Vols. 11–14. *Religion in Life* 24 (Summer 1955): 462–64.

"From Paulinism to Early Catholicism." Review of *The Interpreter's Bible*, Vol. 11. *Interpretation* 10 (July 1956): 347–50.

Review of *Theology of the New Testament*, Vol. 2, by Rudolf Bultmann. *Theology Today* 13 (July 1956): 261–69.

Review of *La tradition: Problème exégétique, historique, et théologique*, by Oscar Cullmann. *Journal of Biblical Literature* 75 (September 1956): 238–39.

Review of *The Early Church*, by Oscar Cullmann. *Journal of Biblical Literature* 76 (June 1957): 172–73.

xxiv • Prepared by Kathleen E. Corley

Review of *Der Staat im Neuen Testament*, by Oscar Cullmann. *Theologische Zeitschrift* 13 (July-August 1957): 305–6.

Review of *Jesus and His People*, by Paul Minear; *Beginning from Jerusalem*, by John Foster; *From Brahma to Christ*, by Lakahmibai Tilak; and *Did Jesus Rise from the Dead?* by James Martin. World Christian Books. *The Journal of Religion* 37 (July 1957): 205.

Review of *Jesus von Nazareth*, by Günther Bornkamm. *Journal of Biblical Literature* 76 (December 1957): 310–13.

Review of *The Gospels: Their Origin and Their Growth*, by Frederick C. Grant. *Interpretation* 12 (January 1958): 79–80.

Review of *The Gospel of Mark*, by William Barclay. *The Journal of Religion* 38 (January 1958): 55–56.

Review of *The Gospel Tradition and Its Beginnings: A Study in the Limits of 'Form-geschichte*,' by Harald Riesenfeld. *Journal of Biblical Literature* 77 (June 1958): 169–70.

"Reorientation and Two Questions." Review of *Understanding the Old Testament*, by Bernard W. Anderson, and *Understanding the New Testament*, by Howard Clark Kee and Franklin W. Young. *The Drew Gateway* 29 (Autumn 1958): 31–34.

"Modern Roman Catholic Scholarship." Review of *Saint Paul. Epître aux Romains: Traduction et Commentaire*, by Joseph Huby. New edition by Father Stanislas Lyonnet, S. J. Verbum Salutis, Vol. 10. *Interpretation* 13 (April 1959): 208–9.

"Recent Research in the Fourth Gospel." Review of *Die Entstehungsgeschichte des vierten Evangeliums*, by Wilhelm Wilkens, and *Untersuchungen zur Menschensohn-Christologie im Johannesevangelium*, by Siegfried Schulz. *Journal of Biblical Literature* 78 (September 1959): 242–52.

"Neo-Liberalism." Review of *Das Wesen des christlichen Glaubens*, by Gerhard Ebeling. *Interpretation* 15 (October 1961): 484–86, 488–91.

Review of *The Prophet from Nazareth*, by Morton S. Enslin. *The Journal of Bible and Religion* 30 (January 1962): 46–48.

Review of *Christ Without Myth*, by Schubert M. Ogden. *Christian Advocate* 6 (February 1, 1962): 11–12. Reprinted in revised abridged form, *The Union Seminary Quarterly Review* 17 (May 1962): 359–62; in revised unabridged form, *Theology Today* 19 (October 1962): 438–44.

Review of *Die religionsgeschichtliche Schule: Darstellung und Kritik ihres Bildes vom gnostischen Erlösermythus*, by Carsten Colpe. *Journal of Biblical Literature* 81 (September 1962): 287–89.

Review of "Jesus Christ," by S. MacLean Gilmour. In *Hastings' Dictionary of the Bible*. Revised edition. *Andover Newton Quarterly*, n.s. 3 (March 1963): 37–39.

"The New Hermeneutic at Work." Review of *Paulus und Jesus: Eine Untersuchung zur Präzisierung der Frage nach dem Ursprung der Christologie*, by Eberhard Jüngel. *Interpretation* 18 (July 1964): 346–59.

"Neither History nor Kerygma." Review of the film *The Greatest Story Ever Told*. *Christian Advocate* 9 (March 23, 1965): 7–8.

Review of *Die Goldene Regel: Eine Einführung in die Geschichte der antiken und frühchristlichen Vulgärethik,* by Albrecht Dihle. *Journal of the History of Philosophy* 4 (January 1966): 84–87.

Review of *The Promise of Bultmann,* by Norman Perrin. In *Christology and a Modern Pilgrimage: A Discussion with Norman Perrin,* pp. 147–52. Edited by Hans Dieter Betz. Claremont, CA: The New Testament Colloquium, 1971; second edition: Society of Biblical Literature and Scholars Press, 1974.

Varia

"Paul as a Modern Church Statesman." *Mississippi Methodist Advocate,* n.s., 9 (Part I, May 16, 1956): 15; (Part II, May 23, 1956): 15–16. Reprinted in other *Methodist Advocates.* Reprinted with the title "Paul and a Current Dilemma." *The Presbyterian Outlook* 138 (September 17, 1956): 5–6.

"How Barth Has Influenced Me." *Theology Today* 13 (October 1956): 364–67.

Newsletter 4, 1965–66. Cambridge, MA: The American Schools of Oriental Research. 5 pp.

Letter to the Editor. *The Progress Bulletin* (Pomona, CA), 24 July 1966, sec. 2, p. 2.

"Claremont Gains Access to Coptic Documents." *Claremont Graduate School and University Center Bulletin* 38 (August 1966): 1–3.

"Discussion of Qumran and Gnosticism." In *Le Origini dello Gnosticismo: Colloquio di Messina 13–18 Aprile 1966,* pp. 387–88. Ed. Ugo Bianchi. Studies in the History of Religions (Supplements to *Numen*), Vol. 12. Leiden: E.J. Brill, 1967.

"Paul W. Lapp, August 5, 1930–April 26, 1970." American Research Center in Egypt. *Newsletter,* no. 74 (September 1970): 2.

"Forward," *The Patmos Monastery Library Project,* pp. 2–3. Claremont, CA: The Institute for Antiquity and Christianity, 1970; 2d rev. ed., 1971.

"Early Christian Manuscripts from the Sands of the Nile." *The UNESCO Courier* 24 (May 1971): 4–10. Simultaneous French and Spanish eds.; subsequent eds. in German, Italian, Russian, Arabic, Hebrew, Japanese, Hindi and Persian.

"International Committee for the Nag Hammadi Codices, Cairo, December 15–18, 1970." American Research Center in Egypt. *Newsletter,* no. 77 (April 1971): 8–10, and *Newsletter,* no. 79 (October 1971): 16–17.

"Annual Report 1969–70 and 1970–71." Institute for Antiquity and Christianity. *Bulletin,* no. 3 (June 1972): i–iii, 8–13, 25–27.

"Annual Report 1971–72." Institute for Antiquity and Christianity. *Bulletin,* no. 6 (February 1973): i–ii, 8–10, 23–25.

"Editing the Nag Hammadi Codices." American Research Center in Egypt. *Newsletter,* no. 91 (Fall 1974): 15–17.

"Foreword," *Nag Hammadi Codices III,2 and IV,2: The Gospel of the Egyptians (The Holy Book of the Great Invisible Spirit),* pp. vii–viii. Eds. Alexander Böhlig and Frederik Wisse in cooperation with Pahor Labib. Nag Hammadi Studies 4. The Coptic Gnostic Library. Leiden: E.J. Brill, 1975.

"Foreword," *Nag Hammadi Codices V,2–5 and VI with Papyrus Berolinensis 8502, 1 and 4*, pp. vii–viii. Ed. Douglas M. Parrott. Nag Hammadi Studies 11. The Coptic Gnostic Library. Leiden: E.J. Brill, 1978 (1979).

"Introduction," "What is the Nag Hammadi Library?" *Biblical Archeologist* 42 (Fall 1979): 201–4.

"For Herbert Braun on his Eightieth Birthday: Jesus and the Immoral Minority." *Die Auslegung Gottes durch Jesus: Festgabe für Herbert Braun zu seinem 80. Geburtstag am 4. Mai 1983 dargebracht von Freunden und Schülern*. Ed. Luise and Willy Schottroff. Mainz: privately duplicated, 1983. Pp. 214, 215–22. Reprint, *Inquiry* 3:3 (Summer 1983): 47–50.

"Vorwort." *Das Johannesevangelium*, by Ernst Haenchen, pp. v–ix. Ed. Ulrich Busse. Tübingen: J.C.B. Mohr (Paul Siebeck), 1980. English trans.: "Preface," *John I: A Commentary on the Gospel of John Chapters 1–6* by Ernst Haenchen, pp. lx–xiii. Ed. Robert W. Funk with Ulrich Busse. Hermeneia. Philadelphia: Fortress Press, 1984.

"Foreword," pp. vi–vii; "The Facsimile Edition of the Nag Hammadi Codices," pp. 29–31; "The Coptic Gnostic Library," pp. 32–36; "Center for Biblical Research and Archives of the Society of Biblical Literature," pp. 55–56; "The Rome-Claremont Cooperative Research on the Archaeology and Literature of Coptic Monasteries," pp. 56–57; "International Photographic Archive of Papyri," pp. 57–58. *The Institute for Antiquity and Christianity Report 1972–80*. Ed. Marvin W. Meyer. Claremont, CA: The Institute for Antiquity and Christianity, 1981.

"Statement Regarding Robert Funk." The Council for the Study of Religion *Bulletin* 12 (December 1981): 143.

"Foreword," *Nag Hammadi Codices: Greek and Coptic Papyri from the Cartonnage of the Covers*, pp. vii–x. Eds. J.W.B. Barns†, G. M. Browne and J. C. Shelton. Nag Hammadi Studies XVI. The Coptic Gnostic Library. Leiden: E.J. Brill, 1981.

"Foreword," *Nag Hammadi Codices IX and X*, pp. vii–x. Ed. Birger A. Pearson. Nag Hammadi Studies XV. The Coptic Gnostic Library. Leiden: E.J. Brill, 1981.

"Introduction," *Faith, Reason and Responsibility*, by Hans Jonas. pp. ix–xiii. Institute for Antiquity and Christianity Studies 1. Claremont, CA: The Institute for Antiquity and Christianity, 1981 (1982). Rev.: "Preface," *The Roots of Egyptian Christianity*, pp. ix–xiii, Ed. Birger A. Pearson and James E. Goehring. Studies in Antiquity and Christianity. Philadelphia: Fortress Press, 1986.

"Claude Frederic-Armand Schaeffer-Forrer (1898–1982): An Appreciation." *Biblical Archeology Review* 9:5 (September-October 1983): 56–61.

"Across 25 years..." *STC Perspectives* (August 1983): 6.

"The Sermon on the Mount/Plain: Work Sheets for the Reconstruction of Q." *Society of Biblical Literature 1983 Seminar Papers*. Ed. Kent Harold Richards. Chico, CA: Scholars Press, 1983. Pp. 451–54.

"Jesus as an Apocalypticist." *Free Inquiry* 4:3 (Summer 1984): 47–49.

"Foreword," *Nag Hammadi Codex III,5: The Dialogue of the Savior*, pp. vii–x. Ed. Stephen Emmel. Nag Hammadi Studies XXVI. The Coptic Gnostic Library. Leiden: E.J. Brill, 1984.

"The Preaching of John: Work Sheets for the Reconstruction of Q." *Society of Biblical Literature 1984 Seminar Papers* 23. Ed. Kent Harold Richards. Chico, CA: Scholars Press, 1984. Pp. 305–46.

Pap. Q. Pp. 1–2 by James M. Robinson, pp. 3–20 by Leif Vaage and Jon Daniels. Claremont, CA.: The Institute for Antiquity and Christianity, 1985.

"Foreword," *Nag Hammadi Codex I (The Jung Codex), Volume 1: Introduction, Texts and Translation*, pp. vii–x; Volume 2: *Notes*. Ed. Harold W. Attridge. Nag Hammdi Studies XXII–XXIII. The Coptic Gnostic Library. Leiden: E.J. Brill, 1985.

"The Mission and Beelzebul: Pap. Q 10:2–16; 11:14–23." With Leif Vaage and Jon Daniels. *Society of Biblical Literature 1985 Seminar Papers* 24. Ed. Kent Harold Richards. Atlanta, GA: Scholars Press, 1985. Pp. 97–99.

"Reconstructing Q: A Lost Collection of Jesus' Sayings," *Connections: A Publication of The Claremont Graduate School* 1:2 "Foreword," *The Formation of Q: Trajectories in Ancient Wisdom Collections*, by John Kloppenborg, pp. xi–xiv. Studies in Antiquity and Christianity. Philadelphia: Fortress Press, 1987. Reprinted in *The Composition of Q*, by John Kloppenborg, pp. xi–xiv. *Occasional Papers*: Number 9. Claremont, CA: The Institute for Antiquity and Christianity, 1987.

"William Hugh Brownlee (1917–1983)." *Early Jewish and Christian Exegesis: Studies in Memory of William Hugh Brownlee*. Pp. vii–viii. Eds. Craig A. Evans and William F. Stinespring. Atlanta, GA: Scholars Press, 1987.

Foreword to *Nag Hammadi Codex II,1–7 together with XIII,2* Brit. Lib. Or. 4926(1) and P. Oxy. 1, 654, 655*, pp. vii–x. Edited by Bentley Layton. Nag Hammadi Studies XX–XXI. The Coptic Gnostic Library. Leiden: E.J. Brill, 1989.

Foreword to *Nag Hammadi Codices XI, XII and XIII*, pp. vii–x. Ed. Charles W. Hedrick. Nag Hammadi Studies XXVIII. The Coptic Gnostic Library. Leiden: E.J. Brill, 1990.

Foreword to Nag Hammadi *Codices III,3–4 and V,1 with Papyrus Berolinensis 8502,3 and Oxyrhynchus Papyrus 1081: Eugnostos and the Sophia of Jesus Christ*, pp. vii–x. Edited and Translated by Douglas M. Parrott. Nag Hammadi Studies XXVII. The Coptic Gnostic Library. Leiden: E.J. Brill, in the press.

Abbreviations

AB	Anchor Bible
BETL	Bibliotheca ephemeridum theologicarum lovaniensium
BZNW	Beihefte zur *Zeitschrift für die Neutestamentliche Wissenschaft*
EBib	Etudes bibliques
GCS	Griechische christliche Schriftsteller
HTS	Harvard Theological Studies
JAC	*Jahrbuch für Antike und Christentum*
LCL	Loeb Classical Library
NF	Neue Folge
NS	New Series
OBO	Orbis biblicus et orientalis
PG	Patrologiae Graecae
PL	Patrologiae Latinae
SBL	Society of Biblical Literature
SJLA	Studies in Judaism in Late Antiquity
SNTSMS	Society for New Testament Studies Monograph Series
TU	Texte und Untersuchungen
WMANT	Wissenschaftliche Monographien zum Alten and Neuen Testament
WUNT	Wissenschaftliche Untersuchungen zum Neuen Testament

Gospel Origins
& Christian
Beginnings

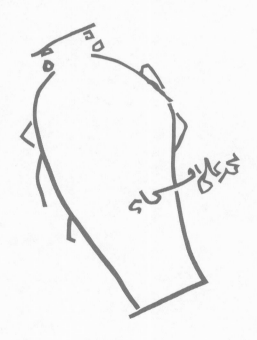

Lord of the Logia

SAVIOR OR SAGE?

Burton L. Mack

0. Introduction

Among his many important contributions to studies of religions in Late Antiquity, two of Robinson's essays strike especially close to the nerve of Christian origins. One is his now famous article from 1964 called "*LOGOI SOPHON*," in which he established the genre of Q as the sayings of a sage. This article has been very influential in Q studies since that time and has provided a solid charter for the Claremont Q project and the SBL Q seminar, which Robinson is currently directing. This aspect of Robinson's work addresses the question of the historical Jesus and builds upon the sayings traditions apart from their incorporation into the synoptic gospels.

The other essay that comes to the quick is Robinson's SBL presidential address of 1981 entitled "Jesus—From Easter to Valentinus (or to the Apostles' Creed)." This essay explored the complex trajectories of Jesus visions from "Easter" into gnostic and other early Christian accounts. The point of departure for this essay was, therefore, not the sayings of the historical Jesus, but the kerygma cited in 1 Corinthians 15. This is Robinson's statement on the other side of the two-pronged scholarly quest for Christian origins, the approach that seeks to determine the "earliest Christology." The kerygmatic approach is usually understood to cast Jesus Christ as a savior.

Toward the end of the Easter essay Robinson took up the critical issue: the relation between the sayings traditions of the historical Jesus, on the one hand, and the vision traditions of the resurrected Christ on the other. One way of relating the two was found on the trajectory that ran from Paul, who "devalued" the "pre-Easter traditions about Jesus," to the Gnostics and Valentinus, where dialogs with the resurrected Lord "replaced the normative role of the sayings of Jesus for primitive Christianity." Another solution, according to Robinson, was the incorporation of the sayings traditions into the synoptic gospels. This move "revalidated the traditional sayings of Jesus" and "reaffirmed their conventional interpretation" for the church.[1]

---

1 Robinson, "Jesus—From Easter to Valentinus," 21.

4 • Burton L. Mack

In order to distinguish between the sayings tradition and the visions tradition, several conceptual problems had required solution, however, including the location of Jesus in time (pre- or post-Easter), the imagination of his appearance ("bodily" or as "luminous spirit"), the form of his communication (sayings or dialogs), and the content of the message (pronouncement or enlightenment). Since Robinson understood the vision tradition to have started with Peter at the very beginning of the church (as 1 Cor 15:5 claims), he assumed that the "Easter experience" affected the sayings tradition from the earliest times. Thus the issue of the two ways of viewing or remembering Jesus eventually came to focus for Robinson not upon the distinction between the kerygma and the synoptic-type gospels, but upon the proper way to interpret the non-synoptic type sayings "gospels" Q and the Gospel of Thomas.

According to Robinson,

> [T]he authors of such collections stand within the post-Easter period, whereas much of their material goes back to the pre-Easter period. Thus they contain things said by Jesus prior to his crucifixion and also things said by the resurrected Christ; and they imply interpretations inherent in the traditions as well as interpretations recently granted to them by the resurrected Christ.[2]

This means that the problem of locating the sayings of Jesus (pre- or post-Easter) was inherent in the sayings traditions themselves. Robinson called this an "ambivalence of the sayings tradition" and noted that neither of the collections was fully appropriate to their eventual assignments because of this ambivalence. Q was pressed into the pre-Easter period of the narrative gospels by the orthodox tradition in spite of the fact that it contained post-Easter sayings. The Gospel of Thomas was accepted by the Gnostics even though it did not specify that the "living Jesus" was the resurrected one, in keeping with gnostic preference for dialog with the resurrected Christ.[3]

Robinson then made the point that neither Q nor the Gospel of Thomas contains any reference to the kerygma of the cross and resurrection, and he concluded that, at this early stage, there was a "lack of concern . . . as to whether the sayings were spoken by Jesus before or after Easter." In each case the lack of concern was possible because some way other than narrative placement with regard to the crucifixion had been found to enhance the sayings with spiritual significance more or less appropriate to the post-Easter situation. In the case of the Gospel of Thomas, Jesus was characterized as "the living Jesus," and for Q the special effect of Jesus' words was attributed to the holy Spirit.[4]

It is to Robinson's credit that he tackled this problem of Christian origins so forthrightly, spelling out the issues so clearly, and finding a way to merge the two traditions (sayings/kerygma) so creatively. Studies since then, however,

2 Robinson, "Jesus—From Easter to Valentinus," 22.
3 Robinson, "Jesus—From Easter to Valentinus," 22–23.
4 Robinson, "Jesus—From Easter to Valentinus," 23.

many of which have been pursued in relation to Robinson's Q project and in conversation with him, have called two assumptions into question that were fundamental for his reconstruction.

One is the assumption of a common "Easter faith" for all forms of the early Jesus movements. The other is the assumption of an apocalyptic mentality as the common denominator for Jesus and the sayings traditions as well as for Paul and the kerygmatic traditions. As Robinson put it,

> The apocalyptic radicalism that lead (*sic*) John the Baptist to lose his head, Jesus to be hung up, and Paul to become a habitué of forty lashes less one . . . could hardly have failed to have left-wing successors down through the first hundred years.[5]

The combination of these two assumptions can be called the apocalyptic-kerygmatic hypothesis of Christian origins, an hypothesis that was firmly in place as a consensus of scholarship when Robinson worked out his proposal.

Since the apocalyptic-kerygmatic hypothesis can no longer be assumed, Robinson's reconstruction of Christian origins needs to be reviewed. The counter thesis will be that Q and the Gospel of Thomas represent Jesus movements that were not born of apocalyptic and kerygmatic persuasions. Thus the present essay will chart the major considerations that have called the hypothesis into question, and it will offer an alternative explanation of the sayings of Jesus within those movements. Emphasis will be placed on those features of the sayings of Jesus that have traditionally been viewed in the light of a "post-Easter" mentality. These include (1) the dramatic pronouncements of prophetic and apocalyptic import, (2) the sense of divine presence, omniscience, and authority of the speaker of the sayings, and (3) the language of the holy Spirit that was used to enhance the divine authority of the sayings in Q. Obviously, if the apocalyptic-kerygmatic hypothesis is no longer adequate, these features of the sayings tradition will have to be explained some other way. [6]

1. Apocalyptic and the Teachings of Jesus

Until recently, the consensus of scholarly opinion held that apocalyptic material was to be found among the sayings of Jesus because Jesus had been an eschatological prophet. This view of Jesus was understood to provide a link to the kerygmatic interpretations of his crucifixion and resurrection: the proclaimer became the proclaimed. The kerygmatic proclamation, it was understood, was both "eschatological" (in reference to the dramatic significance of the resurrection) and apocalyptic (in reference to the future appearance of Jesus and his kingdom). Thus the apocalyptic hypothesis served as a bridge

5 Robinson, "Jesus—From Easter to Valentinus," 6.
6 On the erosion of the apocalyptic hypothesis, see Butts, "Probing the Polling," 110–11; Borg, "A Temporate Case"; Mack, "Kingdom Sayings in Mark"; Mack, *Myth of Innocence*, 57–60.

from the historical Jesus to the kerygmatic Christ. This produced a tidy reconstruction of Christian origins, supported by the assumption of wide-spread apocalyptic fervor in Galilean Judaism and sealed by pointing to the apocalyptic frame of the earliest gospel (Mark).

This reconstruction is now in danger of coming unglued, and that for two reasons. The first is that reference to the kerygma of the cross and resurrection does not occur in Q and the Gospel of Thomas. If one takes this finding seriously and in combination with other early Jesus traditions, it means that Jesus' death was not interpreted as a "saving event" in several movements stemming from Jesus. It also means, further, that the kerygmatic formulation of Christian origins was only one way of understanding Jesus as a founder figure among the many movements of the first century. If this is so, it is no longer helpful to date or distinguish the sayings in Q and the Gospel of Thomas as pre- or post-Easter utterances. "Easter" was, after all, a particular mythologem rooted specifically in the kerygma, a way of imagining the vindi-cation of an innocent martyr for a righteous cause. There is no evidence that the tradents of Q or of the Gospel of Thomas held such a view of Jesus' death as a founding event for their movements.[7]

The other reason for the erosion of the apocalyptic-kerygmatic hypothesis is that studies in Q and the Gospel of Thomas do not support the notion of an apocalyptic Jesus. Q does contain a large amount of material that can be called apocalyptic: woes, judgment pronouncements, prophetic sayings, "eschatolog-ical correlatives," and parables of the eschaton. The Gospel of Thomas is decidedly non-apocalyptic in tenor but does have the disciples asking Jesus many question that assume an apocalyptic frame of reference, which Jesus then subverts or corrects. Thus there can be no question about the existence of apocalyptic material among the sayings of Jesus in these collections. The question is whether this material is early, whether it is traceable to the histori-cal Jesus.[8]

John Kloppenborg's magisterial reconstruction of Q's compositional history has challenged the primacy of apocalyptic in the Jesus traditions. He was able to show that the earliest compositional layer of Q was "sapiential," not apoca-lyptic, and that the apocalyptic material reflected a later phase in the formation of the Q community and its experience of its social world. (The two layers are now being called Q1 and Q2.) The function of apocalyptic language in Q2 is

7 On the non-existence of kerygmatic mythology in Q, see Kloppenborg, "'Easter Faith' and the Sayings Gospel Q."

8 The value of the Gospel of Thomas for a reconstruction of the earliest sayings traditions is evident in the work of the Jesus Seminar and its members, a project begun in 1985 by Robert Funk. Documentation for this assertion is, however, hardly possible at present, for the evidence is distributed piecemeal thoughout many recent books and articles. One can catch the flavor by sorting through the following publications: Crossan, *In Parables*; Crossan, *In Fragments*; B. B. Scott, "Jesus Parable Tradition"; Cameron, "Parable and Interpretations"; Hedrick, "The Treasure Parable"; King, "Kingdom in the Gospel of Thomas"; Butts, "Probing the Polling," and Butts & Cameron, "Sayings of Jesus." On wisdom thinking in the Gospel of Thomas, see Davies, *The Gospel of Thomas*.

quite clear. It serves mainly as a threat of judgment upon those who refused to join the Q movement. Thus Kloppenborg called this layer of material "the announcement of judgement."[9] If this is an accurate description for Q, the function of apocalyptic language in other early Jesus and Christ movements also needs to be reviewed. Perhaps an apocalyptic message should not be thought of as primary for Christian origins at all.

In Paul's letters as well the function of apocalyptic language appears to be secondary, in this case to the primary language and logic of the kerygma. The kerygma of the crucifixion and resurrection of the Christ was based on a logic that did not require an additional apocalyptic projection. Since Paul did use apocalyptic language, the reasons for his doing so require explication. In most cases in Paul the apocalyptic projection functions to undergird a threat of judgment in a way similar to its function in Q2. The difference between the two situations is that Q2 used apocalyptic language to call down threat upon detractors already excluded from the community's new sense of boundary, whereas in Paul the threat was aimed at the community itself. This threat may very well be Paul's own, a threat that shows the measure of his disconcertion with social practices that he considered inappropriate for the Christian community that he imagined as ideal. That the introduction of an apocalyptic frame to the kergyma may have been Paul's own doing is indicated by three considerations. One is that the apocalyptic gospel supports a pattern of dialectical thinking ill-designed to attract people into the community, though it may have worked as a meditation on the tensions that resulted after social formation had taken place. The second is that even his successors in the "Pauline school" found it possible to advance kerygmatic elaboration without an apocalyptic frame. The third is that Paul found it necessary to argue for his apocalyptic gospel and that, where he did set forth an explication (as in 1 Corinthians 15, for instance), he argued for some aspect of the apocalyptic scenario on the basis of analogy to the kerygma, not the other way around.[10]

Neither can the Gospel of Mark be used to argue for the primary importance of an apocalyptic vision at the beginning of the Jesus traditions. Mark's gospel sets non-apocalyptic traditions into an apocalyptic frame and thus achieves their resignification. It is yet another evidence for the use of an apocalyptic projection at a particular juncture of social history in order to justify a social

9 The reference is to Kloppenborg, *Formation of Q*. Kloppenborg has also published *Q Parallels*, an edition of the text that will no doubt become the standard reference work in Q studies. In *Q Parallels* the Q text is divided into units of material and numbered in sequence (S1,S2 . . .). Since Kloppenborg's demonstration of the compositional layers in Q, in *Formation of Q*, the designations Q1, Q2, and Q3 are being used by Robinson's Q project to distinguish these strata. Using this system, the following units in *Q Parallels* can be assigned to Q1: S1, S7, S8(minus Q 6:23c and 6:26b), S9, S10, S11, S12, S13, S14, S21, S22(minus 10:12), S27, S28, S35, S36(?), S40, S41, S42, S48, S49, S54, S56, S60, and S63. All else can be assigned to Q2 with the exception of S6 (The Temptations of Jesus), which belongs to Q3.

10 On the nonapocalyptic logic of the Christ kerygma, see Mack, *Myth of Innocence*, chap. 4.

program in trouble. Mark cannot be used to argue either for an apocalyptic Jesus or for an apocalyptic kerygma at the beginning of the Christian time. [11]

As it appears, then, neither the earliest Jesus traditions nor the earliest kerygmatic formulations made use of apocalyptic language. Apocalyptic language was entertained at points where social formations and programs were in need of additional mythic rationale. The emergence of apocalyptic language among the tradents of Q, for instance, is best explained as a mythic rationalization for their "rejection." A close look at the apocalyptic material in Q2 shows that the apocalyptic projection functioned mainly to support a threat of judgment upon the community's erstwhile detractors, and that the detractors are best described as having been family members, friends, neighbors, and leaders who belonged to synagogues. Since there is no indication in Q1 either of apocalyptic language or of conflict with Judaism in any of its forms, the employment of apocalyptic language must be related to that social situation of distress. [12]

This means that apocalyptic language in the Q tradition is a later, secondary development at a particular stage of social formation and experience. It does not represent the discourse that attracted Q people to the movement in the first place. Neither does it represent the "preaching" of the Q tradents to others. The speeches of judgment composed for Jesus are highly crafted fictions written after other conversations had broken down and decisions had been made either to agree or not to agree about Jesus and the Jesus movement. Those addressed by Jesus in the fictional myth of origins represent partners-in-dialog of the tradents of Q who were no longer listening when the Q community entertained an apocalyptic imagination. The Q community did that not in order to convert the world or to offer their detractors a second chance, but in order to justify their own cause and its future.

In the Gospel of Thomas the situation is quite different. The tradents of these sayings were fully aware of apocalyptic material in the traditions of Jesus' sayings. Several questions put by the disciples to Jesus have to do with an apocalyptic imagination of the future, most frequently in the form of questions about how and when the end will come. In each case Jesus counters the very concern that underlies such questions, usually by means of a reapplication of apocalyptic metaphor to the moment of personal transformation, or to the situation of self-awareness in relation to a *gnosis* about the present constitution of the world.

Scholars have not yet worked out the relation between apocalyptic and wisdom in the compositional and social history of the Gospel of Thomas. It could be argued that the gnosticizing tendency was a reaction to an unhappy apocalyptic period in the tradents' past. This would set the sequence from apocalyptic to wisdom in keeping with Robinson's trajectory, but it would not

11 On the apocalyptic resignification of nonapocalyptic material by Mark, see Mack, "Kingdom Sayings in Mark," and *Myth of Innocence*.
12 On the social history of the Q tradents, see Mack, "The Kingdom That Didn't Come."

establish the primacy of apocalyptic in the Jesus traditions per se. That is because most of the apocalyptic sayings in the Gospel of Thomas are also found in Q, where they are at the secondary level of composition. It seems better, therefore, to see the tradents of the Gospel of Thomas on a sapiential trajectory from the beginning, cultivating the sayings of Jesus as a sage in conscious contrast at some point to other Jesus people who were known to entertain the apocalyptic option. The sapiential sayings turned cryptic in the process of their cultivation wherein Jesus' invitation to be different was eventually internalized as self-awareness.

The point would be that in both cases—the emergence of an apocalyptic imagination among the tradents of Q and the cultivation of an esoteric self-knowledge among the tradents of the Gospel of Thomas—the assumption of an apocalyptic-kerygmatic origin is not necessary. Rather, the generative matrix for the selection, resignification, and additional production of sayings material is to be sought in the social history of these movements. If so, the sharp tenor of Jesus' speech in both Q and the Gospel of Thomas cannot be taken as evidence for some dramatic point of origin in the life of the historical Jesus. The figure of Jesus was recast in keeping with the resignification of the sayings in the course of options taken at various turns in those social histories.

2. Wisdom and the Authority of Jesus

In Q, the characterization of Jesus is different in each layer of the compositional history. This means that the figure of Jesus changed in keeping with the type of sayings material attributed to him. If so, Jesus' authority among the tradents of Q is directly related to the authority granted his teachings.

Q1 contains blocks of sapiential material that can be described as units of elaboration. The core material appears to be aphoristic forms of imperatival address. Thus the earliest layer of Q material is a selection of imperatives attributed to Jesus. That they are aphoristic points to a certain style and élan that may well be indicative of discourse in the presence of the historical Jesus. That they are a select group of imperatives implies an early stage of group formation among those who thought to continue such a style of life as his "followers." A close look at the content shows that the imperatives recommend a pattern of behavior reminiscent of popular Cynics. The arena for such behavior appears to be the public sphere. Attribution to Jesus does not imply an authority different from that regularly acknowledged in Hellenistic times for teachers as founders of a school. [13]

At the level of elaboration in Q1, however, aphoristic imperatives were turned into moral maxims. The arena for performance oscillates from public to private, and the force of the imperative combines the notions of "You can do

---

13 On the attribution of sayings to sages, teachers, philosophers, and founder figures, see Kloppenborg, *Formation of Q*, chap. 7.

it" with "You should do it." One has the impression of a codification of community ethic. Here, at this level, Jesus' authority is enhanced by the simple means of self-reference. He is imagined not only as the author of aphoristic imperatives ("Bless those who curse you"), but as the one who elaborated them into community rules ("Love your enemies, for . . ."). It is thus but a short step to imagine Jesus talking about himself as the one whose words are important for the community ("Every one who hears my words and does them . . ."). It is obvious that Jesus came to be understood as a founder figure with special claim to authority. But the mode of attributing authority to him is not strange when compared with other sayings collections of the time.

In Q2 the situation changes drastically. In order to support the threat of judgment upon the community's detractors, a large epic-apocalyptic frame of reference was worked out. To place Jesus within this frame, some recasting of his character and role was obviously necessary. Three major resignifications are in evidence. One is that Jesus was brought into association with John the Baptist and that both were aligned with the history of the prophets. This move solved several conceptual problems. It not only positioned Jesus correctly with respect to the prophetic strain in the epic history imagined. It also marked his appearance as the beginning of the new time in which the community of Q wanted to find itself. And it solved the problem of imagining how the new apocalyptic rhetoric could be attributed to the traditionally sapiential Jesus.[14]

Another development in Q2 addressed the problem of relating Jesus and his words to the apocalyptic future. The figure introduced at this point was that of the Son of man. The solution was to imagine that Jesus predicted the coming of the Son of man as judge, and that the basis of his judgment would be how one had responded to Jesus (Q 12:8–9). This clever solution was possible without implying any enhancement of the figure of Jesus beyond that of being a special sage and prophet. The notion of his uniqueness was worked out in terms of his special place at the turn of the epic-apocalyptic history.

A third development in the characterization of Jesus can be discerned in a few wisdom sayings that were attributed to him in Q2. These sayings occur in Jesus' answer to the disciples of John (Q 7:35, "Yet wisdom is justified by all her children"), his elaboration on the sign of Jonah (Q 11:31, "Something greater than Solomon is here"), among the woes against the Pharisees (Q 11:49, "Therefore also the wisdom of God said, I will send them prophets . . ."), and at the end of the lament over Jerusalem (Q 13:35, "You will not see me again . . ."). These sayings draw upon the mythology of personified wisdom in order to attribute epic perspective to Jesus' role. In the course of this development, however, Jesus' knowledge of his role is equated with the very knowledge imagined for personified wisdom.

This means that Jesus could easily become a revealer figure without any appeal to an "Easter" mythologem, should the dispensation of special knowl-

---

14 On Q2 as a myth of origin with an epic-apocalyptic frame, see Mack, "The Kingdom That Didn't Come."

edge be of interest to the Q tradents. That it was of interest is documented in the passage where Jesus blesses those who belong to the new order of things, whose eyes have seen the truth that others have not seen (Q 10:21–22). One should note that this enhancement of Jesus' special wisdom is still related to his role as founder figure for a community oriented to his teachings. The knowledge dispensed here is merely the complementary contrast to the knowledge of an apocalyptic judgment that will befall those who reject his teachings. It is a vision of the divine kingdom via reflection from its contrast, the arena of woes.

Accounting for the mythic figure of Jesus in the Gospel of Thomas is a bit more difficult, mainly because both the characterization of Jesus and the application of his teachings were elaborated so programmatically. Jesus is a supernatural revealer whose appearance in the world brought enlightenment to his true disciples. Enlightenment is understood as knowledge of one's self as belonging to an other-worldly order of divine origin and self-sufficiency. Thus the boundary erodes between Jesus as revealer figure and his true disciples as enlightened ones. Comparison with Q is instructive. The tradents of the Gospel of Thomas rejected an apocalyptic interpretation of Jesus' appearance and developed the notion of enlightenment. The claim to enlightenment is highly developed in comparison with the Q2 snippet mentioned above, but it could be understood as a further development of an analogous point of departure. It may be important, however, that the apocalyptic sayings in the Gospel of Thomas are troublesome to the tradents, not as judgment sayings against detractors, but as sayings taken to refer to the destiny of Jesus and the disciples. This may indicate a period of reflection in which the primary function of apocalyptic sayings in the Jesus traditions was no longer appropriate. Left with apocalyptic sayings on their hands, resignification as enlightenment sayings could have been an attractive option.

It should also be emphasized that many sayings in the Gospel of Thomas gain their gnosticizing flavor only in the context of the collection as a whole. If isolated from this context, many sayings are similar to formulations found in Q, and some sayings may even reflect traditions earlier than their counterparts in Q. In a recent dissertation at Claremont, Stephen Patterson succeeded in demystifying approximately one-third of the sayings in a reconstruction of the social behavior of the the Gospel of Thomas tradents. According to his reconstruction, the tradents of the Gospel of Thomas do not look much different from the tradents of Q1. The point would be that the Gospel-of-Thomas tradition may have its roots in a Jesus movement quite similar to that proposed for Q. If so, the process by which Jesus came to be imagined as the divine revelation of self-knowledge can be understood on the Q analogy as a cultivation of his sayings over a rather long period of time in the direction of internalized application.[15]

---

15 On the cynic-like life style reflected in the Gospel of Thomas, see Patterson, "The Gospel of Thomas."

The jump from Jesus as a cynic sage to Jesus as the revealer of esoteric knowledge about salvation has been too great for scholars to imagine without a little help from the resurrected Jesus. If the jump was not taken all at one time, however, but achieved by incremental shifts in characterization, and if the shifts in characterization correlated with changes in the type of instruction attributed to him, the enhancement of Jesus' authority can be explained as the attribution of appropriate authorial roles. This process can certainly be called mythmaking, but none of the mythic features need be derived from the myth of the resurrected Christ. Mythic characterization for divine men and founder figures was a common ingredient in the Hellenistic-Jewish culture of the time. One need think only of Philo's application of many mythic features and functions to Moses as an example of the Hellenistic imagination. None of them required a kerygma of Moses' death and resurrection. All of them stood in the service of enhancing the divine significance of his words.

3. The Holy Spirit and the Sayings of Jesus

Yet a third feature of the teachings of Jesus has been used to link the sayings traditions with the Christ kerygma. It is the reference to the holy Spirit in Q. Since the language of the Spirit occurs in the prophetic tradition, and since it is used in Paul to refer to the presence of the Lord, the link has seemed natural enough. Then, because Jesus is said to baptize with the holy Spirit in Q, and because Luke interprets this as a post-Easter moment, a post-Easter situation for the tradents of Q can be imagined. The result has been to view the tradents of Q as prophets speaking by inspiration of the spirit of the resurrected Jesus. This notion has sometimes been used as well to account for the attribution of newly coined sayings to Jesus as their author.[16]

Confronted with such a congeries of mystification, the social historian simply has to start from scratch. The first observation of significance is that Q1 does not contain any reference to the holy Spirit. The second is that the references in Q2 are meager. The candidates for inclusion are the following:

1. John's Preaching:
"He will baptize you with the holy Spirit and fire" (Q 3:16).
2. Thanksgiving for Revelation:
"In that very hour he rejoiced in the holy Spirit and said, 'I praise you, Father, Lord of heaven and earth, that you have hidden these things from sages and the learned and revealed them to babes'" (Q 10:21).
(Matt 11:25, "At that time Jesus said, 'I praise you . . .'")
3. Confidence in Prayer:
". . . how much more will the heavenly Father give the holy Spirit to those who ask him" (Q 11:13).

16 On the notion of the resurrected Jesus as author by inspiration of the "post-Easter" sayings, see Boring, *Sayings of the Risen Jesus.*

(Matt 7:11, ". . . how much more will your Father who is in heaven give good things to those who ask him.")
4. The Beelzebul Accusation:
   "But if it is by the finger of God that I exorcize demons, then the reign of God has come upon you" (Q 11:20).
   (Matt 12:28, "But if it is by the Spirit of God that I exorcize demons, then the reign of God has come upon you.")
5. Blasphemy of the Spirit:
   "And every one who says a word against the Son of man will be forgiven; but the one who blasphemes against the holy Spirit will not be forgiven" (Q 12:10).
   (Matt 12:32, ". . . but whoever speaks against the holy Spirit will not be forgiven.")
6. The Spirit's Assistance:
   "When they bring you before the synagogues and the rulers and the authorities, do not be anxious how or what you are to answer or what you are to say; for the holy Spirit will teach you in that very hour what you ought to say" (Q 12:11–12).
   (Matt 10:19, "When they deliver you up, do not be anxious how or what you will say; for what you are to say will be given to you in that hour; for it is not you who speak, but the Spirit of your Father speaking through you.")

Three of the six occurrences do not show agreement between Luke and Matthew (Sayings 2, 3, 4). The mention of the holy Spirit in 2 and 3 is suspiciously Lukan, for each agrees with Luke's own conception and theme of the Spirit, and the sayings do not require reference to the Spirit, as the readings in Matthew show. The mention of the Spirit of God in Matthew's version of 4 is suspicious as an anti-anthropomorphic theologumenon. Luke preserves the more difficult, interesting, and appropriate reading. That leaves three sayings, numbers 1, 5, and 6.

The first saying (1) should be read in the light of John's function for the program of Q2. At this stage of Q's compositional history, prophetic and apocalyptic sayings were being combined with the earlier blocks of sapiential material. There is some indication that this new development presented a challenge for the tradents in that the characterization of the older sapiential Jesus had now to include a prophetic role. In the subsequent unit about John and Jesus a significant step was taken toward the conceptual solution of this problem (Q 7:18–35). The unit makes the point that both John and Jesus (prophet and sage) were justified as children of the same wisdom (Q 7:18–35). This assertion helped to join the roles of prophet and sage in the same divine program, but it did not adequately change the characterization of Jesus to that of an apocalyptic preacher. That shift does occur, however, in the announcement that John makes about the kind of baptist Jesus will be (Saying 1 above, Q 3:16). What John says is that Jesus, the coming one, will baptize with both the holy Spirit and fire.

To baptize with fire is explained in apocalyptic metaphor as the burning of the "chaff." When and how that will happen are questions left unanswered. But the theme of fire occurs elsewhere in Q2 as a sign of Jesus' appearance. It occurs, importantly, in the context of sayings on "division" (Q 12:49; cf.

12:51–53). It thus appears that the apocalyptic metaphor (fire) was used both to recharacterize Jesus and to reinterpret the effect of his teachings. Baptizing with fire, applied to the Jesus of the sayings in Q, means that Jesus' words create division.

What baptism with the holy Spirit means is not as clear, but the imagery of the threshing floor provides a clue. The wind separates the wheat from the chaff just as the fire burns the chaff separated from the wheat. If the metaphor of fire refers to the effectiveness of Jesus' speech in regard to the pronouncement of judgment upon the rightly accused, perhaps the metaphor of holy Spirit refers to the effectiveness of Jesus' speech in regard to the defense of the wrongly accused. Later, in Saying 6, the holy Spirit is said to come to the assistance of the accused follower of Jesus. The question is, what kind of speech might that be?

Spirit and prophecy go together, of course, so that the relation between spirit language and effective predictive speech can belong to the metaphor. But there was also a rather strong tradition about the "spirit of wisdom," a metaphor that combined the notion of effective speech with that of special insight into the rhyme and reason of the present orders (inspiration as knowledge). From Sirach, through the Wisdom of Solomon, to Philo, the spirit of wisdom functions as a metaphor for insight into the ways of God in the world of creation, the history of humanity, the social orders, and the secrets of the heart. It does not for that reason cease to function as a metaphor for effective speech. If the metaphor of fire is particularly appropriate to the judgmental effect of Jesus' speech on those outside of the community, the metaphor of the holy Spirit picks up on its capacity to effect insight, discernment, and prophetic clarity for those inside the Jesus movement.

Thus Jesus will "baptize," according to John, by immersing the world in speech. In both applications of the metaphors, it is speech that makes the difference, but the metaphor of fire is overlaid with an imagination of the eschaton, while the metaphor of spirit is more appropriate to the daring activity of speaking in the present.[17] It is extremely important to note that Jesus is not depicted in Q as having bequeathed his or God's spirit to his followers. Neither is there any mention of "bringing spirit upon the earth" in analogy to the saying about the fire. In fact, the later mentions of the holy Spirit in Q treat it as a personification of divine agency in distinction from Jesus. So some conceptual slippage is in evidence between the announcement of John and the rest of Q. Nevertheless, the metaphor works once it is seen that both Jesus' "baptism" "in spirit and fire," as well as the promise about the holy

---

17 The tensive relation between the two terms of the word pair fire/spirit in Q is also true for the background of both in Hellenistic conceptuality (where, for instance, fire and spirit are important concepts in the Stoic system of thought, closely related in cosmologies, but divided in application to eschatology), and in Jewish thinking (where, for instance, fire carries a primary apocalyptic connotation, whereas spirit is a symbol of more universal application).

Spirit "teaching" the follower of Jesus "what to say" (Saying 6), refer to situations in which speech related to the authority of Jesus makes the critical difference.

In Saying 6 the holy Spirit is understood to instruct as well as to empower (in the sense of overcoming anxiety before the rulers of the synagogue), and the situation is understood as trial. Since this situation epitomizes the trauma of the Q community at a particular juncture of their social history, one can safely assume that the accusation has to do with how one stands with respect to the synagogue, given one's loyalty to the Jesus movement. It is obvious that what one said on such an occasion would be critical, because the situation was potentially divisive. Wisdom would be required even if one thought to recall something from the words of Jesus. There is really nothing in Q1 or Q2 that is obviously appropriate for such an encounter, which means that ad hoc "instruction" of some kind would be absolutely necessary. The saying promises that such would occur. The challenge would be to defend one's loyalty to the Jesus movement without further offending the synagogue authorities.

That the instruction is attributed to the holy Spirit does not mean that the tradents of Q were entertaining notions of ecstatic prophecy. It means that the situation in view was considered critical but manageable if correctly assessed. It was critical as an occasion for a speech of defense before one's questioners in the present. It was even more critical in the light of the enormous consequences that loomed when the present moment was placed into the larger apocalyptic frame of reference. The promise comes from Jesus, but he is clearly understood as speaking from the past and therefore absent on the occasion. The promise is therefore cast in terms of the assistance of the holy Spirit. If one's speech on such an occasion confirmed the claims of the movement, drew the boundary issues with the synagogue correctly, and forced the issue of judgment back upon all parties concerned, that would be a holy Spirit speech.

Saying 5 (Q 12:10) is the most difficult of all, for there the issue is what one says *about* the holy Spirit, and a distinction is made between speaking a word against the Son of man and speaking against the holy Spirit. However, if the Lukan order is followed, Q 12:4–12 forms a unit that provides a context for clarification. The unit includes the saying on appropriate fear (Q 12:4–7), the saying about acknowledging or denying Jesus and its eschatological consequence when the Son of man sits in judgment (Q 12:8–9), our Saying 5 (Q 12:10) and our Saying 6 (Q 12:11–12). The language of trial and the theme of anxiety set the tone for a rather comprehensive instruction. The instruction is fully appropriate to the situation reflected in the last saying (6). It is the situation of "trial" before the rulers of the synagogue. In this situation one will be required to give an account of oneself as a member of the Jesus movement. Of the many topics that might come up, three are critical, each for different reasons. One needs to know the consequences when speaking about Jesus, the Son of man, and the holy Spirit.

16 • Burton L. Mack

About Jesus there is no room to maneuver. It is either yes or no with respect
to whether one belongs to the Jesus movement. The consequences are spelled
out clearly. At the eschaton the formula of reciprocity will be exact. Acknowledgment now brings acknowledgment then; denial now brings denial then.

If asked about the Son of man the situation is a bit different. One should not
speak against the Son of man, but if one does it is forgivable. This is at first
curious, but it can be explained. If one takes the two instructions together, a
distinction is being made between Jesus and the Son of man. One denies (or
confesses) loyalty to Jesus; one speaks against (or for) the Son of man. To
"speak a word against" is a rhetorical term that implies the making of a speech,
not just the entering of a plea. It is not at first clear, of course, whether the Son
of man in question is the apocalyptic judge or Jesus in his role as Son of man.
But if the point lies in the distinction between Jesus and the Son of man, it may
not matter which Son of man is intended. The term Son of man, whether
referring to Jesus or to the eschatological judge, describes the apocalyptic
persuasion of the community, and this persuasion was entertained in order to
undergird the threat of judgment upon the rulers of the synagoge. It would
have been very difficult to explain all of that to the very rulers of the synagoge
who presently sat in the seat of judgment. And besides, it was Jesus and his
words that were of first importance. Judgment was a secondary consideration
that applied to those who did not receive his words and "do them." So, even
though one should not speak against the Son of man, it would be forgivable if
one did. The Son of man, apparently, was not yet quite the same as Jesus.

What then of the distinction between the Son of man and the holy Spirit?
One might note the difference between "making a speech against the Son of
man" and the truncated "speaking against the holy Spirit."[18] It is, in any case,
more difficult to imagine the topic of "the holy Spirit" coming up for discussion on such an occasion. But the point must surely be that, in distinction
to what one might or might not say about one's apocalyptic and judgmental
persuasions, one could not afford second thoughts and hasty disavowals with
regard to the holy Spirit; and that must be because the holy Spirit referred to
the wisdom and courage required for coming to speech effectively about Jesus.
One could not speak disparagingly of the holy Spirit and be in a fearless
position when asked about one's loyalty to Jesus. It was the holy Spirit, after
all, who "will teach you in that very hour what you ought to say." These
instructions should therefore not be mystified, as if the Q people expected a
special revelation. They served as a warning about the truly critical nature of
the occasion, and as an assurance that, if one resolved to acknowledge Jesus,
one would find the words for it. The holy Spirit is evident in the fearless
speech in defense of Jesus, his teachings, and the Jesus movement.

18 Reading with Matthew. Speaking against the holy Spirit is called blasphemy in Mark.
Mark's saying is repeated by Matthew in a doublet. Since Luke also reads blasphemy, the
original phrasing cannot be established with certainty. It is possible, however, that both
Luke and Matthew interpreted the saying in the light of Mark.

Apparently, then, the Q tradents were aware of their place in the larger epic-apocalyptic history that they had come to imagine. The epic-apocalyptic mythology was a way of making sense out of some disappointments, and it added a number of imaginative rewards to their investment in the Jesus movement. But it also created some problems of its own. It pushed the reign of God into an apocalyptic future along with the judgments that had to befall those who refused to join their movement. And it positioned Jesus firmly in the past at the turn in the epic history when John appeared. They were left, that is, alone with each other in the midst of an unfriendly world. To fill the time between Jesus in the past and the Son of man to appear in the future, the divine Spirit of wisdom and speech had to be imagined as actively engaged. It is very important to see that this activity was related to speaking for and about Jesus. One might say, therefore, that the community was left alone with the speech of Jesus on their hands. To claim for such speech the presence of the Spirit of God would have been a remarkable solution to the problem of receding horizons.

4. Conclusion

New Testament scholars have traditionally pursued the question of Christian origins from two perspectives. The quest for the historical Jesus has been one approach. The quest for the earliest christology has been the other. The earliest christology has usually been equated with an interpetation of the crucifixion and resurrection. The earliest Jesus traditions have usually been found in the sayings of Jesus. It was Robinson's contribution to these quests to tackle the problem of relating the one to the other. After the two traditions had already been combined in the formation of the gospel with a passion narrative, Robinson's typology of two vision traditions could be used to evaluate the various locations for imagining conversation with the Lord of the logia as the resurrected savior. But for Q and the Gospel of Thomas a certain "ambivalence" was detected. The ambivalence resulted, according to Robinson, from the failure in these traditions to distinguish between the pre-Easter and the post-Easter origins of their sayings. Robinson could phrase the problem that way because of a scholarly consensus about Christian origins. That consensus has been that Easter marked the point of origin for all of the forms of early Jesus movements.

This essay has taken up the question of the evidence for an Easter faith in Q and the Gospel of Thomas, the two collections of the sayings of Jesus with greatest significance for Christian origins. Three factors frequently regarded as evidence for the link between the sayings traditions and the kerygma have been reviewed. They are (1) the incidence and function of apocalyptic language, (2) the divine authority of Jesus, and (3) the language of the Spirit. Each of these features can be explained without relying on the assumption of a kerygmatic interpretation of Jesus' death. The conclusion must be, therefore,

18   •   Burton L. Mack

that in these two traditions at least, movements started from Jesus that were not impelled ideologically by events associated with his death.

Each of the ideological items reviewed in this essay entered the picture only at certain junctures of social experience in need of rationalization. Thus the study has been one about mythmaking in the early Jesus movements. The constant appeal to Jesus as the founder figure of these movements does provide a kind of continuity through the several stages that each reveals. Because Jesus was important to these movements as the author of his sayings, and because his sayings accumulated such astonishing authority, Jesus might be called the Lord of the logia. He came to be seen as an imperious figure, and his sayings became the means for an expected salvation at the eschaton. But for the tradents of Q and of the Gospel of Thomas, the Lord of the logia was not a savior of the dying and rising kind. He was rather a sage whose sayings and the wisdom to be derived from them made all the difference that mattered.

James M. Robinson hosting a reception at the Institute for Antiquity and Christianity

The Sermon on the Mount and Q

SOME ASPECTS OF THE PROBLEM

Hans Dieter Betz

1. The Major Questions

The relationship between the Sermon on the Mount, Matt 5:3–7:27 (henceforth abbreviated: SM), and Q is far more intricate than a superficial view of a synopsis of the New Testament gospels would suggest. James Robinson pointed to the problem years ago in a footnote, when he said: "The cohesion of the collection suggests that the Sermon on the Mount (or Plain) is derived from an oral collection of its own, and did not first come into being in the context of Q. . . . The end seems to be the conclusion of a collection, and this is not simply because of the occurrence there of the term *logoi.*"[1] This way of stating the matter, however, leaves room for several options. Since two texts are involved, the SM and the Sermon on the Plain, Luke 6:20b–49 (henceforth: SP), the question is whether we are dealing with one sermon or two. Which of them is derived from a previous collection? Since that previous collection is said to be oral and thus different from the written Q, how many collections are we to assume? What relationship exists between the presumed oral source and the written Q?

These questions can also be stated in a different way. What relationship exists between the SM and the SP? Was the SM or the SP part of Q? Were both sermons part of different versions of Q, namely Q^{Matt} and Q^{Luke}? Was an earlier Q sermon a source from which both the SM and the SP were developed? Was the SP identical with Q^{Luke}, and did the evangelist Matthew or a pre-Matthean redactor develop the SM from this basis? Or is the SP a secondary reduction of the SM? If one assumes several stages of redaction in Q, the question is whether there ever was an earlier Q sermon or whether the SM and the SP were added at later stages of Q, the SM in Q^{Matt} and the SP in Q^{Luke}. Even if one holds this view, as we do, the similarities and differences in the two sermons must be explained.

Whatever answers one may give to this plethora of questions, they will profoundly affect our understanding of Q as well as of the SM and the SP, not

---

1 Robinson and Koester, *Trajectories,* 94 n. 47.

20 • Hans Dieter Betz

to speak of Matthew and Luke as the final redactional works of which they all
became part. This paper cannot deal with all aspects of these intriguing
questions, but we shall concentrate on one aspect that is often overlooked: The
whole problem, as we know, is as much tied up with the history of scholarship
as it is with the texts themselves.

2. The History of Scholarship

2.1 The basic alternatives

In the history of scholarship the problem of the relationship between the
SM and the SP preceded the Q hypothesis; in fact, it was a factor contributing
to its development. The similarities and differences between the SM and the
SP have baffled scholars since antiquity.[2] Did the two sermons constitute the
same or two different speeches of Jesus? While Origen,[3] John Chrysostom,[4]
Euthymius,[5] and Theophylactus[6] assumed two versions of the same speech,
Augustine,[7] perhaps impressed by Manichaean (and Marcionite?) arguments,
presupposed two separate speeches: one that Jesus gave before the apostles
only (the SM), and the other, a shorter, given before all people (the SP). The
main appeal for Augustine's view was that it was compatible with the doctrine
of inspiration: both sermons could be affirmed as true and accurate. By
contrast, scholars who took Origen's position had to face the problem of the
insufficiency of the shorter SP or had to assume different levels of inspiration.[8]
At any rate, if the fuller account (the SM) was taken to be the more accurate
and complete, it could be integrated with the SP in the form of a gospel
harmony, thus resolving the problem.

2.2 Tholuck and his contenders

This state of things is still presupposed in the learned commentary by
August Tholuck.[9] His work is interesting because he did not work with a
gospel harmony when he wrote his commentary on the SM, and he also knew
that both the SM and the SP are redactional products. Still, he simply ignored
the SP, regarding the SM as the more authentic and more complete account,
although he knew that both were fictional. He insisted that it did not make
much difference. "The peculiar enchantment of the whole of this speech" (sc.
the SM) makes it breathe "the primary and original spirit of Christ."[10]

2 See Tholuck, *Die Bergrede*, 1–6.
3 Origen, *In Matth.* 11.4 on Matt 14:22 (s.v. Klostermann).
4 John Chrysostom, *Hom.* 15.1.
5 Euthymius, *In Matth.*, cap. 5:1–2.
6 Theophylactus, *In Matth.*, cap. 5:1–2.
7 Augustine, *De consensu evang.* 2.19.43.
8 See, e.g., Stier, *Die Reden*, 1.170.
9 Tholuck, *Die Bergrede*, the first edition of which appeared under the title *Philologisch-historische Auslegung der Bergpredigt Christi* (Hamburg: Perthes, 1833).
10 Tholuck, *Die Bergrede*, 8,12,15.

Tholuck's position is directly opposite to the one advocated by Heinrich Ewald[11] and Heinrich Julius Holtzmann,[12] who argued that the SP is shorter and thus more original, while Matthew's SM is the product of secondary expansion and redaction. Was the shorter text closer to historical reality, as Ewald and Holtzmann assumed, or was the Jewishness of the SM the mark of historicity, as Tholuck insisted?[13] In pointing to the Jewish character of the SM Tholuck relied on earlier statements made by Johann Gottfried Herder,[14] who in turn quoted John Lightfoot's[15] and Christian Schöttgen's[16] linguistic proofs that Jesus was a Jew speaking "the Syrian-Chaldaean dialect" as his mother tongue. Because the SM had a Jewish character and the SP had not, even Ferdinand Christian Baur preferred the SM as the more authentic speech of Jesus.[17]

The problem with this debate was, among other matters, that it confused two issues that should be kept apart: the question of the historical origin of Jesus' speech and the question of the textual basis for reconstructing that speech. While Tholuck mobilized his exorbitant scholarly erudition and insisted that the SM was for practical purposes the closest we could get to Jesus' speech, he in fact tried to persuade the reader to believe in a fiction. At the same time, while his commentary went through numerous editions, scholarship had passed beyond it. The state of research at the beginning of the nineteenth century is well summed up in Wilhelm Martin Leberecht de Wette's *Kurze Erklärung des Evangeliums Matthäi,* first published in 1836.[18] According to de Wette, the older consensus of two speeches had been given up in favor of John Calvin's view of one speech recorded in two versions. Both versions were now regarded as redactional compositions. Which best reflected Jesus' original speech? Choosing, however, was not the only option. If Matthew's SM was the evangelist's creation, which source did he revise?

Holtzmann[19] proposed that the original source of the SM was *Urmarkus,* a hypothetical earlier version of Mark, which had the original SM after Mark 3:19; in our Mark this section was omitted, so that we possess only its two secondary elaborations, SM and SP. Luke, according to Holtzmann, took over the original sermon from *Urmarkus* in its entirety and added only the verses 6:39 and 40, whereas Matthew reworked the same *Urmarkus* sermon completely. Thus Holtzmann could claim that the SP was "almost identical" with the source for the SM. When scholarship dropped the *Urmarkus* hypothesis, the hypothetical Q sermon was born and inherited the phrase, "almost iden-

11 Ewald, *Die ersten drei Evangelien,* 207.
12 Holtzmann, *Die synoptischen Evangelien,* 174–78.
13 Tholuck, *Die Bergrede,* 15, agreeing with Baur, *Kritische Untersuchungen,* 585.
14 Herder, *Erläuterungen,* 106.
15 Lightfoot, *Horae Hebraicae,* esp. 173.
16 Schöttgen, *Horae Hebraicae,* "Praefatio" (1, §1–6).
17 See n. 13, above.
18 de Wette, *Kurze Erklärung,* 66–69.
19 Holtzmann, *Die synoptischen Evangelien,* 174–75.

tical with the SP." Holtzmann's basic ideas, however, came from Johann Gottfried Eichhorn's seminal work, "Ueber die drey ersten Evangelien," published in 1794.[20] Eichhorn suggested for the first time that those sections which are common to Matthew and Luke may have come from "a common written source."[21] This source, however, was received by Matthew and Luke not in its original form, but in different versions due to different manuscripts.[22] In other words, these versions have been subject to redactional modifications at the presynoptic level. At the beginning, prior to their modification, this source was in Hebrew or Chaldaic-Syriac, while Matthew's and Luke's version depend on different translations into the Greek. Some of the problems in the sources are due to translation errors.[23] As Eichhorn saw it, Matthew's version of the source (the SM) had been reworked and reflected the needs and views of Jewish Christianity.[24] The problem, therefore, is this: "Only that it is impossible till now to determine whether each addition (sc. in Matthew's SM) has merely been borrowed from another memorandum of the life of Jesus, or whether it has first been written for our Matthew."[25] Differences in style cannot be detected, because Matthew has rewritten it all, and he depended on an earlier Greek translation anyway. "But it is at least probable that the redactor of our Matthew had for some passages something written in front of him."[26] Eichhorn refers to the Lord's Prayer and to other SM passages as examples of possible written sources.[27] It should be clear that Eichhorn's account states the issues and problems as we are discussing them to this day. To use modern terminology, he speaks of Q^{Matt}. In a detailed critique of Holtzmann, Bernhard Weiss[28] disagreed with one of the assumptions of Holtzmann, namely that Luke 6:20–49 contains the original sermon, from which the SM was also developed. He argued that just like Matthew's SM, Luke's SP also showed signs of redaction. Contrary to what had been assumed earlier, the SP does not lack order or suffer from incompleteness, but it represents a composition of its own. Therefore, according to Weiss, SP also "has a secondary character."[29]

2.3 The state of the question around 1850

By the middle of the nineteenth century, some kind of consensus had been reached among critical scholars. It was summarized by Ferdinand Christian Baur in his *Kritische Untersuchungen über die kanonischen Evangelien,* pub-

20 Eichhorn, "Ueber die drey ersten Evangelien," esp. 964–79; idem, *Einleitung in das Neue Testament* 1.439–40; cf. also 1.498–502.
21 Eichhorn, "Ueber die drey ersten Evangelien," 965.
22 Eichhorn, "Ueber die drey ersten Evangelien," 967, 970.
23 Eichhorn, "Ueber die drey ersten Evangelien," 969.
24 Eichhorn, "Ueber die drey ersten Evangelien," 972.
25 Eichhorn, "Ueber die drey ersten Evangelien," 977.
26 Eichhorn, "Ueber die drey ersten Evangelien," 977.
27 Eichhorn, "Ueber die drey ersten Evangelien," 977–78.
28 B. Weiss, "Die Redestücke des apostolischen Matthäus," esp. 52–65. See also his *Das Matthäusevangelium,* esp. 128, 222–23.
29 B. Weiss, "Die Redestücke des apostolischen Matthäus," 55.

lished in 1847.[30] Accordingly, both the SM and the SP are to be regarded as redactional products, and the SP has no advantage over the SM regarding historical originality. Both sermons must be seen at the same level as secondary elaborations, and none is to be given a preferred status. And yet, Baur agrees with David Friedrich Strauss,[31] and even with Tholuck, that in spite of the secondary nature of the SM, this version of the speech preserved the original milieu and conceptuality of Judaism, and it was as yet undisturbed by party factions that had given rise to the Gospel of Luke. Since the *Urmarkus* hypothesis had been given up, the source Q, clearly delineated by the ingenious Christian Hermann Weisse in his *Die evangelische Geschichte,* published in 1838,[32] was indeed the best explanation of the origin of the source underlying both the SM and the SP. The differences between them could then be explained as the redactional operation of the evangelists.

The development of the Q hypothesis does not need to be discussed any further here. Once the idea of a Q source was born, a wealth of studies appeared, all of them attempts at reconstruction of this great unknown source. There were of course also those who rejected the idea, relying instead on the notion of "oral tradition." This line of argument is at present carried on in the Göttingen doctoral dissertation of 1963/64 by Hans-Theo Wrege.[33] Wrege pursues the doubts about a written source Q expressed by his teacher Joachim Jeremias a generation earlier.[34] He contends that oral tradition alone can explain the parallelism of the sayings in the SM and the SP.

2.4 The state of the question around 1900

Wrege's work, however, was outdated when it appeared. He presupposes a certain *status quaestionis* without examining its presuppositions in the history of scholarship. There is no separate investigation of the SP, and he makes no attempts to explain the compositional structure and the parallelism of the arrangement of the sayings in both texts, phenomena that had been noted much earlier in the nineteenth-century debate about the so-called "tradition hypothesis." In fact, Wrege's interests in the oral tradition had already been combined with the Q hypothesis in two important studies on *Die Bergpredigt* by Carl Friedrich Georg Heinrici, which appeared in 1900 and 1905.[35] These works, which have been unduly overlooked by scholarship, analyzed the sayings in the SM and the SP as literary *gnomai,* determining their formal structure, composition, and function. Heinrici's conclusion was that the oral transmission of the sayings of Jesus was carried on by Jesus' disciples for the purpose of collecting and preserving his legacy.[36] The SM and the SP show

---

30 Baur, *Kritische Untersuchungen,* 586–89.
31 Strauss, *Das Leben Jesu,* 1.639–40, 652.
32 Weisse, *Die evangelische Geschichte,* 1.79–85.
33 Wrege, *Die Überlieferungsgeschichte.*
34 Wrege mentions Jeremias and Martin Dibelius as those who have doubts about Q.
35 Heinrici, *Die Bergpredigt,* parts 2 and 3.
36 *Die Bergpredigt,* 2:10, 76–81.

that, while this process was still going on, the move to written sources had occurred at the same time. The two sermons, therefore, must have gone through a period of oral transmission before they were written down. They are not the products of the redaction of the gospel writers Matthew and Luke but are of pre-synoptic origin.[37] Both sermons, according to Heinrici, are "reconstructions, not simply reproductions" of Jesus' teaching.[38] The SM is informed by Palestinian Jewish conditions, while the SP has no relationship to the Jewish environment. The same sayings material has been arranged in different ways, resulting in different documents, because of the different background and interests of their redactors.[39] They are, for this reason, to be treated as independent texts. The SM is close to the environment of Jesus' origin, Jewish Palestine; the SP addresses Gentiles. Both sermons try to communicate Jesus' legacy to different audiences by secondary "reconstructions of a foundational speech of Jesus, in two versions and not depending on a common source."[40]

Unfortunately, however, Heinrici did not state his view forcefully enough,[41] as he was tired of the never-ending battles of the proponents of the oral tradition against those pushing written sources and vice versa, alternatives which he who knew Greek and Roman gnomological literature so well realized were false. Concentrating on the hypothetical source Q, scholarship went in another direction.

Once scholars focused their attention on the reconstruction of the source Q, interest in the SM and the SP as textual units ceased. If the composition of the SM and the SP was taken to be the work of the gospel writers, then the source Q was thought to contain merely the material of the individual sayings that were used in these redactional elaborations. The Q source as a whole, going beyond the SM and the SP, had to have a different structure and composition anyway. Consequently, the SM and the SP became dissolved into Q.

This state of affairs we can observe in the important summary of Q research at the end of the nineteenth century, Paul Wernle's *Die synoptische Frage*, published in 1899.[42] This summary, as everyone agrees, became the starting point for twentieth-century scholarship in this area. According to Wernle, the SM is part of Q, but not in its entirety. Q began with the speech by John the Baptist (Matt 3:7–12//Luke 3:7–9, 16–17), and then continued with the temptation dialogue (Matt 4:3–10//Luke 4:3–12) and "the speech on righteousness" (*Gerechtigkeitsrede*), including the SM sections Matt 5:3–48; 7:1–6, 12–27; with the parallels in SP, Luke 6:20–49; 11:33; 12:58–59; 16:17–18. Beyond this basic material, Q may have included some of Matthew's special traditions (*Sondergut*), in particular Matt 6:1–18 (but not 6:9–15). Wernle was

37 *Die Bergpredigt*, 2:80–81.
38 *Die Bergpredigt*, 2:10.
39 *Die Bergpredigt*, 2:79.
40 *Die Bergpredigt*, 3:2.
41 See Johannes Weiss in his review.
42 Wernle, *Die synoptische Frage*, 224–33.

both cautious and imaginative in his assessment of the question. He did not commit himself to more than assumptions.[43] Yet, he distinguished himself by his keen perception in identifying the problems that needed to be tackled.

Thus he saw the need for working out the compositional structure of Q and found traces of it in three groups of sayings. The function is not chronology but catechesis, so that later sayings are mixed with earlier ones. Wernle thought that Q owed its existence to the need in the new Christian communities for written instruction, since they no longer had contact with Jesus. For these new Christians larger themes or topics served as guidance, such as, "What is the will of God?" or, "What are duties of missionaries?" These topics are of immense historical value to us to get access not to the historical Jesus, but to the oldest Christian theology. Wernle also noticed the lack of a christology but suggested that this lack is deceptive: the sayings about confessing and the Parousia, in fact all sayings, presuppose faith in the messiah Jesus implicitly. One can see from these remarks that assumptions previously held in regard to the SM have now been transferred to Q.

Wernle also recognized that Q had passed through a history before it reached the gospel writers, but the earlier assumption of an Aramaic original was now questioned: "This Q collection was certainly not written in an originally semitic language. The sayings in Matthew and Luke go back to a common Greek source. There is no reason to postulate an Aramaic original. We have to reckon with the possibility that even our oldest records concerning Jesus were in Greek. Since the large Gentile Christian church superseded the oldest church so rapidly, this fact should not surprise anyone."[44] This source Q, according to Wernle, was a redactional product that could be related to the early Christian parties. While the Lukan Q lacks all Judaizing tendencies, the Matthean Q has been influenced by Judaistic tendencies, for which Matt 5:17–20; 10:5–6 and 23:3 are named. "Therefore, the three most important speeches (the speech on righteousness, the one against the Pharisees, and the one for the missionaries) have as their cutting-edge the stamp of Judaism, and this as a matter of principle forbidding any escape such as saying that these words were only casual comments of Jesus. Rather, these three speeches were law for early Christianity."[45]

Wernle believed that the Q source was anti-Pauline in character: "An antithesis against Paul and his work can hardly be missed, when the Christian teachers are measured by their correctness about the law, when mission to the Gentiles and the Samaritans is prohibited, and when even the commandments of the Pharisees are praised."[46] This Judaizing tendency cannot be Matthew's own addition; it must have been part of his source Q.

However, not everything in Q expresses this Judaizing tendency, and there

43 Wernle, *Die synoptische Frage*, 227: "Natürlich sind das alles nur Vermutungen."
44 Wernle, *Die synoptische Frage*, 229.
45 Wernle, *Die synoptische Frage*, 229.
46 Wernle, *Die synoptische Frage*, 229.

are anti-Jewish polemics as well.[47] This can only be the result of a history of redaction, during which a number of contributors added material of hetero-geneous origin and nature.

> As the legacy of Jesus, the Q collection was made for the community and belonged to the individuals who had copies. Everyone had the right to supple-ment or improve it. Presumably, a few exemplars of Q existed, of about equal length. Between the first writing (Q) and the collection that reached Matthew (Q[Matt]) and Luke (Q[Luke]), there were Q[1], Q[2], Q[3], but it would be a vain effort to try to distinguish among them.[48]

Following Wernle, one would have to attribute the differences between the SM and the SP to changes that took place during the history of the transmis-sion of Q. It is not possible to explain every difference, since we do not know what each contributor had in mind.[49] One of the more obvious differences is that SP shows a distance from Judaism and a closeness to Catholicism, which is certainly the work of the evangelist (sc. Luke). By contrast, the SM appears to be preserved by Matthew to a greater degree, so that it reflects more accurately the state of thinking in the primitive church.[50] We of course have only the final stages of the redactions before us. Wernle attributed the first version of Q to the sixties of the first century, when most of the original apostles were still alive. Before this first Q, which was in Greek, lies the oral Aramaic tradition, "until now more the object of speculation than of secure knowledge."[51] This situation was soon to change.

2.5 The debate between Wellhausen and Harnack

Besides Wernle, the other great summary of nineteenth-century research came from Julius Wellhausen, in particular his commentaries on Matthew[52] and Luke[53] and his *Einleitung in die drei ersten Evangelien*,[54] all published in the first years of the twentieth century. From the mass of arguments and hypotheses, Wellhausen, with his analytical mind and merciless criticism, sorted out those results which in his view deserved further consideration. Rather than merely setting forth his own ideas, however, Wellhausen often stated the most important options. Especially valuable for our inquiry are the two editions of his *Einleitung*, the first edition of which served as the basis for Adolf Harnack's seminal study of Q, which appeared in 1907.[55] The second

47 Wernle, *Die synoptische Frage*, 230–31.
48 Wernle, *Die synoptische Frage*, 231.
49 Wernle, *Die synoptische Frage*, 233.
50 Wernle, *Die synoptische Frage*, 233.
51 Wernle, *Die synoptische Frage*, 233.
52 Wellhausen, *Das Evangelium Matthaei*.
53 Wellhausen, *Das Evangelium Lucae*.
54 Wellhausen, *Einleitung*. All four commentaries and the second edition of the *Einleitung* have been reprinted under the title, *Evangelienkommentare*.
55 Harnack, *Sprüche und Reden Jesu*.

edition of Wellhausen's *Einleitung* was changed to a considerable extent and took Harnack's work as well as that of others into account.

Wellhausen's first edition of the *Einleitung* contained a very interesting chapter on the Aramaic foundations of the gospels,[56] a chapter omitted in the second edition. It is in this chapter that Wellhausen launched an idea that, although not new, resulted in an avalanche of studies down to the present day.

> Jesus himself spoke Aramaic, and his words as well as the stories told about him circulated in the congregation of Jerusalem, which also spoke the Aramaic tongue. Therefore, the oral tradition of the gospel was originally Aramaic, and since it is preserved for us only in Greek writing, it underwent a change of language. This is an historical fact, and it can also be demonstrated philologically. The original form of the tradition has not completely disappeared through the transformation and change of the language. Often the semitic idiom shines through the Greek.[57]

If the oral tradition was originally in Aramaic and was transformed into Greek only later, the question is whether Q was originally in Aramaic or in Greek. Cautiously Wellhausen suggested that the gospels may have been preceded not only by an oral Aramaic tradition but even by written Aramaic sources. "It is conceivable [sc. that the gospel writers were familiar with the Aramaic tradition, although what they wrote down was Greek], but the more probable is that the gospel, which was originally in Aramaic, was at first also written down in Aramaic."[58] As proofs Wellhausen refers to linguistic misunderstandings that can be explained as those of an underlying Aramaic substratum. What does this mean for Q?[59]

According to Wellhausen, whose caution cannot be emphasized enough, Luke appears to have preserved Q "more originally,"[60] but of course Luke's material has been translated into Greek. "More original" in Luke is the piece-by-piece assembly of the sayings, whereas Matthew's version of Q has secondary speeches of some length. This then applies also to the SM and the SP. While both sermons show the same arrangement, Luke's SP is "fresher, more condensed, more popular, and less spiritual and biblical."[61] But Wellhausen did not consider the Lord's Prayer, and some other passages, to have been part of Q.[62] Here Matthew is older, because he had access to and preserved the old Jewish-Christian traditions of the church in Jerusalem.[63] Although Matthew wrote his gospel after the destruction of Jerusalem, he has preserved the old Jerusalem traditions of his church, even where he sets them aside or goes

---

56 Wellhausen, *Einleitung* (1905), 14–34: "Die aramäische Grundlage der Evangelien."
57 Wellhausen, *Einleitung* (1905), 14.
58 Wellhausen, *Einleitung* (1905), 35.
59 See Wellhausen, *Einleitung* (1905), 65–73.
60 Wellhausen, *Einleitung* (1905), 67.
61 Wellhausen, *Einleitung* (1905), 67.
62 Wellhausen, *Einleitung* (1905), 67–68.
63 Wellhausen, *Einleitung* (1905), 88–89.

beyond them.[64] It is interesting to see that these old Jerusalem traditions, as Wellhausen conceives of them, are close to, if not the same as, the teachings of the historical Jesus.[65] The second edition of the *Einleitung* (1911), largely in response to Harnack, moved away from the Aramaic hypothesis and paid more attention to the Greek text. The Aramaic prehistory of Q was now seen as a matter of the distant past, while Wellhausen thought that the Greek translation of Q had developed into two recensions before reaching the gospel writers Matthew and Luke.[66] Though Wellhausen still rules out that the Lord's Prayer was a part of the original Q,[67] the fact that both Matthew (6:11) and Luke (11:3) cite the rare term ἐπιούσιος means that both must have used early Greek versions of Q that had the prayer already in Greek.[68]

Wellhausen's response to Harnack is of interest for a number of reasons.[69] Harnack's thesis, that Q reflects more accurately than Mark the teaching of the historical Jesus, urged Wellhausen to emphasize Mark's role in preserving early traditions from the church in Jerusalem.[70] At issue here was not only whether Q is better than Mark as a source for the teaching of Jesus, but also Wellhausen's original thesis about an Aramaic background of the gospel traditions. The issue, therefore, was Aramaic versus Greek, linguistically, culturally, and religiously. As Harnack's primary source Q was Greek, Wellhausen's original gospel traditions were Aramaic. Consequently, Wellhausen's Jesus was not a Christian but a Jew, while Harnack's Jesus more and more looked like a liberal Protestant like Harnack himself.[71] This exchange between Wellhausen and Harnack determined the main options as they are discussed up to the present time in New Testament scholarship; they include the following issues:[72]

1. the language of Q, whether originally Aramaic or Greek;
2. the date of Q, whether earlier or later;
3. the theology of Q, whether Jewish Christian or Gentile Christian;
4. the "image of Jesus" (*Bild Jesu*) projected by Q, whether that of a "conservative Jew" or that of a "liberal" Christian or Jewish-Christian.

The fundamental problem to be considered in conjunction with these options was whether the Q sayings contain the original message of the historical Jesus. If Wellhausen was right that the original Q was in Aramaic, the original words

64 Wellhausen, *Einleitung* (1905), 88–89.
65 Wellhausen, *Einleitung* (1905), 113–15.
66 Wellhausen, *Einleitung* (1911), 60.
67 Wellhausen, *Einleitung* (1911), 59.
68 Wellhausen, *Einleitung* (1905), 68 with n. 1; (1911), 60.
69 Wellhausen, *Einleitung* (1911), 157–76.
70 Wellhausen, *Einleitung* (1911), 168–70.
71 See also my paper, "Neues Testament und griechisch-hellenistische Überlieferung," read at the Annual Meeting of S.N.T.S. at Göttingen, 1987, and to be published in my *Hellenismus und Urchristentum*, 262–69.
72 See also Schmithals, *Einleitung*, 197–201, 224–27.

of Jesus were irretrievably lost,[73] so that the Greek Q represents from the beginning a Hellenization of Jesus' original message.[74] Accordingly, Jesus was to be placed at the end of Judaism,[75] whereas Christianity really began with Paul.[76] This is Wellhausen's basic position and that of others who accept his famous dictum that "Jesus was not a Christian, but a Jew."[77]

Directly opposite is Harnack's view that Q "on the whole is an old source."[78] Q represents a consistent doctrine, mainly Jewish in nature and free from Christian apologetics.[79] It reflects Jesus' original self-understanding and his proclamation. Although the "original" Q was in Aramaic (here Harnack agrees with Wellhausen),[80] its rendering into Greek did not obscure but preserved Jesus' original message. It is, therefore, the oldest and most trustworthy source for recovering Jesus' original message. Consequently, Q is to be preferred to Mark's Gospel, which reflects Christian theology.[81] For Harnack, the Jesus of Q was the first Christian, not Paul.[82]

This exchange between Harnack and Wellhausen drew up the battle lines for the later twentieth century. How strongly people felt about the famous dictum of Wellhausen can be seen from the fact that they felt compelled to accept or reject it. For instance, Heinrici, who was hesitant about Q, nevertheless felt obliged to side with Harnack when he concluded his second study on the SM by saying, "Jesus is not the last Jew, but the creator of a new, authentically rooted religion; he is the first Christian (Rom 8:29)."[83] Bultmann, on the other side, endorsed Wellhausen's dictum at the beginning of his *Theologie des Neuen Testaments*, which began to appear in parts in 1948.[84]

Harnack's work on Q, published in 1907, drew from the conclusions of Wernle (1899) and Wellhausen (1905) that the time had come for the reconstruction of the Greek text of Q. As regards the SM, it appears in Harnack's list of Q texts as a rubric called "The most significant parts of the SM,"[85] but in fact the rubric covers only separate sayings, as elsewhere in Q. Harnack concluded from the textual comparison that the arrangement of the sayings common to

73 Wellhausen, *Einleitung* (1911), 168.
74 Wellhausen, *Einleitung* (1905), 14; (1911), 103–4.
75 Wellhausen, *Einleitung* (1911), 98.
76 Wellhausen, *Einleitung* (1911), 99, 102–4, 147–53.
77 Wellhausen, *Einleitung* (1911), 102: "Jesus war kein Christ, sondern Jude." Cf. 103.
78 Harnack, *Sprüche und Reden Jesu*, 162.
79 Harnack, *Sprüche und Reden Jesu*, 163–64.
80 Harnack, *Sprüche und Reden Jesu*, 171.
81 Harnack, *Sprüche und Reden Jesu*, 173.
82 Harnack, *Sprüche und Reden Jesu*, 173. See also Harnack's programmatic statements in his *Das Wesen des Christentums*, 10–11 (in Bultmann's reedition of 1950), against making the religion of Jesus "a religion of miserabilism." As Harnack says in an added note from 1908 (in Bultmann's reedition of *Das Wesen*, 180–85), his *Sprüche und Reden Jesu* of 1907 had clarified his earlier somewhat vaguer notions in *Das Wesen des Christentums* of 1900, esp. p. 13.
83 Heinrici, *Die Bergpredigt*, 3:98: "Jesus ist nicht der letzte Jude, sondern der Schöpfer einer neuen, wurzelechten Religion; er ist der erste Christ (Röm. 8,29)."
84 Bultmann, *Theology*, 1.
85 Harnack, *Sprüche und Reden Jesu*, 126: "Die bedeutendsten Teile der Bergpredigt."

the SM and the SP, when they differ, should follow the SM as the more original order, but that the sayings peculiar to Matthew and not in Luke could not have been part of Q.[86] Thus, the "original Q Sermon" would have contained all sayings common to the SM and the SP. While Luke had the right number of sayings, but had them dispersed in his Q, Matthew had the right arrangement in his SM.[87] Neither the SM nor the SP, however—as Harnack sets them up—have any consistency as textual units, but they simply are traditional names for sequences of sayings, as elsewhere in Q.[88] Using the name "Sermon on the Mount" is therefore misleading in a description of Q.

For Harnack, the SM as a whole is the work of the evangelist Matthew. Arguing against Wellhausen's connection of the SM with the formulation of the "gospel" ($\epsilon\dot{v}a\gamma\gamma\dot{\epsilon}\lambda\iota\nu$) in Mark 1:15, Harnack denied that the SM is more than a cluster of sayings, and that it has anything like a common theme.[89] While this seems clear enough, Harnack is able to tolerate strange contradictions.

In the face of all that has been reported so far, he can also reaffirm the traditional view about the SM: "That which in the SM has been put at the beginning of Jesus' proclamation bears the stamp of undiluted authenticity. One can only be amazed that at the same time when Paul was active and when apologetic questions and the problem of the law were urgent, Jesus' proclamation as moral preaching was remembered and kept in force."[90] This remembrance is attributed to the continuing impact of the "image of Jesus" upon the early Christian church. This image of Jesus is reflected in the material, even though it is not identical with specific sayings or clusters of sayings. Therefore, Harnack can even provide a sketch of a "theology" of Q, which pertains to the Q sermon as well and which contains even the rudiments of a "christology."[91] At this point, it seems that Harnack's and Wellhausen's views come close together.

In the SM, which as a whole surpasses the level of a prophetic manifesto, only at two points does the person of Jesus come to the fore. He himself calls his doctrine the light that belongs on the lampstand, so that it shines for all. And he identifies obedience toward his commandments with the doing of the will of the Father; with this it is decided whether a person builds his house on the rock or on the sand. By contrast, merely saying, "Lord, Lord" has no value.[92]

As Harnack indicates by putting brackets around the term "Sermon on the Mount," the SM has ceased to exist as a concrete text. It now simply signifies

86 Harnack, Sprüche und Reden Jesu, 127.
87 Harnack, Sprüche und Reden Jesu, 128–29.
88 Harnack, Sprüche und Reden Jesu, 129.
89 Harnack, Sprüche und Reden Jesu, 138–46.
90 Harnack, Sprüche und Reden Jesu, 146.
91 Harnack, Sprüche und Reden Jesu, 162–64.
92 Harnack, Sprüche und Reden Jesu, 164.

the force of Jesus' "image" reflected in the words of the master generally.[93] When he cites specific passages for verifying this image, however, he usually refers to SM passages. If this seems odd, if not self-contradictory, the practice continues in much of the following scholarly literature, to say nothing about popular treatments. Although the SM was and is called a Matthean construction, it continues to serve as a unified body of material representing Jesus' original teaching.[94] There are other problems in Harnack's work.

Harnack agreed with Wellhausen, Nestle, and others when he assumed that the original Q was written in Aramaic and represented a collection of sayings of Jesus from the period before 70 CE.[95] This assumption would imply that those sayings belonging to the Q sermon (i.e., sayings common to the SM and the SP) are Greek translations of Aramaic antecedents. As it turns out, however, precisely those sayings are Greek in character and outlook, while the supposedly later accretions of Matthew (in the SM) represent old Jewish-Christian ideas. As Wellhausen in his critique seems to be aware,[96] this strange inconsistency calls Harnack's construction into question. Clearly, further studies would follow at this point.

2.6   Tendencies in the twentieth century

Among these studies there appears to have been a growing tendency to move Jesus and his teaching away from Judaism. This took quite different forms: by letting him pronounce his messianic self-understanding, by having him break with the Torah or all Judaism, or by having him teach straight Christian doctrine. The idea that Jesus was "not Jewish but Christian" reached its absurd climax in the infamous address by Walter Grundmann on *Die Frage der ältesten Gestalt und des ursprünglichen Sinnes der Bergrede Jesu*,[97] followed by the book *Jesus der Galiläer und das Judentum.*[98] According to Grundmann, Jesus was not a Jew but a Galilean, hence an Aryan preaching the "gospel" of the *Deutsche Christen.* The Jewish Jesus of the SM was termed a later, secondary, and illegitimate "fabrication" by Jewish Christianity. This theory was too absurd to be believable, but the issues have remained unresolved to this day. Was Jesus "orthodox," as the SM claims, or a "non-normative," or a "Galilean"

---

93 See on this issue my paper, "The Problem of Christology in the Sermon on the Mount," to be published in the *Festschrift* for Hendrikus W. Boers.

94 This is also true of Harnack's *Das Wesen des Christentums*, esp. 6, where even later he continues to refer to "Jesus Christus und sein Evangelium," apparently meaning the SM (see his additional note from 1908 on p. 180 of Bultmann's reedition of *Das Wesen des Christentums*). Wellhausen's keen observation that neither Q nor the SM, for that matter, uses the term "gospel" (εὐαγγέλιον) (*Einleitung* [1905], 108–15; [1911], 98–104, 147–53, 153–76) is left undiscussed by Harnack (*Sprüche und Reden Jesu,* 170–74). In fact, the issue raised by Wellhausen, which text should be named to identify Jesus' "gospel," remains unresolved even today.

95 Harnack, *Sprüche und Reden Jesu,* 171–72.

96 See his *Einleitung* (1911), 157–76.

97 Grundmann, *Die Frage der ältesten Gestalt.*

98 Grundman, *Jesus der Galiläer,* esp. 16–17, 25, 165–75, 200–201.

Jew?[99] Should the SM be treated as part of Jewish theology of the first half of the first century, or of early Jewish Christianity? Does the SM contain the "gospel" in any form, or is it the illegitimate child of "rejudaization"?[100] Was Marcion right or wrong?

Those who regard the SM and the SP as creations by the gospel writers Matthew and Luke have solved the problem in the sense that the Christian character of both texts has been safeguarded. The almost passionate commitment by some more conservative scholars to what they call "redaction-criticism" finds its explanation here.[101] Those who engage in research on Q, specifically on the christology of Q, find that the same problems recur in different ways. Was the christology of Q, if there is one that can be called by this term, a Christian or a Jewish form of belief? There is thus far no clear picture that critical scholarship can deliver.[102] Since Harnack, research has moved ahead at many points relevant to the issues of the SM and the SP in their relationship with Q. The field of options, however, has been determined by Wellhausen and Harnack, who sharpened the results of the scholarship of the eighteenth and nineteenth centuries. The way they set up the options still dominates present scholarship.

3. The Present Options

Given the present state of scholarship, which are the options now available for determining the relationship between the SM, the SP, and Q? Since we do agree that the SM and the SP were part of Q, we begin with the most common of today's assumptions:

1. There was one source Q, which had an early form of the Sermon (Q Sermon) identical, or nearly identical, with Luke's SP.[103] Matthew's SM would then be the evangelist's revision and expansion of the Q Sermon, observable as SP; for his revision Matthew used other special traditions (*Sondergut*). Some of these special traditions show signs of pre-Matthean redaction. The question of how this pre-Matthean redaction can be distinguished from Matthew's own redaction is still unanswered.

2. There was one source Q containing a sermon identical or nearly identical with the SM. The SP would then be the result of Luke's revision and reduction. This option has no advocates today, and rightly so.

3. There was one source Q, which was substantially different from either the SM or the SP, so that both are redactional revisions by Matthew or Luke.

99 For more recent information see Udo Schnelle, "Jesus, ein Jude," with bibliography.
100 See Stauffer, "Jesus, Geschichte und Verkündigung," esp. 14–17.
101 See, especially Stanton, "Origin and Purpose," 181–92; also his review of my *Essays on the Sermon on the Mount;* Carlston, "Betz on the Sermon on the Mount," 47–57.
102 See on this problem Polag, *Die Christologie;* Schweizer, "Jesus Christus I. Neues Testament," esp. 697–98; Sato, *Q und Prophetie,* esp. 301–2, 373–75.
103 See also Kloppenborg, *Formation of Q,* 171–90. Summing up the consensus, Kloppenborg is aware of its hypothetical character. The same is true of his *Q Parallels,* 22–47.

Those scholars who hold that the Q Sermon was not completely identical with SP in fact subscribe to this option. Conceivably this earlier Q Sermon was written first in Aramaic, so that the SM and the SP are separate translations into Greek, based on the needs of the branches of the later church. The problem with this option is that neither SM nor SP can be shown to be a complete translation from the Aramaic

4. Whatever the origins of Q may have been, the evangelists Matthew and Luke received the source Q in the form of two recensions, one containing the SM and the other containing the SP. This option presupposes that Q has gone through a history of development. In the course of this history the earlier Q source was modified in different ways due to different traditions. This means that the similarities and differences of the SM and the SP are the result of pre-synoptic redaction rather than of the redaction of the evangelists. The conclusion would be that the original Q contained some form of a sermon which, however, cannot be recovered. This original sermon may have been in Aramaic or Greek, or first in Aramaic and then in Greek.

5. The SM and the SP were formulated first independently of Q as separate collections of sayings. At a later stage of Q's development they were joined to Q (SM to Q^{Matt}; SP to Q^{Luke}). The analogy for this process would be the inclusion of smaller collections of sayings into larger ones, as we find it in the growing collections of Greek gnomologia.

6. The SM and the SP were formulated first independently from Q as separate collections of sayings and never became part of Q. It was only the evangelists Matthew and Luke who drew them from special traditions (*Sondergut*) and included them in their gospels along with Q. This option would come close to a multiple-source theory.

4. Conclusion

Which of these options is the most probable one, considering all aspects of the problem, is not easy to say. The following considerations may help to formulate a solution.

1. Both Matthew and Luke make use of Q elsewhere in their gospels, so that the Two-Source-Hypothesis can best explain the parallel transmission of the sayings. The conclusion would be that what is true of the majority of the materials should be assumed also for the SM and the SP.

2. The SM and the SP are located at about the same place in both gospels to which they belong. They are introduced by a narrative framework (Matt 4:24–5:2 and Luke 6:17–20a), and they are followed by the story of the centurion at Capernaum (Matt 8:5–13; Luke 7:1–10). This immediate sequence of textual units parallel in Matthew and Luke must have been the same in Q. Consequently, there must have been some kind of sermon in Q.

3. The SM and the SP are two substantially different elaborations of basically similar materials (beatitudes, interpretation of the love command, Golden

Rule, sayings on judging, parable of the two trees, and parable of the two builders). These materials are presented in roughly the same order. As elaborations the SM and the SP have an integrity of their own, compositionally, functionally, and theologically. It is not possible to explain all the differences and similarities between them as redactional changes made in one or the other, either by expansion or reduction. The internal consistency and integrity of the SM and the SP precede the efforts of the gospel writers Matthew and Luke.

4. The internal evidence shows theological ideas that, although agreeable to the evangelists, have not sprung from their own minds. The SM is characterized by a consistent Jewish-Christian theology of an earlier period, remaining consciously within the terms of Jewish theology. The evangelist Matthew assigned the SM the important place of Jesus' first programmatic speech in the Gospel, but this evangelist also relativized and historicized the SM in this way. On the whole his gospel serves not only to preserve the SM and other older sources, but also to reinterpret, revise, and correct them. The SP shows less tension with Luke's own theology than does the SM with Matthew's. While in harmony with Luke's own views, the SP is characterized by a Greek cultural orientation, especially through its ideas about education; these ideas precede Luke.

5. In terms of their function, both the SM and the SP originally served educational purposes. The SM is conceived for disciples coming from a Jewish background, while the SP speaks to minds formed by Greek ideas. Both are *epitomai,* specifically designed for this purpose. The role of the SM and the SP in their present contexts of the Gospels of Matthew and Luke is that of "speeches." Both evangelists, however, must have been aware of their original function because they have Jesus address the disciples after they have been called. Matthew shows Jesus as he delivers the SM to Peter and his brother Andrew, and to James and John, the sons of Zebedee (Matt 4:18–22; 5:1–2), whereas the Twelve (disciples and apostles) receive the mission instruction (Matt 10:1–5). Differently, in Luke the Twelve (disciples and apostles) are chosen first and then given the SP (Luke 6:12–16, 20a). At any rate, their role as speeches is secondary and due to their narrative frameworks; their primary function was educational.

All things considered, the evidence of the SM and the SP as well as the results of modern scholarship on Q favor the solution that the evangelists Matthew and Luke obtained their respective "sermons" from the versions of Q available to them, Q^Matt and Q^Luke respectively. The SM and the SP were joined with Q at an advanced stage of development of Q. This fits with the growth of Q by inclusion of new materials, a kind of collection of collections.

Nomos *and* Ethos
in Q★

John S. Kloppenborg

The name of James M. Robinson will, perhaps more than any other, be mentioned in connection with the ending of monopolies, most especially those associated with the Nag Hammadi materials. He has, however, contributed importantly to the dissolution of other monopolies. The task of imagining Christians origins, which had long been conducted almost exclusively with reference to the New Testament canon, must now attend to other materials that faded from view either though historical accident or by ecclesiastical censure. This revolution is due in no small part to Robinson's essays, and those of his collaborator, Helmut Koester, in *Trajectories through Early Christianity*. The theological monopolies associated with the term *kerygma* that were already under attack in his essays of the sixties[1] had all but collapsed by the time of Robinson's SBL presidential address of 1981.[2] Robinson has also prodded the academy to abandon the coziness of unilinear models for imagining Christian origins and to embrace the incomparably messier—but also richer—model of multiple trajectories emanating from a complex generating matrix comprising the words and deeds of John, Jesus, and their followers and the sapiential, apocalyptic, thaumaturgic, and gnostic configurations that were invoked to interpret the significance of these persons and their words. In each of these developments, the sayings gospel (Q) has played a decisive role.

In the 1983 Vosburgh Lectures at Drew University Robinson raised in passing the problem of Q and the Torah.[3] There he observed that Q does not represent Jesus as consciously repudiating the Torah; but on the other hand, it does not invoke Torah as a source of proof-texts. The framer of Q is neither a Mark nor a rabbi. Instead, Q depicts Jesus as the exponent of a radicalized or idealized Torah. Here, Robinson puts his finger on a matter that touches on both the soteriology and the sociology of the sayings gospel.

Indeed, although there has been a virtual avalanche of literature on Paul and the Law, little systematic has been said on how the sayings gospel

★ I wish to thank Leif Vaage for his useful comments on earlier drafts of this paper.
1 "Basic Shifts in German Theology"; "Kerygma and History in the New Testament."
2 "Jesus—From Easter to Valentinus."
3 "The Sayings of Jesus: Q," 32.

conceives of the Torah. This in itself is not too surprising. As far as it can be reconstructed, Q has little to say in regard to individual laws or indeed the Torah as a whole. Q lacks Markan-type controversies that account for Jesus' non-observance of the Sabbath laws and regulations concerning purity. And unlike Paul, Q does not reflect on the position of the Law within the scheme of salvation.

Initially these facts could lead to two mutually exclusive conclusions. Either Q takes for granted the validity of the Torah and therefore never engages such legal issues; or it ignores the issues with which Mark and Paul struggled, because the Torah does not figure importantly in the soteriology and paraenesis of the community. In one case we would arrive at a Torah-observant Jewish Christianity and in the other a community in which covenant and Law are not important categories.

Of these two options, most interpreters appear to have favored the former. Recently Robert Wild suggested that two of Q's woes against the Pharisees— Luke 11:39–41 (on purifying cups) and 11:42 (on tithing)—reflect not, as is usually assumed, the controversies of Christians with Pharisees, but of *Christian Pharisees* with other Pharisees or with other Christians.[4] Q indeed focuses precisely upon those issues—tithing and the observation of purity laws outside the Temple—which lay at the heart of Pharisaic self-understanding. Even if Q 11:42 (to use Lukan versification) criticizes those who tithe meticulously for neglecting more important matters, it nonetheless accepts the need to tithe, as is made clear by the phrase, "these you ought to have done without neglecting the others." Wild interprets Q 11:39–41 similarly. The importance of the purity of vessels and utensils is not in dispute; it is only set within a more comprehensive context of divine demands. Q's attention to the issues at the core of Pharisaic piety suggests that its criticisms are made from *within* a Pharisaic context. Wild compares similar debates between Hillel and Shammai on the circumstances under which various items are subject to tithe and on the halakah regarding impurity.[5]

To grant Wild's hypothesis that "Christian Pharisees" were influential in the formation of the Q Woes (Q 11:39–52) immediately raises other questions. Did such Christian Pharisees also understand the Torah to be the definitive and authoritative expression of divine will? And did they understand salvation —or more properly, sanctification—to consist in the faithful observance of Torah, however they may have interpreted the import of individual laws? Wild does not pursue these issues. Siegfried Schulz, however, proposes an understanding of Q as an expression of the "messianic Torah and *halakah* of Jesus" and claims that for Q the saving event is located in Jesus' "messianic Torah, his prophetic-apocalyptic word, and his priestly instruction."[6]

---

4 Wild, "The Encounter between Pharisaic and Christian Judaism," 113–17.
5 See Neusner, *Rabbinic Traditions about the Pharisees before 70*, 1:303–40, and esp. "First Cleanse the Inside," 486–95.
6 Schulz, "Die Bedeutung des Markus," 138–39.

Although Schulz distinguishes two strata in Q, an early "Palestinian Jewish Christian" (Q¹) and a later "Hellenistic Jewish Christian" stratum (Q²),[7] he sees no significant shift in the understanding of the Torah. For both the Torah remains absolutely binding both in its ethical and in its cultic aspects. Schulz assumes that the community practiced circumcision and tithing, observed kashruth and Pharisaic purity laws, frequented the Temple, and observed the Passover (rather than primitive Christian sacraments).[8] It was not an abrogation of the Torah that led to Q's disagreements with Pharisees, but rather Q's radicalized Torah-observance. In opposition to Deut 24:1 and current Pharisaic practice, divorce was disallowed; the ordinary means of retaliation and retribution permitted by the *lex talionis* were eschewed; and the demands of mercy and love—even of one's enemies—were given more prominence than cultic observance, though the latter was by no means rejected.[9] Accordingly, Jesus was viewed as the eschatological Torah-exegete and as the coming Son of man.

The impulse for such radicalized Torah-observance derived, according to Schulz, from the Parousia expectation that dominated community consciousness. And the earliest stratum of Q had not yet taken the decisive theological step of interpreting the *earthly Jesus* kerygmatically. This, for Schulz, did not occur until a later stratum of Q, when Jesus was understood as the envoy of Sophia *par excellence*.[10] The theological program of Bultmann looms large in this view of Q. For Schulz as for Bultmann, the earliest Palestinian community (Schulz: Q¹) had not yet drawn the boundary between itself and Judaism.[11] Fulfilment of the Law remained the condition of salvation,[12] and christology focused on Son of man expectation. Schulz describes Q¹ in precisely the terms which Bultmann uses for the earliest community that had not yet explicitly grasped Jesus' person and fate as "*the* eschatological occurrence in Paul's sense" and for that reason "was in danger of remaining a Jewish sect."[13]

1. Pharisaic Halakah and the Q-Woes

It is the Q woes and especially Q 11:39–41 and 11:42 that Schulz and others adduce in support of the thesis that the Q community was Torah-observant.[14] Since Lührmann, however, it has been recognized that the redaction of the

7 Schulz's division has been criticized extensively by Paul Hoffmann in his review and by the present author in "Tradition and Redaction," 34–62.
8 Schulz, *Spruchquelle*, 169, 485.
9 Schulz, *Spruchquelle*, 172–73. Robinson ("Judaism, Hellenism, Christianity," 244) seems to concur with Schulz's proposal that Q radicalized rather than rejected the Torah, although he also notes that "Q does not seem to be more comfortably Jewish. . . ."
10 Schulz, *Spruchquelle*, 482–83.
11 Bultmann, *Theology*, 1:53; Schulz, *Spruchquelle*, 171.
12 Bultmann, *Theology*, 1:54–55; Schulz, *Spruchquelle*, 167–68.
13 Bultmann, *Theology*, 1:37 (emphasis original).
14 Thus P. D. Meyer, "The Community of Q," 68–69, 87–88; Luz, "Die wiederentdeckte Logienquelle," 533; Schelkle, "Israel und Kirche im Anfang," 89–90.

woes emphasizes not simply a disagreement with Pharisaic halakah, but a sharp polemic against *all Israel* for her rejection of Q's prophetic preaching (Q 11:49–51).[15] That is, what may have begun as controversy with Pharisaic groups has been broadened substantially at the stage of the assembling of the woes into the present form of Q 11:39–52. This literary observation in itself should serve as a caution against generalizing the implications of two pre-redactional components of a cluster of Q sayings into a conclusion about the final redaction of Q as a whole.

1.1   Q 11:39–41: On purifications

Although there are some differences in wording between Matt 23:25–26 and Luke 11:39–41, the shape of Q's woe is still visible. "Woe to you Pharisees, for you purify the outside of the cup and the dish, but the inside is full of rapacity and self-indulgence. Did not the maker of the outside also make the inside? Purify the inside (of the cup), and its outside will also be clean (or: and all will be clean for you)."[16] Schulz takes the view that "the ceremonial law" is neither abrogated nor treated as a secondary issue. The force of the woe is to assert only that ritual purity must accord fully with ethical purity.[17]

---

15 Lührmann, *Redaktion*, 43–48.
16 Reconstruction: *Q 11:39*. Matthew has assimilated this woe to the structure of those in 23:13, 15, 23, 27 by introducing the justification of the woe-cry with ὅτι and by placing the verb καθαρίζετε immediately after ὅτι. Second, since he prefers adverbial uses of ἔσωθεν (cf. 7:15; 23:27, 28; see Gundry, *Matthew*, 465; Schenk, *Die Sprache des Matthäus*, 282), he is obliged to omit the article, transpose δέ and ἔσωθεν, and change Luke's (=Q's) γέμει into a plural. However, since πονηρ- words are elsewhere favored by Matthew (Gundry, *Matthew*, 647; Schenk, *Die Sprache des Matthäus*, 161), there is little reason for him to have altered Luke here; therefore Matthew's ἀκρασίας is probably original.
    Q 11:40. Harnack (*Sayings*, 101), Schulz (*Spruchquelle*, 96–97), and Schenk (*Synopse*, 76) exclude both Luke 11:40 and Luke 11:41/Matt 23:26 from Q. Schulz argues first that no reasons can be given for Matthew's omission of Luke 11:40 and that 11:40 contains Lukan vocabulary (ἄφρων, ποιέω of divine creative activity), and second that Matt 23:26 and Luke 11:41 represent independent amplifications of the Q woe by Matthew and Luke. However, the presence of a parallel to Luke 11:40 in GThom 89 (not in the form of a woe!) makes it difficult to regard 11:40 as Lukan. Moreover, ἄφρων occurs only here and at 12:20, which may derive from Q (see Kloppenborg, *Q Parallels*, 128), and ποιέω is used immediately of the potter and only metaphorically of God. Bultmann (*History*, 131–32) argues that Matthew omitted 11:40 because he did not understand the sentence, while Gundry (*Matthew*, 465) more plausibly urges that Matthew's polemical tone led to the omission of the didactic question in Luke 11:40.
    Q 11:41. The agreement between Matthew and Luke in extending the discussion of inside vs. outside and, in particular, in the use of an imperative (καθάρισον/δότε) followed by a final clause which promises complete cleanness suggest strongly that something of the same structure existed in Q. Luke's δότε ἐλεημοσύνην (cf. Luke 12:33; Matthew is different) is suspect as redactional. Moreover, Luke's formulation completely abandons the metaphor of washing cups and dishes. To this extent Matthew's version is probably more original, though his second person singular verb should probably be restored to a plural (Polag, *Fragmenta*, 54 reads καθαρίζετε).
17 Schulz, *Spruchquelle*, 97–98. Schulz follows the lead of Braun, *Spätjüdisch-häretischer und frühchristlicher Radikalismus*, 2:12.

This conclusion, however, seems unjustified. Q 11:39–41 indeed betrays knowledge of the Pharisaic view that in matters of purity, vessels are divided into inner and outer parts.[18] Neusner has convincingly demonstrated that the Q saying can only be directed at the Shammaite opinion (which was dominant before 70 CE) that the inside and outside of cups function autonomously and that either or both might be clean or unclean. Under such circumstances, care must be taken while handling the outside (or the handle) of the cup that one's hands do not contaminate the liquid clinging to the rim of a cup and thereby render the inside of the cup unclean.[19] The Hillelite view, which treated the outside of cups as permanently unclean (*y. Ber.* 8:2), accordingly held that the state of the inside of the cup was decisive. Q 11:39–41 is meaningful only to someone who takes for granted that the outside of vessels *can* be cleansed or that the state of the outside may (indirectly) affect the inside. This is not the Hillelite position.

Does this imply that Q criticized Shammaite Pharisees from a Hillelite standpoint? Hardly. While Q 11:39–41 acknowledges the Pharisaic distinction regarding cups, it immediately reduces this distinction to an absurd caricature and diverts the discussion onto an ethical plane by treating vessels as metaphors. No one, either Hillelite or Shammaite, would hold that cleaning the outside of a vessel would render the inside clean; moreover, since cleansing was normally done by immersion in a *mikveh* pool, it would have been virtually impossible to wash only the outside of a vessel.[20] And the mention of rapacity and self-indulgence is obviously not appropriate to eating utensils: something else is at issue.

Nevertheless, Q 11:39–41 maintains the metaphor of vessels throughout and creates double significations for several elements of the saying. Its logic is important to observe. It begins not as Matthew does by focusing on the hypocrisy of the Pharisees and the *danger* they represent,[21] but with the sheer contrast between outside and inside, a contrast that is deemed to be self-evident both for vessels and for the metaphorical significations that they have. Q 11:40 then ridicules the distinction of outside/inside by appealing to the process of the production of cups and, by analogy, lampoons any system which partitions human existence into discrete realms. The concluding imperative serves then to underscore the lack of a strong boundary, either in matters of table utensils or in human matters. Fluid boundaries, based on the fact of creation, permit "purity" an unobstructed movement.

18 *M. Kel.* 25.1, 7.
19 Neusner, "First Cleanse the Inside," 486–95. The schools' opinions and their rationale are detailed in *m. Ber.* 8.2, *m. Kel.* 25.1, 7; *y. Ber.* 8.2, and *b. Ber.* 52b.
20 *M. Miqw.* 5.6; 6.2, 5, 6. Mark 7:4 speaks of the immersion (βαπτισμός) of cups. See Maccoby, "The Washing of Cups," 5.
21 This is also the dynamic of Matt 23:23–24 (Pharisaic halakah identifies small defilements, only to permit great ones); 23:27 (outward beauty vs. inward corpse-uncleanness); 23:28 (outward righteousness vs. inward lawlessness); 23:29–33 (outward piety vs. inward homicidal intentions).

The Q woe betrays knowledge of Shammaite distinctions, but no sympathy with them. By subverting the boundaries between inside and outside and by diverting attention to ethical issues, Q is actually undermining the entire system of purity that depends for its existence on a well-defined taxonomy of the cosmos. In its use of lampoon, Q resembles some of the cynic criticism of ritual,[22] but in its substance, Q approaches Pseudo-Phocylides' sentiments: ἁγνείη ψυχῆς, οὐ σώματός εἰσι καθαρμοί ("purifications are for the purity of the soul, not [for the purity] of the body," 228).[23] To invoke the terms καθαρίζω or καθαρμοί in this manner is to take terms belonging to a realm of discourse that pays close attention to the state of bodies and bodily orifices and to redeploy them in a realm which implicitly denies the utility of rigid controls on the body—both the social body and the physical one. This is not simply a redefinition of the system of "purity" but a rejection of it.

1.2 Q 11:42: On tithing

The other woe that bears on Q's attitude toward the law is Q 11:42. It appears that Matthew rather than Luke has preserved the original list of spices to be tithed: mint (ἡδύοσμον), dill (ἄνηθον) and cummin (κύμινον). Luke agrees in the mention of mint but has rue (πήγανον) instead of dill, and every herb (πᾶν λάχανον) instead of cummin. The latter divergence is best understood as a typically Lukan generalization.[24] The change from dill to rue is perhaps due to the fact that dill (ἄνηθον, ἄννητος) was less familiar to Luke than rue. Theophrastus (Historia plantarum 9.7.3) lists dill among the aromatic herbs which are not native to Europe, whereas πήγανον is well known.[25]

On the other hand, it is Matthew who added the phrase "the weightier things of the law" (τὰ βαρύτερα τοῦ νόμου), consistent with his understanding of the law of love as the canon for interpreting the Law. In their descriptions of what the Pharisees neglect, Matthew and Luke concur in naming κρίσις ("justice"). Matthew adds ἔλεος ("mercy") and πίστις ("faith[fulness]"), while Luke has ἀγάπη τοῦ θεοῦ ("love of God"). The prominence of mercy (ἔλεος, always understood as God's demand[26]) in Matthean redaction (9:13; 12:7) makes its appearance suspect here. Luke has no aversion to the term, which he normally uses to mean God's display of mercy (1:50, 54, 58, 72, 78), and thus there would have been no reason for Luke to have substituted love (of God), which occurs only here in Luke-Acts had he found mercy in his Vorlage.

22 See Diogenes Laertius 6.42: "Seeing someone perform religious purification, he said, 'Unhappy man, don't you know that you can no more get rid of errors of conduct by sprinklings than you can of mistakes in grammar?'" 6.63: "Someone having reproached him for going into dirty places, his reply was that the sun too visits cesspools without being defiled." I owe these references to Vaage, "The Woes in Q," 5–6.
23 See the discussion of this in Van der Horst, The Sentences of Pseudo-Phocylides, 258–60.
24 For documentation of this tendency see Cadbury, Style and Literary Method, 115–18.
25 Theophrastus, Historia plantarum (s.v. Enquiry), 1.3.4; Nicander, Alexipharmaca, 49. If the ruling of m. Šebi. 9.1 is in effect, Luke is also incorrect in assuming that either rue or "every herb" was to be tithed.
26 Przybylski, Righteousness in Matthew, 100–101.

Faith(fulness) (πίστις), however, may be pre-Matthean. While the term is important in Matthew's redaction, it is used redactionally to denote the belief of those seeking (or performing) miracles. Here, by contrast, it means "faithfulness" or "fidelity." Luke seems unfamiliar with this latter sense and for that reason may have omitted the word.

The trio of words κρίσις, ἀγάπη τοῦ θεοῦ, and πίστις probably reflect the Hebrew terms *mišpāt, hesed*, and *'emûnāh* which occur together in the Hebrew bible denoting both attributes of God and expectations of humankind.[27] The qualification "of God" in Q indicates that the perspective is theocentric rather than anthropocentric. Q's accusation is that the Pharisees neglect *God's* justice, love, and fidelity and the demands that these impose upon humankind. By contrast, Matthew construed the terms as divine demands which the Pharisees do not obey. Luke, however, preserved the original theocentric dimension of the Q saying.[28] Accordingly, it seems preferable to reconstruct Q 11:42b with Luke's παρέρχομαι ("disregard," "overlook") rather than with Matthew's ἀφίημι ("abandon"), which appears to reflect Matthew's accusation that his opponents are violating the basic demand of the Law. Hence, I propose the following reconstruction:

> Woe to you, Pharisees, for you tithe mint and dill and cummin and disregard the justice and love of God (and faithfulness). These you ought to have done without neglecting the others.

There are several important points to be made regarding the Q saying. First, the woe begins with Pharisaic practice but, as with the woe concerning purifications, immediately directs attention to God's activity as a means of refocusing the question of how humans ought to view themselves and their obligations. Like Q 6:27–35, which finds the warrant for merciful action in the *imitatio Dei*, Q 11:42 invokes the justice and love of God as a warrant for human action. It could be added that elsewhere in the Q tradition, the examples of divine generosity (11:9–13), providence (12:4–7), and nurture (12:24–31) are invoked as the basis for imitation or consolation.

Of course, Pharisees would rightly retort that their tithing and the extensions of biblical purity laws are *also* grounded in an attribute of God, namely, holiness. The dispute between Q and the Pharisees thus turns on the norms of theological and ethical hermeneutics; but Q shows no special concern for legal hermeneutics. The Torah and its interpretation are not at issue; this is only

---

27 As attributes of God: Pss 89(88):15 (*sedeq* [δικαιοσύνη, "righteousness"], *mišpāt* [κρίμα, "judgment"], *hesed* [ἔλεος, "truth"], *'emet* [ἀλήθεια]); 111(110):7 (*'emet* [ἀλήθεια], *mišpāt* [κρίσις]); Hos 2:21–22 (*sedeq* [δικαιοσύνη], *mišpāt* [κρίμα], *hesed* [ἔλεος], *'emûnāh*, "faithful" [οἰκτρίμων, "merciful"]); *Ps. Sol* 18:3–4: (τὰ κρίματά σου, ἡ ἀγάπη σου, "your judgments, your love"). As demands placed on humans: Mic 6:8 (*mišpāt* [κρίμα], *hesed* [ἔλεος]); Zech 7:9 (*mišpāt* [κρίμα], *'emet* [οἰκτρίμων], *hesed* [ἔλεος]); Hos 12:7 (*hesed* [ἔλεος], *mišpāt* [κρίμα]); 4:1 (*'emet* [ἀλήθεια], *hesed* [ἔλεος]).

28 Thus McNeile, *Matthew*, 335. Schulz (*Spruchquelle*, 101) thinks that it is Luke who has introduced this perspective.

true for Matthew. Neither Q's criticism of the Pharisees nor its counter-proposal is obviously nomocentric.

This raises a second point: What is Q's view of tithing? Schulz argues that Q fully approved the Pharisees' practice and like them required even the tithing of herbs.[29] This is unlikely. Like Q 11:39–41, this woe engages in rhetorical exaggeration and caricature. That it accurately reflects current tithing practice is most unlikely. Even a cursory glance at the Mishnaic discussions of tithing is sufficient to indicate that there was no unanimity in regard to the liability of *any* of the items of 11:42a. The ruling that the dill plant was liable to tithe (*m. Ma'aś.* 4.5) derives from Eliezer (b. Hyrcanus).[30] His view was based on the principle that the act of cultivation is decisive rather than any unstated intention regarding the use of the product or parts thereof. Yet this principle was open to dispute as related rulings of Akiba show (*m. Ma'aś.* 4.6). In any case, it is difficult to imagine that Eliezer's view was universally adopted. Though there is no ruling on the matter, it is likely that an uncultivated (and perennial) crop such as mint would have been regarded as exempt by many.[31] *M. Demai.* 2.1 includes cummin in the *demai*-produce to be tithed; but this ruling is unattributed and therefore its date is uncertain.

The tactic of this woe resembles that of 11:39–41. The framers of these woes know that Pharisees discuss the susceptibility of parts of vessels to uncleanness and the susceptibilities of various produce to the tithe. But the woe conjures up absurd spectres: someone washing *only* the outside of a cup, or someone tithing in a way that corresponds neither with the actual practice of all Pharisees nor even with that of any particular house or school. The point is sheer ridicule.

The third point concerns 11:42c. This phrase is widely construed by commentators as evidence of a Torah-observant Q community.[32] It is equally widely suspect as an interpolation by an anxious Jewish-Christian redactor of Q.[33] The clause fits awkwardly with a saying which is already complete in itself (11:42ab). It is all the more awkward in a collection of woes which otherwise

29 Schulz, *Spruchquelle*, 101–3.
30 Neusner (*Eliezer ben Hyrcanus* 1:71; 2:175) classifies the tradition as "fair" (i.e., not among the "best" or "better" traditions) but notes that its logic is consistent with Eliezer's rulings elsewhere. See also Jaffee, *Mishnah's Theology of Tithing*, 135–40.
31 According to *m. Sebi.* 7.1 mint leaves (*dandanah*) were subject to the Sabbatical year law on the grounds that it was fit for human or animal consumption. The same text exempts it from the law of removal because it is a perennial and therefore is never deemed to have disappeared from a field. No clear statement exists in regard to its liability to tithe. However the ruling of *m. Sebi.* 9.1 which exempts other wild crops suggests that wild mint is exempt from tithes. Since such crops are not cultivated, there is no question either of the intention of the grower or even of the plain sense of his act. See further Newmann, *The Sanctity of the Seventh Year*, 137–50, 179–97.
32 On the basis of absence of the Luke 11:42c in Codex Bezae and Marcion several commentators argue that the phrase belonged neither to Luke nor to Q but was a Matthean interpolation. Thus Harnack, *Sayings*, 101; Wellhausen, *Das Evangelium Lucae*, 61; Manson, *The Sayings of Jesus*, 98.
33 Thus Bultmann, *History*, 131; Hoffmann, "Anfänge," 148 n. 33; Zeller, *Logienquelle*, 69; Schenk, *Synopse*, 76; Polag, *Die Christologie*, 80.

interpret Pharisaic actions in a uniformly negative way. Q 11:42c differs from the remainder of 11:39-42, 44 by casting its gaze beyond the Pharisees to another audience to warn them that *not everything* that the Pharisees do is entirely wrong-headed and to be disregarded. Moreover, the use of the verb *poiein* in connection with the items of 11:42b shows that these have now been construed (as in Matthew) as divine demands, rather than as divine attributes which create ethical demands.

What was the intention of the glossator who added 11:42c? Given what was said above regarding the contrived nature of the accusation of 11:42a, it is scarcely likely that the glossator of Q meant to enjoin upon the Q group a tithing practice that surpassed in scrupulousness each and every Pharisee! On the contrary, the intention of the gloss is, at most, to affirm the importance of tithing as it is articulated in Num 18:12 and Deut 14:22-23. But perhaps it is more an "e.g.," signalling more generally the allegiance of the glossator to Torah.

If 11:42c is an interpolation, it is important to ascertain the point in the literary evolution of Q at which this addition occurred, and correspondingly, the point in the history of the community when it was deemed necessary to re-inforce tithing practice. Obviously, this question cannot be answered in isola-tion. It it necessary to determine on the basis of a redactional analysis of the Q materials whether there is a discernible stage in Q's literary evolution when similar concerns over the validity of individual laws (or the Law as a whole) were expressed. What may be said at this point is that none of the extended compositions shows a tendency either to buttress admonitions by means of an appeal to the Torah or to frame them in such a way as to contrast the admonitions with the Torah. This is true of the programmatic opening sermon (Q 6:20b-49), the commissioning speech (Q 9:57-62; 10:2-16),[34] the instructions on prayer (11:2-4, 9-13) and anxiety (12:2-12, 22-31), the con-troversies with "this generation" (11:14-26, 29-32, 39-52 [minus 11:42c]), and the two apocalyptic collections (12:39-59; 17:23-37). This in itself sug-gests that nomistic concerns are foreign to the formative components of the Q tradition and appear only at a later stage, probably the result of local social interactions in a Jewish environment where it became advantageous or neces-sary to affirm the Torah in some way. As will be seen, anxious reflection on the theological trajectory of Q is in evidence elsewhere in the collection.

2. Q 16:16-18

The most direct statements regarding the validity of the Law are found in a brief cluster of sayings in Q 16:16-18. This cluster is not part of a longer Q-

34 If Luke 10:8 ("eat what is placed before you") comes from Q (thus Laufen, *Die Doppelüberlieferung,* 219-20; Uro, *Sheep among the Wolves,* 83) the implication would be that Q's missionaries at least had abandoned the observance of kashruth. Meyer's suggestion ("The Community of Q," 68) that the missionaries are only exempted from the prohibitions against eating untithed food is improbable.

composition and is not clearly related to its surrounding context. It is preceded by the parable of the lost sheep (15:4–7) and the proverb about serving two masters (16:13) and is followed by a series of sayings treating scandal (17:1–2, 3–4), faith (17:6), and the coming of the Son of man (17:23–37). The original location of the first saying, 16:16, is disputed. Some authors argue that it originally belonged with Q 7:18–35 where Matthew placed it.[35] However, it is difficult to overcome the force of the observation made long ago by Johannes Weiss that if Luke had seen 16:16 in its present Matthean location (in a cluster of sayings about John the Baptist), it is hard to imagine why he would have moved it to its current context.[36] There is hardly any doubt, however, as to the extent of Lukan redaction of the saying, and most authors hold that Matthew reproduces the saying better than Luke apart perhaps from inverting the order of the two clauses.[37]

A plausible reconstruction of the three sayings is:

16:16a   The Law and the Prophets were until John.[38]
16:16b   From the days of John until now, the Kingdom of God suffers violence and the violent take it by force.[39]
16:17   I say to you, until heaven and earth pass away, not one serif will pass from the Law.
16:18   Anyone who divorces his wife (and marries another) commits adultery. And whoever marries a divorcée commits adultery.[40]

With regard to the divorce saying, two points are important. First, this saying should not be construed as implying an abrogation of the Law. Indeed the saying prohibits what Deut 24:1–4 permits. However, Q 16:18 is not framed in such a way as to confront the Torah text directly and in any event, it is an example of the imposition of more stringent demands than the Torah requires, not of allowing what the Torah prohibits. Q does not violate the

---

35 E.g., Harnack, *Sayings*, 16; Lührmann, *Redaktion*, 27–28; Schenk, *Synopse*, 44.
36 J. Weiss, *Die Predigt Jesu vom Reiche Gottes*, 192.
37 See Schulz, *Spruchquelle*, 262; Hoffmann, *Studien*, 51–52.
38 Matthew's version, "for the prophets and the Law prophesied until John" (11:13) emphasizes the prophetic character of the scriptures and avoids the impression of the abrogation of the Law. Both features are probably due to Matthew. See Trilling, "Täufertradition," 276–79; Schulz, *Spruchquelle*, 261 and the literature cited there.
39 There is virtual unanimity that Matt 11:12bc (apart from "of the heavens") represents Q. See Schulz, *Spruchquelle*, 261–62; Polag, *Fragmenta*, 74–75. There is more dispute concerning whether Luke's ἀπὸ τότε ("from then," only here in Luke-Acts) or Matthew's ἀπὸ δὲ τῶν ἡμερῶν Ἰωάννου (τοῦ Βαπτιστοῦ) ἕως ἄρτι ("from the days of John [the Baptist] until now") is from Q. "From the days of John" is not demonstrably Matthean (*pace* Trilling, "Täufertradition," 277–78): it appears in *Sondergut* at 2:1 and 23:30 and is from Q at 24:37. Moreover, if we assume that 16:16a and 16:16b are originally independent sayings (see Schlosser, *Le Règne de Dieu*, 516–17), 16:16b requires both a beginning and a link to provide an eventual connection to 16:16a. The Matthean version supplies both. Thus also Schenk, *Synopse*, 44.
40 The reconstruction of Q 16:17–18 is that of Polag, *Fragmenta*, 74. It agrees substantially with the reconstruction of Schulz, *Spruchquelle*, 114 (16:17), 118–19 (16:18).

Torah any more than the authors of the *Cairo Damascus Covenant* (CD 4.20, 21), who considered divorce and remarriage to be a matter of successive polygamy.

Second, if the stringent divorce saying is not framed as rejection of the Torah, neither is it presented as an explication of Deut 24:1. It belongs tradition-historically with other Q sayings such as the prohibitions of retaliation and violence (Q 6:27–31) that are better understood as sapiential than as intentional "intensifications of the Torah."[41] Of course such admonitions go far beyond most conventional wisdom, as indeed Q 16:18 goes far beyond contemporary Jewish understandings by equating divorce (and remarriage) with the capital offense of adultery. The stringency of these admonitions has as its presupposition the dawning of God's dominion and the radically new ethos that it brings. The divorce saying thus serves as a pointer to this ethos, as do sayings such as Q 6:27–35 or 16:13.

Q 16:16 shares a similar perspective. Although Wernle took it as a Hellenistic saying that implied the abrogation of the Law,[42] this is probably not its intention, at least in its Q form (16a + 16b). Instead the saying concerns *heilsgeschichtliche* periodizing: the time of the "Law and Prophets" ended with John; and with John's appearance the time of the Kingdom had come.[43] It implies too that the position of the "Law and the Prophets"—a summary reference to Old Testament preaching[44]—is relativized in the era of the Kingdom. Polag comments:

> In any event it is certain that the Kingdom is contrasted with the Scripture, and indeed it becomes clear that the Kingdom is independent of the Law and the Prophets, i.e., the scriptures understood as a norm for conduct; obviously it is a matter of God's new intervention that alters the situation and represents a new claim of God upon humankind.[45]

This intensified claim of God upon humankind is perfectly consistent with a host of Q sayings, including Q 6:27–35 and Q 16:18. There is no doubt, however, that to a later editor 16:16a might be cause for concern. Matthew's rewording of the statement shows that it continued to pose a problem for him. Q 16:17 appears to be one attempt on the part of an editor of Q to obviate the possibility of an antinomian interpretation of Q's parenesis. This saying interposes itself between two sayings that evince the theme of the new situation that the Kingdom brings about (16:16, 18). Indeed 16:13, which radically opposes service to God with service to wealth, seems also to be formulated from this perspective. In other words, Q 16:17 is intrusive in 16:13–18, just as 11:42c

41 See Lohfink, "Jesus und die Ehescheidung," 207–17.
42 Wernle, *Die synoptische Frage*, 229. The same interpretation is adopted by Streeter, *The Four Gospels*, 233, and Barth, "Matthew's Understanding," 64.
43 See on this Lührmann, *Redaktion*, 26–29; Schenk, *Synopse*, 44.
44 For references see Fitzmyer, *The Gospel According to Luke X–XXIV*, 1116.
45 Polag, *Die Christologie*, 79 (my translation—JSK).

intrudes into the original collection of woes. Both glosses express the same anxiety regarding the enduring validity of the Law.

3. A Nomocentric Redaction of Q?

At what stage in the composition of Q did such concerns arise? While it is usual to think that the further one traces the tradition back the more "Jewish" it becomes and the greater the likelihood of nomocentric piety, this does not appear to be the case with Q. Almost a century ago Paul Wernle characterized Q as the product of a Greek-speaking church and, more significantly, of a non-Jewish community. In order to explain the transition from Q to Matthew, Wernle posited a "Judaizing form" of the collection (Qʲ), which contained sayings such as Matt 5:17-20, 10:5-6, and 23:3.[46]

One may recognize a thorough "methodological anti-Judaism" in Wernle's reconstruction of Q, which he declared to contain "the free, almost revolutionary gospel of Jesus himself" with no admixture of "Judaism."[47] Nevertheless, his suggestion is not without merit even if it requires considerable nuancing. Both of the sayings that express concern over the validity of legal observance (11:42c; 16:17) appear to be glosses added to obviate difficulties created by earlier sub-collections within Q. Furthermore, there is little evidence from the larger compositional units within Q—the inaugural sermon (Q 6:20b-49) for example—of a nomocentric piety. On the contrary, salvation is a matter of obeying Jesus' words (6:46-49), not of maintaining oneself within the framework of the covenant. This suggests that at its earliest stages, Torah observance was not an issue, but only became one in the later stages.

A clue to locating the stratum at which this concern emerged may be provided by the Temptation story (Q 4:1-13). There is now a broad consensus that the story is the latest addition in the evolution of Q.[48] While several features distinguish this pericope from the rest of Q, one is important for our purposes. No other Q text employs Old Testament quotations (in Septuagintal form) preceded by the formula, "It is written," in an argumentative context. And apart from 7:27 Q refers to the OT allusively rather than by direct quotation. Though the Temptation account is not a "halakic dispute" as it has incongruously been termed, the story does presuppose the validity of Torah texts for settling arguments and for determining behavior. Hermann Mahnke aptly observes that the account presents Jesus not so much as learned in the Torah as obedient to it.[49] This is very near the perspective from which Q 11:42c and 16:17 are formulated. In this light, it seems a plausible solution to

46 Wernle, *Die synoptische Frage*, 229-31.
47 Wernle, *Die synoptische Frage*, 230.
48 For detailed argumentation see Mahnke, *Versuchungsgeschichte*, 186-87; Polag, *Die Christologie*, 146-51; Zeller, "Die Versuchungen Jesu," 61-62; Jacobson, "Wisdom Christology in Q," 40.
49 Mahnke, *Versuchungsgeschichte*, 198.

locate the additions of these two glosses at the same (late) stage at which the Temptation story was added.

4. Law and Salvation in Q

The assertions that Q reflects a Torah-observant Jewish Christianity or that it presents Jesus as a radicalizer of the Torah depend in large measure upon elements in Q that are rather late additions to the collection. So too they presuppose, tacitly or not, that the conviction that salvation or sanctification is mediated in the context of the Law and the covenant was a common denominator that is to be assumed unless there is reason to suppose otherwise. Such a view would find support in E. P. Sanders' ambitious attempt to discover "covenantal nomism" as the basic pattern of religion in both Palestinian and Hellenistic Judaism.[50] Hellenistic Judaism, however, resists the attempt to impose the categories of covenantal nomism, as Collins has convincingly demonstrated.[51] *Pseudo-Phocylides* and *Pseudo-Menander* attach no significance to the covenant, and while a view of law is presupposed, it is one of a universal moral law lacking any references to specifically Jewish observances. On the Wisdom of Solomon, Collins comments;

> The primary distinction is not between Israel and the gentiles but between the righteous and the wicked. While Israel is presented as the paradigm of the righteous, it is not necessarily an exclusive paradigm.[52]

The sayings gospel not only lacks any inclination to demark Jews from Gentiles, but depicts Gentiles such as the centurion (7:1–10) and the Ninevites and the Queen of the South (11:30–32) in a favorable light. And as in these Hellenistic Jewish documents, neither the Covenant nor the Torah has a determinative function in the symbolic universe constructed by Q, though "Israel" and terms related to it remain important, especially in the later strata of Q (3:8; 13:28–29; 22:28–30) although even here the boundaries of "Israel" are rather fluid (cf. Q 7:9; 13:28–29). Salvation is better understood on the model of *paideia* provided by antique sapiential genres and chriae collections. The goal of instruction is the assimilation of an ethos that is ultimately grounded in divine order. In the idiom of Egyptian instructions the goal is to "do Maʿat, speak Maʿat"; in the Hebrew biblical tradition, it is to pursue and learn from Sophia. There is no hint that the Torah mediates between the divine and the cosmos. On the contrary, intuition of the divine is directly available in the observations of the transactions of human families (Q 11:9–13), of birds and plants (12:4–7, 22–31), and of the indiscriminate goodness of

---

50 E. P. Sanders, *Paul and Palestinian Judaism*; "The Covenant As a Soteriological Category."
51 Collins, *Between Athens and Jerusalem*; "Cosmos and Salvation," 121–42.
52 Collins, *Between Athens and Jerusalem*, 185.

the sun and rain (6:35). The sayings gospel directs attention to the ethos of the divine and enjoins imitation and emulation.

Since this new ethos is depicted as radically dissimilar from the old, Q engages in polemic and lampooning to underline that difference. The woes (and Q 16:16) function importantly in this respect. It would seem, however, that to a later eye and in another situation some of Q's statements appeared troublesome and steps were taken to mitigate their implications. Even though the basic soteriological thrust of Q is not substantially revised by these later additions of Q 11:42c, 16:17 and 4:1–13, these glosses do have the effect of bringing Q closer to the orbit of a nomocentric view and are, perhaps, steps in the direction of Matthew.

James M. Robinson and his longtime friend and mentor E. C. Colwell (Photograph courtesy of the Institute for Antiquity and Christianity)

Q and Its Relatives

Helmut Koester

A new era of research on the Synoptic Sayings Source began a few years ago under the leadership of James Robinson with the "Seminar on Q" of the Society of Biblical Literature. As I was drawn into this work, it became clear to me that one of the major problems relating to Q is the investigation of its predecessors and relatives. This article is the first installment of my attempt to contribute to the solution of this problem. As the inspiration for this study derives from several decades of a shared path, it is appropriately dedicated to the scholar and friend to whom I owe more than words can express.

John Kloppenborg[1] has described with great mastery the history of a particular document, the Synoptic Sayings Source (Q). His thesis is convincing. The story of Q begins at the moment at which sayings of Jesus are for the first time composed in the literary genre of "wisdom instruction," albeit an instruction that is not "wisdom of order" but "wisdom of the kingdom" and thus an eschatological—but not prophetic—challenge to the order of society. Kloppenborg then traced the further development of this sapiential book. In the second stage the older document is absorbed into a "chriae collection" in which prophetic announcement of judgment and polemic defense radicalize the contrast between the Q community and "this generation." In the final stage, the addition of the narrative of the temptation transforms the book into a pre-biographical writing in which the instruction is legitimized by the proto-typical behavior of the sage Jesus.

This clarifies one segment of the development of the sayings traditions related to Jesus. It answers a very important question, namely that of the formative literary genre that consolidated a considerable portion of those sayings that found their way into the Gospels of Matthew and Luke. This is a very helpful working hypothesis for the assessment of various other complexes of sayings that are in some ways related to those found in Q but are not dependent upon either Q or those later gospels that incorporated Q. The history, development, and function of these other complexes still remain to be written. A relationship of these complexes to Q does not necessarily exist with

---

1 Kloppenborg, *Formation of Q.*

respect to the literary genre that was the catalyst for the formation of Q. But these complexes contain a number of sayings also used in Q, and they may be involved in the formation of Q as well as other gospel literature.

I will discuss the following complexes to which I shall give only descriptive designations at this stage of the inquiry:

1. The 1 Corinthians complex.
2. The esoteric wisdom of parables.
3. Forerunners of Q and the Gospel of Thomas.

There are three other complexes that deserve discussion but will be left out of consideration in this paper: (1) Sayings in the Gospel of Thomas that—independently of Q—have found their way into the Gospel of Matthew and into the Gospel of Mark. (2) Sayings shared by the Gospel of John, the Gospel of Thomas, the Dialogue of the Savior, and other gnostic writings.[2] (3) The sayings used in the Apostolic Fathers and other early Christian documents and their relationship to the synoptic tradition. Thus, this paper can only be a small contribution to the difficult question of the formation and transmission of sayings in their earliest stages.

1. The 1 Corinthians Complex

In an earlier essay, I have explored the appearance of the tradition of sayings in gnostic writings.[3] In that context I stumbled upon the surprisingly close relationship of several revelation sayings with the peculiar terminology used by Paul in 1 Corinthians 1–4. We are dealing, in particular, with sayings that employ the terminology of "hidden and revealed." The most prominent of these appears in Matt 11:25–26=Luke 10:21–22:

> I praise you, Father, Lord of heaven and earth,
> that you have hidden these things from the *wise and understanding* ($\sigma o\phi\hat{\omega}\nu$
> $\kappa a\grave{\iota}\ \sigma\upsilon\nu\epsilon\tau\hat{\omega}\nu$),
> but have revealed them to the *unlearned* ($\nu\eta\pi\acute{\iota}o\iota\varsigma$).

It is certainly a Q saying, but its position and function in Q are problematic.[4] The saying is not necessarily characteristic for the formative stage of Q, and it fits poorly into its later stages. On the other hand, attestation of such sayings elsewhere is abundant. The small sayings collection in Mark 4 contains such a saying (Mark 4:22). Matt 13:35 ("I will utter what has been hidden . . .")

2 See my essay, "Gnostic Sayings."
3 "Gnostic Writings."
4 See Kloppenborg, *Formation of Q,* 201–3. Here and in the following, I will usually avail myself of the convenient opportunity of referring to the excellent discussions of the problems by Kloppenborg, rather than rehearsing the entire earlier debates about individual Q sayings.

employs this terminology,[5] and a parallel to Mark 4:22 appears in the Gospel of Thomas (sayings 5 and 6).

Allusions in 1 Corinthians 1–4 to this group of sayings are striking. Matt 13:35, ". . . what has been hidden from the foundations of the world," has its closest New Testament parallel in 1 Cor 2:7 ("the hidden wisdom which God has predetermined before the ages"). The term "unlearned" ($\nu\dot{\eta}\pi\iota os$, Matt 11:25 par=Q/Luke 10:21) is used in 1 Cor 3:1 but rarely elsewhere in Paul. The same applies to $\sigma o\phi o\grave{\iota}\ \kappa a\grave{\iota}\ \sigma v\nu\epsilon\tau o\acute{\iota}$ of the same passage from Q, for which the only New Testament parallel is the Isa 29:14 quotation in 1 Cor 1:19. The contrast between hidden and revealed is employed in 1 Cor 4:5: ". . . the Lord who will illumine the hidden things of darkness and reveal the counsels of the hearts." This can well be understood as a commentary on Mark 4:22.

To these striking relationships of Paul's language in the first chapters of 1 Corinthians to a Q saying must be added the occurrence of the strange "quotation from scripture" in 1 Cor 2:9 ("what eye has not seen and ear has not heard . . ."), which is paralleled in the Gospel of Thomas (saying 17), in the Dialogue of the Savior (140:2–4), and elsewhere.[6] This saying, however, not only appears in the same form in gnostic writings, it has also made its way into Q in a somewhat altered form in which it appears in Matt 13:16–17=Q/Luke 10:23–24,[7] i.e., immediately following upon the previously quoted Q parallel to the Pauline language employed in 1 Corinthians 1–4.

Finally, there is the ironic reference of Paul to the Corinthians as the ones who have already been satisfied, who have already become rich, and who *have become kings* ($\dot{\epsilon}\beta a\sigma\iota\lambda\epsilon\acute{v}\sigma a\tau\epsilon$) without him (1 Cor 4:8). The verb $\beta a\sigma\iota\lambda\epsilon\acute{v}\epsilon\iota\nu$ ("to reign") is used elsewhere in 1 Corinthians only of Christ (15:25).[8] Not only is this characterization of the Corinthians possibly an ironic rendering of the famous saying of GThom 2, it must also be remembered that the democratization of the concept of kingship genuinely belongs to Jewish wisdom language.[9]

In my essay of 1980, I have suggested that these affinities of 1 Corinthians 1–4 with certain wisdom sayings may indicate the use of some kind of Jewish

---

5 On the question of the relationship of Matt 13:35 to its assumed source, Ps 77:2 (LXX), see Stendahl, *School of St. Matthew,* 116: the sentence is quoted in a form "differing entirely from the LXX and the later Greek versions."

6 Attention to this was drawn first by Robinson, "Kerygma and History in the New Testament," 42–43.

7 This might imply that the more original wording of Q 10:23–24 is found in GThom 17 and 1 Cor 2:9.

8 Otherwise Paul uses the verb of the believers only in Rom 5:17–21. There it is the believers' rule on the basis of their having received grace, whereas in 1 Corinthians 4 those who already are kings are asked whether they can boast of anything they have not received.

9 See especially Wisdom's invitation in Prov 9:6, where at least some important manuscripts read $\dot{a}\pi o\lambda\epsilon\acute{\iota}\pi\epsilon\tau\epsilon\ \dot{a}\phi\rho o\sigma\acute{v}\nu\eta\nu\ \acute{\iota}\nu a\ \epsilon\dot{\iota}s\ \tau\grave{o}\nu\ a\dot{\iota}\hat{\omega}\nu a\ \beta a\sigma\iota\lambda\epsilon\acute{v}\sigma\eta\tau\epsilon$ ("leave off simple-mindedness, that you may reign forever"). Editors consider this as an intrusion from Wis 6:21 and prefer the reading $\zeta\acute{\eta}\sigma\epsilon\sigma\theta\epsilon$ ("you will live"). But even if the latter is the original reading, the former reading may have circulated very early.

wisdom book that had the status of "scripture." This would explain Paul's quotation formula "as it is written" in 1 Cor 2:9 as well as the close affinity to Old Testament passages that is evident in Matt 13:35 (cf. Ps 77:2) and 1 Cor 1:19 (also introduced by "it is written"; cf. Isa 29:14). However, whatever appears here as some kind of scriptural reference—surprisingly remote in wording from the respective scriptural passages in all instances—is certainly, at the same time, a collection of wisdom sayings with multiple attestations in the sayings traditions. The connections to Q material do not go beyond Q 10:21–24. The other sayings to which Paul alludes in 1 Corinthians 1–4 do not belong to Q: Matt 13:35; Mark 4:22; GThom 2, 5–6, and 17. The topic of the revelation of hidden wisdom is at best marginal in Q, but it unites all the sayings to which Paul alludes in this context.

Whatever the Corinthians used here may be related to the sayings tradition by another element, namely the recourse to the authority of certain persons: Paul, Apollos, Cephas, possibly Christ (1 Cor 1:12; 3:4–5, 22). This phenomenon is still one of the most puzzling conundrums of New Testament scholarship.[10] If the thesis of a particular sayings tradition current among the Corinthians is plausible, there are three elements that together call for an answer: (1) The Corinthians knew a number of sayings that they understood as the revelation of hidden wisdom and life-giving knowledge. (2) Paul explicitly rejected the suggestion that his calling had anything to do with baptism (1 Cor 1:15–17); the claim of belonging to a specific person may have been connected with the relationship of the initiate to his/her baptizer.[11] (3) The question of the earliest appearance of the claim to apostolic authority can be answered: Papias, The Gospel of Thomas, The Apocryphon of James, and even Ptolemy's Letter to Flora show that apostolic authority, appealed to with the name of specific apostles, played a role in the transmission of sayings of Jesus, especially in gnostic circles.[12]

If all three observations can be combined, the conclusion would be that Paul faced a Corinthian faction in which believers claimed that baptism was their initiation into a mystery. They understood particular apostles as their mystagogues from whom they received sayings that revealed life-giving wisdom. The dual role of the baptizing mystagogue and the guarantor of a tradition of wisdom sayings is quite natural. Both the action and the sayings can be understood as μυστήριον ("mystery"). Paul's arguments against this under-

---

10 As is well known, the literature on this problem is as immense as is the number of unsatisfactory suggestions for a solution. For a brief survey, see Conzelmann, *1 Corinthians*, 33–34.

11 Here and in the following note I must refer to my own previous publications, simply because this problem has concerned me for a long time. In my review of Wilckens, *Weisheit und Torheit*, I have made the suggestion that the Corinthians understood the apostolic authorities to whom they referred, and possibly also Christ, as mystagogues who initiated them through baptism into the mystery of the new faith.

12 This thesis was first put forward by von Campenhausen, *Formation*. I have expanded this suggestion in my article, "La tradition apostolique."

standing of salvation become much clearer if they are understood against this background. The well-attested reading μυστήριον instead of μαρτύριον ("witness") in 1 Cor 2:1,[13] as well as Paul's reference to Christ's crucifixion as the "hidden mystery predetermined by God before the ages," become understandable.[14] Nowhere else does Paul speak about the cross of Christ in such terms. But an interpretation of 1 Corinthians 1–4 is not the object of this essay.

2. The Esoteric Wisdom of the Parables

Q certainly contained a number of similes and brief parables.[15] Of the parables from the Markan parable chapter, the "Mustard Seed," occurs also in Q (13:18–19). But two elements are missing in Q: (1) most of the longer narrative parables that appear in Mark 4, Matthew 13, and in the Lukan travel section;[16] (2) the understanding of the parables as esoteric mystery instructions.[17]

The understanding of parables as "mysteries" that are accessible only to the circle of initiates is clearly present in Mark 4:11–12. These verses are not part of the Markan redaction but belong to the older collection of parables that Mark incorporated into his writing. In the preserved text of the canonical Gospel of Mark, the singular μυστήριον is used in order to characterize the entire parable teaching of Jesus as the esoteric revelation of *the* mystery of the kingdom. However, the Matthean and Lukan reproduction of Mark 4:11, i.e., Matt 13:11 and Luke 8:10, apparently preserve the original wording of their Markan *Vorlage* in their use of the plural: the μυστήρια ("mysteries") of the kingdom. Each of the parables is such a mystery saying, demanding interpretation that is given only to the initiate.

While a tradition that understands the parables as mysteries has not found its way into Q, it is present in the Gospel of Thomas. Saying 62, "It is to those that are worthy of my mysteries that I tell my mysteries. Do not let your left hand know what your right hand is doing," introduces three parables: saying 63 (Rich Fool), saying 64 (Invitation to the Banquet), and saying 65 (Wicked Husbandmen). The introductory saying and the three parables must have formed a unit before they were incorporated into the Gospel of Thomas. The

13 Shunned by previous editions of Nestle's *Novum Testamentum Graece,* but now correctly adopted by Aland in the 26th edition.

14 Elsewhere in Paul, the singular μυστήριον is used only of specific sayings (cf. 1 Cor 13:2; 15:51), never of the event of Christ's crucifixion or of the gospel as a whole. The latter use appears for the first time in the Pauline corpus in Eph 3:3–4, 9; 6:19.

15 See the list of Q pericopes in Kloppenborg, *Formation of Q,* 74–76.

16 The most striking exception is the parable of the "Invitation to the Banquet" (Q 14:16–24). Whether the somewhat longer parable or example story of the "Rich Fool" (Luke 12:16–21) was a part of Q is debated; see Kloppenborg, *Q Parallels,* 128–29; Kloppenborg himself is inclined to include this pericope in Q.

17 See the comment of Kloppenborg (*Formation of Q,* 134) about Mark's implicit rejection of "Q's understanding of Jesus' public preaching as an adequate ground for repentance and faith."

author of this gospel does not make any effort to exploit the concept of parable as mystery. Moreover, there are a number of other parables scattered throughout this gospel that are presented without any special reference to their esoteric character.

All three parables of this small collection have synoptic parallels; but it seems unlikely that either the author or the redactor of Q, or any of the authors of the synoptic gospels, knew them as a unit. GThom 63 (Rich Fool) appears only in Luke (12:16–21) and belongs either to the Lukan special materials or to Q.[18] GThom 64 (Invitation to the Banquet) appears in Matt 22:1–10 and Luke 14:16–24 and is most probably a part of Q;[19] but it may belong to the later redaction of Q and not to its formative stage.[20] On the other hand, GThom 65 (Wicked Husbandmen) has come into the synoptic tradition through the Gospel of Mark (12:1–9=Matt 21:33–41=Luke 20:9–17).

Thus, it seems as if there is no plausible relationship between the transmission history of the three mystery parables of GThom 62–65 and any earlier building blocks that preceded the composition of Q and of the synoptic gospels.[21] However, there is a special connection between the Gospel of Thomas and the Gospel of Mark. In both writings, the parable of the Wicked Husbandmen is followed by the saying about the stone rejected by the builders that has become the cornerstone (GThom 65 and 66; Mark 12:1–9 and 12:10).[22] Mark 12:10 is often considered as a redactional Markan addition;[23] but this may be questioned. Mark 12:1–11 was inserted by Mark into a context of a traditional collection of apophthegmata (11:27–12:37). Mark 12:12—directly tied to 12:13—provides the Markan redactional transition that leads back into the interrupted context of the source. Mark 12:10–11, however, does not seem to serve any such redactional function; it must have been part of the parable before it was brought into this context. The introduction to this parable in Mark 12:1 provides a clue: Καὶ ἤρξατο αὐτοῖς ἐν παραβολαῖς (plural!) λαλεῖν ("And he began to speak to them in parables"). This is an

---

18 Kloppenborg (*Q Parallels*, 128) includes this parable in Q but encloses it in parentheses and notes that most authors do not include it. It is not treated seriatim in Kloppenborg, *Formation of Q*. Since there is no Matthean parallel, a conclusive argument is difficult.

19 See Kloppenborg, *Q Parallels*, 166.

20 Kloppenborg, *Formation of Q*, 229–30, 242.

21 It is true that the parables of the Wicked Husbandmen and of the Invitation to the Banquet appear next to each other in the Gospel of Matthew, though not in the same sequence as in the Gospel of Thomas (Matt 21:33–41 and 22:1–14). But this is purely accidental, since Matthew drew the former from Mark, following the Markan sequence, and the latter from Q. The two are connected in Matthew because Matthew himself gave both parables the same interpretation—rejection and punishment of Israel. This interpretation is certainly secondary with respect to the parable of the Invitation to the Banquet, possibly also with respect to the parable of the Wicked Husbandmen if GThom 65 has preserved its more original form.

22 See the discussion of this parable of the Gospel of Thomas in its relationship to Mark 12 in Fallon and Cameron, "Gospel of Thomas," 4221–23.

23 Bultmann, *History*, 177, 419, and most commentaries.

introduction for a collection of parables, not for a single parable.[24] Though it is impossible to say anything more about the character of the collection from which Mark drew this parable, it can be assumed that it must have been related to the one used by the Gospel of Thomas.

It is, of course, tempting to posit a major source in which parables were collected under the heading "mysteries (of the kingdom)." There are parallels to two of the parables of Mark 4 in the Gospel of Thomas: Mark 4:3–9 (Sower)=GThom 9; Mark 4:30–32 (Mustard Seed)=GThom 20.[25] But they do not appear in the context in which the Gospel of Thomas introduces parables under the heading of "mysteries." On the other hand, other synoptic parables also have their analogies in the Gospel of Thomas, especially those added by Matthew to the Markan parable chapter: Matt 13:24–30 (Tares)=GThom 57; Matt 13:33 (Leaven)=GThom 96; Matt 13:44–46 (Hidden Treasure and Pearl)=GThom 109, 76; Matt 13:47–50 (Dragnet)=GThom 8. Nowhere are these parables associated with the concept of "mystery," but they are presented as parables of the "kingdom" in all instances except GThom 8 and 9. Only the latter appears in the synoptic tradition as a "kingdom" parable. In all other instances, the Gospel of Thomas and the synoptic parables agree in designating them as parables of the "kingdom."

One must, therefore, conclude that the Gospel of Thomas knew at least two different parable clusters, one designated as "mystery parables," the other circulating as "parables of the kingdom." Although Q includes some parables that appear in each of these two collections, it does not seem likely that Q was acquainted with either one of them.

3. Q and the Gospel of Thomas

Among the sayings of the Gospel of Thomas that have parallels in the synoptic gospels, by far the largest number are sayings that Matthew and/or Luke has drawn from the Synoptic Sayings Source.[26] There are at least thirty-six sayings that belong in this category, possibly as many as forty-five, if one includes the Q–Mark overlaps and those sayings that Luke may have drawn from Q, although there are no Matthean parallels. On the other hand, there are only fourteen sayings that the Gospel of Thomas shares with Mark (seven-

---

24 Matt 21:33 and Luke 20:9 noticed the awkwardness of the plural and corrected the text accordingly.

25 Missing is the parable of the Seed Growing Secretly, Mark 4:26–29, unless the brief phrase of GThom 21d ("When the grain ripened, he came quickly with his sickle in his hand and reaped it") can be considered as a parallel. However, this parable may not have been a part of the original Markan parable chapter. It is not reproduced by either Matthew or Luke.

26 The following count is approximate, because in some instances it is debated whether a saying of the Gospel of Thomas is indeed a variant of a synoptic saying. Instances in which the Gospel of Thomas quotes the same saying more than once have been counted as only one parallel.

teen if the Q–Mark overlaps are counted), thirteen that it shares with Matthew only, and six that have parallels only in Luke.[27]

Although, however, Q contains the largest numbers of parallels to the Gospel of Thomas by any count, the total number of sayings with parallels only in either Matthew or Mark (or possibly Luke) is substantial. Taking a minimalist position on Q, thirty-six certain Q parallels compare with a total of thirty-six parallels in the three synoptic gospels apart from their uncontested Q materials. As there are also a number of sayings in the Gospel of Thomas with parallels only in John and an additional number of possibly quite early sayings without parallels in the canonical gospels, it is obvious that the Gospel of Thomas cannot simply pass as a variant or as an early form of the Synoptic Sayings Source, nor is it possible to consider Q as the source of any of the sayings of the Gospel of Thomas.

Nevertheless, the consideration of Q parallels in the Gospel of Thomas is as instructive as it is puzzling if two questions are asked: (1) To which layer of the development of Q do the parallels in the Gospel of Thomas belong? (2) Are there any instances in which the wording of the sayings in the Gospel of Thomas can help to decide the more original wording of a Q saying? In the following, I shall discuss the first question; some remarks with respect to the second question will be offered in an appendix.[28]

3.1 Specific cases

A good portion of the Q parallels in the Gospel of Thomas are wisdom sayings and community instructions that appear in the formative stage of Q, which Kloppenborg has identified as the "Sapiential Speeches."[29] I shall use Kloppenborg's analysis of the formation of Q as my working hypothesis and shall list the sayings here in the order in which they appear according to the most likely original order of Q:[30]

Saying	Matthew	Luke	Thomas
Blessed are the poor ...	5:3	6:20b	54
Blessed are the hungry ...	5:6	6:21	69b
Blessed when they hate you		(6:22)	68
Blessed when they persecute	5:11		68, 69a[31]

27 Most of the last group are considered to be Q sayings by most scholars. It is interesting to observe that most scholars are more likely to assign sayings to Q if they are preserved by Luke alone, while sayings of Matthew are rarely considered to derive from Q unless they are paralleled in Luke.
28 A good summary of research to date on the relationship of the Gospel of Thomas to the synoptic gospels, including the relationship to Q, is presented by Fallon and Cameron, "Gospel of Thomas," 4195–4251. See this recent publication for further literature on the questions discussed below.
29 See Kloppenborg, Formation of Q, 171–245.
30 See Kloppenborg, Q Parallels, passim.
31 Because Luke 6:21, 22 and Matt 5:11 form a cluster in GThom 68 and 69, all three synoptic sayings are candidates for inclusion in Q.

If someone takes away . . .	5:42	6:30	95
Golden rule	7:12	6:31	6b
Blind leading the blind	15:14	6:39	34
Splinter in your brother's eye	7:4	6:42	26
Good tree, good fruit	7:16–18	6:43–44	43, 45
	12:33–35		
Foxes have their dens . . .	8:20	9:58	86
Large harvest, few workers	9:37–38	10:2	73
Eat what they serve, heal the			
sick . . .	10:8,14	10:9–11	14b
Seek and you will find	7:7–8	11:9–10	2, 92, 94
Hidden and revealed	10:26	12:2	5, 6b
Proclaim from the rooftops	10:27	12:3	33a
Blasphemy against the father	12:32	12:10	44
. . . what you shall wear	6:25	12:22	36
Heavenly treasure	6:19–21	12:33–34	76b
Invitation to the Banquet	22:1–10	14:16–24	64[32]
Hate your father and mother	10:37	14:26	55, 101

Of sayings of the Gospel of Thomas that have parallels in the secondary layer of Q, "The Announcement of Judgment,"[33] many are wisdom sayings or community rules that do not reveal any polemical intent as they appear in the Gospel of Thomas:

Saying	*Matthew*	*Luke*	*Thomas*
"Blessed the womb . . ."		11:27–28	79a[34]
Lamp not under a bushel	5:15	11:33	33b
Eye lamp of the body	6:22–23	11:34–36	24
Wash outside of the cup	23:25	11:39–40	89[35]
Divide my inheritance		12:13–14	72
First last and last first	20:16	13:30	4b[36]
. . . serve two masters	6:24	16:13	47a
Mountain, move from here	17:20	17:6	48
Whoever has, will be given	25:29	19:26	41

Also the parables of the Gospel of Thomas with parallels in Q do not reveal any signs of polemical or apocalyptic intent:

32 This is the only parable that Kloppenborg (*Formation of Q,* 229–30) includes in one of the "Sapiential Speeches" of Q. On the other Q parables, see below.

33 See Kloppenborg, *Formation of Q,* 102–70.

34 GThom 79b quotes as the second half of 79a, "For there will be days when you say, 'Blessed are the womb which has not conceived and the breasts which have not given milk.'" A parallel to this saying appears in Luke 23:29. If GThom 79a+b preserves the original form of this saying, it could be classified as eschatological, though it does not express polemic or judgment.

35 In GThom 89 there is no reference to the Pharisees at all. The saying may have been a community rule or an allegorical saying derived from such a rule.

36 GThom 4b is a proverbial statement of reversal without any reference to an eschatological dimension. The context of Q/Luke 13:28–29 is not presupposed.

Saying	Matthew	Luke	Thomas
Householder and the thief	24:43–44	12:39–40	21, 103[37]
Mustard Seed	13:31–32	13:18–19	20[38]
Leaven	13:33	13:20–21	96
Lost Sheep	18:12–14	15:3–7	107
The Rich Fool		12:16–21	63

The remaining sayings of the Gospel of Thomas that have Q parallels appear in sections of Q that Kloppenborg has identified as "The Announcement of Judgment." Two are related to John the Baptist in Q:

Saying	Matthew	Luke	Thomas
"Reed shaken by the wind"	11:7–8	7:24–26	78
John greatest born by a woman	11:11	7:28	46

The first, as it appears in the Gospel of Thomas, has no explicit relationship to John the Baptist. It could be understood as a general statement about the exclusion of the rich, and Q's use of this saying in the context of sayings about John the Baptist may be secondary. The second names John the Baptist explicitly and contrasts "the child of the kingdom" with John. Whatever its origin, it demonstrates that the "Announcement of Judgment" sections of Q have incorporated free sayings that speak about the newness of Jesus' message. Also the saying Q/Luke 10:23–24 ("Many prophets and kings desired to see what you see . . .") belongs in this category. It is uncertain, however, whether GThom 38 ("Often have you desired to hear these sayings . . .") can be considered a parallel or variant of this Q saying. This saying belongs more appropriately in the context of the traditional cluster that is shared by the Gospel of Thomas and the Gospel of John.[39]

Controversy with the Pharisees is evident in two sayings of the Gospel of Thomas: "The Pharisees have the key of knowledge . . ." (Matt 23:13//Q/Luke 11:52=GThom 39), and "Woe to the Pharisees, for they are like a dog sleeping in the manger of oxen . . ." (GThom 102). While there is no synoptic parallel

37 In Q, this parable is clearly eschatological and has been assigned by Kloppenborg (*Formation of Q*, 148–51) to one of the "Announcements of Judgment." In the Gospel of Thomas, where this parable is quoted twice (21 and 103), an original eschatological meaning may have been implied, but it speaks of the guarding of the treasure rather than of watchfulness. Cf. Kloppenborg (*Formation of Q*, 149): "Thomas interprets the parable in its more natural sense: Watchfulness against 'the world' will prevent the loss of one's 'goods' (presumably γνῶσις ['knowledge'])." There is also no parallel to the reference to the coming of the Son of man of Q/Luke 12:40.

38 This as well as the following parables are not assigned by Kloppenborg (*Formation of Q*) to either the "Sapiential speeches" or the "Announcements of Judgment" in Q. As they appear in the Gospel of Thomas, they are clearly wisdom parables.

39 GThom 38 concludes with a sentence ("There will be days when you will seek me but will not find me") that has been used several times in the Gospel of John (7:34, 36; 8:21–22; 13:33); but see the "Appendix" on the possible relationship of Luke 17:22 to GThom 38.

to the latter saying, the first is paralleled in an "Announcement of Judgment" section of Q; however, there it is formulated in the second person, introduced by "Woe." Probably this formulation is not necessarily a structural part of the tradition of sayings about the Pharisees that the Gospel of Thomas and Q (and also Matthew!) share,[40] though GThom 102 is also introduced by "Woe."[41]

The "Announcement of Judgment" sections in Q/Luke 12:39–59[42] and Q/Luke 17:20–37[43] contain three sayings each that are paralleled in the Gospel of Thomas:[44]

Saying	Matthew	Luke	Thomas
Cast a fire on the earth	—	12:49	10
Not come to bring peace	10:34–36	12:51–53	16
You judge earth and sky	16:2–3	12:54–56	91
The kingdom is in your midst	—	17:20–21	3, 113b[45]
Kingdom . . . behold over here . . .	24:26	17:23	113a
Two will be on a couch	24:40	17:34	61a

Most of these sayings are "eschatological" in character because they announce a crisis moment related to Jesus' coming or to the reception of his word. However, this moment of crisis is never some expected future event, but always the present situation. It is remarkable that the Q sayings of these sections that speak about the coming of the Son of man (Q/Luke 17:24, 26, 30) and the references to the Son of man in Q parallels (Q/Luke 12:40) are missing from the sayings of the Gospel of Thomas. Thus the future eschatological or "apocalyptic"[46] interpretation of such sayings as it is evident in Q has not yet touched the formulations of the parallels in the Gospel of Thomas.

3.2 Conclusions

Considering all Q parallels in the Gospel of Thomas, it is extremely difficult to formulate a conclusion about the relationship of these sayings in the two documents. The answer to the first question posed above ("To which layer of the development of the Synoptic Sayings Source do the parallels in the Gospel

40 Also Kloppenborg (*Formation of Q,* 144) suggests that "the woe-oracle form is a secondary construction of Q redaction."
41 On GThom 89 ("Wash the outside of the cup . . .") see above. It is not certain that the Gospel of Thomas knew this saying as part of the tradition about the Pharisees.
42 Kloppenborg, *Formation of Q,* 148–54.
43 Kloppenborg, *Formation of Q,* 154–66.
44 Also the parable Q/Luke 12:39–40=GThom 103 (cf. 21) belongs to the context of the first of these sections; see above.
45 The inclusion of Luke 17:20–21 in Q is debated; see Kloppenborg, *Formation of Q,* 155, and *Q Parallels,* 188. There is no Matthean parallel. But GThom 113 seems to be related to both Luke 17:20–21 and 17:23 (even to Luke 17:22). See the discussion of these sayings in the "Appendix."
46 On the appropriateness of the term "apocalyptic" for the designation of Q's eschatology, see Kloppenborg, "Symbolic Eschatology."

of Thomas belong?") is not entirely clear. The majority of the sayings in the Gospel of Thomas appear in the more original layer of "Sapiential Speeches" or resemble sayings of that layer of Q. More than thirty of the Q parallels of the Gospel of Thomas (including the parables) are sapiential in their character and lack any future eschatological component. A few of the sayings are polemical insofar as they reveal an attempt to distinguish the followers of Jesus from the followers of John the Baptist and from the Pharisees. The remainder of the relevant parallels in the Gospel of Thomas can be legitimately called "eschatological," insofar as they describe the crisis situation created by Jesus' words, but—in contradistinction to Q—they lack any of the future or apocalyptic orientation that characterizes their employment in the secondary stage of Q (the "Announcement of Judgment").

It can be said with confidence that the Q parallels in the Gospel of Thomas always represent, or derive from, more original forms of those sayings. Not only is there no trace of redactional features of Q in these sayings of the Gospel of Thomas, but they are also either core sayings of the respective sections of Q in which they occur or free sayings added at a later stage of the development of Q. But to reconstruct any kind of a source for Q from the sayings of the Gospel of Thomas would not do justice to the complex nature of the traditions and sources used in the two documents. Q obviously had access to sayings that have no parallels in the Gospel of Thomas. On the other hand, the Gospel of Thomas includes materials that lie outside the traditions to which Q had access (cf. especially the parables and the sayings shared with the Gospel of John).

The investigation of the sayings shared by Q and the Gospel of Thomas leads into the very earliest period of the transmission of these sayings. Here, as also in the preceding two sections of this study, the most remarkable feature is the great diversity of the complexes and clusters of sayings at the formative stages of the transmission. Yet, some clusters of sayings that Q and the Gospel of Thomas share can be identified with some confidence.[47] The first is identical with the materials that now are included in Luke's "Sermon on the Plain"; of the Q materials of this section the following appear also in the Gospel of Thomas: Q 6:20b, 21, 22, 30, 31, 39, 40, 42, 43–44. One or two clusters of materials paralleled in the Gospel of Thomas appear in Luke 11 and 12: Q 11:27–28, 33, 34–36, 39, 52; 12:2, 3, 10, 13–15, 16–21, 22, 33–34, 39–40, 49, 51–53, 56. Perhaps also Q/Luke 17:20–21, 23, 34 belong to a more original unit of sayings in the tradition preceding both Q and the Gospel of Thomas. It is remarkable that there is not a single instance of sayings from the Gospel of Thomas paralleled in these sections of the Gospel of Luke that cannot be assigned to Q with a high degree of probability. In the case of Q

---

47 In almost no instance is it helpful to observe the order in which Q parallels appear in the Gospel of Thomas. But that is more a problem of the composition of that gospel than a concern for the identification of sayings clusters used for its composition.

11:27–12:56 some of these sayings belong to sections identified as "Sapiential Speeches" by Kloppenborg, while others are more properly to be understood as "Announcements of Judgment." However, it has been argued above that some of the materials that Q has incorporated into the latter sections were originally wisdom sayings or community rules; in an earlier edition of Q they could have been part of Sapiential Speeches.

A confirmation of this hypothesis is the observation that some of the parallels of Q in the Gospel of Thomas that appear outside these sections belong to different clusters of the earliest tradition. That is most evident with respect to some of the parables. Two of the parables shared by the Gospel of Thomas and Q belong to a group of Thomas parables that also appear in Matthew 13. The following list will make this evident:

Saying	Matthew	Luke	Thomas
Parable of the tares	13:24–30		57
Mustard seed	13:31–32	13:18–19	20
Leaven	13:33	13:20–21	96
Hidden treasure	13:44		109
Parable of the pearl	13:45–46		76a
Parable of the dragnet	13:47–50		8

The two parables reproduced in Q are not typical Q material[48] but an instance in which Q happened to incorporate casually two parables from a collection that was reproduced more fully by Matthew and by the Gospel of Thomas.[49]

Appendix:
The Gospel of Thomas as Witness for Original Readings of Q

In all instances in which the Q parallels in the Gospel of Thomas agree with either Matthew or Luke, one must assume that such agreements represent the wording of the more original versions of those sayings and thus the text of Q. It is, of course, possible that the transmission of the text of the Gospel of Thomas and/or its Coptic translation was influenced by the text of the canonical gospels. In the following, I will present a number of instances in which parallels between Q and the Gospel of Thomas suggest reconstructions of Q. These reconstructions either diverge from the most probable Q text that has been presented by Kloppenborg, *Q Parallels,* and by others or address previous uncertainties that have existed in the reconstruction of Q.

---

48 It is interesting to observe that Kloppenborg (*Formation of Q*) does not assign these Q parables to any particular stage of the development of Q.

49 The parables of the Gospel of Thomas without synoptic parallels may have been derived from the same collection.

Saying	Matthew	Luke	Thomas
Lamp not under a bushel	5:25	11:33	33b

Luke 11:33 εἰς κρυπτήν ("out of sight") has a correspondence in GThom 33b. . . . εἰς κρυπτήν . . . οὐδὲ ὑπὸ μόδιον ("nor under a bushel basket") may have been the original reading of Q.

| Wash outside of the cup | 23:25 | 11:39–40 | 89 |

The text of GThom 89 argues for the inclusion of Luke 11:40 in Q, although a parallel in Matthew is missing.

| . . . have key of knowledge | 23:13 | 11:52 | 39 |

In this woe of the speech against the Pharisees, the Greek text of POxy 655, as reconstructed on the basis of the Coptic translation of GThom 39, argues for the following text as the original text of Q: Φαρισαῖοι καὶ γραμματεῖς ("Pharisees and scribes"=Matthew), ἤρατε τὴν κλεῖδα τῆς γνώσεως ("you have taken away the key of knowledge"=Luke).

| Householder and the thief | 24:43–44 | 12:39–40 | 21, 103 |

GThom 21b presupposes the verb γρηγορεῖν ("watch") (Matt: ἐγρηγόρησεν ["he would have watched"], missing in Luke).

| Not come to bring peace | 10:34–36 | 12:51–53 | 16 |

The text of GThom 16 argues for ἦλθον βαλεῖν εἰρήνην ("I have come to cast peace"=Matthew; Luke: εἰρήνην . . . δοῦναι ["to give . . . peace"]) as the original text of Q 12:51a. In the second half of the saying, one usually wants to choose between μάχαιραν ("sword," Matthew) and διαμερισμόν ("division," Luke). However, the text of GThom 16 suggests that Q 12:51b presented both terms. Furthermore, GThom 16 includes among its terms also "fire"; though certainly secondary in that context, it might indicate that its source coupled the two sayings Luke 12:49 (= GThom 10) and 12:51. That would be a strong argument for the inclusion of Luke 12:49 in Q.[50]

| You judge earth and sky | 16:3 | 12:56 | 91 |

GThom 91 supports the inclusion of τῆς γῆς ("of the earth," only Luke) and the reading τὸν καιρὸν τοῦτον ("this time," Luke; Matthew: τὰ σημεῖα τῶν καιρῶν ["the signs of the times"], for Q 12:56.

| Mustard Seed | 13:31–32 | 13:18–19 | 20 |

As in Matthew, the version of the parable in the Gospel of Thomas emphasizes the smallness of the mustard seed. This emphasis is missing in Luke, and the Matthean version is usually seen as due to influence from Mark 4:31.

| Invitation to the Banquet | 22:1–10 | 14:16–24 | 64 |

The absence of the invitation to the poor (Luke 14:21) in GThom 64 confirms that it is secondary, most likely inserted by Luke.[51] On the other hand, the excuse of the first guest in GThom 64 ("Some merchants owe me money . . .") seems to be equally tendentious and secondary.

---

50 See furthermore Kloppenborg, Q Parallels, 142, and Formation of Q, 151.
51 This has been frequently asserted; cf. Bultmann, History, 175.

Hate your father and mother   10:37   14:26   55, 101
   If the text of GThom 55 can be trusted, this saying was originally formulated in
   two parallel clauses, the first ending with οὐ δύναται εἶναί μου μαθητής ("he is not
   able to be my disciple," preserved only in Luke), the second with οὐκ ἔστιν μου
   ἄξιος ("he is not worthy of me," preserved only in Matthew). "One might suggest
   that Gos. Thom. 55 represents more accurately, at least in terms of its concluding
   clauses, the Q version."[52]

Serving two masters   6:24   16:13   47a
   GThom 47a presupposes a Greek text that included the term οἰκέτης ("house
   slave," only in Luke, missing in Matthew).

Mountain, move from here   17:20   17:6   48
   Matt 17:20, μετάβα ἔνθεν ἐκεῖ, καὶ μεταβήσεται ("move from here to there, and it
   will move"), should be considered the original reading of Q 17:6, while Luke's
   uprooting of the sycamore fig tree is secondary, and its planting ἐν τῇ θαλάσσῃ
   ("in the sea") an intrusion from Mark 11:22.

The kingdom is in your midst   ——   17:20–21   3, 113b
... and you will not see it   ——   17:22   38
Kingdom ... behold over here ...   24:26   17:23   113a
   As indicated above (n. 45), the inclusion of Luke 17:20–21 in Q is debated, and
   there is almost a consensus against an inclusion of Luke 17:22.[53] The easiest solution would exclude Luke 17:20–21 altogether as probably Lukan creation and
   reject Luke 17:22–23//Matt 24:26 as formulations dependent upon Mark 13:21–
   23.[54] However, Luke 17:23 is certainly confirmed for Q through the parallel in
   Matthew.[55] The repetition of "Behold, here it is . . ." in Luke 17:21 and 23 suggests that both passages reproduce what was originally *one* single saying such as
   GThom 113, from which also οὐκ ἔρχεται ἡ βασιλεία τοῦ θεοῦ μετὰ
   παρατηρήσεως ("the Kingdom of God does not come with signs to be observed by
   empirical observation," Luke 17:20) is derived; cf. also GThom 3 for Luke 17:21.
   Finally, GThom 38b ("There will be days when you look for me and do not find
   me") may have been the basis for Q/Luke 17:22.

Two will be on a couch   24:40   17:34   61a
   ἐπὶ κλίνης ("on a couch") is the correct reading. Matthew's ἐν τῷ ἀγρῷ ("in the
   field") is influenced by Matt 24:18=Mark 13:16.

Whoever has, will be given   25:29   19:26   41
   The almost verbal agreement between GThom 41, Luke 19:26, and Mark 4:25
   demonstrates that Matthew's expanded text is secondary.

52 Fallon and Cameron, "Gospel of Thomas," 4221.
53 See Kloppenborg, *Q Parallels*, 192.
54 Lührmann, *Redaktion*, 72.
55 Matthew reproduces Mark 13:21–23 in Matt 24:23–25 and then edits the Q variant
    (= Luke 17:23) in order to avoid repetition.

The Gospel of Thomas
and the New Testament

John H. Sieber

0. Introduction

When James M. Robinson first introduced me to the Gospel of Thomas some twenty-five years ago, there were certain assumptions that a majority of writers took for granted: (1) that Thomas was dependent on the New Testament for most of its Jesus sayings; (2) that Thomas was written about 140 CE; (3) that Thomas was a gnostic book. Today few of the scholars who study Thomas would hold all three of those opinions (with the most disagreement on the third), and the change is due in part to the work of Robinson on the genre he calls *Logoi Sophon* (Wisdom Sayings). This article will survey how those changes of opinion have occurred, with special attention to the arguments for the independence of Thomas from the New Testament.

The Gospel of Thomas has been of such interest because its 114 sayings provide a rich new vein of material for those who have been engaged in the study of the sayings of Jesus preserved in the synoptic gospels, Q, and the Apostolic Fathers. In Thomas we have had for the first time in modern scholarship a copy of an apocryphal gospel that has direct bearing on our study of the canonical gospels and the Jesus tradition.

Both its similarities to those gospels and its differences from them are easily recognized. Thomas contains many of the sayings of Jesus already familiar previously from the New Testament, often with almost identical wordings; for example, GThom 34, "Jesus said: If a blind man leads a blind man, both will always fall down into a pit," is clearly very much like the Matthean form of a Q saying: "Avoid them, they are leaders of the blind; and if the blind lead the blind, both will fall into a pit" (Matt 15:14/Luke 6:39).

Yet Thomas' version of the Parable of the Net is so different from the canonical parable of Matt 13:47–49 that it is not immediately clear whether we are dealing with one or two parables. GThom 8 reads:

And he said: The Man is like a wise fisherman who cast his net into the sea, he drew it up from the sea full of small fish; among them that wise fisherman found a large, good fish; he threw all the small fish into the sea; he chose the large fish without regret.

It was both the similarities of Thomas' sayings to New Testament materials and its differences from them that spurred the initial debate about the Gospel of Thomas and the New Testament that began over a quarter of a century ago, the debate over whether the New Testament gospels were or were not the sources of Thomas' synoptic-like sayings.

1. Dependent or Independent?

Two contrary opinions about the origins of Thomas' sayings have been held. In the early years after the publication of the Coptic text in 1958 scholars such as Gilles Quispel and Hugh Montefiore were quick to claim Thomas as a new source of Jesus sayings.[1] Before long those opinions were largely rejected, and many concluded that Thomas was a secondary witness to the synoptic tradition, i.e., it derived its versions of the sayings of Jesus from the canonical gospels. On the basis of evidence that Thomas lacks the editorial traits of the synoptic evangelists, another group of scholars has come to hold the view once again that Thomas represents a sayings tradition that not only was not dependent on the canonical gospels but also developed in a different way from Q. (Thomas is similar to Q but not Q.) The discussion that follows centers on methodological issues of this problem rather than on providing a review of the opinions of all those who have written on the topic.[2]

Most of those who have championed the view that Thomas is dependent on the New Testament for its synoptic sayings did their work in the early 1960s. R. M. Grant and D. N. Freedman, writing in 1960, argued that Thomas' synoptic sayings are examples of the same type of exegesis used by Naasene Gnostics.[3] They noted that, according to Hippolytus (*Refutations,* V,1) these Gnostics accomplished their exegetical goals by interweaving several synoptic passages (usually drawn from very different contexts) or by rearranging the sequences of the sayings. Grant–Freedman's analysis of GThom 14a provides an example of how they discover both types of Naasene exegesis in Thomas. GThom 14a reads:

> Jesus said to them: When you fast, you will beget sin for yourselves, and when you pray, they will condemn you, and when you give alms, you will do evil to your spirits.

According to Grant–Freedman the introductory questions in Thomas deliberately reverse the order of alms, prayer, and fasting given by Matt 6:1–18, i.e.,

---

1 Quispel, "The Gospel of Thomas," and "L'évangile selon Thomas"; Montefiore, "A Comparison of the Parables."
2 See Robinson, "From Q to Thomas," 142–64, for a more thorough historical review.
3 Grant–Freedman, *The Secret Sayings.*

they rearrange the order of the sayings, while the remainder of the saying is composed by the interweaving of Luke 10:8–9 and Matt 15:11. Many others have also attributed the difference in Thomas' sayings to some form of gnostic exegesis of canonical texts. Since such theses can "explain" almost any anomaly as due to the strangeness of Gnostics without providing a logical argument for such interweaving, this method has not proved very fruitful.

The Grant-Freedman thesis as such has not been widely accepted by others. Haenchen, who also wished to argue for the dependency of Thomas, pointed out that Thomas was totally unconcerned with the main Naasene doctrines reported by Hippolytus and could hardly be counted as a Naasene work.[4] Other considerations also show that Thomas' text cannot be as easily explained as Grant-Freedman supposed. Their first argument about the rearranging of the order of the topics totally ignores the larger fact that the three sayings of Thomas that could be dependent on Matthew 6, GThom 6a, 14a, and 62, are widely separated from one another in Thomas but are closely connected with their neighboring sayings in Thomas itself by catchword connections. Thus, Thomas does not appear to be a document artificially constructed from written sources, as Grant-Freedman assumed; on the contrary, it appears to be a genuine collection of sayings with features such as the catchwords that point to an origin in an oral tradition. Furthermore, the form of GThom 14 in which Jesus makes a statement most likely represents a later stage of oral development than does the form of the saying in Matthew 6, where others initiate the discussion, so that Thomas does not seem to have developed out of a written source such as Matthew 6 at all. Finally, Thomas does not show any interest in the only certain Matthean redactional trait in the canonical passage, a concern for righteousness.[5]

Haenchen himself argued that Thomas represented a gnostic altering of sayings remembered freely from the canonical gospels, but he never presented a detailed analysis of the texts of the sayings in support of that thesis. Thus, although his conclusions about the gnostic themes of Thomas might explain the choice of sayings included in the collection, they do not explain why Thomas might have preferred the memory of Matthew's text here or of Luke's there. These two attempts at using gnostic exegetical methods (if indeed we can know much about them) show that they are not very much help in trying to understand the relationship of Thomas' text to the New Testament.

The most significant study that has argued for Thomas' dependence on the New Testament is that of Wolfgang Schrage.[6] Schrage moved the discussion onto a much firmer methodological basis. He contended that the question can only be decided on the basis of the form-critical and redactional evidence for each saying. Yet when he found that such evidence was not conclusive for many sayings, he turned also to a textual critical comparison of Thomas'

---

4 Haenchen, "Literatur zum Thomasevangelium," 169–72, 318–19.
5 Sieber, "Redactional Analysis," 14–15, 49–55.
6 Schrage, Das Verhältnis.

Coptic texts with those presented by the Coptic versions of the New Testament.

Although Schrage delineated the nature of the methodological problem much more clearly than his predecessors had done, his understanding of what constitutes redactional evidence led him too easily to the conclusion that most of Thomas' sayings show signs of dependence on the New Testament. Whenever he could show that Thomas' text appears to be a mixture of readings from the synoptic gospels (chiefly from Matthew and Luke), he was certain to claim at least some of those readings as redactional traces that proved Thomas' use of those gospels.

His analysis of GThom 16 provides a typical example. The saying itself reads:

> Jesus said: Men possibly think that I have come to cast peace on the world, and they do not know that I have come to cast divisions on the earth, fire, sword, war. For there shall be five in a house, three shall be against two and two against three; the father against the son, and the son against the father, and they shall stand as solitaries.

Schrage argued that the words "to cast" and "sword" come from Matthew's redactional work in Matt 10:34–36 and that "think," "divisions," "father . . . son," "son . . . father," and the repetition of "I have come" are derived from Luke's work in Luke 12:51–53.[7] Yet none of those words or phrases which he singled out can with any confidence be assigned to the editorial work of either evangelist, i.e., they are not attributable to the special vocabularies of Matthew or Luke, nor to their compositional methods, nor to the theological intent of either. Thus, Schrage accepted too many readings as redactional and incorrectly concluded that many of Thomas' sayings were dependent on the New Testament.

At the same time, with one paragraph in his Introduction Schrage dismissed any discussion of the question of ordering of the sayings by the synoptic evangelists. The issue was not relevant, he wrote, because the arrangement of sayings in Thomas is so enigmatic as to be explainable only on the grounds of some gnostic exegesis.[8] Yet the arrangement of materials in certain sequences, the use of framing techniques and other literary devices, the use of special vocabularies, these are often the editorial traits of the synoptic evangelists about which there is the most agreement by scholars. If one could show that Thomas was dependent on Matthew's arrangement of sayings into five sermons, for example, then one would have solid redactional evidence that Thomas knew and used Matthew. But neither that particular bit of evidence nor any other relating to the ordering of sayings in Thomas exists. Only in the case of a few sayings (mostly twin parables), and almost always with some

7 Schrage, *Das Verhältnis*, 57–60.
8 Schrage, *Das Verhältnis*, 6–7.

intervening materials, is Thomas' order of sayings similar to that of a canonical gospel. In fact even when most of the sayings from a given synoptic passage are in Thomas, the ordering of them in Thomas is randomly different from that in the synoptic gospel.[9] Thus, by dismissing the question of order as due to gnostic exegesis Schrage ignored significant evidence that ran counter to his thesis.

In a similar way his use of form-critical evidence must be called into question. With regard to many sayings Schrage was able to show that Thomas' form of the saying represented in traditional form-critical terms a development later than that of the synoptic form. From that observation he went on to draw the conclusion that Thomas must have taken the synoptic saying from the canonical gospel and then expanded it, rather than considering as a serious option the possibility that Thomas may represent a later stage in the development of a different oral tradition.

Since there are several possible ways of understanding it, secondary development within a saying does not in and of itself constitute an adequate argument for dependence. Those like Schrage who use secondary forms as evidence of dependence also tend to ignore those instances where Thomas' sayings seem to represent an earlier form of the saying than those preserved by the New Testament. It is also the case that all such traditional form-critical judgments are now being called into question by the work of oral-tradition specialists who contend that there is no such thing as an "original form" in an oral tradition because each oral performance is unique.[10]

Finally, Schrage's use of textual evidence from the Coptic versions of the New Testament presents a serious methodological problem. Even if Thomas' text should occasionally betray some dependence on other Coptic versions of the same saying, this fact would tell us something only about influences on the Coptic version of Thomas. It certainly provides no information about the sources of Thomas, which was clearly composed in Greek.[11] For example, GThom 55 and 101 in Coptic read literally, "be a disciple *to me*"; Matthew and Luke both have the Greek genitive "my," but the Sahidic New Testament passages read the same "to me" as Thomas. For Schrage the agreement with the Sahidic New Testament proves a dependence of Thomas on the New Testament, but surely at the most it shows only that the Coptic translation of Thomas may have been influenced by the Sahidic New Testament, or that the Coptic translation of Thomas may have influenced the Sahidic translators of the New Testament.[12]

By the time that Schrage's work appeared in print late in 1964 I had already made considerable progress in my own investigation of the question of whether or not Thomas gave evidence of the editorial traits of the synoptic

9 See Koester, "GNOMAI," 132, for Luke 11:27–12:56; and Davies, *The Gospel of Thomas,* 7–8, for Mark 3:35–4:34.
10 Kelber, *Oral and Written Gospel,* 30.
11 Cf. Robinson, "From Q to Thomas," 161.
12 Cf. Rudolf, "Gnosis," 361.

evangelists, using a methodology adapted from the work of Helmut Koester.[13] For me the definition of an editorial trait was much narrower than for Schrage; in the main such a trait had to be something related to the ordering of sayings, to the literary style or the special vocabulary of an evangelist, or most importantly to the theological concerns or intentions of one of the evangelists. Thus, I had rejected as redactional not only most of the readings that Schrage accepted but also phrases such as the "kingdom of heaven," known mostly in Matthew but not a Matthean trait because it was presumably Jewish in origin.

Similarly I had found that the words and phrases generally being accepted as traits by the redactional critics were missing in Thomas. In the parallels to GThom 31 (POxy 1, 6), to take one example, traits such as Luke's use of "amen," his dislocation of the passage from the Markan order to place it earlier in Jesus' story, his use of the Isaiah 61 materials are all missing. At the same time the reading of *dektos* ("acceptable") in the Greek version of this Thomas saying where Mark/Matthew have *atimos* (without honor) had been seriously proposed as the use of a Lukan trait. My conclusion was that *dektos* is not redactional because it is not related to Luke's special vocabulary or to his theology.[14] Anderson's form-critical argument that the saying about a physician not healing himself is a Lukan construction also cannot be maintained, because the many rabbinic and classical parallels indicate that the saying was a proverb in its own right.[15] Thus, I accepted the much earlier opinions of Wendling and Bultmann that the Oxyrhynchus version of these sayings was not dependent on either Mark or Luke.

When that stricter definition of editorial traits was applied in a saying-by-saying analysis of Thomas, it became clear that very few of Thomas' sayings exhibited anything that could be attributable to the work of the synoptic evangelists, at least as that redactional work is accessible to us.[16] Thus, in the spring of 1966 I wrote:

> The conclusion of this dissertation is, therefore, that there is very little redactional evidence, if any, for holding that our Synoptic Gospels were the sources of Thomas' synoptic sayings. In the great majority of sayings there is no such evidence at all. This overwhelming lack of editorial evidence suggests that Thomas' ultimate sources must have been an oral tradition or traditions (to which the catchwords still evident in Thomas witness), which existed independently of the written Synoptic Gospels.[17]

Nothing that has happened in the interval has convinced me to disregard that methodology or to withdraw that opinion.

Indeed, others working independently have buttressed the conclusion

---

13 Sieber, "Redactional Analysis." Cf. Köster, *Synoptische Überlieferung.*
14 Against H. Anderson, "Broadening." Cf. Fitzmyer, *The Gospel According to Luke I–IX,* 527–28, who in 1981 continued to accept Anderson's position.
15 Nolland, "Classical and Rabbinic Parallels."
16 Robinson, "From Q to Thomas," 162, continues to caution that Thomas must be approached saying by saying.
17 Sieber, "Redactional Analysis," 262–63. Cf. Crossan, *Four Other Gospels,* 36–37.

reached at that time. Koester's opinion, as expressed by him in the 1971 quote given below, has been maintained by him ever since:

> Since no peculiarities of the editorial work of Matthew, Mark, or Luke are recognizable in these proverbial sayings of *Thomas,* there is no reason to assume that they were drawn from the synoptic gospels.[18]

Crossan has isolated Markan traits in the parable of the mustard seed and in the saying about rendering to Caesar what is Caesar's, traits that are conspicuous by their absence in Thomas.[19] Kelber, working on a different question altogether, notes for Mark 6:1–6 that its double emphasis on the family, which he identifies as a Markan trait, is absent from Thomas 31.[20] Similar opinions have been expressed by Stevan Davies, Ronald Cameron, and others.[21]

As of the date of this article (1988), almost all those who are currently still at work on Thomas have come to hold that it represents an independent tradition.[22] That opinion has in turn been the basis for a rich new understanding not only of the Gospel of Thomas but also of the New Testament, for we now have a clearer understanding of the variety of christologies and traditions in first- and second-century Christianity against which to view the New Testament. It is to that set of topics that we now turn our attention.

2. Gospel of Thomas as Alternative Trajectory

James M. Robinson was the first to advance the thesis that the Gospel of Thomas was another representative of the wisdom-sayings genre to which Q also belonged. He has continued to develop and refine that proposal, often in conversation with Helmut Koester.[23] Koester has written largely on Thomas itself, showing among other things how its sayings have been transformed from wisdom sayings into gnostic ones.[24]

One of the other results of the work of the various scholars who have pursued Thomas as an independent tradition is that for them the date of Thomas has been set back from ca. 140 CE into the second half of the first Christian century, the dating suggested originally by Grenfell and Hunt for the Oxyrhynchus fragments of Thomas.[25]

---

18 "One Jesus," 181–82; cf. Koester, *Introduction,* 2:154; see also, Robinson, "From Q to Thomas," 143–49.
19 Crossan, *In Parables,* 48–49; "Mark 12:13–17," 397–401.
20 Kelber, *Oral and Written Gospel,* 102–3.
21 Davies, *The Gospel of Thomas,* 4; Cameron, *The Other Gospels,* 24; Attridge, "Gospel of Thomas."
22 Cf. Tuckett, *Nag Hammadi and the Gospel Tradition,* esp. 3–9, 149–63, who accepts the possibility of Thomas' independence while rejecting it for the other Nag Hammadi works.
23 Robinson, "LOGOI SOPHON"; "From Q to Thomas." Koester, "One Jesus," 166–68; *Introduction,* 2:169–75.
24 Cf. Davies, *The Gospel of Thomas,* for the view that Thomas is still wisdom and not gnostic.
25 See Robinson, "From Q to Thomas," 142–64, for the arguments pro and con.

Although Robinson's thesis is based on the conviction that Thomas, or at least most of its sayings, comes from a source other than the canonical gospels, his own concern has been to define and characterize the genre of collections of wisdom sayings (*logoi sophon*), a genre to which both Q and Thomas belonged. In the end his work on such wisdom collections has aimed at showing that the genre provided "a congenial point of departure, a seedbed, an impetus" through which some strands of early Christianity were led into Christian Gnosticism.[26]

The traditional model for the development of Gnosticism has been that it was a second-century offshoot of the normative Christian kerygma represented in the main by the New Testament. What Robinson, Koester, and others have provided for students of the New Testament is a viable alternative to that traditional model, a picture of early Christianity that envisions two sets of rival Jesus-sayings traditions, one represented by Q and the synoptic tradition, the other by Thomas, each developing along its own trajectory. It remains to be seen whether other such traditions can also be uncovered.

The ideological connection for such a trajectory between wisdom and Gnosticism was already laid out by Robinson in the "LOGOI SOPHON" article. In "From Q to Thomas" he has now accepted as well the need for a sociological explanation of how the shift from wisdom collection to gnostic gospel might have occurred.

> The sociological substructure presupposed in Gnosticism, namely an ascetic lifestyle, seems particularly related to the bearers of the sayings of Jesus: wandering, begging charismatics.[27]

In particular he finds congenial the suggestions of M. Eugene Boring about the role of those wandering prophets, although calling some of his arguments "strained." Those wanderers eventually had to settle down, and in the process some of them at least became Christian Gnostics. Robinson concludes:

> Just so itinerant prophets may initially have wandered from pillar to post, with at best a home base to which to return as part of a "circuit," but with nowhere to rest their heads or to be sure of a square meal while "out in the field." But a generation or so later some of the households that had taken them in had become house churches, until the network of such local congregations would gradually come to represent the rule rather than the exception. Thus the itinerant charismatic would increasingly become an exception to be monitored and ultimately to be given an honored, limited, and thereby domesticated role in the development that led to Christian monasticism—and Gnosticism.[28]

---

26 Robinson, "From Q to Thomas," 134–35. Cf. Robinson's recent attempt to reconstruct a wisdom christology on the basis of this thesis in an essay titled, "Very Goddess and Very Man."
27 Robinson, "From Q to Thomas," 135.
28 Robinson, "From Q to Thomas, 141.

This sociological argument can be strengthened with the addition of another set of observations. In a study of contemporary Melanesian cargo cults, groups that hold or have held millenarian views similar in type but not content to the apocalyptic viewpoints of the early Christians, Peter Worsley has shown that none of those cults was able to sustain its apocalyptic zeal over an extended period of time.[29] After a fairly limited amount of time under the leadership of a charismatic individual, they either ceased to function altogether or became a more traditional institution, usually political in nature, and transferred their ultimate hopes to a distant future. Such successful transformations from active to passive millenarism happened, according to Worsley, not because the apocalyptic hopes of cargo went unfulfilled, not because of some major sociological crisis, but because the very nature of that hope created a new sub-set of society, a new group, which then took on a life of its own as a part of life in this world.

> The revolutionary energy is drained from them; they become passive. The Day of the millenium is pushed farther back into the remote future; the kingdom of the Lord is to come, not on this earth, but in the next world; and the faithful are to gain entrance to it not by fighting in the here and now with their strong right arms but by leading quiet, virtuous lives.[30]

Such a transformation from an active millenial cult to a passive one is very close to what Robinson describes as his model for the trajectory of the wisdom–Gnosticism tradition represented now in its later stages by the Coptic version of the Gospel of Thomas.

If millenarian groups metamorphose as Worsley contends, then one aspect of the study of the Thomas tradition that requires more attention in Robinson's thesis is the eschatological nature of the early stage of the tradition. He himself mentions the fact that the tradition originally had some eschatological elements in it, usually with references to Koester's work, but seems not to accord much importance to it. While Koester emphasizes the originally eschatological nature of many of the sayings in Thomas, his interest has largely been in comparing that eschatology to Q's eschatology. He has shown that Thomas' Kingdom-of-Heaven views are not the same as the Son-of-man eschatology of Q and also that, in many sayings in Thomas, that eschatology has been "interpreted in such a way that they point to the presence of revelation both in recognition of oneself (GThom 3, 113) and in the person of Jesus (91)."[31] Yet neither Robinson nor Koester has emphasized sufficiently the importance of this eschatological strain for the original stages of the Thomas tradition. It began not just as a wisdom collection in the mold of Proverbs or Sirach, but as a wisdom tradition with a significant eschatological component that helps

29 Worsley, *Trumpet Shall Sound,* ix–lxix, 221–56.
30 Worsley, *Trumpet Shall Sound,* 231.
31 Koester, *Introduction,* 2:153; "One Jesus," 169–75.

explain, among other things, the ascetic lifestyle of its prophets. Koester cites as originally eschatological sayings 3, 10, 16, 82, 91, and 113 but does not draw out the implications of that eschatology for that early stage. Surely there are many other sayings as well that may have once been eschatological in nature, sayings such as 18, 21, 23, 36, 37, 40, 44, 47b, 51, 57, 61, 68, 73, 79, 88, 91, and 98. Further study of this aspect of the Thomas tradition and of its relationship to the transformation of wisdom into Gnosticism might prove a fruitful line of inquiry.

In fact, the very act of committing the tradition to writing, an act that Kelber has shown to have been hostile to the Q tradition's theology, was almost certainly also an important part of the process by which the eschatology of Thomas was transformed into an emphasis on inner revelation.[32] As the communities brought into existence by the wandering prophets became more established and as the number of prophets decreased, the need for a written tradition would have increased. Once written down, that tradition would have lost the creative spontaneity of the oral tradition, a spontaneity that could maintain an eschatological intensity in a way a written document could not. Thus, from that point on the Thomas tradition would have been more open to the "spiritualization" of its hopes. So it is that Kelber can write near the end of his study that he finds himself in substantial agreement with the thesis of Robinson and Koester about the relationship of Thomas and the New Testament:

> The discovery of *Thomas,* a sayings collection itself, could well be taken to corroborate the Q hypothesis, but it also brought with it full consciousness of the absence of the genre in the canon. In view of the genre's triumphant rise in Gnosticism, its unacceptability to the canonizers except by mediation through the written gospels is all the more significant.[33]

Robinson finds this agreement helpful.[34] Both Robinson–Koester and Kelber trace the trajectories of a wisdom sayings tradition, Kelber of Q with its transformation by Mark into a death and dying gospel, Robinson and Koester of the tradition known to us through a few Oxyrhynchus fragments and now also through the Coptic Gospel of Thomas, a later stage of that same tradition. Thus, the discussion of the relationship of Thomas and the New Testament has been raised to a different level from that earlier and much more limited debate about the independence of Thomas from the New Testament.

32 Kelber, *Oral and Written Gospel,* 31, 90–139, 184–99.
33 Kelber, *Oral and Written Gospel,* 199.
34 Robinson, "From Q to Thomas," 174.

VI

Authorial Presence and Narrator in John

COMMENTARY AND STORY*

Charles W. Hedrick

1. Narration and Interpretation

Compared to the synoptic gospels, the author of John has a more sophisticated compositional technique and frequently resorts to a particular narrative device to control the story so as to insure that the reader gains a "proper" understanding of it. Though the narrative device has long been recognized as a distinctive feature of the Gospel of John, few published works in the past twenty-five years have been devoted exclusively to its study. It has been described as explanatory comments, "asides," "footnotes,"[1] and parentheses. Recently it has been examined in connection with the literary criticism of John under the discussion of "the narrator" and "his point of view."[2]

A. E. Garvie may serve as an example of one earlier study. In 1922 he discussed the feature under the rubric of "comments by the evangelist."[3] Except to designate the device as a "comment," Garvie does not offer a definition. He identifies twenty-eight passages as "comments" and groups them for study under six types.

In 1960 M. C. Tenney, in a short article, defined the device as:

> explanatory material which is not directly involved in the progress of the narrative. This material is by no means irrelevant to the main thrust of the Gospel, but is parenthetical. If it were omitted, the main theme of thought would remain largely unaltered, although the parenthetical material has a definite value for understanding the meaning of the gospel. . . . They are sentences or paragraphs of explanatory comment, interjected into the running narrative of the story, and

---

* For JMR on his 65th birthday: In gratitude, appreciation, and admiration.
1 Tenney, "Footnotes of John's Gospel"; O'Rourke, "Asides in the Gospel of John."
2 Wead, *Literary Devices,* 15–49. See also Culpepper, *Anatomy,* 15–49 and Wuellner, "Narrative Criticism." Wullener ("Narrative Criticism," 68–69) refers to this phenomenon as "overt comments by which the implied author becomes audible."
3 Garvie, *Beloved Disciple,* 14–29. Garvie makes a distinction among comments by the evangelist (14–29), insertions by the redactor (38–60), and the reminiscences and reflections of the "witness" (61–77). See Van Belle, *Les parenthèses,* 19–57 for a survey of the principal studies of the phenomenon.

74

obviously intended to illumine some casual reference, or to explain how some important statement should be understood.[4]

Tenney identified fifty-nine passages, which he classified into ten types.

Some twenty years later (1979) J. J. O'Rourke appropriated both the classification of Tenney and his criteria for identifying the narrative device.[5] In his study O'Rourke challenged the classification of certain passages under Tenney's types while adding to the total number of "asides."

In 1983 A. R. Culpepper added a few "intrusive comments" to the lists of Tenney and O'Rourke and correctly noted that the asides are only one of the rhetorical features through which the narrator of the gospel communicates the story to the reader.[6]

In 1985 a much needed monograph on the device was published by Gilbert Van Belle.[7] Van Belle attributes the "parentheses" not to a second and different hand, but to the author of the text, because of their homogeneity of style and because they reflect the primary themes of Johannine theology.[8] His judgment in this regard contrasts with the general consensus of scholarship as to the unity of the gospel. The phenomena (asides, footnotes, digressions, parentheses, etc.) in many instances are usually accounted for in contempory scholarship by various source and redaction theories, as Van Belle well knows.[9] Van Belle classifies his approximately 165-plus parentheses into seventeen types.

This narrative device is quite common in the literature of antiquity. One finds parallels to it among the Greek and Roman rhetoricians. Two rhetorical forms, the *parenthesis* and *apostrophe*, appear to function as the "asides" in John have been understood to function. The *parenthesis* is the insertion of one sentence in the midst of another, where it interrupts the thought of the passage and disrupts its natural syntax.[10] The *apostrophe* appears to be a turning aside from the formal address to the judge at a trial to attack an adversary, or it consists of statements intended to divert the attention of the hearers (at the trial) from the question before them.[11] To these one might also add "digression" ($\pi\alpha\rho\acute{\epsilon}\kappa\beta\alpha\sigma\iota\varsigma$)[12] and "amplification" ($\alpha\check{v}\xi\eta\sigma\iota\varsigma$).[13] What is, perhaps, more

4 Tenney, "Footnotes of John's Gospel," 350.
5 O'Rourke, "Asides in the Gospel of John," 210–11.
6 Culpepper, *Anatomy*, 18.
7 *Les parenthèses;* see the review by Hedrick. Most recently C. J. Bjerkelund has made a study of a special group within the explanatory comments, clauses beginning with $\tau\alpha\hat{v}\tau\alpha/\tau\sigma\hat{v}\tau\sigma$: *Tauta Egeneto.* He discusses 1:28; 2:11; 4:54; 6:69; 7:39; 8:20; 10:6; 11:51; 12:16; 12:33; 12:41 as "precision clauses" (*Präzisierungssätze*).
8 Van Belle, *Les parenthèses*, 206–8.
9 See his valuable survey of scholarly judgments on the "parentheses" in the literature: *Les parenthèses*, 61–104.
10 Quintilian, *Oratio*, 8.2.15; 9.3.23.
11 Quintilian, *Oratio*, 4.1.63; 9.2.38; cf. Cicero, *Ad Herennium*, 4.15.22.
12 Quintilian, *Oratio*, 9.1.26–36.
13 Aristotle, *Rhetoric*, 1.9.38–41.

significant for the present study is that explanatory "asides" are a common narrative feature in ancient Greek and Roman novels and historical narrative,[14] although little attention has been paid to their function in the narrative of these ancient genres.[15] And one also finds that explanatory "asides" are common in the synoptic gospels and Acts as well.[16]

Tenney's definition for this narrative feature, while basically accurate, may be refined as follows: It is comprised of intrusive word(s), sentence(s), or paragraph(s) of explanatory or clarifying commentary included in the narrative as direct address to the reader. In general, it is to be characterized by "telling" about the story as opposed to the "showing" of the story. It is easiest to identify when it intrudes into the narrative to such an extent that the dramatic showing of the story is momentarily suspended. The word(s), sentence(s), or paragraph(s) that occupy the space between the two segments of the breeched story line provide for the *reader* (as opposed to personalia in the story) information that an author regards as significant for the *reader's* "understanding" of the story.

This narrative feature in the Gospel of John at its most extreme I shall designate as *hermeneia* (ἑρμηνεία), a designation that is already used in John to describe the function of certain of these parenthetical comments (cf. John 1:42; 9:7; and 1:38, 41). Of course not every "explanation" in John would be considered *hermeneia* in the technical sense in which I am using it here. For in narrating a story some explanation would be required for the clarity of the "showing" (viz. 2:1), and hence such explanations as these are not *digressions* in a narrow sense; they are novelistic features that belong properly to the showing of the story. The *hermeneiai*, on the other hand, as I define them in this paper, are characterized by a suspension of the dramatic showing of the story and the intrusion of a "voice" that stands some distance from the story, reflecting on it from that distant and different perspective. The difference between *hermeneia* and story can best be expressed by the perspective from which you as reader "see the action." Are you standing beside an unselfconscious narrator of the tale at the scene of the drama seeing the action as it

14 See in particular the following Roman novels: Lucius Apuleius, *The Golden Ass*, and Petronius, *Satyricon*. In the early Greek novels it is used less frequently, but in ways that seem closer to its usage in the Gospel of John: Achilles Tatius, *Leucippe and Clitophon;* Longus, *Daphnis and Chloe;* Dio Chrysostom, "The Hunter's Tale" in *The Euboean Discourse or The Hunter;* Xenophon, *An Ephesian Tale;* Heliodorus, *Ethiopica;* Chariton, *Chaereas and Callirhoe.*

15 See, for example, Perry, *Ancient Romances;* Hägg, *Novel in Antiquity;* and G. Anderson, *Ancient Fiction.*

16 Some of the more obvious are: Mark 5:42b; 7:3–4; 7:11b; 7:19b; 13:14b; 15:16b, 22b, 34b; 16:4b; Matt 1:23b; 24:15b (=Mark 13:14b); Luke 2:23; 3:23b; 7:29–30; 8:29b; 19:25; Acts 1:15, 18–19; 4:36b; 11:36b; 13:8b; 27:37. There is also an explanatory aside in John 8:6a (τοῦτο . . . κατηγορεῖν αὐτοῦ ["this . . . to accuse him"]) in the well-known non-Johannine passage 7:53–8:11. See Metzger, *Textual Commentary*, 219–22. The phenomena are only now being investigated in the gospels and Acts: See Hedrick, "Narrator and Story in the Gospel of Mark: *Hermeneia* and *Paradosis*," and Sheeley, "Narrative Asides in Luke-Acts."

happens, or do you stand some "distance" from the events and have them explained and evaluated for you by a self-aware interpreter?

What follows is a listing of all asides as identified by Garvie, Tenney, O'Rourke, Van Belle, and myself.[17] Garvie finds approximately twenty-nine, Tenney fifty-nine, O'Rourke 109, Van Belle 165 plus; and I find 121. We frequently disagree as to what constitutes asides. In each instance the number of asides can only be approximate, because they have generally been reported by chapter and verse, rather than by subdividing the verse. The method of reporting used by Van Belle, i.e., using sigla in the text of John's gospel, is certainly the clearest. Where it was possible in the designation of what I consider an aside, I have adopted Van Belle's subdivision of verses. The Greek text cited in the chart below indicates specifically what I consider the limit of the aside. Question marks indicate that the verse is included with some uncertainty.

John	Garvie	Tenney	O'Rourke	Van Belle	Hedrick
1:2			X (?)		
1:6–8			X	X	
1:9			X (?)		
1:10b				X	
1:12b-13			X	1:12c-13	
1:14		X	1:14b	1:14bc	
1:15			X	X	
1:16		X	X		
1:17–18			X		
1:23d				X	
1:24			X (?)	X	X [all]
1:28			X (?)	X	X [all]
1:38		X	X	1:38g	X 1:38g [ὃ λέγεται . . . διδάσκαλε]
1:39				1:39e	1:39e [ὥρα ἦν ὡς δεκάτη]
1:40				X	
1:41		X	X	1:41d	1:41d [ὅ ἐστιν . . . χριστός]
1:42		X	X	1:42e	1:42e [ὃ . . . Πέτρος]
1:44			X (?)	X	X [all]
1:48	X				
2:6				X	2:6b [κατὰ . . . Ἰουδαίων]
2:9		X	2:9b	2:9cde	2:9de [οἱ δὲ . . . ὕδωρ]
2:11		X	X	X	X [all]
2:17	X		X	X	X [all]
2:21—22	X	2:22	X	X	X [all]
2:23-25	(24–25)	(24–25)	X	(24–25)	X [all]

17 My initial conclusions were arrived at without prior consultation with the studies by Tenney, O'Rourke, and Van Belle. I then worked through their material adding from their analyses several of the *heremeneiai* that I had missed. I have excluded the prologue (1:1–18) from this analysis as constituting a special problem.

John	Garvie	Tenney	O'Rourke	Van Belle	Hedrick
3:1b				X	
3:16–21		X	X	X	
3:23–24			(24)	(23c,24)	(23c,24) [23c: ὅτι . . . ἐκεῖ; 24: all]
3:26d				X	
3:31–36	X?	X	X	X	
4:2		X	X	X	X [all]
4:4					X [all]
4:6d				X	X [ὥρα . . . ἕκτη]
4:8				X	X [all]
4:9		X	X	4:9f	4:9f [οὐ . . . Σαμαρίταις]
4:18	X				
4:22				X	
4:23			X	4:23ad	
4:25		X	X	4:25c	4:25c [ὁ λεγόμενος χριστός]
4:27				X	
4:44	X		X	X	X [all]
4:45d				X	
4:46ab				4:46b	X [ἦλθεν . . . οἶνον]
4:54		X	X	X	X [all]
5:2			X	5:2c	5:2c [ἡ ἐπιλεγομένη . . . βηθζαθὰ]
5:9d				X	X [ἦν δὲ . . . ἡμέρᾳ]
5:13d				X	
5:16					X [all]
5:18	5:18c			5:18d	X [all]
5:19–29	X				
5:25			X	5:25b	
6:1b					X [τῆς Τιβερίαδος]
6:2					X [all]
6:4			X (?)	X	6:4b [ἡ ἑορτὴ τῶν Ἰουδαίων]
6:6		X	X	X	X [all]
6:10c				X	
6:15					X [all]
6:17c–18				X	
6:22a				X	
6:23		X	X (?)	X	X [all]
6:27d				X	
6:31bc				X	
6:33				X	
6:39–40				X	
6:46				X	
6:59		X	X	X	X [all]
6:61a					X [εἰδὼς . . . αὐτοῦ]
6:64		X	6:64b	6:64bcd	6:64bcd [ᾔδει . . . αὐτόν]
6:71		X	X	X	X [all]
7:1				7:1bc	X [all]

John	Garvie	Tenney	O'Rourke	Van Belle	Hedrick
7:2		X	X (?)		
7:4ab				X	
7:5		X	X	X	X [all]
7:9				X	
7:13					X [all]
7:22			X	7:22bc	7:22bc [οὐχ . . . πατέρων]
7:30			X		7:30b [καὶ οὐδεὶς . . . αὐτοῦ]
7:38–39	X	7:39	7:39	7:38b,39	7:39 [all]
7:43–44					X [all]
7:50			X	X	7:50b	7:50bc [ὁ ἐλθὼν . . . αὐτῶν]
8:20		X	X	X	X [all]
8:27	X	X	X	X	X [all]
8:30				X	X [all]
8:35			X	X	
9:7			X	X	9:7c	9:7c [ὃ . . . ἀπεσταλμένος]
9:8b				X	
9:13b				X	
9:14		X	X	X	X [all]
9:18c				X	
9:22–23			X		X [all]
9:24b				X	
10:6		X	X	X	X [all]
10:12fg				X	
10:22–23		X	X	10:22b	10:22b [χειμὼν ἦν]
10:27b				X	
10:35b				X	X [καὶ . . . χραφή]
10:39					X (?) [all]
10:40bc				10:40b	10:40c [καὶ ἔμενεν ἐκεῖ]
10:42					X [all]
11:2		X	X	X	X [all]
11:3			X		
11:5			X	X	X [all]
11:13			X	X (?)	X [all]
11:15b				X	
11:16			X	11:16b	11:16b [ὁ . . . Δίδυμος]
11:18–19		X	11:18	X	11:18 [all]
11:20d				X	
11:30		X		X	X [all]
11:31bc				X	
11:38cd				X	
11:41	X				
11:49b				X	
11:51–52	X	11:51	X	X	X [all]
11:54					X [all]
11:57				X	

John	Garvie	Tenney	O'Rourke	Van Belle	Hedrick
12:1bc				X	X [ὃν ... Ἰησοῦς]
12:2bc				X	
12:4			X	12:4c	12:4c [ὁ μέλλων ... παραδιδόναι]
12:6		X	X	X	X [all]
12:9e				X	
12:14c–16	12:15	12:16	X	X	X [14c: καθώς ... γεγραμμένον; 15–16: all]
12:17–18				X	X [all]
12:21b				X	
12:33			X	X	X [all]
12:36de				X	
12:37–43	12:38–41	X	X	X	X [all]
12:50a				X	
13:1	X		X		X [all]
13:2	X		X ?	13:2bc	13:2bc [τοῦ ... Ἰσκαριώτου]
13:3	X		X (?)		X [all]
13:10c				X	
13:11		X	X	X	X [all]
13:18b–19	X				
13:23		X	X		
13:27			X		13:27a [καὶ ... σατανᾶς]
13:28–29		13:28	X	X	X [all]
13:30			X	13:30c	13:30c [ἦν δὲ νύξ]
14:22		X	14:22b	14:22b	[οὐχ ὁ Ἰσκαριώτης]
14:26bc				X	14:26b (?) [τὸ πνεῦμα ... ἅγιον]
14:27c				X	
14:29	X				
15:5d				X	
15:25	X				X (?) [all]
15:26bc				X	
16:13a				X	
16:32ade				X	
17:3	X			X	X (?) [all]
17:6cd				X	
17:10ab				X	
17:12	X				17:12b [καὶ οὐδεὶς ... πληρωθῇ]
17:23ab				X	
18:2				X	18:2b [ὁ ... αὐτὸν]
18:4	X				18:4b [εἰδὼς ... ἐπ' αὐτὸν]
18:5b			X (?)	18:5e	18:5e [εἱστήκει ... μετ' αὐτῶν]
18:8–9	X		18:9	18:9	18:9 [all]
18:10		X	18:10b	18:10e	18:10e [ἦν δὲ ... μάλχος]
18:13			X (?)	18:13b	18:13b [ἦν ... ἐκείνου]
18:14		X	X	X	X [all]
18:15			X (?)		
18:16			X	18:16c	

John	Garvie	Tenney	O'Rourke	Van Belle	Hedrick
18:18c				X	
18:26			X (?)	18:26b	18:26b [συγγενὴς ... ὠτίον]
18:28			X	18:28bcde	18:28b [ἦν δὲ πρωΐ]
18:32	X			X	X [all]
18:40		X	X	18:40d	18:40d [ἦν ... λῃστής]
19:13		X	X	19:13d	19:13d ['Εβραϊστὶ ... Γαββαθά]
19:14		X	19:14a	19:14ab	19:14ab [ὥρα ... ἕκτη]
19:17		X	X	19:17b	19:17b [ὃ ... Γολγοθα]
19:20			X (?)	19:20c	19:20b [ὅτι ... 'Ιησοῦς]
19:23degh			X		
19:24	X		X	19:24def	19:24def [ἵνα ... κλῆρον]
19:27c				X	
19:28	X		X	19:28b	19:28b [ἵνα ... γραφή]
19:29a				X	
19:31		X	X	19:31ad	19:31d [ἦν ... σαββάτου]
19:35		X	X	X	X [all]
19:36–37	X	19:36	X	X	X [all]
19:38			X	19:38c	19:38c [ὢν ... 'Ιουδαίων]
19:39			X	19:39b	19:39b [ὁ ... πρῶτον]
19:40			X	19:40c	19:40c [καθὼς ... ἐνταφιάζειν]
19:42		X			
20:2			X		
20:8b				X	
20:9		X	X	X	X [all]
20:16		X	X	20:16e	20:16e [ὃ ... διδάσκαλε]
20:17c				X	
20:24			X	20:24b	20:24b [ὁ ... Δίδυμος]
20:30–31		X	X	X	X [all]
21:1				X	
21:2			X	21:2ce	21:2bc [ὁ ... Δίδυμος]
21:4c				X	
21:7		X	X (bis)	21:7g	
21:8		X	X (?)	21:8bc	21:8bc [οὐ ... διακοσίων]
21:11d				X	
21:12			X (?)	21:12cde	21:12cde [οὐδεὶς ... ἐστιν]
21:14		X	X	X	X [all]
21:17b					X (?) [ἐλυπήθη ... με]
21:18–19a		21:19	21:19	21:19ab	21:19a [τοῦτο ... θεόν]
21:20			X (bis)	21:20efg	21:20efg [ὃς ... σε]
21:23		X	X	21:23cdefg	X [all]
21:24–25		X	X	X	X [all]
Total	29	59	109	165	121

Below I propose a new classification of the asides based on specific function in the narrative. The classification does not aim at a synthesis of the feature to the "lowest common denominator" but will designate each function of the aside as a narrative "type." Through the use of this feature a narrator:

    I. locates particular events with a topographical site: 1:28; 6:23; 6:59; 8:20a; 12:1bc; 19:20b; 21:8bc;

   II. explains Hebrew and Aramaic words: 1:38g; 1:41d; 1:42e; 4:25c; 6:1b; 9:7c; 20:16e;

  III. explains the time of an event: 1:39e; 4:6d; 5:9d; 9:14b; 10:22b; 13:30c; 18:28b; 19:14b;

  IV. explains Jewish religious customs: 2:6b; 6:4b; 19:31d; 19:40c;

   V. clarifies, or further explains, the significance or success of events or sayings: 2:11; 3:23c; 3:24; 4:2; 4:44; 4:54; 7:22bc; 7:30b; 7:43–44; 8:20b; 8:30; 10:35b; 10:42; 10:39; 11:51–52; 17:3 (?); 19:35; 20:30–31; 21:14; 21:25;

  VI. cites (and sometimes explains) or alludes to "Old Testament" passages as proof texts that clarify events or sayings: 2:17; 12:14b–16; 12:37–43 (see under XI); 13:18b; 15:25 (?); 17:12b; 19:24def; 19:28b; 19:36–37;

 VII. explains the "true" meaning, cause, or intent of a saying of Jesus: 2:21–22; 6:64bcd; 6:71; 7:39; 8:27 (also under XII); 11:13; 12:33; 13:11 (cf. VIII); 21:19a; 21:23;

VIII. clarifies the inner motivation and inner feelings of Jesus: 2:23–25; 6:6; 6:15; 6:61a; 7:1; 11:5; 13:1; 13:3; 13:11; 18:4b (cf. VII);

  IX. adds new information to clarify a preceding statement: 4:4; 4:8; 4:9f; 11:30;

   X. provides the Hebrew term for a given location: 5:2c; 19:13d; 19:17b;

  XI. explains thoughts, motives, and character of personalia in the story: 2:9de; 2:23; 5:16; 5:18; 6:2; 7:5; 7:13; 8:27 (also under VII); 9:22–23; 10:6; 12:16–18; 12:42b–43 (see under VI); 13:2bc; 13:27a; 13:28–29; 14:26b (?); 18:40b; 19:38bc; 20:9; 21:12cde; 21:17b;

 XII. makes a brief statement indicating a passage of time, change of location, or indicates a brief interlude in the action of the story: 4:46ab; 10:40c; 11:54;

XIII. identifies personalia in the story: 1:24; 1:44; 7:50bc; 11:2; 11:16b; 12:4c; 14:22b; 18:2b; 18:5e; 18:10e; 18:13b; 18:14; 18:26b; 18:40d; 19:39b; 20:24b; 21:2bc; 21:20efg; 21:24;

XIV. clarifies distances between locations: 11:18;

 XV. cites sayings of Jesus as "proof texts": 18:9; 18:32.

2. Toward Identifying the "Hermeneut"

Considerably more than half these explanations simply clarify aspects of the story being shown in the dramatic presentation,[18] and hence function *inside* the dramatic presentation, i.e., the story being shown in the Gospel of John. They describe aspects of dramatic presentation in terms of setting, scenes, characterization, plot, etc., i.e., information that is not easily showable or

18 To this category I assign the following: 1:28, 38g, 39e, 41d, 42e, 44; 2:6b, 9de, 11, 23–25; 3:23c, 24; 4:4, 6d, 8, 9f, 25c, 46ab, 54; 5:2c, 16; 6:1b, 2, 4b, 6, 15, 23, 59, 61a, 64bcd; 7:1, 13, 30b, 43–44, 50bc; 8:20, 30; 9:7c, 22–23; 10:6, 22b, 39, 40c, 42; 11:2, 5, 16b, 18, 30, 54; 12:1bc, 18, 37; 13:1, 30c; 14:22b, 26b; 18:4b, 10e, 13b, 14, 26b, 28, 40d; 19:13d, 14b, 17b, 20b, 31d, 38bc, 39b, 40c; 20:16e, 24b; 21:2bc, 8bc, 12cde, 17b, 20efg.

knowable in terms of dramatic presentation; in short, they function to intensify a reader's visualization of the dramatic action. While they are diegetic (digress) rather than mimetic (mimic) and hence take on distance and a different perspective from the showing of the story, they nevertheless function inside that act of narrating.[19]

Certain of these explanations, however, take on a much greater distance from the story being shown.[20] This second more distant narrative voice seems much more self-conscious as a personality vis-à-vis that voice that merely intensifies the visualization of the dramatic presentation of the story. The interpretive observations on the dramatic presentation made by this voice are not technically a part of the story being shown. They are not designed to help the reader understand the dramatic presentation in terms of the story world being portrayed; that is to say, they do not clarify aspects of plot, character, scene, event, or setting of the narrative of the Gospel of John in order to facilitate the showing. Indeed they seem to derive from, and to address, a second narrative world, since they impose on aspects of the story being shown in the Gospel of John values, explanations, and insights that are not an immediate natural part of the dramatic *mimesis* of John's showing; neither do they clarify aspects of that story within the showing. They derive from a second intermediary narrative world unstated in the Johannine dramatic presentation of the story of Jesus, except for these few *hermeneiai* that *reflect back* on the Johannine showing through the unstated intermediary world.[21]

To illustrate, I shall briefly discuss three of the *hermeneiai* where this metadiegetic feature can best be seen. John 2:21–22 is a spiritualizing explanation of a difficult saying of Jesus. In 2:19 Jesus says that he will raise up "this temple" in three days if it is destroyed. The explanation understands what may be a traditional saying of Jesus on the Jerusalem temple (cf. Matt 26:61; 27:40; Acts 6:13–14) as an allegorical figure for the resurrection of the body of Jesus.[22] It would appear that there are two levels of meaning to the text. Level one, the level of dramatic presentation, seems to reflect a simple literal understanding of the logion on the destruction of the temple (2:19): Jesus predicts that he will rebuild the temple facility if it is destroyed. This is the way the "Jews," the auditors of Jesus in the showing, increduously understand 2:19. At

19 See Genette, *Narrative Discourse,* 162–70, 227–43.
20 1:24; 2:17, 21–22; 4:2, 44; 5:9d, 18; 6:71; 7:5, 22bc, 39; 8:27; 9:14; 10:35b; 11:13, 51–52; 12:4c, 6, 14c–17, 33, 38–43; 13:2bc, 3, 11, 18b–19, 27a, 28–29; 15:25; 17:3, 12b; 18:2b, 5e, 9, 32; 19:24def, 28b, 35–37; 20:9, 30–31; 21:14, 19a, 23–25.
21 That is to say, those *hermeneiai* listed in note 20 above. See Genette, *Narrative Discourse,* 227–43.
22 The original saying would have alluded to the destruction and rebuilding of the temple (a theme well known in late Judaism, cf. 1 Enoch 90:28–29; Tob 14:4–5), perhaps with some reference to its rebuilding as a miraculous act (i.e., in "three days"). Compare the late Jewish tradition that Solomon had built the original temple "miraculously" with the aid of demons. See Conybeare, "Testament of Solomon." See the note in Duke, *Irony,* 50 and 181, n. 73) to the affect that the "weight" of 2:21–22 "overshadows" the prophetic irony of 2:19.

this level, except for the reference to "three days" (though not "on the third day"), there is no hint or allusion to the resurrection of Jesus.[23]

Level two, on the other hand, stands some distance from the dramatic showing of the scene and provides the reader with the *sensus plenior* of the saying of Jesus in 2:19: It is a reference, says the hermeneut, to the resurrection of the physical body of Jesus. This "fuller," authoritative meaning, however, does not arise from a natural understanding of the simple literal meaning of the traditional logion; rather, it derives from standard early Christian theology and the interpreter's own personal faith; and it is *superimposed* over the conclusion to the dramatic scene. In the interpreter's "reading" of the logion it becomes, even in the dramatic scene, a Christian witness, a prediction of the resurrection of Jesus (2:21), the meaning of which his disciples only "recall" *after* the resurrection (2:22), strongly suggesting that it may have been understood differently before the resurrection, and hence within the memory of the hermeneut. John 2:22 suggests that the fuller meaning of the traditional saying in John 2:19 was arrived at by the disciples some distance from the time of the statement and only after reflection and study of the scriptures. The function of 2:21–22 is to identify the true meaning of the difficult saying in 2:19, since without the clarification the reader might be misled into thinking that Jesus was talking about the destruction and rebuilding of the Jerusalem temple building.[24] It is difficult to know what function, if any, the saying in 2:19 had in the showing of the story, since the dramatic action concludes with it and the dramatic presentation of the incident in 2:13–20 is never resumed after the hermeneut's interpretation of the saying in 2:21–22.

John 4:2 is a blatant contradiction of 4:1 and hints at a negative view of water baptism, a concept that is closely paralleled by the narrator's description of the spiritual baptism of Jesus in 1:29–34. It is, quite frankly, puzzling why a "narrator" would state that Jesus himself actually baptized his followers (3:22 and 4:1) and then clearly contradict these statements for the reader at 4:2 (or, if one prefers, clarify 3:22 and 4:1 by affirming that they do not "mean" what they actually say). If the "narrator" did not want to give the impression that Jesus himself baptized disciples (as appears to be the case in 4:2), why does (s)he state affirmatively that Jesus baptized disciples at 3:22 and 4:1? Clearly here we have two distinct narrative levels. The Johannine "showing," dramatically portrayed in the narration, depicts Jesus baptizing disciples, but in a remarkable clarification another "voice" flatly rejects this dramatic portrayal of the story to provide another way of understanding it. This particular contradiction reflects extremely negatively on the reliability of the narrator's dra-

---

23 Since John does not share the synoptic tradition of resurrection after three days (to John 19:31–20:1 compare Matt 12:40; 27:63; Mark 8:31) the probability of the traditional character of the allusion is increased.

24 See the discussion of the passage by Bultmann, *The Gospel of John*, 126–27 and Cameron, *Sayings Traditions*, 116–19.

matic showing of the story. The clash is so great that the verse (4:2) is regularly regarded as redactional.[25]

John 7:21–22 presents the reader with an interesting and unnecessary contradiction. 7:22a asserts that Moses authorized circumcision. In the sense that Moses was traditionally believed to have written the Torah (Genesis-Deuteronomy), it is a true statement, because circumcision is prescribed in Torah (viz., Lev 12:3). But in a narrow sense, it is not true, because circumcision was prescribed by Yahweh to Abraham before Moses (Gen 17:9–14). The hermeneutical voice (7:22bc) that interrupts a statement by Jesus in the dramatic portrayal (i.e., two corresponding parts of a compound sentence [7:22a, d] joined by καί ["and"]) in order to "correct" the oversight by Jesus in the first half of his statement (at 7:22a) is clearly not made by the character Jesus in the dramatic portrayal. It is rather a voice that directly addresses the reader for the purposes of clarification/correction. The way the adjustment to the story is made is perplexing. The awkward way the "oversight" is corrected could easily have been avoided had the word "Moses" simply been changed to read "the Fathers," or by adding the phrase "you believe that" before "Moses"—that is to say, if the story had been conceptualized and shown as the interpretive voice apparently would have preferred, there would have been no need for the awkward disruptive explanation. As it now appears in the narrative, the clarification/correction seems to have been added, almost as an afterthought, in order to correct an earlier overlooked deficiency in the narrative proper.[26]

How is one to accommodate the distance between this second group of *hermeneiai*,[27] and the story world of the Gospel of John? The customary way is to posit a hypothetical redactor to accommodate certain *hermeneiai*, like 4:2 and 7:22bc, where the distance seems so great that one can no longer think of a single "author." Or to put it more simply: Where the text blatantly contradicts itself, one tends to attribute the correction to a hand other than the original author. In other cases, where the distance is not as great, like for example 5:9d or 5:18, it is easier for the reader to accommodate the *hermeneiai* to the story and to argue that the narrator is drawing valid conclusions from the dramatic presentation. In such cases one does not find it necessary to posit a second redactional layer.

Of course, if Van Belle's analysis of the *hermeneiai* as being consistent with the language world of the gospel as a whole be correct,[28] it makes less convincing any argument that appeals to a later different editor, since syntax, vocabulary, and style are a major part of the evidence that helps one to isolate a different redactional hand.

25 See Van Belle, *Les parenthèses*, 70.
26 It is regularly regarded as redactional; see Van Belle, *Les parenthèses*, 79.
27 See note 20 above for a list of these *hermeneiai*.
28 Van Belle, *Les parenthèses*, 206–10.

Can the *hermeneiai* be accounted for in terms of literary criticism without appeal to a later redactor? The first group of explanations[29] is really no problem in this regard. They suit admirably the kind of explanatory comments by narrators of tales that one is accustomed to find in narrative fiction.[30] In such instances the (author through the) narrator (that has been created for this purpose) addresses the reader directly for the purpose of story control or enhancement. The second group, what I call *hermeneiai*, on the other hand, does not suit well the character of a narrator showing a tale. These explanations do not arise as clarifications of the story within the context of the story world being shown. They arise at some distance from the story in the context of a different narrative world with different values (viz., John 2:19-22: Rebuilding the temple=rising from the dead), and in a real sense as an aside to the reader they actually subvert the story being "shown" by the narrator. In those instances where this interpretive narrative voice intrudes into the narrative it is clearly in control. Indeed, it changes the story, interrupts dialog, and even speaks over the closure of dramatic scenes, thus replacing the dramatic conclusion of the "showing" with interpretive commentary.

Recent literary criticism of the Gospel of John has appropriated the literary categories developed in the discussion of fictional narrative and applied them to the Gospel of John.[31] R. A. Culpepper understands the *hermeneiai* as deriving from "an evangelist who used material derived from an authoritative source, and [from] at least one redactor who later edited the evangelist's gospel, as is commonly supposed by Johannine scholarship."[32] This authorial "committee," as Culpepper calls it, tells the story through a narrator "who speaks in the prologue, tells the story, introduces the dialog, provides explanations, translates terms, and tells us what various characters knew or did not know."[33] In other words, the primary narrator who "shows" the story and the "interpreter" who tells the reader what to think at given points in the narrative are one and the same.[34]

I find such a distance in perspective, however, between what I would describe as the first narrative voice, which shows the story and clarifies it within its own context at certain points, and that of the authoritative interpretive voice, which corrects and clarifies the first narrator's showing of the story, that I would have to describe them as *two* voices. The distance in perspective is so great that the "committee" (to use Culpepper's word) speaks with a divided voice. Hence, if my analysis of the *hermeneiai* above is correct, two *different* voices should be recognized in the narrative, i.e., two different narrators, one of which could be Culpepper's "redactor." But to treat them as a

---

29 See note 18 above for these *hermeneiai*.
30 See in particular the discussion by Booth, *Rhetoric*.
31 Culpepper, *Anatomy,* and Wuellner, "Whispering Wizard."
32 Culpepper, *Anatomy,* 16.
33 Culpepper, *Anatomy,* 17.
34 Culpepper, *Anatomy,* 17-18.

single voice obscures the distance at which each stands from the story and thereby overlooks a distinction that is important for understanding the narrative.

One possibility for explaining the two voices in the narrative is to attribute the more distant voice of the *hermeneiai* to the author.[35] Is it possible that an author might become audible in such a way as to correct or compete with the principle narrator? Or to put the question somewhat differently, and probably more accurately, how much distance in perspective is required before one can say that the author has cast aside the narrator's guise (or perhaps better: has unconsciously let it slip aside momentarily) to speak more or less in his/her[36] own persona? Does an author ever enter audibly into the story in competition with the principal narrative voice(s) that (s)he originally created to show the story?

Literary critics make a distinction between the historical figure that puts the narrative together and what they call the "implied author." The "implied author" is generally recognized as the "author" as (s)he is

> reconstructed by the reader from the narrative. He is not the narrator, but rather the principle that invented the narrator, along with everything else in the narrative, that stacked the cards in this particular way, had these thing happen to these characters, in these words or images. Unlike the narrator, the implied author can *tell* us nothing. He, or better *it*, has no voice, no direct means of communicating. It instructs us silently, through the design of the whole, with all the voices, by all the means it has chosen to let us learn.[37]

Hence, according to Chatman, the implied author cannot speak but is merely an image conveyed to the reader by the whole of the work itself.[38] In other words, by definition the "implied author" has no voice and may take no overt part in the action of the narrative, but is merely a mental construct developed by the reader from the sum total of information that is provided in the narrative. Hence there may be as many "implied authors" as readers, or one author may project in different works different images of him/herself. And these "images" may bear no relationship at all to the actual historical figure that wrote the texts.[39]

On the other hand, according to Wayne Booth, the author that the reader infers from a text (i.e., the so-called "implied author") may speak and frequently does intrude into the narrative and address the reader directly, frequently with overt commentary.[40]

---

35 Wuellner, "Narrative Criticism," 68–69.
36 On the gender of narrators see Hedrick, "Narrator and Story," 253–57.
37 Chatman, *Story and Discourse,* 148; see also Culpepper, *Anatomy,* 15–16.
38 See also Culpepper, *Anatomy,* 16, and Rimmon-Kenan, *Narrative Fiction,* 86–89.
39 See Chatman, *Story and Discourse,* 148.
40 Booth, *Rhetoric of Fiction,* 8, 25, 27, 70–71, 169–209.

These differences [between the real author and the implied author, the author's second self] are most evident when the second self is given an overt, speaking role in the story.[41]

Of course, Booth does not mean that the reconstructed image "speaks," but that the author (whoever that may be) addresses the reader in various ways through the narrative and that address, whether secret or overt, clandestine or direct, becomes part of the data from which the reader infers the author, as implied by the text. Such "address" would include the slant from which the story is told, statements made by characters in the "showing" (these characters then become "reflectors" for the [implied] author's view), and narrative voices that address the reader self-consciously and directly outside of and apart from the dramatic showing of the story.[42]

Why an author becomes audible in a given text would have to be determined from that text, but one reason for the frequent occurrence of such is the narrator's "unreliability," a common feature of narrative fiction. The term "unreliability" is one that derives from Booth,[43] but Chatman's description is succinct:

> What makes a narrator unreliable is that his values diverge strikingly from that of the implied author's; that is, the rest of the narrative—"the norm of the work"— conflicts with the narrator's presentation, and we become suspicious of his sincerity or competence to tell the "true version." The unreliable narrator is at virtual odds with the implied author; otherwise his unreliability could not emerge.[44]

The "unreliability" of the narrator appears most clearly when one finds in the narrative either "corroborating or conflicting testimony" in support of, or in conflict with, the narrator.

> Both reliable and unreliable narrators can be unsupported or uncorrected by other narrators . . . or supported or corrected. . . . Sometimes it is almost impossible to infer whether or to what degree a narrator is fallible; sometimes explicit corroborating or conflicting testimony makes the inference easy. Support or correction differs radically, it should be noted, depending on whether it is provided from within the action, so that the narrator-agent might benefit from it in sticking to the right line or in changing his own views . . ., or is simply provided externally, to help the reader correct or reinforce his own views as against the narrator's. . . .[45]

I understand Booth's "corrected" and "conflicting testimony" that is "provided externally" (i.e., as opposed to "within the action") in the above quote to refer

---

41 Booth, *Rhetoric of Fiction*, 71.
42 See Booth, *Rhetoric of Fiction*, 180. Booth notes that the French novel by Marcel Ayme, *La jument verte*, has two narrators. See also in particular Booth's discussion of *The Liar* by Henry James (*Rhetoric of Fiction*, 347–54) and *The Aspern Papers*, also by James (*Rhetoric of Fiction*, 354–64).
43 Booth, *Rhetoric of Fiction*, 158–60, 300–309, 339–74, 422–34.
44 Chatman, *Story and Discourse*, 149.
45 Booth, *Rhetoric of Fiction*, 159–60.

to overt intrusions into the narrator's story that consciously correct the narrator or supply for the reader information lacking in the narrative so as to cast a different light on the story being narrated. Such "corrections" appear to be a common feature of narrative fiction.[46]

One good example of a narrator's unreliability is found in the 20th century novel, *The Power and the Glory,* by Graham Greene. The principal narrator describes the main character of the novel, a priest, celebrating Mass:

> The Latin words ran into each other on his hasty tongue: he could feel impatience all round him. He began the Consecration of the Host (he had finished the wafers long ago—it was a piece of bread from Maria's oven). . . .[47]

It is not really clear who is responsible for the parenthentical aside that clarifies the true character of the Host being served by the priest (i.e., that it was simply bread and not wafers). It could be the principal narrator's ironic statement, pointing out in a direct address to you the reader just another instance of the priest's disreputable character. If it is the principal narrator's comment, the intent of the statement would seem to be that the priest not only has failed his church in his moral life but has also desecrated even the Mass by using the bread baked by the (immoral) mother of his own illegitimate child! It seems more likely, however, that it is due to the (implied) author who, inadvertently letting his narrator's guise momentarily slip, speaks in his own persona to contradict the narrator's story so as to give the reader an insight into the priest's true character. Neither the threat of imminent arrest nor the lack of the usual wafers prevents the priest from continuing to serve his people. He uses chipped cups instead of a chalice, a packing case instead of an altar, an earthen-floored hut instead of a church, and a piece of common bread instead of wafers.[48] The difference in perspective between this parenthetical aside and the perspective of the usual narrator is great indeed.

This incident is only a minor example of how totally unreliable the narrator of this novel actually is. (S)he repeatedly tells the reader how bad the priest is when the reader can see clearly from the actions of the priest how good he is. For example, the narrator has the priest make the following reflection upon his kindly reception by German Protestants after escaping to Las Casas from the severe religious persecution in the neighboring state of Mexico. The priest reflects:

> How odd it had seemed at first to be treated as a guest, not as a criminal or a bad priest. These people were heretics—it never occurred to them that he was not a good man. . . .[49]

---

46 Booth, *Rhetoric of Fiction,* 422–34. See also the discussion by Benstock, "Margin," 204–9.

47 Greene, *Power and Glory,* 97–98.

48 For other asides see Greene, *Power and Glory,* 16, 18, 23, 39, 72, 97, 157, 159, 180, 183, 193, 200, 204, 206, 279.

49 Greene, *Power and Glory,* 235; cf. 257, 258, 262, 270, and 283.

But the entire tone of the novel, and particularly the unselfish actions of the priest, inform the reader in contradiction to the narrator's presentation of him that the priest is, on the contrary, a very good man. In this story the norm of the narrative (i.e., how the narrative is put together) betrays the narrator's unreliability in his characterization of the priest. Or to put it differently, and more accurately, the narrator of the tale diverges radically from the norm of the work.

Such explanatory asides in which (implied) author may be able to be distinguished from narrator can also be found in the early Greek novels. For example, in *Clitophon and Leucippe* (ca. CE 300) one finds such explanatory clarifications. In one instance[50] Clitophon has been arrested and is in jail; there is a plot to induce Clitophon to reveal certain information by securing the services of a second inmate who, as a fellow prisoner, would gain Clitophon's confidence and thus induce Clitophon to talk. The fellow begins to complain and tries to lead Clitophon into a conversation. Clitophon, however, as narrator of the incident says:

> However, I paid little attention to what he said between his groans; but one of our fellow-prisoners (for in misfortune man is a creature always inquisitive to hear about another's woes; community of suffering is something of a medicine for one's own troubles) said to him: "What was the prank that Fortune played you? I dare say you met with a piece of bad luck, and did nothing wrong, if I may judge from my own misfortunes." So saying, he related his own story, the reason why he was in prison. However, I paid no attention to any of his talk.[51]

The proverb-like observation on human nature, rather common elsewhere in the novel, that interrupts and digresses from the principal incident being narrated by Clitophon could actually belong to three different figures. It could, of course, be Clitophon's own astute observation on human nature; but appearing as it does interrupting Clitophon's narrative, freezing the action of the scene, and clarifying the motivation for a third prisoner's brief discourse before the discourse is made makes this interpretation suspect. The intrusive material could easily have been incorporated as a more natural part of Clitophon's narration had it followed the next-to-last sentence in the segment quoted above; for example:

> So saying, he related his own story, the reason why he was in prison, for in misfortune man is a creature always inquisitive to hear about another's woes; community of suffering is something of a medicine for one's own troubles. However, I paid no attention to any of his talk.

Even after the intrusive material is placed in this more natural position in the speech of Clitophon, however, one is still struck by the lack of appropriate-

50 Achilles Tatius, *Clitophon and Leucippe*, 7.1–2.
51 Achilles Tatius, *Clitophon and Leucippe*, 7.2.3–4.

ness of the observation. The "proverb" in itself describes the sense of comfort produced in an auditor upon *hearing* of the suffering of others; "misery loves company" we might say. But as the proverb is actually used in the text, and also even in its more natural position where it can comment upon the stories of both prisoners, it explains the motivation for *telling* of one's misfortune rather than for *hearing* of the misfortunes of others.

If it is Clitophon's aside, then it would have directly addressed his only auditor, the fictional author (Achilles Tatius?) and assumedly the principal narrator who allows Clitophon to tell his tale in the first person (1.1-3). As a comment to the fictional author/narrator, however, it seems inappropriate, since it really has nothing to do with Clitophon's story, and since such moralisms would tend to bore an auditor who wanted to enjoy the pleasures of a love story (1.2.3). In any case the plot to entrap Clitophon is clear without it; it appears to be entirely gratuitous as far as Clitophon's story is concerned. The aside makes more sense as the saying of the principal narrator who allows Clitophon to tell his tale through him in the first person (1.1-3) and who interrupts Clitophon's narration at various points to provide, among other things, learned digressions (diatribes) on various subjects for the moral edification of the (implied) readers.[52]

Such asides actually make better sense, however, as intrusions by the (implied) author of the text. It is difficult to see them as statements of the fictional author consciously so created by the (implied) author, since the tale never returns to the fictional author met in 1.1-3. The narrative is abruptly concluded (8.19.3) by Clitophon without any futher reference to the fictional frame established in 1.1-3. Hence one is led to conclude that the (implied) author does not maintain throughout the tale by Clitophon the illusion of the fictional frame, with which (s)he began. And this conclusion strongly suggests that in at least some of the more diatribic digressions the implied author has simply let the "narrator's guise" slip momentarily and speaks in his/her own persona.

In a recent study Tamara Eskenazi has analyzed characterization in Ezra-Nehemiah from a literary perspective.[53] On the one hand, she finds that in Ezra-Nehemiah the "omniscient narrator" seeks to identify Ezra as a "reliable narrator,"[54] but on the other hand the omniscient narrator uses similar tech-

---

52 As examples of diatribic digressions that seem to arise metadiegetically rather than in the context of Clitophon's tale compare: on providence (1.3.2-3); on sleep (1.6.2-4); on the myth of Cadmus (2.2.1-3.1); on the discovery of purple dye (2.11.4-8); on the Egyptian ox (2.15.3-4); on shame, grief, and anger (2.29.1-5); on weeping (3.11.1-2); on the Egyptian clod (3.13.3); on pity and friendship (3.14.3-4); on tears (6.7.4-8); on rumour and slander (6.10.4-5); on anger and love (6.19.1-7); on flesh wounds and soul wounds (7.4.4-5); on the water of the Styx (8.12.1-9). The (implied) author is more careful in other instances to cast his/her diatribes as speeches of characters in the narration; for example, compare Clitophon's digression on the crocodile (4.19.1-6), and the messenger's learned description of the Phoenix (3.25.1-7).

53 *In an Age of Prose,* 127-54.

54 *In an Age of Prose,* 135.

niques "to deflate Nehemiah."[55] One can also observe a similar phenomenon in the Chronicler's use of the Deuteronomist's narrative. While Eskenazi stops short of describing Nehemiah as an "unreliable" narrator, it seems clear from her analysis that such is the net effect of the "omniscient narrator's" undermining or subversion of Nehemiah's story.

These examples of extraneous narrative voices in ancient and modern texts, voices that compete with the principle narrator of the story, are important for the *hermeneiai* in John for two reasons: they show that the literary technique is a common feature of narrative, and that it was not unknown to ancient writers who may, therefore, be expected to have used the technique as well.

The *hermeneiai* in John's gospel, i.e., those intrusive comments that do not derive from the "principal narrator" of the showing of the story,[56] do seem to function much as the examples from narrative fiction that I have cited above. Through these intrusive comments the hermeneut:

1) improves the showing of the story by clarifying what is apparently conceived as obscurity in the story's showing (1:24; 5:9d, 18; 7:5; 8:27; 9:14; 11:13; 12:33); 2) corrects errors made by the principal narrator (4:2; 7:22bc; 21:14); 3) clarifies the dramatic presentation where the reader might be misled (4:44); 4) tells information that the narrator has simply not shown (6:71; 12:4c; 18:2b, 5e),[57] or may not know (7:39; 11:51–52; 12:6, 17, 42–43; 13:2bc, 3, 11, 27a, 28–29; 17:3; 21:19a); 5) tells information that could not have been part of the dramatic presentation since it derives from subsequent reflections on that presentation (hence, it is information that the narrator of the first story "did not know") (2:17, 21–22; 10:35b; 12:14c–16, 38–41; 13:18b; 15:25; 17:12b; 18:9, 32; 19:24def, 28b, 35–37; 20:9, 30–31; 21:23, 24–25).[58]

The intrusions of the hermeneut seem to qualify the principal narrative voice of the Gospel of John (if not totally, certainly in part) as an "unreliable" narrator; that is to say, the narrator who shows the primary story diverges strikingly from the "norm" of the story, as it is construed by the hermeneut. Indeed the hermeneut's concluding summaries (20:30–31; 21:24–25) constitute both praise and criticism of the dramatic presentation. The "story" (i.e., the description of the "signs" done by Jesus in the presence of the disciples— 20:30) written by the disciple bearing witness to them (i.e., the principal narrator of the story—21:24) in this book (i.e., the principal narrator's story as corrected, clarified, and expanded from the perspective of the hermeneut's

55 *In an Age of Prose*, 135.
56 Or perhaps better the narrator of the "first story." See note 20 above.
57 The narrator of the principal story clearly knows the tradition that Judas is the betrayer, since that feature is part of the dramatic presentation in John 13:21–26, 30. I have included these constant explanatory reminders of Judas's betrayal with the hermeneut rather than with the narrator of the principal story because they fit the hermeneut's "vendetta" against Judas in other places (viz., 12:6; 13:2).
58 The hermeneut categorically tells the reader that the sort of information included in item 4 was *not* known at the level of the dramatic presentation, since the disciples of Jesus only came to this knowledge sometime later after reading "the scriptures" and "remembering" what Jesus had done (viz., 2:17, 21–22; 12:14c–16; 20:9, 21:23).

more mature information and faith—20:30) are "true" (21:24), but they do not tell the "whole" story, either in the sense of completeness (20:30; 21:25) or in the sense of accuracy—since they were written just for the purpose of an evangelistic witness (20:31). This limited purpose naturally compromised a more complete "showing" and "telling" of the story (20:31; 21:25).

3. Conclusion

This paper has shown that narrative asides that "correct" or "improve" a story are a common feature of narrative fiction in both contemporary and ancient literature. It has argued that what is traditionally understood as the later editing of the Gospel of John by a hand other than the original "author," i.e., its redaction,[59] is readily understandable within the conventions of narrative criticism. If a narrative analysis of the Gospel of John can account for what has been traditionally seen as redactional levels in the text without recourse to (a) hypothetical redactor(s), it raises questions about aspects of the redaction-critical methodology with regard to the Gospel of John.

Other historical questions are raised as well, particularly with regard to the reliability of the story. For example, when the principal narrator tells the reader in certain of the asides what no one in real life could possibly know (i.e., what characters in the story are thinking and feeling and when their motivation is explained), the modern reader wonders how reliable that information is—since the technique belongs to the craft of fiction, drama, and art more so than to the historian's method, though to be sure ancient and modern historians as well use the technique. On the other hand, when the hermeneut "adjusts" the principal narrator's presentation, the average reader tends to follow the "omniscient" hermeneut rather than the "fallible" narrator. But who can really know that the authoritative "telling" is actually more reliable than the showing? Or to put it another way, if one thinks in terms of tradition and interpretation, why should one think that the hermeneut's distance actually provides a more reliable (historical) perspective than the (traditional) story being interpreted? The (implied) author, who carries the reader with him/her in the authoritative voice of the hermeneut, allows no question about how the narrator's story should be understood. But is it not possible that the (implied) author's "heavy-handed" use of intrusive commentary is due to the fact that the story that the principal narrator shows in the Gospel of John actually subverts the (implied) author's (later) understanding of the story? The uncritical reader tends to accept the hermeneut's interpretation as the final authoritative word on whatever subject (s)he addresses, while critical scholarship tends to ignore much of the commentary as later redaction by a different hand. If this study has validity, however, it would appear that the study of the Gospel of John in its present form should rather begin with what has been generally disregarded as later extraneous redaction.

---

59 See, for example, Brown, *The Gospel According to John I–XII,* cxxxvi.

The Youth in Secret Mark and the Beloved Disciple in John

Marvin W. Meyer

Although James Robinson's research has not focused specifically upon the enigmatic Secret Gospel of Mark, it might have. After all, during his career Robinson has directed his attention to the Markan tradition, manuscript discoveries and reconstructed stories of the discoveries, and the impact of newly-discovered documents upon our knowledge of Christian origins. In all these respects the Secret Gospel of Mark touches upon themes characteristic of the scholarly career of the person whom these essays honor. In the present essay I shall attempt to evaluate the significance of this secret gospel for the study of the Johannine "Beloved Disciple".

1. The Discovery

As James Robinson has presented the stories of the discoveries of the Nag Hammadi Codices and of the Bodmer Papyri, so also Morton Smith has told of his manuscript discovery in the Judean desert. In the summer of 1958, Smith recounts, some seventeen years after he had first visited the Greek Orthodox Monastery of Mar Saba in 1941, he returned to the monastery with the permission of the Patriarch Benedict, in order to study and catalogue the manuscripts housed there. Smith's colorful account of his discovery deserves to be quoted at some length:

> Then, one afternoon near the end of my stay, I found myself in my cell, staring incredulously at a text written in a tiny scrawl I had not even tried to read in the tower when I picked out the book containing it. But now that I came to puzzle it out, it began, "From the letters of the most holy Clement, the author of the *Stromateis*. To Theodore," and it went on to praise the recipient for having "shut up" the Carpocratians. The *Stromateis,* I knew, was a work by Clement of Alexandria, one of the earliest and most mysterious of the great fathers of the Church—early Christian writers of outstanding importance. I was reasonably sure that no letters of his had been preserved. So if this writing was what it claimed to be, I had a hitherto unknown text by a writer of major significance for early Church history. Besides, it would add something to our knowledge of the

94

Carpocratians, one of the most scandalous of the "gnostic" sects, early and extreme variants of Christianity. Who Theodore was, I had no idea. I still don't. But Clement and the Carpocratians were more than enough for one day. I hastened to photograph the text and photographed it three times for good measure.[1]

Smith's account raises three issues for our consideration.

1. When Smith mentions the question of the authenticity of the Mar Saba letter of Clement ("if this writing was what it claimed to be"), he inadvertently anticipates the controversy that has swirled around this text and the issue of its authenticity. From the well-known statements of Quentin Quesnell[2] to the more recent dispute over insinuations in Per Beskow's *Strange Tales about Jesus*,[3] the scholarly discussions concerning the Mar Saba manuscript have been conducted within the context of expressed doubts and uncertainties about the authenticity of the text. While uncertainties remain, it is noteworthy that a number of scholars increasingly seem inclined to accept the text as an ancient letter of Clement. Smith himself notes, in a review article surveying some 150 publications on the letter of Clement and the Secret Gospel of Mark, that "most scholars would attribute the letter to Clement, though a substantial minority are still in doubt."[4] At least four scholars (John Dominic Crossan, Helmut Koester, Marvin Meyer, Hans-Martin Schenke[5]) have gone into print assuming the authenticity of the text. Such an assumption of authenticity is also the "working hypothesis" (the phrase is Crossan's) of the present essay.

2. Smith indicates that he made the discovery by himself, in the privacy of his monastic cell, and to this day Smith apparently remains the only scholar who has seen the actual text. At least one other scholar, Thomas Talley, tried to see the text in January of 1980, but he has written that his attempts were frustrated.[6] I heartily agree with the observation of Crossan in this regard: "The authenticity of a text can only be established by the consensus of experts who have studied the original document under scientifically appropriate circumstances."[7] That independent scholarly examination and verification of the authenticity of the Mar Saba letter has yet to be accomplished.

3. Smith writes that he photographed the letter of Clement, "three times for good measure." His photographs are reproduced in both his scholarly and his popular editions of the text,[8] and to date these personal photographs are the

1 Smith, *The Secret Gospel*, 12–13.
2 Cf. Quesnell, "The Mar Saba Clementine," and "A Reply to Morton Smith," as well as Smith, "On the Authenticity of the Mar Saba Letter of Clement."
3 Cf. Smith, "Regarding *Secret Mark*."
4 Smith, "Clement of Alexandria and Secret Mark," 451.
5 Crossan, *Four Other Gospels*, 89–121; Koester, "History and Development of Mark's Gospel"; Meyer, "The Youth in the *Secret Gospel of Mark*"; Schenke, "The Mystery of the Gospel of Mark."
6 Talley, "Liturgical Time in the Ancient Church," 45.
7 Crossan, *Four Other Gospels*, 100.
8 Smith, *Clement of Alexandria and a Secret Gospel of Mark*, 449, 451, 453; *The Secret Gospel*, 38.

only published facsimiles of the Mar Saba letter of Clement. The adequate publication of the text in facsimile edition also needs to be undertaken, so that scholars may be able to examine the clearest possible reproductions of the document. The accomplishment of this task will not give scholars access to an actual ancient copy, since the copy of the Mar Saba letter seems to have been made "about 1750, plus or minus about fifty years," according to the scholars who examined the photographs and attempted to date the scribal hand.[9] Yet a facsimile edition of the text at least will allow more scholars to see reproductions of the letter of Clement and draw their own conclusions from the evidence thus presented.

2. The Document

The Mar Saba letter attributed to Clement of Alexandria was written in cursive Greek on two and a half pages at the back of a printed edition of the letters of Ignatius of Antioch (Voss, *Epistulae genuinae*). As copied, the document preserves only a fragment of the letter of Clement to Theodore. In the letter Clement as heresiologist commends the recipient for his opposition to the gnostic Carpocratians, and the style and contents of the heresiological letter are reminiscent of Clement's *Stromateis* and *Protreptikos pros Hellenas*. While he is exposing the foul deeds of the Carpocratians, Clement declares that they make use of an edition of the Gospel of Mark that Carpocrates falsified. Clement charges that after Carpocrates obtained from a Christian presbyter in Alexandria a copy of the Gospel of Mark ("the secret gospel," $\tauο\hat{υ}$ $\muυστικο\hat{υ}$ $ε\dot{υ}αγγελίου$, 1v,6), he interpreted it "according to his blasphemous and carnal opinion" and polluted it by "mixing the most shameless lies with the undefiled and holy words" (1v,7–9). In contrast to this falsified edition, Clement specifies two other editions of Mark that are true and authoritative: the public version of the Gospel of Mark, which seems, from Clement's account, to be identical or nearly identical with the present canonical Gospel of Mark; and the Secret Gospel of Mark, an equally authentic version of Mark that functioned as "a more spiritual gospel for the use of those being perfected" (1r,21–22).

According to Clement, the Secret Gospel of Mark is an edition of the gospel that seems to be only slightly longer than public Mark. Clement cites two relatively brief sections found in Secret Mark but not in public Mark. Conceivably Clement may have known of other passages peculiar to Secret Mark and may have referred to such passages in a portion of his letter that has not survived. Yet in the extant fragment of his letter Clement indicates nothing to support such a possibility, and he appears to be turning away from the discussion of the passages unique to Secret Mark in the final lines of the fragment ("Now then, the interpretation that is true and in accordance with the true philosophy . . .," 2r,17–18).

---

9 Smith, *Clement of Alexandria and a Secret Gospel of Mark*, 1.

The first section of Secret Mark quoted by Clement (1v,23–2r,11) is to be located immediately after Mark 10:34 and reads as follows[10]:

And they come into Bethany, and a certain woman, whose brother had died, was there. And she, coming, bowed down before Jesus, and says to him, "Son of David, have mercy upon me." But the disciples rebuked her. And Jesus, angered, went with her into the garden where the tomb was, and immediately a loud voice was heard from the tomb. And approaching, Jesus rolled away the stone from the door of the tomb. And immediately going in where the *youth* (νεανίσκος) was, he stretched out his hand and raised him, taking hold of his hand. But the youth, looking upon him, loved him and began to beseech him that he might be with him. And going out of the tomb, they came into the house of the youth, for he was rich. And after six days Jesus gave him instructions, and when it was evening the youth comes to him, wearing linen on his naked body. And he stayed with him that night, for Jesus taught him the mystery of the kingdom of God. And rising from there, he returned to the other side of the Jordan.

The second section of the Secret Gospel of Mark (2r,14–16) is to be located within Mark 10:46. Secret Mark 10:46 then may be reconstructed to read as follows:

And he comes into Jericho. And the sister of the youth whom Jesus loved and his mother and Salome were there, and Jesus did not receive them (fem.). And as he was leaving Jericho with his disciples and a large crowd, Bartimaeus, son of Timaeus, a blind beggar, was sitting by the side of the road.

The most recent studies on Secret Mark by Crossan, Koester, Meyer, and Schenke interpret the fragments of the secret gospel in dramatically different ways, but they are in agreement on several matters. As noted above, these studies assume the authenticity of the Mar Saba letter as an ancient text and direct serious attention to the letter of Clement and the Markan fragments imbedded within it. Further, these studies are unanimous in recommending a redaction-critical approach to Secret Mark, in order to evaluate the place of the secret gospel within the Markan redactional tradition. And these studies also all advocate the priority of the text of Secret Mark to that of canonical Mark. As Koester puts it, "The conclusion is unavoidable: Canonical Mark is derived from Secret Mark. The basic difference between the two seems to be that the redactor of canonical Mark eliminated the story of the raising of the youth and the reference to this story in Mk. 10:46."[11] The evidence marshalled by Koester and others to support this contention need not be rehearsed here. Suffice it to say that peculiar redactional traits of canonical Mark are mirrored in the surviving two sections of Secret Mark.

Elsewhere I have argued that a careful reading of the Secret Gospel of Mark exposes a sub-plot in Secret Mark that is present in only a truncated form in

10 Here and elsewhere the translation is mine, based upon the Greek text in Smith, *Clement of Alexandria and a Secret Gospel of Mark,* 448, 450, 452.
11 Koester, "History and Development of Mark's Gospel," 56.

98 • Marvin W. Meyer

canonical Mark. This sub-plot features the story of a paradigmatic *youth* (νεανίσκος), and the story functions to communicate Secret Mark's vision of the life of discipleship as that is exemplified in the career of the youth. Five pericopae (Mark 10:17–22; Secret Mark section 1; Secret Mark section 2; Mark 14:51–52; Mark 16:1–8), each connected to the others by means of a series of literary links, serve to advance the story of the youth. The elimination of the story of the raising of the youth in the redaction of canonical Mark thus fractured the integrity of the sub-plot and left the youth fleeing naked (Mark 14:51–52) and the youth in the tomb (Mark 16:1–8) for scholars to worry over.

This story of the youth in Secret Mark also brings to mind features of the Gospel of John. Ever since the initial publication of the Mar Saba letter, scholars have noted that the account of the raising of the youth in Secret Mark is remarkably similar to the story of the raising of Lazarus in John 11. According to Secret Mark, a youth of Bethany (cf. John 11:1) dies, and his sister comes to Jesus and greets him (cf. John 11:20ff.; in John Martha comes and Mary stays at home). Jesus *is angered* at the disciples' rebuke (Secret Mark 1v,25, ὀργισθείς; in John 11:33, 38 forms of the verb ἐμβριμάομαι are used, a verb that commonly functions as a synonym or near-synonym of ὀργίζω). Jesus goes to the tomb in a garden (perhaps cf. John 19:41), and there is the call of a *loud voice* (φωνὴ μεγάλη, Secret Mark 2r,1; in John 11:43 Jesus himself cries with a *loud voice*, φωνῇ μεγάλῃ). Jesus removes the stone from the door of the tomb (according to John 11:41, "they took away the stone"), and raises the youth (cf. John 11:41ff.).

That there is a relationship between the Markan story of the youth and the Johannine story of Lazarus seems quite evident. Smith has argued that "there can be no question that the story in the longer text of Mk. is more primitive in form than the story of Lazarus in Jn."[12] I am convinced by Smith's argument; other scholars[13] are not. As Smith points out painstakingly, the Markan story of the youth in the Mar Saba text lacks the details we expect in a more developed tradition (personal names, descriptions of features of the miracle, etc.), and shows no evidence of specifically Johannine redactional traits (vocabulary, delay of the miracle, aretalogical self-predication).[14] To Smith's wide-ranging arguments Crossan adds the claim that it is plausible to read the miracle story of Secret Mark as a more primitive version of the story than that of John 11, and that John 11 may well manifest a secondary use of three themes: the loud voice, the anger or strong emotion of Jesus, and the garden.[15]

An additional parallel between the Markan and Johannine miracle stories should be highlighted. According to the Secret Gospel of Mark, *the* resurrected *youth looked upon Jesus and loved him* (ὁ δὲ νεανίσκος ἐμβλέψας αὐτῷ ἠγάπησεν αὐτόν, 2r,4), and the youth in turn is described as the νεανίσκος

12 Smith, *Clement of Alexandria and a Secret Gospel of Mark,* 156.
13 Cf. Brown, "The Relation of 'The Secret Gospel of Mark' to the Fourth Gospel"; Bruce, *The "Secret" Gospel of Mark.*
14 Smith, *Clement of Alexandria and a Secret Gospel of Mark,* 148–63.
15 Crossan, *Four Other Gospels,* 105–6.

"whom Jesus loved" (ὃν ἠγάπα αὐτὸν ὁ 'Ιησοῦς, 2r,15), a description that compares well with the statement of Mark 10:21 ("And Jesus, looking upon him, loved him," ὁ δὲ 'Ιησοῦς ἐμβλέψας αὐτῷ ἠγάπησεν αὐτόν). This statement about the rich youth of Mark 10:17–22 seems especially significant: Only here in the synoptic gospels is it specifically said that Jesus loves a given disciple or candidate for discipleship; and this pericope, as I have posited, is linked to the other Markan pericopae in the sub-plot of the youth in Secret Mark. In the Gospel of John, Lazarus also is said to be loved by Jesus in four passages: (1) Lazarus is the one *whom* Jesus *loved* (ὃν φιλεῖς, 11:3); (2) Jesus *loved* (ἠγάπα) Martha, her sister, and Lazarus (11:5); (3) Jesus calls Lazarus "our friend" (or: "our loved one," ὁ φίλος ἡμῶν, 11:11); and (4) those around say of Jesus, "Behold, how he loved him!" (ἴδε πῶς ἐφίλει αὐτόν, 11:36).

If, then, the Markan figure of the youth and the Johannine figure of Lazarus constitute the one "whom Jesus loved," how do these characters in turn relate to the Johannine figure of the Beloved Disciple? To the provocative issue of the Beloved Disciple we now turn.

3. The Beloved Disciple in John

A certain disciple loved by Jesus, "another disciple," and unnamed disciples are all mentioned in the Gospel of John, and all have been said to be important for the interpretation of the role of the Johannine Beloved Disciple. Here we shall attempt to gather these three sorts of references and assess their significance for our understanding of the Beloved Disciple.[16]

1. The Beloved Disciple is explicitly referred to in four passages in the Gospel of John. First, in the account of the Last Supper, Jesus announces that one of the disciples will betray him. The disciples in general are uncertain, but one disciple discovers who the betrayer will be: "One of his disciples, whom Jesus loved (εἷς ἐκ τῶν μαθητῶν αὐτοῦ . . . ὃν ἠγάπα ὁ 'Ιησοῦς), was reclining in the bosom of Jesus. So Simon Peter beckons to him to ask who it might be of whom he speaks. So leaning thus on the breast of Jesus, he says to him, 'Lord, who is it?'" (13:23–25). Jesus proceeds to give indication to the confidant that Judas is the one who will betray him (13:26). Secondly, according to the Johannine passion narrative, several women were standing by the cross, as were two others: "So Jesus, seeing his mother and *the disciple whom he loved* (τὸν μαθητήν . . . ὃν ἠγάπα) standing near, says to his mother, 'Woman, behold, your son.' Then he says to the disciple, 'Behold, your mother.' And from that hour the disciple took her to his own house" (19:26–27). Thirdly, after the crucifixion, according to John 20:1–2, Mary Magdalene goes to the tomb of Jesus, only to discover that the stone had been moved. "So she runs and comes to Simon Peter and to *the other disciple, whom Jesus loved* (τὸν ἄλλον μαθητὴν ὃν ἐφίλει ὁ 'Ιησοῦς), and says to them, 'They have taken the

---

16 The bibliography on the Beloved Disciple is extensive. Cf. the sources listed in Brown, *The Gospel According to John I–XII*; Schenke, "Function and Background."

lord from the tomb, and we do not know where they have laid him'" (20:2). Peter and "the other disciple" (ὁ ἄλλος μαθητής, 20:3) run to the tomb, and although "the other disciple" reaches the tomb before Peter (20:4) and looks within, he himself does not enter until Peter has done so. "So then the other disciple, who came to the tomb first, also entered, and he saw and believed" (20:8).

In the appendix (or epilogue) to the Gospel of John (chapter 21) occurs the fourth passage that refers to "the disciple whom Jesus loved." After the resurrection Jesus reveals himself to his disciples and has direct exchanges with Peter on the theme of love and with the Beloved Disciple. At 21:7 it is the latter who recognizes Jesus: "So *that disciple whom Jesus loved* (ὁ μαθητὴς ἐκεῖνος ὃν ἠγάπα ὁ Ἰησοῦς) says to Peter, 'It is the lord.'" Later in the chapter that disciple is identified with the intimate disciple at the Last Supper (13:23–26):

> Peter, turning, sees the disciple whom Jesus loved following, who also was leaning on his breast at the supper and said, "Lord, who is it that is going to betray you?" So Peter, seeing him, says to Jesus, "Lord, what about him?" Jesus says to him, "If I want him to remain until I come, what is that to you? As for you, follow me." So this saying spread to the brothers, that this disciple is not to die, but Jesus did not say to him that he was not to die, but rather, "If I want him to remain until I come, what is that to you?" (21:20–23).

Finally, the author of the appendix writes that this disciple is the witness who stands behind the tradition: "This is the disciple who bears witness concerning these things and who has written these things, and we know that his witness is true" (21:24).

2. In two passages John describes an anonymous disciple as "the other disciple" (ὁ μαθητὴς ὁ ἄλλος) or "another disciple" (ἄλλος μαθητής). According to John 18:15 "another disciple" along with Peter followed Jesus; "that disciple was known to the high priest, and he entered the courtyard of the high priest with Jesus." Then "the other disciple" went out and spoke to the maid at the door, so that Peter also could enter (18:16). In John 20:1–10, as noted above, "the disciple whom Jesus loved" is called, in four instances, "the other disciple" (20:2, 3, 4, 8).

3. In two additional passages unnamed disciples are presented in the Gospel of John. In 1:37–42 two of John the Baptist's disciples follow Jesus: One is identified as Andrew, the other is unnamed. As the most reliable reading of John 1:41 puts it, "He (i.e., Andrew) *first* (πρῶτον) finds his own brother Simon. . . ." The inferior reading πρῶτος, supported by א* and other manuscripts, could allow—or so it has been suggested—the translation, "He (i.e., Andrew) is the first to find his own brother Simon," thus implying that the unnamed disciple (John the son of Zebedee?) also finds his brother (James?).[17]

---

17 Cf. Brown, *The Gospel According to John I–XII*, 75–76.

Again, according to John 19:35 an unnamed eyewitness is the guarantor of the truth of the crucifixion account, perhaps in particular the interpretive elements unique to John (blood and water, possibly also no broken bones): "The one who has seen has borne witness."

How might we evaluate these several Johannine references and their significance for our understanding of the Beloved Disciple? We begin with the unnamed disciple of John 1:37–42: That figure may be dismissed immediately from our consideration, since there is very little evidence, and none of it compelling, that would lead us to suppose an identification of the companion of Andrew with the Beloved Disciple. The reference to "the disciple whom Jesus loved" in John 21 clearly seems to be the work of the redactor, who is supremely interested in tying the motif of the Beloved Disciple to the authorship of the gospel. Such a general observation seems safe enough after the seminal work of Rudolf Bultmann.[18] John 19:35 similarly seems to be a redactional gloss (so also Bultmann), for both its apparent intention and its wording resemble John 21:24. In any case, John 19:35 does not describe the eyewitness either as "the disciple whom Jesus loved" or as "the other disciple." Whether "the other disciple" of John 18:15–16 is to be related to the Beloved Disciple is not obvious. The fact that "the other disciple" of John 20:1–10 is equated with "the disciple whom Jesus loved" suggests the plausibility of a similar equation in John 18, as might the additional parallels between John 18:15–16 and John 20:1–10 (in these two passages "the other disciple" is depicted with Peter, precedes Peter, and finally allows Peter to enter the courtyard of the high priest in chapter 18 or the tomb of Jesus in chapter 20). The two other references to the Beloved Disciple (John 13:23–26; 19:26–27) portray a disciple who is intimate with Jesus, close to Jesus in life and in death. Whatever may be the background of the character of the Beloved Disciple, at key points in these chapters this figure is presented in a personalized manner as a model disciple who is near Jesus.

4. Conclusion

"The figure of the Beloved Disciple is admittedly one of the great puzzles in the mysterious Fourth Gospel."[19] With these words Schenke turns to his own study of the place of "the disciple whom Jesus loved" in John. Many have attempted to identify the Beloved Disciple with a particular historical figure (e.g., John the son of Zebedee, John Mark, John the Presbyter, or, in the case of the disciple in John 18:15–16, a disciple with priestly connections); since Bultmann some have suggested that the Beloved Disciple in John 21 (cf. also 19:35) is an authoritative historical figure, in the Johannine school, whom the redactor of John identifies as the eyewitness and author of the gospel. Now

---

18 Bultmann, *The Gospel of John,* esp. 483–86.
19 Schenke, "Function and Background," 114.

Schenke has combed the Nag Hammadi texts for other figures who resemble the Beloved Disciple, and he proposes that Mary Magdalene, James the Just, and Judas Thomas also function as beloved disciples in one way or another in gnostic texts. In the *Gospel of Philip* (NHC II,3), for example, it is said concerning Mary Magdalene that "[Christ loved] her more than [all] the disciples [and used to] kiss her [often] on her [mouth]" (63,34–36; the reconstruction of these lines is made more secure by the well-preserved lines at 64,1–5). Elsewhere in the *Gospel of Philip* Mary Magdalene is termed the "companion" or "consort" (κοινωνος) of Jesus (e.g., 59,9). Such a relationship between Mary Magdalene and Jesus in gnostic traditions is confirmed by the *Gospel of Mary* (BG 8502,1; cf. 10,1–9; 17, 15–18, 15). In other gnostic documents James the Just, the brother of Jesus, is said to be especially close to Jesus (cf. the *Apocryphon of James* [NHC I,2], the *First Apocalypse of James* [NHC V,3], the *Second Apocalypse of James* [NHC V,4], and the Gospel of Thomas [NHC II,2] logion 12). Most notable for Schenke are the descriptions of Judas Thomas in the Gospel of Thomas (cf. logion 13) and the *Book of Thomas* (NHC II,7). In the *Book of Thomas* Jesus addresses Thomas as his brother (con/caн) three times (138,4, 10, 19), and at 138,7–8 Jesus also calls Thomas "my twin and my true companion (or: friend)," ΠΑϹΟΕΙϢ ΑΥΩ ΠΑϢΒⲢⲘⲘⲎⲈ, which Schenke translates back into Greek as σὺ εἶ . . . ὁ φίλος μου ὁ ἀληθινός, or, following Johannine syntax, σὺ εἶ ὃν φιλῶ ἀληθῶς (second person) or αὐτός ἐστιν ὃν ἐφίλει ἀληθῶς ὁ ᾿Ιησοῦς (third person).[20]

Schenke concludes, on the Beloved Disciple, that "the Beloved Disciple passages are only a simple fiction of the redactor," and he may very well be right. He continues:

> Reference is made to the alleged Beloved Disciple in the same way as the Pastorals refer to Paul. The function of the Beloved Disciple is to ground the Fourth Gospel (and the tradition of the Christian group in which it originates and has its influence) in the eyewitness testimony of one who was especially intimate with Jesus. This kind of deception may find its explanation and, what is more, its justification, only within a particular historical situation of conflict. The circumstances, however, do not point to a conflict within the group, but rather to a confrontation with another Christian (Petrine) tradition.[21]

Schenke's evaluation of the Beloved-Disciple passages suggests that they all have been edited by the redactor, not only John 21 but also John 13:23–26 and John 20:1–10 (Schenke also places John 19:35 with these passages). This interpretation rightly acknowledges the way in which the Beloved Disciple usually accompanies and outranks Peter in the Gospel of John.

At 19:26–27, however, the Beloved Disciple does not appear alongside Peter, but rather is described at the cross with the mother of Jesus. Schenke

---

20 Schenke, "Function and Background," 123.
21 Schenke, "Function and Background," 119.

observes, "The intention of 19:26–27 is to have the Beloved Disciple, in the dying-hour of Jesus, appointed his successor on earth."[22] That is accomplished by means of this scene that allows the Beloved Disciple to be adopted, as it were, into the family of Jesus, so that he becomes the brother of Jesus. This observation, then, allows Schenke to turn to the figure of Judas Thomas as a close disciple and beloved brother of Jesus and to propose that he may have served as the prototype (Schenke uses the term "historical model") for the Johannine Beloved Disciple. If this is the case, then the role of Thomas would be doubled in the Gospel of John, since the figure of Thomas also appears in John 11:16; 14:5, 22(?); 20:24, 26–28; 21:2. Schenke sees no difficulty in such doubling and concludes, "Finally it seems easy to reverse the whole question and to look upon the conspicuous role that Thomas plays in the text of the unrevised Fourth Gospel as created under the influence of the same Syrian Judas Thomas tradition, which, then, would have affected the Fourth Gospel at two stages in its development."[23]

Schenke's basic thesis concerning the fictional character of the Beloved Disciple is persuasive, in a certain way of considering it, and his reconstruction of the function of the Beloved Disciple in John is at least a plausible alternative to Bultmann's, but I find his argument on the background of "the disciple whom Jesus loved" to be weak. To be sure, gnostic documents show that other figures such as Mary Magdalene, James the Just, and Judas Thomas could be singled out, in a general way, as beloved disciples, that is, as disciples judged to have a special role and authority within the Christian tradition. To this extent the motif of the Beloved Disciple may have a fairly wide application within various early Christian communities. In order to identify Judas Thomas as the "historical model" for the Beloved Disciple in John, however, Schenke must engage in what seems to me to be a forced reading and interpretation of texts on Thomas, in particular the opening page of the *Book of Thomas* from the Nag Hammadi library. Further, his insistence upon reading the Beloved Disciple passages "backwards" (i.e., from chapter 21 back to the other passages) allows for an important way of establishing a redactional uniformity to the passages on "the disciple whom Jesus loved," contrary to Bultmann, but it also may prevent him from giving appropriate attention to another passage that will elucidate the background of the Beloved Disciple. That passage is John 11, with its account of Lazarus, the beloved follower of Jesus who, we have seen, seems to be linked literarily with the youth in the Secret Gospel of Mark.

Schenke, too, raises the issue of the Markan youth and the Johannine Beloved Disciple, but he dismisses the parallels as being only apparent. He raises three objections,[24] and each may be answered. (1) He emphasizes the

22 Schenke, "Function and Background," 119.
23 Schenke, "Function and Background," 125.
24 Schenke, "Function and Background," 120–21.

difference between the youth's loving Jesus in the first section cited from the Secret Gospel of Mark and Jesus' loving the Beloved Disciple in John. But Schenke virtually ignores the significance of the second section of Secret Mark cited by Clement (with its reference to "the youth whom Jesus loved" [ὁ νεανίσκος ὃν ἠγάπα αὐτὸν ὁ 'Ιησοῦς], 2r,15) and also does not recognize the Markan sub-plot and the place of Mark 10:21 (with its reference to Jesus loving the rich youth) within the sub-plot. (2) Schenke stresses that the love of Jesus for the Johannine Beloved Disciple has an exclusive quality, while the love for the Markan youth does not. In the Secret Gospel of Mark, we might reply, the claims to exclusivity may be subtler, but they still are there. After all, Secret Mark characterizes the youth as a disciple of paradigmatic significance and describes him as one "whom Jesus loved" over against the women whom Jesus did not receive. (3) Schenke points out the differences in role between the Markan youth, representative of cultic interests (i.e., baptism and initiation), and the Johannine Beloved Disciple, a more historicized figure. These distinctions are valid (although we should not ignore the cultic interests of John 13), but they stem mainly from the redactional development of the youth in Mark and of the Beloved Disciple in John.

Hence, I propose that the prototype or "historical model" of the Beloved Disciple may best be understood to be the paradigmatic youth who is presented as the νεανίσκος in Secret Mark and as Lazarus in John. By suggesting this thesis I am building, in part, upon the position of Bultmann and others who have asserted that the Beloved Disciple as depicted by the Johannine evangelist (as opposed to the figure developed by the redactor) "is an ideal figure."[25] I am also appreciative of the scholars who previously have seen the clear ties between Lazarus and the Beloved Disciple.[26] Just as the youth in Secret Mark embodies Mark's vision of the life of discipleship, so also Lazarus as Beloved Disciple illustrates the ideal of the follower of Christ who has been raised to new life. This symbolic disciple is depicted in a less developed manner in Mark and in a more expanded and historicized fashion in John. Very possibly this idealized figure emerged from an early aretalogical source (cf. pre-Markan miracle stories, or the pre-Johannine Semeia-Quelle), and the figure was taken over and adapted by Mark and John. In John the author or redactor not only developed the story of beloved Lazarus to meet the needs of the gospel. The author or redactor (subsequently?) also introduced the Beloved Disciple into several other portions of the evolving gospel, perhaps in more than one stage, the result being an increasingly historicized presentation of the Beloved Disciple as the witness, authority, and even author (cf. 21:24) of the gospel. This presentation discloses an ideal disciple who surpasses Peter and who "saw and believed" at the tomb (20:8) but who in turn

25 Bultmann, *The Gospel of John*, 484. Cf. also Brown, *The Gospel According to John I–XII*, xciv–xcv, also 924: "There is little doubt that in Johannine thought the Beloved Disciple can symbolize the Christian."
26 E.g., Filson, "Who Was the Beloved Disciple?"

is surpassed by the implied readers, who are pronounced blessed as "those who have not seen and yet have believed" (20:29). Thus the youth in the Secret Gospel of Mark may shed important new light on the Gospel of John and may encourage us to reevaluate, once again, the place of the Beloved Disciple within that gospel.

James M. Robinson with Birger Pearson (Photograph courtesy of the Institute for Antiquity and Christianity)

viii

Strategies of
Social Formation
in the Gospel of Luke

Petr Pokorný

1. The Model of Social Relations

The Gospel of Luke has often been called a social gospel, for it is full of texts dealing with social problems, from Mary's Magnificat to the stories about the Good Samaritan or poor Lazarus. In some respects this also applies to the Book of Acts written by the same author. In keeping with the old tradition we shall call him Luke.

The social motifs are not simply created by Luke, but their selection and interpretation express his theological view at a time when the church had to cope with the long-term prospect of its way through history.[1] For Luke the Kingdom of God is the common expression of both Jesus' proclamation and the post-Easter message as in Acts 19:8; 28:31; and Luke 4:43. In the synoptic tradition, the Kingdom of God is a keyword for a multi-dimensional reality, and Luke has stressed that it also includes a vision of social justice, which is expressed in two ways.

1.1 Eschatological exchange

First, Luke availed himself of a semantic code, which is mostly used in a parenetic context. It is the code of eschatological exchange, which could be characterized by the saying, "The last will be first and the first last" (Luke 13:30 par.), expressing the eschatological reappraisal of contemporary values. In the *Apocalypse of Ezra* (5:42) a similar saying expresses the universality of the last judgement, which will apply to all generations, like the second coming of Jesus Christ as found in 1 Thess 4:15–17. In Luke the apocalyptic background is still recognizable, but the intention of the saying is to give a warning to those of God's people who do not do God's will, and in the wider Lukan context it also expresses the relativity of given social discrepancies. In the view of the Kingdom of God, the poor are blessed and the rich are warned (Luke 6:20–26), the hungry will surely be filled with good things and the rich sent

---

1 Conzelmann, *Mitte*, 80ff.; Bovon, *Luc*, 21ff.; Fitzmyer, *The Gospel According to Luke I– IX*, 171ff.; Rese, "Das Lukas-Evangelium," 2300ff.

empty away (Luke 1:53). The rich man is humiliated and poor Lazarus raised up to heaven (Luke 16:19–31). This is a consistent thread of an early Christian tradition that Luke must have taken over from a Christian group that also knew the sayings of Jesus from the source Q. Most probably, some sayings such as the four woes (Luke 6:24–26) were even formulated in this setting. An expectation of social exchange obviously shaped the entire life of such groups, which in their social structure can to some degree be compared to the Essene community from Qumran.[2] The members of such groups considered themselves as the "humble" (ταπεινοί—Luke 1:52) or "poor" (πτωχοί—Luke 6:20).[3] A literary parallel are the *poor* (Coptic ϩΗΚΕ) from the *Acts of Peter and the Twelve Apostles* (NHC VI,*1*). They win the precious pearl, since they are not burdened by their riches.[4] The motifs of wandering and of bread for a single day[5] hint at the groups of prophets who, unlike Qumran people, wandered from one Palestinian village to another,[6] keeping their distance from the civilization of the Hellenistic cities with its *greed* (πλεονεξία—Luke 12:15) and consumerist life (Luke 15:13). Luke tried to remind the church of the legacy of these groups. He introduced Jesus as a child of poor parents (Luke 2:7), and in the parable about the Great Supper he spoke of the promised raising up of the poor.[7] In Luke we even meet elements of encratite practice abolishing marriage.[8] Luke did not concentrate only on this trajectory, but he appreciated it.

1.2 Compensation

The second means used by Luke to express the structure of Christian hope is the concept of compensation. It expresses the hope more deeply than does the code of eschatological exchange. According to this concept the Kingdom of God is the realm of social justice. Luke found an expression of it in Isa 40:4, where we read about the raising up of the valleys and the lowering of the mountains (Luke 3:5). Originally a metaphor of an eschatological royal road towards the new land of promise it became for Luke an expression of the Kingdom of God itself. The *lowering* (ταπεινοῦν) of mountains is the humbling of those who make themselves great (Luke 18:14; cf. 1:48), and the raising of valleys means the overcoming of poverty and humiliation. Yet it is more than a mere warning for the rich and proud, and more than consolation for the humble and poor. The image of leveled land also expresses the result of eschatological compensation, the structure of the new creation where there

2 Braun, *Qumran*, 1.143ff.
3 Cf. also 1QM 14,7; *Pss. Sol.* 5:2,11; 10:6; 1 Enoch 99–105; nevertheless we cannot prove that the members of these groups also called themselves "the poor"; see Keck, "The Poor," passim.
4 NHC VI,*1*; 3,1–5,1; 7,25ff.; 10,8ff.
5 NHC VI,*1*; 10,19; 5,28ff.; cf. Luke 11:3.
6 Theissen, "Wanderradikalismus," 84ff.
7 Luke 14:15–24; GThom 64; cf. Matt 22:1–10.
8 Luke 14:26; 17:27; 20:34–36; Acts 24:25; Klauck, "Armut," passim.

will be neither oppressors nor oppressed, neither rich nor poor. This can be derived from the following parenetic passage (Luke 3:10f.).[9] This is why Luke (6:17) has introduced the collection of sayings of Jesus—the parallel to the Matthean Sermon on the Mount—as words pronounced on a level place, i.e., on the eschatological plain. He tried to express that those sayings contain the rules of a new age when the social discrepancies will be leveled. The expanded quotation of Isaiah 40 in Luke 3, containing the sentence on eschatological leveling, is quite probably the key to understanding the theological function of the Lukan frame of sayings in Luke 6:20ff.[10] From this point of view the meaning of the beatitudes of the poor and woes of the rich is not simply to interchange their positions, but to proclaim new and just relations: "There should be no poor among you" (Deut 15:4a). What we have said about Luke's idea of social hope on the basis of Luke 3:5 and 6:17 can be supported by further indirect evidence. In the parable about the Prodigal Son, the house of the father is characterized as a place where all have bread enough (Luke 15:17), and at the beginning of his public activity Jesus reads and comments on Isa 61:1–2a—a text dealing with the year of the Lord's favor. This meant restoration of just relations among humans (Luke 4:18ff.).[11] The most convincing argument for such a model of social equality in Luke is his report on the life of the earliest Christian community in Jerusalem:

"All the believers were together and had everything in common" (Acts 2:44).[12] "Now the company of those who believed were of one heart and soul, and no one said that any of the things which he possessed was his own, but they had everything in common, and with great power the apostles gave their testimony to the resurrection of the Lord Jesus, and great grace was upon them all. There was not a needy person among them, for as many as were possessors of lands or houses sold them and brought the proceeds of what was sold and laid it at the apostles' feet; and distribution was made to each as any had need" (Acts 4:32–35).[13]

This undoubtedly reflects the trends in earliest Christianity evoked by the expectation of imminent eschatological change;[14] but in Luke this memory was pointed out and reshaped so that it might represent an archetype for social relations.[15] Thereby Luke demonstrated one dimension of God's mercy, since mercy has to be shared (Luke 6:36).

Historically it is an idealized image created by Luke, but theologically it is the eschatological structure put into history as a pattern and promise at the same time. What in Mark 10:30 is an anticipation of the eschatological reward in "this age" and what is expressed very briefly in the Lukan parallel (Luke

9 Kahl, *Armenevangelium*, 176–77.
10 Mánek, "On the Mount," passim.
11 Pilgrim, *Good News to the Poor*, 64ff.; Esler, *Community*, 164ff.
12 Translation: New International Version.
13 Translation here as well as page 110 and page 117: Revised Standard Version.
14 Hengel, *Eigentum*, 39–42.
15 Horn, *Glauben und Handeln*, 40–41; cf. Degenhardt, *Lukas*, 168–69.

18:30),[16] Luke has developed in his image of early Christian social life. Such an egalitarian program is at variance with economic tendencies towards profitability[17] and cannot change the wider society, but as a model of a christocentric community it contributed to the group identity of early Christians.[18]

2. Parallels in Antiquity

To discover the intention of the Lukan pattern of social justice, we need to compare it with similar concepts in ancient religions and philosophy.

2.1 Qumran

The community of goods as described in Acts 2 and 4 is often compared with the community of goods among the Essenes at Qumran.[19] In both cases the members of the community shared all their possessions, and the groups considered themselves to be the people of God and most probably the spiritual temple with spiritual sacrifices. That is why they have no possessions, like all the tribe of Levi.[20] The Christians also gathered in the temple (Acts 2:46). However, there are also striking differences. First, both texts are of a different literary genre. Acts 2:44–45 and 4:32, 35 are summaries[21] in which Luke tries to characterize the first pure and classical response to the Easter and Pentecost events, whereas the *Manual of Discipline* (1QS) is a set of instructions concerning common life.[22] According to Luke, the sharing of possessions was spontaneous, according to the *Manual* it was regulated by legal orders.

2.2 Greek mind

Another comparable text, which is often quoted in commentaries on Acts 2:44–45, is the third chapter of Plato's *Republic* (3.416C–E, cf. 5.464D). In Plato's ideal city the class of warriors and *officers* of state ($\phi\acute{v}\lambda\alpha\kappa\epsilon\varsigma$) must not gain any personal possessions. Robert von Pöhlmann in his "History of the Social Question"[23] characterized these ideas as a kind of ancient socialism. But this is a false opinion, since Plato's ideal city is organized strictly according to the various classes. The warriors consume what has been produced by artisans, who do not share their possessions.[24] So the Platonic utopia is not any analogy to the Lukan image of the first Christians. Nevertheless Pöhlmann is correct

---

16 Schottroff und Stegemann, *Jesus,* 149ff.
17 Kippenberg, *Religion und Klassenbildung,* 155.
18 Pilgrim, *good News to the Poor,* 147ff.
19 1QS 1,1–13; 6,16–25; 7,6–7; Josephus, *Bellum Judaicum* 2.122; for a survey see Braun, *Qumran,* 1.143ff.
20 Klauck, "Gütergemeinschaft," 67.
21 Conzelmann, *Apostelgeschichte,* 31, 38.
22 Klauck, "Gütergemeinschaft," 66–67.
23 Pöhlmann, *Geschichte,* 84ff.
24 See the criticism of Pöhlmann's theories in Asmus, *Antichnaya filosofia,* chap. IV,7.

on one point: In Hellenism and in the early period of the Roman Empire some social utopias, including those that proclaimed sharing of all possessions, were linked with the Platonic heritage.

The Pythagorean tradition, which for centuries survived in secret associations and re-emerged in the first century CE, also derived the community of goods from Platonic ideas. According to the report of the Neoplatonist Iamblichus of Chalkis, the Pythagorean community of goods had a general significance: It was an expression of righteousness. All the members of the community supported common needs, and if need be they offered all their possessions. The "alienation" (ἀλλοτρίωσις) of common goods is there the root of injustice.[25] The parallels between this text and Acts 2 and 4 are obvious:

ἀρχή τοίνυν ἐστὶ δικαιοσύνης μὲν τὸ κοινὸν καὶ ἴσον καὶ ἐγγυτάτω ἑνὸς σώματος καὶ μιᾶς ψυχῆς ὁμοπαθεῖν πάντας καὶ ἐπὶ τὸ αὐτὸ τὸ ἐμόν φθέγγεσθαι καὶ τὸ ἀλλότριον . . . ἴδιον δὲ οὐδεὶς οὐδὲν ἐκέκτητο.

The origin of righteousness derives from a sharing in common, an equality, where all have the same close affection (for one another) as in one body and one soul; thus, they refer to the same thing as "mine" and "yours." . . . No one possessed anything as their own.[26]

πάντες δὲ οἱ πιστεύοντες ἦσαν ἐπὶ τὸ αὐτὸ καὶ εἶχον ἅπαντα κοινά . . . τοῦ δὲ πλήθους τῶν πιστευσάντων ἦν καρδία καὶ ψυχὴ μία, καὶ οὐδὲ εἷς τι τῶν ὑπαρχόντων αὐτῷ ἔλεγεν ἴδιον εἶναι, ἀλλ ἦν αὐτοῖς ἅπαντα κοινά.

And all who believed were together and had all things in common. . . . Now the company of those who believed were of one heart and soul, and no one said that any of the things which he possessed was his own, but they had everything in common.[27]

Under the partial influence of early Christian traditions the idea of *equality* (ἰσότης) and sharing *in common* (κοινότης) reappeared in the social concept of the gnostic teacher Epiphanes, the son of Carpocrates.[28]

Luke must have been familiar with both the social life of the community in Qumran and the Platonic-Pythagorean ideas. Both these traditions influenced his image of the first Christian congregation in Jerusalem. From Essenes he knew about the practice of common life, and the idea of common responsibility and sharing is derived from the Greek traditions that we have discussed.

25 Iamblichus, *de vita Pythagorica* 30.168; cf. Theissen, "Die soziologische Auswertung," 37. In some respect Iamblichus developed the widespread idea about the sharing of *possessions among friends* (κοινὰ τὰ φίλων); e.g., Plato, *Republica* 4.424A; *Phaedrus* 279C; Euripides, *Orestes* 735; Plutarch, *Coniugalia praecepta* 34; Cicero, *de Officiis* 1.16; Diogenes Laertius 8.10; cf. 10.11. For further evidence see also Mealand, "Community of Goods," passim.
26 Iamblichus, *de Vita Pythagorica*, from 30.167 and 168.
27 Acts 2:44 and 4:32; cf. Klauck, "Gütergemeinschaft," 72–73.
28 Clemens Alexandrinus, *Stromateis* 3.7.1–4; Hauschild, "Christentum und Eigentum," 40–41.

3. Lukan Theological Frame

The Lukan idealized report about the life of the first Christians in Jerusalem not only was influenced by a number of Jewish and Hellenistic traditions, but also appears in a specific theological and literary frame through which Luke tried to resolve the problem of history and God's revelation in Jesus Christ.

Against the background of the Jewish apocalyptic expectation, from which Christian theology took over its basic language (resurrection, Messiah, new age, etc.), the post-Easter reality seemed to introduce a kind of "telescoped" eschatology. The ages overlap: The conditions of the old age survive, but in Jesus Christ the future has already been present; the eschatological dimension has been revealed in history. Paul was already aware of it, but Luke, even if his theological reflection was not so penetrating as Paul's, dared to draw wider consequences for the concept of history. The revelation in Jesus Christ no longer marks the apocalyptic end of history. "The end will not be at once" (Luke 21:9). Hans Conzelmann was right when he proclaimed that according to Luke, Jesus Christ becomes the center of time.[29] Less convincing is Conzelmann's thesis about Luke as theologian of "salvation history," who has divided history into three parts: before Christ, the earthly presence of Christ, and the history of the church.[30] Luke did not intend to write a continuous church history. He concentrated his attention on Jesus Christ as God's revelation and on the apostolic time, which is the archetype of the true reception of the revelation. These are the criteria for all further Christian witness. The story of Paul was included because Paul, being no apostle himself,[31] took over the apostolic mission from Acts 1:8.[32] According to Acts 1:1, 21–22, Jesus is the beginning and norm for the post-Easter witness, and according to Acts 2:4 the Pentecostal experience is the norm for all the subsequent manifestations of the spirit (11:15). So the summaries in Acts 2 and 4 are primarily a part of the ideal pattern of Christian behavior.[33] It is neither a mythical archetype, as was the community of soil in the Golden Age[34] nor a speculative one like Plato's *Republic* or the Utopias of Euhemerus or Iamblichus. For Luke as a Christian the eschatological archetype is a part of history. Undoubtedly many of the early Christians used to share their possessions at least to some degree. An indirect witness is Lucian of Samosata mocking the credulity of Christians who from their common goods support the suffering people.[35] But above all the Lukan report about the first Christians in Jerusalem expresses the challenge of revelation in Jesus Christ, which happened in history. According to

---

29 Conzelmann, *Mitte*, 146–47; Esler, *Community*, 64ff.
30 Esler, *Community*, 8.
31 Brox, *Zeuge*, 53ff.
32 See Acts 13:47.
33 It is more than a model of a fulfilled prophecy, as maintains Johnson, *Literary Function*, 192ff.
34 Ovid, *Metamorphoses* 1.135.
35 *de Morte peregrini* 13.

the rules of ancient historiography, which was always written with an educational intention,[36] Luke idealized the first reaction to Pentecost. In reality the Jerusalem congregation soon needed support from other congregations.[37] But the image in Acts is a part of historized eschatology as the ideal response to revelation.

4. The Reality

There is visible tension in the Lukan image of the early church. On the one hand there is the eschatological compensation and sharing of all possessions,[38] and on the other hand there are rich rulers and officers like Sergius Paulus (Acts 13:7–12) who become Christians and obviously remained in their luxurious houses, supporting the socially underprivileged Christians, as their patrons.[39] On the one hand is the demand of discipleship in absolute poverty, on the other hand the collection of alms for the benefit of the poor in Jerusalem (Acts 11:27–30). On the one hand Jesus Christ is expected to "bring down rulers from their thrones" (Luke 1:52), on the other hand his parents obey the decree of Caesar Augustus (Luke 2:1ff.), and Paul appeals to the Emperor to decide his plea (Acts 25:11).[40] There are transitions between such extremes. The chief tax collector Zacchaeus, when he accepts Jesus, decides to give half of his possessions to the poor,[41] and Ananias and Sapphira were expected to declare frankly what part of their possessions they would put at the disposal of the congregation (Acts 5:1–11). A historically valuable note about women supporting Jesus and his disciples in Luke 8:1–3 reveals that the traveling group of Jesus' followers was dependant on settled groups of wealthier persons,[42] and Luke was certainly no radical charismatic himself.[43] How did he reconcile the two tendencies theologically?

4.1 Various sources

We can deal with this problem by pushing it theologically aside, i.e., by ascribing the ideal image and the realistic one to various sources, or to a source and to Luke himself, for example. In that case the "moderate" view would reflect the later period, in which the original imminent expectation faded.

---

36 This esp. Polybius proclaimed as the father of pragmatic historiography in the introduction to his Universal History.
37 Gal 2:10; Georgi, *Geschichte*, 22–23; Gewalt, "Exegese," passim.
38 See also Luke 5:11—giving up "all" (πάντα), which is stressed by Luke himself (Luke 12:33; 18:22); cf. Pilgrim, *Good News to the Poor*, 87.
39 Judge, *Social Pattern*, chap. 6; Meeks, *First Urban Christians*, 52–53; Esler, *Community*, 61ff.; Luke himself was supported by Theophilus—Luke 1:3; Acts 1:1.
40 It was Schroeder who formulated this problem: "Haben Jesu Worte . . .," passim.
41 Luke 19:8; Pilgrim, *Good News to the Poor*, 129. Pilgrim concentrates on the "realistic" features of Lukan social strategy.
42 Theissen, *Soziologie der Jesusbewegung*, 21ff. About the wealthier Christians see Hengel, *Eigentum*, 69–70.
43 Horn, *Glauben und Handeln*, 187. On the whole, Horn tries to diminish the radicality of Luke's social demand.

This explains much, but it is not yet any solution of the problem. Luke must have had an idea of how these different attitudes are related to each other.

4.2 Inconsistency of Luke?

A possible answer, theoretically, is to criticize Luke as an inconsistent theologian who gave up the gospel of the poor in favor of the compromise that was necessary in order that the church, which consisted of former Jews and pagans, might survive.[44] Nor can this view be rejected as totally false, since Luke has taken the given situation very seriously. Nevertheless our first task is to investigate how Luke coped with it theologically.

4.3 Different situations

According to Walther Schmithals, the radical social demands in Luke are conditioned by a situation of persecution.[45] But Luke omitted the references to the oppression, which were contained in his sources.[46] He may have done it for apologetical reasons, but in that case his radical demands would be incomprehensible. So this is not the way towards a solution of the problem.

4.4 Various addressees

4.4.1 H.-J. Degenhardt.   According to H.-J. Degenhardt, the radical demands of Jesus in the sense of the *consilia*, "advice," as it was formulated in later Christian tradition, were destined for the disciples as a special group, and Luke applies them to the Christian officials and missionaries; whereas, the other exhortations in the sense of *praecepta*, "demands," as, e.g., alms and the love of one's neighbor in general, are intended for all Christians. The beatitudes apply to a special group of poor who consciously gave up their possessions, whereas the woes are aimed at the rich who oppose Jesus.[47] This is an inaccurate solution. Jesus certainly distinguished between his disciples and other people, but his promises,[48] as well as his demands,[49] express the radical and total character of his eschatological challenge.[50] The function of the "Blessed are you poor, since yours is the Kingdom of God" (Luke 6:20) is to characterize the Kingdom of God as a realm where there will be no poverty.[51] The radical demands, even if they were developed as direct instructions in some ascetic Jewish-Christian groups, were not understood by Luke as intended for Christian leaders only. He even underlined that this applies to the "crowds" (Luke 14:25). So we cannot identify ourselves with Degenhardt's solution.

4.4.2 Luise Schottroff.   Another attempt at distinguishing various groups

---

44 So, e.g., Kahl, *Armenevangelium,* 165ff, 195.
45 Schmithals, *Einleitung,* 356.
46 Cf. Luke 8:13 with Mark 4:17; and Luke 18:30 with Mark 10:30.
47 Degenhardt, *Lukas,* 211–22; cf. 50–51, 53.
48 E.g., the beatitude of the poor, Luke 6:20.
49 E.g., the saying about the "hating" of one's parents, etc.—Luke 14:26 par.
50 Perrin, *Rediscovering,* 141–42.
51 Bovon, *Luc,* 412.

of addressees of Jesus' sayings and of different bearers of the two threads of tradition was submitted by Luise Schottroff. According to her, the exhortations to love one's enemies and to give up possessions are intended for the wealthy Christians, whereas the beatitudes are directed at the poor.[52] While Degenhardt tried to blunt the social edge of the gospel tradition, Schottroff has sharpened it. But in Luke 6:27 the new saying is simply addressed to the poor of 6:20–23 after the inserted woes, which were intended for the absent rich people (6:24–26). The same people are blessed and exhorted to love their enemies.

We have to suppose that the Gospel of Luke addressed various groups, but the differences between them are not identical with the difference between the ideal and blessed image of social life and the report about the real life of Jesus' disciples and the early church in Luke and Acts.

4.5 Editorial intention

The inner tension in the Lukan image of the Christian social life must be a part of Lukan editorial intention. He obviously tried to confront the ideal archetype, which was linked with the centre of time, with its secondary effect in history. We have to discuss this strategy in a separate section. Anyway, the aim of the confrontation was to exhort and to teach.

5. Lukan Social Strategy

5.1 Exhortation

First, Luke took advantage of the differences in Christian traditions by taking the radical pattern as the norm for subsequent history. The history with its absurdities (the rejection of Jesus, tension between Jewish and Hellenistic Christians, etc.) is not the norm in itself, even if it is a history of a church that is successful in mission, and even if the history is narrated in a harmonized way. The original response to Easter and Pentecost is the point of view from which the life of the church has to be judged. This classical period of christocentric theocracy[53] is understood as an exhortation to take up a new attitude towards possessions. After the parable of the rich fool we read a warning against greed, which also includes the exhortation "to be rich with God" (Luke 12:21), and twice we read about exalting the humble and humbling the exalted.[54] The poor and oppressed[55] are those who are protected by God, as in a number of Psalms[56] or in Qumran.[57] In this respect Luke

---

52 Schottroff und Stegemann, *Jesus*, 145, 149–50.
53 Depicted also by help of some older radical ideas and sayings.
54 Luke 14:11=SLuke; Luke 18:14=Q.
55 Πτωχός, πένης; in Hebr. ānî or ānāv.
56 E.g., Ps 25:16=LXX 24:16.
57 4QpPs 3,10–11 to Ps 37:21–22; that is what Lohse, "Das Evangelium," passim, and Johnson, *Sharing possessions*, 32ff., have stressed; cf. also Karris, "Poor and Rich," 124–25.

merely developed an older tendency towards spiritual evaluation of poverty. In one stream of Christian moral teaching it developed into a theory of inner distance towards possessions, which was also widespread in Hellenistic Jewry.[58] Principally this attitude was compatible with social differentiation inside the church, as was later expressed by Clement of Alexandria in his *Quis dives salvetur?*[59]

Although this tendency is present in Lukan writings, it does not express the author's main intention. Luke does not consider the classical pattern of community of goods to be only an expression of trust in God. The demand to give up property (Luke 14:33; 12:33; cf. Matt 6:19) is intended as a real challenge for the readers and as an exhortation to real social solidarity. Luke even radicalized some exhortations concerning social behavior.[60]

Nevertheless, even this was not the deepest intention of Luke when he bound together the ideal image of the classical period and the more or less realistic telling of history. His aim was not only to contrast the archetype with the reality. This is palpable only in a few passages,[61] but on the whole, Luke also presents the compromises in a positive way. The collection organized for the starving Christians in Jerusalem is certainly rather the giving of alms than the sharing of possessions, but it is still characterized as providing relief (Acts 11:27–30; 12:25). Lydia in Philippi is praised for hosting the missionaries (Acts 16:15), even if she did not give up her goods etc.[62] So exhortation is not the main intention of Luke's social strategy.

5.2 A model of effective grace

Luke obviously understood the alms for the poor, the support for those who proclaim the gospel (e.g., Luke 8:3; Acts 16:15; 17:4, 12), the collection for relief in the famine (Acts 11:27–30), and the support of widows (Acts 6:1ff.) as a demonstration of effective influence of God's revelation in Jesus Christ upon history. He certainly considered the collection for the starving to be a response to Jesus' proclamation of the Kingdom of God and to Pentecost. It was a very indirect and sometimes even inconsistent response, but it demonstrated to later generations that the gospel is not a mere idea. What happened in the centre of time is effective in subsequent history, and the Holy Spirit "works" in all dimensions of life, including the social sphere. Its activity may be weakened by human inconsistency and overshadowed by great movements and the decisions of rulers (Luke 2:1–2; 3:1–2), but nevertheless the new age has really started. The *Leitmotif* in world history of this age is the acts of mercy,

58 E.g., *Pseudo Phocylides* 106–15.
59 Hauschild, "Christentum und Eigentum," 36–37.
60 Cf., e.g., Luke 5:11 with Mark 1:20 par. or Luke 14:26 with Matt 10:37.
61 For example we can observe an intended contrast between the image of sharing in Acts 4 and the story of Ananias and Sapphira in Acts 5.
62 Cf. Tabitha in Joppa—Acts 9:36; Klauck, "Armut," 5–17.

reconciliation, and hospitality accompanying the public proclamation of the Kingdom of God (Acts 26:26).

The realism of Luke is not any simple accommodation to the conditions of this world. It is the Kingdom of God in its coming that is the axis of history, and it is the full sharing in the early community that corresponds fully to God's grace and that remains, according to Luke, the undeniable norm for all social activity. This way Luke hinted at the strategy of Christian social responsibility,[63] which was otherwise expressed in individual exhortations to support the common need.[64] In the world of today, in which the disproportion between developed and undeveloped nations, including Christians in developed and undeveloped nations, is becoming the main problem, the Lukan view of economic sharing as a necessary consequence of ecumenical communion becomes topical once again.

It seems as if Luke had recognized the necessity of interaction between the intention (in our case grace, as fully shared among humans) and the real function of a social model in history as it was described by contemporary sociology. Without the radical norm, the activity would degenerate and accommodate, and the group could lose its identity. Without the real social activity, which necessarily includes compromises, the group would be isolated as a sect.[65]

6. Theological Background

The theological background of the Lukan social strategy depends on the theological frame of his work as a whole, in which the apostolic age is the age of the classical and inspired response to the revelation in Jesus Christ.[66] Paul is the last representative of this period, and his farewell to the elders in Ephesus, which is his spiritual testament,[67] reveals the main theological features of Lukan social strategy. Paul declares that he did not claim any support from the Christian congregations[68] but worked with his own hands,[69] in order that he might support himself and his companions (Acts 20:33–35a). Now he faces hardship including the sacrifice of his own life when testifying to the gospel of grace (20:22–24). This is the blending of the ideal Christian of the apostolic age and the ideal of the disciple of Jesus. Paul also warns against false teachers who will distort the truth of the Gospel and break up the Christian community

---

63 Later it was Basil of Caesarea and Gregory of Nazianzus who supported the Lukan idea of social sharing—unfortunately solitary phenomena in the church of that time; see Hauschild, "Christentum und Eigentum," 43–44.

64 Rom 12:13; Gal 6:6; Phil 4:14–15; 1 Tim 6:18; Heb 13:16; 1 Clem 48:6; Barn 4:10; Did 4:8; Popkes, "Gemeinschaft," 1133–34.

65 Cf. Theissen, "Theoretische Probleme," passim; Klauck, "Armut," 46–47.

66 See above, section 3.

67 Michel, Abschiedsrede, 48ff.

68 Cf. 1 Cor 9:1–18.

69 Cf. 1 Cor 4:12.

(20:29–31). Indirectly we learn that the ideological counterpart of social disintegration is discrimination in teaching: The false teachers obviously kept some parts of Christian teaching for a special group only. This must be the reason that Paul declares that he always taught in public what was necessary for salvation (20:20).[70] Sound social behavior is linked with sound teaching. The very grace of God is a grace shared in all respects with other men and women. This is the deepest theological background of both mission and social responsibility. Paul's testament at Miletus culminates with a maxim declared as a saying of Jesus. It is the summary of Luke's social strategy: "It is more blessed to give than to receive" (Acts 20:35). The maxim itself has many parallels in ancient philosophy.[71] The most contemporaneous parallel is in Seneca (*Epistulae* 81.17). The context there is clearly stoic, but by taking up this well-known maxim and declaring it to be a saying of Jesus, which of course cannot be ruled out, Luke tried to demonstrate that the gospel is the fulfillment of basic human destiny (cf. Acts 17:16ff.). Jesus as the Son of God is also the true new Adam (cf. Luke 3:23–38), an incarnation of the destiny of all humankind —of the one family of God (Acts 17:28). To repent and turn towards God is therefore to overcome the alienation caused by sin and to become human indeed. The maxim from Acts 20:35 is in fact only a second part of Lukan ethics. The first, the vertical one, is expressed in the maxim, "to obey God rather than men" (Acts 5:29; cf. 4:19), which is especially valid within God's people.[72] Both these maxims have a similar shape:

πειθαρχεῖν δεῖ θεῷ μᾶλλον ἢ τοῖς ἀνθρώποις
"We must obey God rather than men" (Acts 5:29).

μακάριόν ἐστι μᾶλλον διδόναι ἢ λαμβάνειν
"It is more blessed to give than to receive" (Acts 20:35).

The first one also has parallels in the Greek tradition, particularly in Plato's Apology of Socrates. There, Socrates says that he obeys God rather than the Athenians, even if he likes them:

". . . πείσομαι δὲ μᾶλλον τῷ θεῷ ἢ ὑμῖν
"I shall obey God rather than you" (*Apol.* 29C).[73]

Expressed briefly, Lukan ethics says that to obey the one and true God means also to share possessions, and that the deepest motivation for sharing is to turn towards the true God, who is the source of sharing.[74] The event in which both the dimensions of life, i.e., communication with God and with

---

70 This may be an allusion to a gnostic or pre-gnostic teaching; Talbert, *Luke*, 49ff.
71 Thucydides 2.97.4; Plutarch, *Moralia* 173D; 778C; Aelian, *Varia Historia* 13.13; cf. Barn 19:8 etc.; see also Talbert, *Luke*, 90–91.
72 Conzelmann, *Mitte*, 127.
73 Hommel, "Herrenworte," passim.
74 Luke 10:22; 22:27; Bovon, *Luc*, 427.

other humans, meet, is the Lord's Supper (see Acts 2:42–47), where the Christians "remembered"[75] the unique service of Jesus for others. We can say that it was a "remembrance of the future"—a contemporization of the "today" of Jesus' presence, of the centre of time. In the light of this concept of the Lord's Supper, all meals became significant, especially the meals of Jesus' tradition: Luke 7:36–50; 9:16–17; 11:37–54; 14:1–24; 15:23–24; 19:1–10; 22:4–38; 24:29–43. The "remembrance" also included a model as well as a mighty impulsion for sharing bread justly in daily life, too (cf. Acts 6:1–4). The "today" ($\sigma\acute{\eta}\mu\epsilon\rho\sigma\nu$) of Jesus' earthly presence[76] becomes "perpetualized" through the Holy Spirit and transformed into an "each day" ($\kappa\alpha\theta$' $\acute{\eta}\mu\acute{\epsilon}\rho\alpha\nu$) of Christian conversions (Acts 2:47), of taking the cross (Luke 9:23), of prayers for bread (Luke 11:3; cf. Matt 6:11), and of sharing it (Acts 2:46; 6:1).[77] Thus Lukan social strategy is closely linked with his theology.

7. Addendum

Only after I have written this article I came across the monograph of David P. Seccombe, *Possessions and the Poor in Luke-Acts.* Studien zum Neuen Testament and seiner Umwelt. Linz: A. Fuchs, 1982, which I consider to be a good contribution to our problem. My article can be considered a complementary expansion of his conclusions.

75 Luke 22:13–20 parr.
76 Luke 2:11; 4:21; 19:5, 9; 23:43; Conzelmann, *Mitte,* 169–70.
77 The rediscovery of the Lord's Supper as an anticipation of the Kingdom of God and as mutual sharing led towards re-shaping society in later periods of church history also, especially in the Czech reformation: Molnár, "L'évolution," passim. For the impact of Lukan social ideas in the ancient church see Klauck, "Armut," 45–47.

First Jesus Is Present, Then the Spirit

AN EARLY CHRISTIAN DOGMA AND ITS EFFECTS

Douglas M. Parrott

In Luke-Acts and John there is a clear division between the time of Jesus and the time of the Holy Spirit. The division can also be found, though less obviously, in Matthew. It assumes that the Spirit is present in Jesus alone during his ministry and that it does not become available to his followers until after Jesus' physical departure. This essay questions whether this belief is an accurate reflection of history and, when it appears that it is not, asks how and why it developed and what the effects of it were on the shape of the Gospel traditions.

1. Description of the Division

The most dramatic description of the division between the time of Jesus and the time of the availability of the Spirit is found in Acts 1 and 2. The resurrected Jesus, during the forty days he spends with the eleven disciples in Jerusalem, predicts that they will be baptized in the Holy Spirit (1:5), which makes it clear that at that time they do not then have the Holy Spirit. When he ascends, there is a ten-day period when they are without both Jesus and the Holy Spirit. Finally the day of Pentecost arrives and they are all dramatically filled with the Holy Spirit (2:4). From then on the Holy Spirit is available to be conferred on others by them and by those whom they authorize.

In the Gospel of John, this division of time is also described, but in a way different from that of Acts. In his farewell address before the crucifixion, Jesus tells his followers in Jerusalem: "It is to your advantage that I go away, for if I do not go away, the Counselor (παράκλητος) will not come to you; but if I go, I will send him to you" (16:7).[1] The Counselor is otherwise defined as "the spirit of truth" five verses later. Here it is clear, as it was in Acts, that the followers do not yet have the Counselor. After the crucifixion, when Jesus appears to his disciples in Jerusalem, he himself fulfills the prediction: "And when he had said this, he breathed on them and said to them, 'Receive the Holy Spirit'"

---

1 The RSV, 2d ed., is used throughout, unless otherwise indicated. Where Greek is quoted, it is from the UBS *Greek New Testament*, 3d corrected edition.

119

(20:22). Note the main differences from the account in Acts: In John, the prediction is given before the crucifixion; and, then, after the crucifixion, the Spirit is conferred by Jesus without prolonged delay while he is still with his followers.[2]

In Matthew, there is a similar time division, although it is not as dramatically signaled as in John or Acts. After the crucifixion, when the disciples go up the mountain in Galilee, Jesus appears, announces that all power has been given him, and commissions them. His final words are, "Lo, I am with you always, even to the end of the age" (28:20). Before the crucifixion he had been with them physically. Now, he says, from that point on he will continue to be with them; the reader is left to assume that this will be in a different form. Among early Christians, that form would probably have been understood as the Spirit, as we will see.[3] Here, in contrast to the other accounts, the locus is changed, and the prediction and the conferral of the Spirit appear to be collapsed into one incident.

Nothing similar to this division between the time of the earthly life of Jesus and the availability of the Spirit is found in Mark or Q. Nor is there any mention of it in Paul.[4]

At the heart of these three accounts is the post-resurrection conferral of the Spirit on the disciples, and the accounts vary so widely from one another that one is led to the conclusion that there is no one historic occurrence to which they all refer. Ernst Haenchen arrived at the same conclusion when he compared just the Pentecost narrative in Acts and the Johannine account: Luke, he

---

2 Although an ascension is announced in 20:17 ("I am ascending to my Father . . ."), it appears that the reader is not to think that it happens until after the conferring of the Spirit, which takes place "on the evening of that day" (20:19). The similarity and differences between John and Luke are noted by Lake, "Note IX," 105, n. 2. While not ignoring the differences, Brown dwells on the functional similarities (*The Gospel According to John XII–XXI*, 1038–39).

3 G. Barth, in commenting on this verse, does not mention the Spirit but speaks of the promise of "the abiding presence of Jesus in the congregation" and insists that "divine support is not referred to in a merely figurative sense." Finally, however, what is meant, in his view, is "the word of proclamation," which does not suggest as close a connection with the person of Jesus as the text implies (Bornkamm, Barth, Held, *Tradition and Interpretation*, 135–36).

  The baptismal formula here (". . . in the name of the Father, Son, and Holy Spirit" [vs 19]) does suggest a distinction between Son and Spirit, if taken in a later orthodox trinitarian sense. Eusebius regularly omits mention of both the command to baptize and the formula when quoting this verse, which has led to speculation that these elements may be scribal additions, although there is no textual evidence for that view. (See the discussion in Bornkamm, Barth, Held, *Tradition and Interpretation*, 134.) It is perhaps better to assume that the passage is original and to interpret it in a late first century CE context where baptism in the name of Christ had become standard and where Christian baptism was understood as normally conferring the Holy Spirit (see Acts 2:38). "Father" would seem to be an addition, but quite understandable in the context of the Gentile mission, where converts would have been expected to affirm belief in the one creator God revealed in the Old Testament. Thus understood, the baptismal formula presents no obstacle to thinking of vs 20 as referring to Christ/the Holy Spirit.

4 A distant reference to it might be contained in 2 Cor 5:16, but that seems unlikely in view of the context.

said, "could not count on much help from sources: there was no ancient or uniform tradition."[5] Rather, the conferral accounts appear to rest upon the prior conviction that there was in fact the dramatic division of time we have referred to. That this was a consciously held conviction in the latter part of the first century is clear from a statement of a late Johannine editor—perhaps the final one. Commenting on the invitation of Jesus, "If anyone thirst, let him come to me and drink" (7:37), he writes: "Now this he said about the Spirit, which those who believe in him were to receive; for as yet the Spirit had not yet been given because Jesus was not yet glorified" (7:39).[6] In other words, the writer is asserting that Jesus could not have offered the Spirit when he spoke, because that was prior to the time when he (the editor) believed it to have been given to his followers.[7]

It is notable that this conviction is not expressed in the earliest sources: Mark, Q, and Paul (although, as we shall see below, it influenced Mark and Q). That suggests that it became fully articulated only in the generation following the apostles.

In the next major section, we shall examine whether this conviction in fact corresponded to the experience of Jesus' earliest followers. But first we must be clear about the dimensions of the conviction. There appear to be three parts to it:

1. The belief that *the Holy Spirit was active in Jesus during the time of his earthly ministry.* That affirmation is reflected in the account of the visible descent of the Spirit upon Jesus at the time of his baptism, which is found in Mark and Mark's parallels in Matthew and Luke. It is also found in John, though without the depiction of the baptism. This story makes clear that there was a fundamental difference between what occurred to Jesus and what was said to have happened to others, namely, that they were on some occasion or other "in the Spirit," or "filled with the Spirit." John is probably interpreting the account as it was originally understood when he has the Baptist say that the Spirit descended and remained on Jesus (1:33).[8] The statement of the heav-

---

5 *Acts,* 173.
6 The text of vs 39b reads, οὔπω γὰρ ἦν πνεῦμα, ὅτι . . ., which literally means "for Spirit was not yet, because. . . ." There is general agreement that, given the context, this can only mean that the Spirit was not yet available. Bultmann believes that vs 39b could be a gloss, but not 39a (*The Gospel of John,* 303, n. 5). Many modern commentators accept the verse as factually correct. E. F. Scott does so for a conjectural historical reason: "This conception was doubtless based on the historical fact that the disciples did not become aware of the new power until some time after the Crucifixion" (*Spirit in NT,* 194–95). Others offer essentially theological reasons for acceptance: Barrett, *John,* 329; Dunn, *Baptism,* 20; Brown, *The Gospel According to John I–XII,* 161 and 324.
7 E. F. Scott writes: "It was the accepted belief of the early church that the Spirit had been promised by Christ to his people, and had been bestowed on them after his death" (*Spirit in NT,* 62); similarly, Dodd, *Interpretation,* 222.
8 This point is also made in the apocryphal Gospel to the Hebrews: "When the Lord ascended from the water, the whole fount of the Holy Spirit descended and rested upon him, and said to him, 'My son, in all the prophets I was waiting for you, that you might come, and that I might rest in you. For you are my rest; and you are my firstborn son, who reigns forever'" (trans. in Throckmorton, *Gospel Parallels,* 11).

enly voice, that Jesus is the beloved son, in the synoptics is probably designed to clarify the uniqueness of what occurred, namely, that the coming of the Spirit upon him establishes him in an intimate and permanent relationship with God.

2. The belief that *the Spirit's presence was limited to Jesus during the time of his ministry.* C. K. Barrett and others have observed this in regard to Luke. Barrett writes, "Jesus is in his time the only bearer of the Spirit."[9] But what is true of Luke is true as well of the other gospels, including, in this regard, Mark. There is no indication during his ministry that anyone beside Jesus has even a temporary experience of the Spirit. One might have expected, for example, that, in the synoptics, the disciples would have been granted the Spirit when they were sent out on their two missions; but there is no mention of that. All we are told is that Jesus gives the disciples "authority" over the unclean spirits (Mark 3:15 and 6:7 and parallels in Matthew and Luke).[10]

For Luke, the baptism seems to have marked the time when the Spirit began to limit itself to Jesus exclusively.[11] Prior to that there are statements in Luke of the activity of the Spirit in others. We are told in the birth narrative, for example, that John the Baptist would be filled with the Holy Spirit from his mother's womb (1:15), and later, at the ceremony of purification, we hear that Simeon has the Holy Spirit (2:25).[12] But nothing similar is to be found after Jesus' baptism. For Matthew, the time of Jesus' exclusive possession of the Spirit seems to begin with his conception (1:18).[13]

3. The belief that *the Spirit could only be conferred on others after Jesus' crucifixion,* when he was either not visible or visible in a transformed state. This is a corollary of the last point and one we have already noted. These, then, are the constituent elements of the conviction that was accepted among the second generation of Christians, whose beliefs are reflected in Luke-Acts, John, and Matthew.

2. Historical Evidence

The question we must next explore is whether the conviction squares with the historical evidence. It assumes that Judaism at the time of Jesus, or at least during the time of his ministry, was without manifestations of the Spirit. It also assumes that Jesus, during his ministry, did not confer the Spirit on those who

---

9 *Holy Spirit,* 101. Similarly, Conzelmann, *Theology,* 179, 184.
10 Jeremias understands the granting of authority to "presuppose that the possession of the spirit has been communicated to the disciples" (*NT Theology,* 79). One can believe that Jesus did indeed confer the Holy Spirit on his disciples. The important point to note here, however, is that explicit reference to it has been suppressed.
11 For John, in whose gospel the baptism is not depicted, a similar function would have been served by the testimony of the Baptist about seeing the Spirit descend and rest upon Jesus (1:32–33).
12 See also Luke 1:41 and 1:67.
13 Caution is necessary about this conclusion because the reference to the conception begins Matthew's narrative (i.e., it comes directly after the genealogy). Hence one cannot make the same kind of before-and-after comparison that is possible with Luke.

became his followers or give instruction regarding life in the Spirit that was relevant at the time it was given.[14] Are these assumptions correct?

A. Since the time of Herman Gunkel's classic, *Die Wirkungen des heiligen Geistes nach der populären Anschauung der apostolischen Zeit und der Lehre des Apostels Paulus,* published a century ago, scholarship has by and large accepted his assessment of Judaism during that period. "Where the literature of Judaism refers to activities of the spirit, the concern is almost always with prophecy, vision, wisdom, and so on. . . . Worthy of special note is the fact that such activities of the Spirit ('prophecy, vision, wisdom, and so on') are for the most part events of long ago. . . . Judaism distinguished itself from ancient Israel and from the Christian community by the fact that it produced no, or, stated more cautiously, only very few pneumatic phenomena."[15]

The traditional assessment, however, can no longer be accepted. There is, first, the evidence brought forward by Geza Vermes in his *Jesus the Jew.* In his chapter called "Jesus and Charismatic Judaism," he particularly focuses on those within Judaism in the general period of Jesus who claimed to have powers that derived from immediate contact with God, i.e., who were charismatics. He mentions as two prominent examples Honi the Circle-Drawer, from the first century BCE and Hanina ben Dosa, a Galilean from the next century, who may well have been a contemporary of Jesus. The texts suggest that Honi was primarily a worker of nature-miracles and that Hanina was a healer. Although neither seems to have had a significant teaching ministry, and although the term Holy Spirit is not mentioned either by Vermes or in the texts he quotes, both had powers that the tradition attributed to their intimacy with God. Vermes concludes that it is undeniable "that a distinctive trend of charismatic Judaism existed during the last couple of centuries of the Second Temple."[16] Additional support for this comes from a Q saying found in the account of Jesus' response to those who claimed that he was casting out demons by the power of Be-el'zebul: "If I cast out demons by Be-el'zebul, by whom do your sons cast them out?" (Luke 11:19). This saying recognizes that others were also engaged in exorcistic activity, although no conclusion can be drawn from it about claims concerning the Holy Spirit, much as they may seem to be implied.

Another consideration is the evidence of the Dead Sea Scrolls. The writer of some of the Hymns, whether the Teacher of Righteousness or some other Essene leader, was convinced that he had received the Holy Spirit; for example, in Hymn 21: "Thou hast shed Thy Holy Spirit upon me that I may not stumble."[17] In addition, the Qumran Community as a whole, as David E. Aune has observed, "was convinced that the Spirit of God, an eschatological

---

14 For the uncritical acceptance of this concept, see n. 6.

15 The English translation is quoted, *Influence of the Holy Spirit,* 21. More recently Jeremias has expressed similar views, citing Jewish texts about the ending of prophecy and discounting contrary evidence ("Qumran is no more than an exception." [!]) (*NT Theology,* 80–82). Similarly, Stronstad in *Charismatic Theology,* 38.

16 *Jesus the Jew,* 69–79.

17 1QH 7,6–7 (Vermes's translation in *Dead Sea Scrolls,* 173); see also 1QH 14,25 and 17,26.

gift, was present and active in their midst."[18] One place where this can be seen is in the description of the experience of the initiate in the Manual of Discipline, where it says that "he shall be cleansed from all his sins by the spirit of holiness uniting him to his truth" (1QS 3,7–8).[19]

Finally, one should not overlook the fact that late Jewish apocalyptic literature attests that there were those who felt that they received visions and divine messages by the Spirit, even though they did not wish to make these known in their own name.

There is ample evidence, then, of the belief in Palestine during the time of Jesus about the present activity of the Spirit. That means that it is unlikely that anyone, during Jesus' own time, would have thought that the Spirit was confined to him.

B. The further question is whether Jesus' ministry was more than a demonstration of his own possession of the Holy Spirit, as the belief assumes. Is there evidence that it also entailed his intention to confer the Holy Spirit on others? There are two passages that, taken together, support the view that it did.

1. Mark 1:8. "I have baptized you with water, but he will baptize you with the Holy Spirit"—the prediction of John the Baptist just before the baptism of Jesus. Mark contains no subsequent mention of Jesus' baptizing with the Holy Spirit.[20] The saying was probably preserved primarily because it testified to the superiority of Jesus; but, recognizing that, it is difficult to believe that it would have been kept even so, had there not been some basis for it in the experience of Jesus' followers.[21] Luke, who follows what is probably the secondary version of the prediction, which he would have found in Q (the coming one "will baptize in Holy Spirit and fire," 3:16),[22] appears to understand it as being

18 *Prophecy,* 133; see also endnote 205 for that page.
19 Vermes's translation (*Dead Sea Scrolls,* 75).
20 The dialogue in 10:38–40, with its questions to James and John about drinking "the cup that I drink" and being "baptized with the baptism with which I am baptized," is clearly, in the context, a veiled way of speaking about martyrdom.
21 Schweizer states that "Mark undoubtedly found the fulfillment of this saying in the outpouring of the Spirit on the community" (*TDNT,* 6.398), which begs the question of whether there was in fact such an outpouring and whether Mark was aware of any of the accounts of it.
22 It has often been suggested that the original version of the saying was "I have baptized you with water, but he will baptize you with fire." Mark would have presumably interpreted that to refer to Christian baptism and substituted "Holy Spirit" for "fire." Subsequently, Matthew and Luke would have combined the "original" version with Mark. On this reading, it is not clear what role Q would have played. (See Bultmann, *History,* 111.) Scobie's objection to this view seems decisive. He notes that it "involved the coincidence of both Matthew and Luke making an identical conflation, whereas normally, since Matthew and Luke use identical Greek, it would be assumed that both were drawing on Q" (*John the Baptist,* 70, n.1).
     As to the frequent suggestion that the Q version is to be preferred to Mark (for references, see Dunn, *Baptism,* 8, nn. 1, 2; also, Chevallier, *Souffle de dieu,* 97–108), it should not be overlooked that Q's understanding of Jesus was that he was the eschatological judge who came beforehand to reveal the terms of the judgment to those who would listen (e.g., Matt 7:21–27/Luke 6:46–49; Matt 24:26–28/Luke 17:23–24, 37; Matt 25:14–30/Luke 19:12–27). This is so close to the image of the coming one predicted in

e**r****t****y****,** **T****h****e****n the Spirit** • 125

fulfilled after the crucifixion, in the gift of the Spirit at Pentecost, which came
with "tongues as of fire" (Acts 2:3–4). But there is a problem with Luke's
understanding, from the point of view of Mark. As Robinson has noted, in
Mark the prediction was to be fulfilled for those listening to John the Baptist,
whom John had previously baptized, i.e., who were John's disciples.[23] Yet
there is no evidence, at least in the synoptics, that this was true of those
mentioned in Acts as having received the Spirit at Pentecost. (In the Gospel of
John, two had been—one unnamed, the other, Andrew [1:35–40]). Another
problem is that the Marcan version of the prediction assumes that the one who
would baptize with the Holy Spirit would be an historical personage, like John
himself, i.e., not a heavenly being (Christ, seated at the right hand, as in Acts,
or Q's eschatological judge). The prediction in Mark, then, raises expectations
in the discerning reader that are not fulfilled in the accounts in the synoptics or
Acts.

2. The same is not true of the Gospel of John, however. There we are
explicitly told that Jesus baptized: "After this Jesus and his disciples went into
the land of Judea; there he remained with them and baptized" (3:22). This is
reaffirmed in two other passages—3:26 and 4:1. As to the historical reliability
of these passages, Raymond E. Brown, in his commentary on John, has
observed: "We believe that iii 22–30 . . . gives us very reliable information
about the early days of Jesus, material not preserved in the Synoptics. . . .
There is no plausible theological reason why anyone would have invented the
tradition that Jesus and his disciples once baptized."[24] Since in these passages
the Gospel does not distinguish between the way Jesus baptized and the way
John did, we are probably meant to assume that Jesus baptized with water. But
does the writer expect us to think that Jesus' baptizing was confined to that?

We have already noted that at the beginning of the Gospel the writer has
John the Baptist say, "He who sent me to baptize with water said to me, 'He on
whom you see the Spirit descend and remain, this is he who baptizes with the

the Q version of John's prophecy that one might reasonably suspect that the original
prediction had been modified by the Q community to conform to it.

The objection to Mark's version, that it simply refers to Christian baptism, seems
based on reading Mark from the point of view of the later Acts, where the ascended Jesus
is depicted as pouring out the Spirit. That, however, is a late conception about the source
of the Spirit. When Paul speaks of the source of the Spirit, he always refers to God: 1 Cor
2:12; 2 Cor 1:22; 5:5; Gal 3:5; 4:6; 1 Thess 4:8. The probable reason for Paul's view, as
we shall see, is that he identifies Christ and the Spirit.

23 *Problem of History in Mark*, 26.
24 *The Gospel According to John I–XII*, 155. Bultmann is somewhat more reserved. He
acknowledges that vs 22 could be based on tradition, but it could also be an invention of
the evangelist: "He wanted to give a pictorial representation of the rivalry between the
two Baptist sects by setting Jesus and John alongside each other as Baptists." But this
argument is weak, because it is not at all clear that the gospel writer was interested in
representing the rivalry; his primary concern was to use the testimony of John to show
the uniqueness of Jesus. The account of Jesus' baptizing activity became an occasion for
the writer to make this point once more (see also 1:19–37) (Bultmann, *The Gospel of
John*, 168).

Holy Spirit'" (1:33). Thus the early readers of John would have assumed, as C. H. Dodd and others have noted, that Jesus baptized not only with water but also with the Spirit.[25] The situation itself, as portrayed by John, makes it probable that that accurately reflects what occurred. It would be hard to understand why Jesus would have been winning a larger number of disciples than John, including some who had already been John's disciples (as predicted in Mark!), had he not been offering something significantly different and, in the minds of new followers, better. These passages in John, then, provide evidence for Jesus' baptizing activity, which was lacking in the synoptics, and strengthen the belief that he baptized both with water and the Spirit.

One other point should be made in support of this view. The distinctive thing about baptism in the early church according to Luke, other than the formula used in the course of it, was that it normally involved immersion in water and conferral of the Holy Spirit. Scholars have discussed a number of possibilities for the origin of this rite.[26] The simplest explanation, however, remains that it originated with Jesus himself.[27]

To summarize, the conviction, embedded in Matthew, Luke-Acts, and John, that Jesus alone possessed the Spirit during the time of his ministry is contrary to the evidence that we have considered showing that Palestinian Judaism had within it other individuals whose actions could reasonably be interpreted as manifestations of the Spirit, and that there was at least one group that believed that the Spirit was present in their midst. It is also contrary to the indications that remain in the gospels that Jesus himself practiced baptism and the conferral of the Spirit.

3. Origin of the Belief

If that is the case, and there is no historical basis for "first Jesus is present, then the Spirit," then, somehow the belief must be accounted for. We have noted that it does not come to full expression until the generation after the apostles. What developments led up to that point? Three steps can be traced.

1. The first would have been the immediate post-crucifixion experience of Jesus as a spiritual presence. The consensus among scholars is that the earliest tradition about the experience of the risen Christ is contained in the accounts handed on by Paul in 1 Corinthians 15. There, Paul lists himself among those who have experienced Christ. Since his experience, as reflected upon in that

---

25 Dodd, *Interpretation*, 310; Lightfoot, *St. John's Gospel*, 119; Cullmann, *Baptism*, 79–80. The contrary position has been argued by: Dunn, *Baptism*, 20–21; Goguel, *Jean-Baptiste*, 92–94; R. Meyer, *Der Prophet*, 115. Although, as we have seen, a late editor had theological reasons for thinking that Jesus could not have conferred the Spirit (7:39), we may presume that early readers of the Gospel would have read a version without 7:39.
26 See New, "Note XI."
27 "If . . . baptism were practised with the approval of Jesus, it becomes easier to explain why, immediately after Pentecost, baptism took its place as the normal rite of entry into the Christian community" (Flemington, *NT Doctrine of Baptism*, 31).

chapter, alluded to in Gal 1:15–16 (ὅτε δὲ εὐδόκησεν [ὁ Θεὸς] . . . ἀποκαλύψαι τὸν υἱὸν αὐτοῦ ἐν ἐμοὶ . . . "When it pleased God . . . to reveal his son *in me*. . . ."), and graphically portrayed three times in Acts (9:1–19; 22:3–16; 26:9–18), seems to have been of a spiritual presence, it has generally been concluded that that was what the other witnesses to the resurrection experienced, too.[28]

2. The second step would have been the identification of the resurrected Christ with the Spirit. Evidence for this in Paul has frequently been noted.[29] In 1 Cor 15:45, the resurrected Christ is called a πνεῦμα ζῳοποιοῦν, "a life-giving spirit." Earlier in the same letter, where Paul makes an argument against Christians frequenting prostitutes, he asserts that "he who is united with the Lord (meaning Christ) becomes one spirit with him" (6:17). Two verses later, he identifies the Spirit within Christians as the Holy Spirit (6:19). In Rom 8:9–10, he once again identifies Christ with the Spirit, which he also calls in the same passage both the Spirit of God and the Spirit of Christ. And in 2 Cor 3:17, in a passage about which there has been some debate, he seems to be making the same identification: "The Lord is the Spirit," he says, or, in another equally possible translation, "The Spirit is the Lord."[30] And in the following verse, also, the Lord and the Spirit are identified.[31]

28 Fuller, *Resurrection Narratives*, chap. 2.
29 Gunkel, *Influence of the Holy Spirit*, 111–16; Lake, "Note IX," 106; Dunn, "1 Corinthians 15:45," 132–41; Robinson, "Jesus—From Easter to Valentinus," 12–13. E. F. Scott exhibits some ambivalence. At one point, he denies "that Paul anywhere identifies the Spirit and Christ" (*Spirit in NT*, 182), but shortly thereafter he finds himself admitting that "it may therefore be said that in effect Paul identifies Christ and the Spirit" (*Spirit in the NT*, 183); and still further on, summing up Paul's view, he writes, "The historical Christ becomes a universal presence, dwelling in the hearts of men; while the Spirit ceases to be a vague supernatural principle, and is one, in the last resort, with the living Christ" (186).
30 E. F. Scott insists that the whole passage where this verse is found means to say that whereas Moses gave the written law, Christ gave the living Spirit. "'The Lord is the Spirit' may thus be regarded as a condensed way of saying 'the Lord represents the new rule of the Spirit.'" Scott also notes that the verse should be considered a commentary on the Old Testament verse, which Paul has just quoted (although not very exactly). Quotation marks ought therefore to be inserted: "Now 'the Lord' signifies the Spirit" (*Spirit in NT*, 181). Barrett follows Scott on both points. However, he argues that, for Paul, "Lord" in 3:16 refers both to Christ and to the Holy Spirit. Thus, in vs 17, Paul chooses to emphasize the function that is appropriate to the Spirit. Barrett takes this position because otherwise, he believes, an unacceptable doctrinal conclusion would have to be drawn, namely, that Paul's view was binitarian rather than trinitarian (*2 Corinthians*, 122–23). The problem with Scott's and Barrett's view is that Paul does not give the hearer/reader any clue that vs 16 is to be thought of as a passage from scripture to be commented upon. Providing such clues seems to be his regular practice. Moreover, elsewhere in Paul's letters the term Lord is used exclusively of Christ, except in quotations from the LXX, where Lord is used of God. The likelihood, then, is that Paul intends to identify Christ and the Spirit in vs 17a. (Similarly, Foerster, *TDNT*, 3.1091; and Schweizer, *TDNT*, 6.417–20.)
31 The identification is not complete, for Paul. He seems to distinguish between his initial experience of the risen Christ (Gal 1:12–16), which involved revelation, and his experience of the Spirit, who is Christ, which does not involve revelation. As he speaks of it in Romans 8 and Galatians 5, Spirit seems to operate on a level different from that

It is important to note that Paul nowhere feels compelled to argue that this is the case. The most reasonable explanation for that is that it was a conviction that his readers/hearers shared with him. Moreover, since Paul refers to it in the letter to the Christians in Rome, most of whom had never heard him speak, it seems likely that it was a conviction that went beyond the Pauline churches.

Further evidence for the identification of Christ and the Spirit is found in what seem to be early editorial levels of John.

> I will not leave you desolate; I will come to you. Yet a little while, and the world will see me no more, but you will see me; because I live, you will live also. In that day you will know that I am in the Father, and you in me, and I in you (14:18–20). Abide in me, and I in you (15:4). He breathed on them, and said to them, "Receive the Holy Spirit" (20:22).

The first passage suggests that the spiritual presence in the lives of Jesus' followers after his death will be Jesus himself. This is made clear again in 15:4. The last verse indicates not only that Christ gives the Spirit, but that the Spirit (the Greek word for which has as its root meaning "wind" or "breath") is that which Christ himself breaths out, i.e., it is his spiritual essence. Putting that together with the other verses leads to the conclusion that at some stage in its development, the Johannine community believed that the resurrected Christ and the Holy Spirit were one.[32]

We are justified, then, in thinking that the identification of Christ and the Holy Spirit was widely held among Christians in Paul's time and later.

It may be that the development of this belief was spurred by the serious challenge of a piety that related the Spirit somehow to the Torah rather than to Christ. That is the kind of piety that Paul seems to be contending with in 2 Corinthians 3, where he contrasts the fading splendor of the dispensation of condemnation—the Mosaic Law—with the greater splendor of the dispensation of righteousness (3:9), using the language of light that often expresses the experience of the Spirit.[33] It is in this context that Paul makes the assertion that "the Lord is the Spirit." His point, as Bultmann notes, is that true piety understands the Spirit in terms of Christ.[34]

of words, providing, at a deep level of the psyche, a sense of assurance in relation to God and a motivational direction, to which Paul refers as love.

32 Dodd notes the difference between 20:22 and the earlier passages (in the Gospel) predicting the giving of the paraclete in the farewell discourses and suggests that they are from a different tradition (*Interpretation*, 430).

33 See Georgi, *Opponents*, 317–19 (note particularly the summary, 394–403).

34 *2 Corinthians*, 96–98; Dunn makes the same point in "1 Corinthians 15:45," 141. In Acts and John there is evidence of a later view about the risen Christ and the Holy Spirit in which they are seen as separate and distinct: Christ resides with God in heaven, and the Holy Spirit is given to believers either by Christ himself, or by God, at Christ's request (Acts 2:32–33; John 14:16–17). This conviction may have arisen as a result of the threat that new revelations from Christ "through the Spirit" would undermine the authority of the increasingly fixed body of apostolic tradition.

3. Thinking of Christ as the Holy Spirit would have led to an increasingly difficult conceptual problem for many within the developing Christian community when they thought about the historical Jesus. How could Jesus have conferred the Spirit during his lifetime when he *was* the Spirit in fleshly form? Could he have parceled out portions of himself without destroying his own integrity? The negative answer to that question would have led to something like the following formulation of the belief that we have been discussing: The historical Jesus, as the enfleshed Spirit, came to demonstrate his nature to the world; only when he accomplished that and put off the flesh would he have been able to resume his universal character, to be in all places, and to enter into all persons who were willing to receive him.[35]

Alongside this conclusion, and supporting it, would have been the early conviction of the uniqueness of Jesus, which is dramatically expressed in the synoptic gospels in the transfiguration account (Mark 9:2-8 and parallels). At bottom, that account asserts that Jesus is not just another prophet in the line of Moses and Elijah; rather he is unique in being the Son of God, who alone is to be attended to. To have shown Jesus as a baptizer and a conferrer of the Holy Spirit would have compromised that portrait, since it would have confused the role of Jesus with that of his disciples, who were doing those things as well.

We have examined the three steps that would have led to the belief that we have called "first Jesus, then the Spirit." The early post-crucifixion experience of Christ as a living spiritual presence was followed by the identification of that presence with the Holy Spirit. And this in turn would have led to the twin convictions that during his earthly life, Jesus did not dispense the Spirit to others, and that the Spirit was only given after his death.

4. Effects of the Belief on the Tradition

We must now turn to an examination of the final question of our study: the effects of the "first Jesus, then the Spirit" belief on the shape of the gospel tradition in the synoptics and John, and how these effects are to be accounted for.

4.1 Synoptics

As we have seen, there is a complete omission of the accounts of Jesus' baptizing activities in the synoptics. Were it not for the brief mention of them in John, we would have no hint of them. If we may assume that they were in

---

35 There is an obvious parallel here to the developing wisdom christology, whose growth in Q and Matthew has been traced by Robinson in his essay "Jesus as Sophos and Sophia." It seems unlikely that the conception of Sophia played a role at the beginning of the development we have examined, because the expansion of the Sophia myth seems to have taken place in the diaspora (particularly in Egypt, where the Wisdom of Solomon attests to it). At some point, it appears, the Spirit and Sophia trajectories met and syncretism of some sort occurred. (1 Corinthians, where Paul confronts it, lets us glimpse this process at an early stage.)

fact part of his ministry, as we have argued above, the only way this omission can be accounted for is that during the period of oral transmission a major part of the early community did not wish to use, and thereby preserve, such accounts. John gives us a good example of the sense of discomfort that some in the Johannine community had about the accounts. Immediately following 4:1, which refers to Jesus making and baptizing more disciples than John, an editor adds "although Jesus himself did not baptize, but only his disciples." The editor thus denies the clear meaning of the text.[36] One can assume that a similar belief-based skepticism operated broadly while the tradition behind the synoptics was still in a more or less fluid state.

If we recognize that these accounts were suppressed, it is not difficult to take the next step and imagine that sayings having to do with conferral of the Spirit and life in the Spirit might also have been suppressed, and for the same reason.[37] There is only one saying in the synoptics that seems to relate to the conferral of the Holy Spirit—a Q passage, whose indirectness might have helped preserve it: the saying about the unclean spirits and the clean and empty house (Luke 11:24-26/Matt 12:43-45). It is about a person who has had an evil spirit exorcised but who has done nothing to replace it with something else that could prevent the evil spirit from returning. The "something else" is not specified, but it is hard to imagine what it could be except the Holy Spirit.

36 Dunn recognizes that 4:2 was added because of the twin convictions that "Jesus' baptism is Spirit-baptism and the Spirit was not yet [given]." But he uses the word "fact" to refer to these convictions (*Baptism*, 21), which begs the question. Brown, who understands 4:2 as editorial, suggests that the final redactor might have been concerned that John the Baptist's followers could have used the verses about Jesus' practice to contend that he was only imitating John (*The Gospel According to John I-XII*, 164). The Gospel, however, has already prepared the way for the account of Jesus' baptizing activity, and for distinguishing between it and that of the Baptist, in 1:33. Furthermore, the account is intended to show that Jesus is increasing and John is decreasing (3:30)—a point that is lost if Jesus did not baptize. Thus, it seems that the editorial insertion would have been counterproductive. Haenchen holds that the reason the editor did not deny that Jesus baptized when it was first mentioned (3:22) is that the activity would have been meaningless to him, since the Spirit could not have been conferred with it in view of the assertion in 7:39; it was only when the baptizing activity was emphasized in 4:1 that he felt compelled to comment (*John 1*, 21). Others who regard 4:2 as editorial: Bultmann, *The Gospel of John*, 176; Dodd, *Interpretation*, 311, n. 3; Barrett, *John*, 230; Jeremias, *NT Theology*, 45.

37 The lack of such sayings was remarked by E. F. Scott (*Spirit in NT*). "The evangelists...," he wrote, "report only a few sayings, and these of a doubtful character, in which he makes reference to the Spirit" (71-72). He then offers an explanation. "There is no indication that he (Jesus) thought of his teaching, or his relation to God, or the new life he offered to men, in terms of the Spirit (77). . . . If such sayings are not preserved it can be for no other reason than that they were never spoken (!) (78)." Why should this be so? (a) "The habits of religious thought and language which he shared with his age. . . . Since the Old Testament the doctrine of the Spirit had fallen into the background" (78). (b) "It was not entirely congenial to his own mind" (79). Spirit removed God to a distance. (c) "The religion of Jesus was not metaphysical. . . . Communion with God was ethical" (79). "That tranquility, that consistent elevation of thought and feeling which are manifest in the whole life of Jesus. . . . Gusts of religious emotion were foreign to Jesus. . . . Fellowship with God . . . was . . . his habitual mood" (79-80). "In a real sense the Spirit rested upon Jesus, and for that reason he was unconscious of its presence" (80).

One need not think that a deliberate purging took place. Rather the process described by form criticism was probably at work. The community used traditions from Jesus to convey its message to outsiders, to teach members, and to worship. In the process, many of the traditions, not yet considered sacred, were modified, taking on distinctive forms. But selection also occurred. As John attests, some of the traditions were not used ("Now Jesus did many other signs in the presence of the disciples which are not written in this book" [20:30]) and as a result, were lost. Within the synoptic community, it appears that this occurred with the accounts of Jesus' baptizing activity and teachings about the Spirit.

4.2 John

As to the tradition behind John, the situation was different. Some references to Jesus' baptizing activities were preserved, as we have seen above—if only for the purpose of showing the superiority of Jesus to John the Baptist. In view of the skepticism of the late editor, which we have noted, it is perhaps surprising that they survived even then. We should probably assume that they were part of a corpus of Johannine traditions that had achieved a high level of community acceptance and use before the editor responsible for 4:2 began his work.[38] We can suppose that there were other traditions about Jesus' baptizing activity that were not as firmly fixed in the tradition and that therefore did not survive.

Just as some recollections of the baptismal activity were preserved in John, some authentic Spirit sayings also appear to have survived there. The dialogue with Nicodemus contains the following:

Unless one is born of water and the Spirit, he cannot enter the kingdom of God. That which is born of the flesh is flesh, that which is born of the Spirit is Spirit. The wind blows where it wills, and you hear the sound of it, but you do not know whence it comes or whither it goes; so it is with everyone who is born of the Spirit (3:5–8).

In the dialogue with the Samaritan woman we find others:

Every one who drinks of this water will thirst again, but whoever drinks of the water that I shall give him will never thirst; the water that I shall give him will become in him a spring of water welling up to eternal life (4:13–14).[39] The hour is coming, and now is, when the true worshipers will worship the Father in spirit and truth, for such the Father seeks to worship him. God is spirit, and those who worship him must worship in spirit and truth (4:23–24).

---

38 The corpus must not, however, have attained the status of sacred scripture, or the editor would not have felt free to comment as he did.
39 Here water is a symbol for Spirit; see 7:37–39.

Still another Spirit saying is found in 7:37: "If any one thirst, let him come to me and drink."[40]

4.3 Two communities

What occurred to these accounts and sayings tells us something about the two communities that we have broadly identified as the synoptic and the Johannine. The synoptic community at a relatively early date put aside the traditions about Jesus as one who baptizes and confers the Holy Spirit and focused on preserving traditions from Jesus' ministry that were relevant to his role in the divine plan and that could be understood as underscoring his uniqueness, as we have observed. The Johannine community, on the other hand, was only influenced by the belief that we have been examining at a relatively late point. It therefore lived a longer time with traditions that the synoptic community had discarded.

The early situation in which each community found itself no doubt contributed to this difference. The synoptic community appears quite early to have confronted divergent views about Jesus among adherents ("Who do men say that I am?" [Mark 8:27]), as well as opposition from official Judaism; no doubt this was the community of Peter and James, so many of whose post-resurrection traditions are found in Acts. It may be that the Johannine community was somehow sheltered from these problems for a time,[41] although eventually it had to deal with them, too—but in its own way.

5. Conclusion

We have found in Luke-Acts, John, and Matthew a division of time between the ministry of Jesus and the early Christian community having to do with the Holy Spirit. It is confined to Jesus during his ministry; after the resurrection it is conferred upon the apostles and through them upon the rest of the community. The accounts of the conferral itself were so different that it was reasonable to think that there was no historical event behind them, but that they arose from a prior belief in the truth of the time division mentioned above. Our examination of evidence from Judaism of the period and in the gospel accounts themselves led to the conclusion that the belief did not reflect historical reality. In particular we found reason to think (1) that contemporaries of Jesus would not have shared the conviction that the Spirit was restricted to Jesus during his lifetime, and (2) that based upon evidence in John, Jesus did baptize and confer the Holy Spirit on others during his earthly ministry.

We explored the development that might have led to the belief and concluded that there were three steps to it: the experience that Jesus' followers

---

40 See Barrett, *John*, 233–34, 329.
41 For a similar conclusion, but through a different line of reasoning, see Martyn, *John in Christian History*, 102.

had of him as a spiritual presence in the post-crucifixion period; the identification of Christ and the Holy Spirit; and the tension of conceptual difficulties concerning the historical Jesus caused by this identification, combined with the need to assert Jesus' uniqueness.

Finally we focused on the effects of the belief on the gospel tradition and attempted to understand the "shape" of the tradition transmitted by the synoptic community, on the one hand, with its lack of accounts of Jesus' baptizing activities and its failure (with one exception) to preserve teachings about the Spirit; and of the Johannine community, on the other, which kept remnants of accounts about Jesus baptizing, and some of his teachings about the Spirit.

In sum, then, the identification of "first Jesus is present, then the Spirit" as a religious conviction rather than as an historical fact has allowed us to discern a generally unrecognized aspect of Jesus' ministry. It has also allowed us to see how this conviction influenced what was and was not preserved of the accounts about Jesus' activities and his teachings.

Prophecy and Women
Prophets in Corinth

Antoinette Clark Wire

The reconstruction of early Christian prophecy has been very much shaped by Paul's description of spiritual gifts in 1 Corinthians, particularly by his conviction that the gift to be sought is intelligible prophecy that builds up the community. James Dunn in *Jesus and the Spirit* and David Hill in *New Testament Prophecy* each develop on this basis a homogeneous picture of the normative Christian prophet, who turns out to be what we would call a preacher. Under the title of *Prophetie und Predigt im Neuen Testament,* Ulrich B. Mueller does a comprehensive form-critical study of the tradition of judgment and salvation preaching from the Deuteronomistic history to John the Baptist, Jesus, and Paul, adding significantly to our understanding of Paul's preaching. But because Mueller takes Paul's description of prophecy as his starting point, Paul's preaching again becomes the gauge for early Christian prophecy.

This general consensus identifying Christian prophecy and proclamation has recently been broken by two important studies. Gerhard Dautzenberg's *Urchristliche Prophetie* traces Christian prophecy back to a two-stage process that he finds reported in Jewish apocalyptic sources: A mystery or vision is experienced and then receives an equally inspired interpretation. Interpretation of the law had been a tradition in the synagogue, and groups like the Essenes and Therapeutai were inspired to interpret the scriptures apocalyptically or allegorically. Some apocalyptic Jews and Christians applied these interpretive skills to visions and revelations as well as to texts. As Dautzenberg sees it, Paul's struggle in Corinth was simply to sustain this inspired but orderly two-stage practice in an increasingly non-Jewish environment.

David Aune's encyclopedic study, *Prophecy in Early Christianity and the Ancient Mediterranean World,* goes a step further by recognizing the positive contribution of Greek prophecy to Christianity. His book opens with a thorough study of Greek prophetic places, personnel, and forms of speech before considering Jewish and Christian prophecy. Rather than taking Paul's description of prophecy as normative for the church, he makes a catalogue of all early Christian prophetic oracles—words attributed to the divine or received by

134

inspiration that give special knowledge and may be set off from their contexts by prophetic formulas. Yet his careful form-critical study of the 107 extant early Christian oracles turns out to be of limited value for reconstructing prophecy in Corinth. This is in large part because most surviving oracles are from the later periods of the Revelation of John, Shepherd of Hermas, and the Odes of Solomon, but also because he makes no equally thorough analysis of the communal functions of these forms. Yet Dautzenberg and Aune have pointed us in the direction of prophecy as an early Christian experience of inspiration and communication, often with multiple stages or participants and with identifiable forms of speech. This more specific view of Christian prophecy can now be tested and sharpened by new studies of particular phenomena and texts.[1]

The greatest obstruction to reconstructing the prophecy of the Christians in mid-first-century Corinth has been the authority of the text as canon. Those who take time to interpret 1 Corinthians are committed in advance to accept what they hear Paul say, so they hear Paul say only what they can accept. This has distorted text-critical work, historical reconstruction, and hermeneutics.

When establishing the 1 Corinthians text, scholars have on the whole rejected Winsome Munro's thorough surgery on Paul's writings to excise what she considers a patriarchal pastoral editing,[2] and neither have they accepted narrower interpolation theories that dissociate Paul from the arguments for women's head-covering.[3] But at the one point in 1 Corinthians where Paul's words can in no way be integrated into twentieth-century theology, interpolation theories are still the primary resort.

Three major arguments have been made for taking the silencing of women in 1 Cor 14:34–35 as a later interpolation in Paul's letter, one textual argument and two literary arguments. The textual argument cannot finally sustain itself, as is widely recognized.[4] Although in certain Latin and Greek-Latin manu-

---

1 Reiling's *Hermas* is an earlier study focusing on a specific text; Callan's "Prophecy and Ecstasy" studies one phenomenon; J. Panagopoulos's *Prophetic Vocation* represents recent collections of essays.

2 On Munro's *Authority in Paul and Peter* see Elliott's review and Dijkman, "I Peter." For another radical proposal see Walker, "Theology."

3 See Murphy-O'Connor, "I Corinthians 11:2–16," in response to Walker, "I Corinthians."

4 The major proponents of an interpolation theory propose a longer interpolation for literary reasons, dismissing the appearance of the two verses at the chapter's end as a copyist's effort to improve an already interpolated text: Conzelmannn, *1 Corinthians*, 246, n. 54; Dautzenberg, *Urchristliche Prophetie*, 271, n. 58. Others who weigh the textual argument seriously do not consider it able to demonstrate an interpolation: Ellis, "The Silenced Wives," 218–20; Wolff, *An die Korinther*, 140–43. Ellis's conclusion that 1 Cor 14:34–35 is Paul's own gloss leans heavily on the survival of a marginal reading into the sixth century Vulgate Codex Fuldensis. This misreads the Fuldensis manuscript, whose corrector adds 14:36–40 in the margin before 14:34, probably in response to the surviving Old Latin order in the vulgate predecessor of Codex Reginensis by which Fuldensis was corrected. Here Ranke's edition of *Codex Fuldensis* is supported by microfilms of the manuscript against the reading reflected in Metzger, *Textual Com-*

scripts surviving from the sixth century onward these two verses are found at
the end of the chapter (as in one twelfth-century Greek text), this early
dissenting tradition is too narrow, interdependent, and tendentious to be taken
as evidence that these two verses began as a marginal gloss that was then
inserted in two different places. It is narrow in that early evidence is all in
Latin-speaking contexts, interdependent in that many of its witnesses omit in
common other sections of the epistles,[5] and tendentious in that this entire
Western tradition makes a number of obvious corrections of adjacent sentences, so that, for example, it is "eleven" rather than "twelve" who see the
risen Lord (15:5).[6] The simplest explanation of the textual variant is an
omission of these verses, whether accidental or editorial, in the Greek source
of the Old Latin and bilingual tradition, an omission immediately caught and
reinserted below after the section.[7]

The second argument for an interpolation, that the passage does not fit into
its immediate literary context, is no stronger. Dautzenberg has shown that the
form used to silence uninterpreted tongues and simultaneous prophecy is also
followed when silencing the women: A rule on who can speak is stated and
then applied in a conditional clause and accompanied before or after by an
explanation.[8] (Any argument that women as a topic are out of place here
assumes that women are not key figures among the prophets and speakers in
tongues whom Paul has been discussing.)

The third argument, that the passage does not fit into the wider literary

mentary, 565. For the best defense of an interpolation to date see Fee, *First Corinthians*, 699–708.

5 Nestle-Aland, *Novum Testamentum Graece*, 689–90, 714.

6 This is the reading in D*FG latt sy/hmg. Other examples: "As in all the churches of the saints" becomes "as I teach in all the churches of the saints" in 14:33 (FG afg vg/mss Ambst); "spirits of the prophets" becomes "spirit of the prophets" in 14:32 (DFG Psi* 1241/s *pc* ad vg/mss sy/p Ambst); "command of the Lord" reads simply "of the Lord" in 14:37 (D*FG bdg Ambst); and "if you hold on" becomes "you ought to hold on" in 15:2 (D*FG abdg Ambst). See also 15:47 and 51.

7 The consensus of scholars working in the Old Latin and Greek-Latin manuscripts is that the four surviving bilingual manuscripts of 1 Corinthians, DEFG, represent only two Greek witnesses that are themselves so close that a single Greek archetype is assumed. Although the Latin in the bilinguals is not dependent on these Greek manuscripts but represents an already long-evolving Old Latin tradition, it turns out to be very close to the Greek archetype already mentioned, indicating a strong probability of a single Greek source behind both the Old Latin and the Greek archetype of the bilinguals (Frede, *Altlateinische Paulus-Handschriften*, 88–101; Fischer, "Das Neue Testament," 24–26, 67–73, 80–83). This narrow base of the variant tradition is evident in my being unable to find any Old Latin manuscript placing these verses in the numerical order. Although the Aland *Greek New Testament* cites it/dem x z in the numerical order, these are now recognized as essentially Vulgate texts: Metzger, *The Early Versions*, 295, 302, 306. We must wait for the eventual collation of 1 Corinthians in the Vetus Latina edition at Beuron (Freiburg: Herder) for an evaluation of this variant in the entire Old Latin tradition.

8 Dautzenberg, *Urchristliche Prophetie*, 254–55; yet for other literary and hermeneutical reasons, Dautzenberg himself proposes a complex interpolation theory compassing 14:33b–38: *Urchristliche Prophetie*, 257–73, 397–98; *Frauen*, 193–96.

context, conflicting specifically with 1 Cor 11:5 where Paul speaks of women praying and prophesying, is as strong as Paul is in every way consistent. Paul's arguments, however, are consistent in the directions in which they point and in the situation that they assume, but not in the rationales that he provides, witness his argument on idol food,[9] or, as we shall see, on spiritual gifts. So here his instructions on women covering their heads and on women not speaking both point in the same direction of restricting women's worship roles, and both assume the same situation, that women in Corinth are prophesying and praying. It does not violate Paul's canons of consistency that he first argues from scripture and propriety for women prophets' covering their heads and then argues from the same authorities for their silence.

The authority of 1 Corinthians as canon has also warped the way scholars reconstruct the Corinthian Christians. Although the worst heretic-baiting of Paul's opponents has given way to more erudite discussions of their proto-gnosticism or Hellenistic dualism, Corinthian thought and practice are still taken as the contrasting foil for Paul's virtue.[10] His rhetoric is taken at face value without considering that both ethos and pathos, his self-presentation in strength and his playing for their sympathy, are themselves efforts to persuade. Interpreters assume that where the Corinthians are called presumptuous Paul is modest, where they are contentious he is irenic, where they are otherworldly he is "incarnational." In fact, accusations in a debate are often mutual rather than contrary. If one party in an argument appeals to the common good, to experience, and to scripture, it is probable that the other party is doing the same. Yet scholars, for all their sophistication, continue to analyze Paul's writings as if they were descriptive and normative discourse exposing mistaken views, rather than as letters by one person working to persuade others whose commitments or priorities differ.

Finally, on the hermeneutical front the kind of authority attributed to this text has been a major hindrance. Where any writer's view is taken as a divine oracle and the text is determined and the letter-writing situation reconstructed to make that oracle at least tolerable to our ears, two further sacrifices are made. The claims to legitimacy by other voices in the debate are denied in advance, robbing us of a sympathetic presentation of their challenges; and Paul's arguments cannot be heard and weighed to determine whether they are convincing or not—the possibility of an unconvincing argument having been

9 At one point Paul argues that eating such food endangers the eaters who idolatrously devote to demons—even to non-existent demons—what should be devoted to God (10:14–22). Then he says that this eating endangers the observer, who might take demons seriously, but is no problem for the believer who eats (10:23–30).

10 Schmithals, *Gnosticism*, simply assumes "the Corinthian heresy" and seeks to determine its nature. The burgeoning literature linking the Corinthians to the Hellenistic wisdom tradition as seen in Philo provides important new leads. Yet stereotypical theological judgments can prevent a balanced assessment of Corinthian theology. See Horsley, *"Pneumatikoi"* and "Spiritual Eliteism," and occasionally Pearson, "Terminology." In this area James M. Robinson's willingness to champion theological pariahs points in another direction. Note Georgi's recent apologies to the Corinthians in *Opponents*, 345.

excluded in advance—so that even the best argument cannot evoke the event of persuasion. Therefore a church or society today with this view of scriptural authority does not extend and develop the richness of the debates among the first century prophets and apostles. Instead both sides in the modern struggle claim against each other the single authority of a biblical writer, who is thus forced into grotesque wrestling with himself. And if there is any substantive debate on the contemporary issue, it takes place in terms of the human or natural sciences, where there is hope that authority can be determined by persuasive argument.

To reverse this unfortunate history it may be helpful to turn our attention away from the biblical authors. Rather than rushing to put the "Humpty Dumpty" of our Pauline theology back together again after it is clear that he silenced the women, we can let the women prophets take our eye. In the restoration of their voices Paul will be needed as a servant, and such an indenture may be an appropriate way for him to move back toward full participation in the debate. This article applies a rhetorical analysis to Paul's argument concerning the spiritual in order to seek in Paul's ways of persuasion for the people whom Paul wants to persuade.[11] Of course it is the Corinthians as Paul understands them whom we meet in this way, not their self-conscious-ness or their reality in the eye of God. But our good fortune is that Paul is a persuader by trade and is strongly motivated here not to miss his aim. We will follow as Paul's attention turns from all the spiritual in Corinth to the prophets among them and then strictly to the women among the prophets. Whether his focus on them is broad, mid-range, or sharp, each argument provides impor-tant data about how women prophesied in Corinth.

Paul heads his argument in 1 Corinthians 12–14 "concerning the spiritual," by analogy to his earlier "concerning what you wrote about," suggesting that "the spiritual" was a topic of their letter to him (12:1; 7:1; cf. 7:25; 8:1; 16:1, 12; cf. 1 Thess 4:9, 13; and 5:1). The way Paul responds to their topics and slogans throughout this letter shows that he is not answering polite questions but questioning bold answers. His practice is to affirm their claims in theory and immediately to qualify them in practice (6:12; 7:1–2, 27–28a; 8:1–3; 10:23–24; 16:12). Here he concedes their claim to be "spirituals" by warning that people like them, once captivated by speechless idols—however that was possible—should not forget that the truly spiritual are known by their speech.

---

11 It is hoped that this very rudimentary analysis will stimulate more comprehensive and technical analyses of the types of rhetorical arguments in 1 Corinthians, so as to sharpen our view of its rhetorical situation. Classical rhetorical categories may be favored for their normative influence at the time (Lausberg, *Handbuch;* used in H. D. Betz, *Galatians*) or contemporary rhetorical categories for their effectiveness as a descriptive tool today (Perelman and Olbrechts-Tyteca, *New Rhetoric;* used in Siegert, *Argumentation*). My forthcoming *The Corinthian Women Prophets: A Reconstruction through Paul's Rhetoric,* Fortress Press, 1990, takes the latter path. This kind of study should in turn provoke further literary, historical, and cross-cultural studies. Also see the recent dissertations by Margaret M. Mitchell at the University of Chicago and Dale B. Martin at Yale University and their forthcoming publications.

So a person saying "Jesus is Lord" can no more lack God's spirit than one who says "Jesus is cursed" can have it. Paul's reduction of the spiritual here to this lowest common denominator of those who say "Jesus is Lord" is not necessarily the style of the Corinthians. They may have a lot more to say, or they may see their ability to speak in the spirit as what sets them off from the speechless state rather than their saying any certain words. But it is clear that they share in some way the acclaiming of Jesus. Otherwise Paul could not assume their unity in the confession of this Christ, on the basis of which he immediately goes on to build his primary argument for the distribution of gifts. Yet the way Paul chooses to accept their acclamation—not without deflating them by recalling their past and by pointing out that no one in the spirit says less— shows that they project a considerable confidence and creativity in the spirit.

To stress that gifts are distributed, Paul repeats three times the word "distinctions" and four times the phrase "to one this, to another that," following these with the elaborate image of the interdependent parts of the body. Clearly his point in the rest of the chapter is not the unity but the diversity in Christ. In this context even the baptismal formula loses its key negative particles.[12] Rather than saying that those baptized into Christ are *"neither* Jew nor Greek, *neither* slave nor free, *not* male and female"* (Gal 3:28; cf. Col 3:11), here Paul writes, "We are all baptized into one body, whether Jew or Greek, slave or free." The distinctions are not cancelled out but integrated into Christ.

Further, the distinction of male and female is not even integrated but disappears. Because an oral formula such as this one is flexible, as the three surviving versions of the baptismal saying attest (Gal 3:27–28; 1 Cor 12:12–13; Col 3:9–11), the particular usage can only come from some exigency in the situation of use. In the context of integrating differences, this omission could mean that Paul does not want male and female distinct yet integrated. But in women's head-covering and silencing he calls for just such integration of the distinct functions of each sex. In fact, Paul's effort to stabilize sexual relationships by appeal to the way slave and free and Jew and Greek remain what they were when called (7:18–25) suggests that he could be implying distinct male and female integration here by appeal to such integration of other groups. Then not making it explicit is strange, unless Paul does not want to evoke in any way what this part of the baptismal formula means in Corinth. Some have argued that the Corinthian Christians claimed to recover in baptism a full androgynous humanity as it was before the fall into physical sexuality.[13] The letter itself at least suggests that the women in Corinth who prayed and prophesied without covering their heads were claiming to function as God's image in Christ—because Paul tries to reverse this conduct by calling the male alone God's image (11:7). If so, the new creation story told at baptism about putting on Christ, God's human image who is *not* "male and female," had the

12 There is a rather wide consensus that a baptismal formula is being quoted in Gal 3:27–28; 1 Cor 12:12–13; and Col 3:10–11. See H. D. Betz, *Galatians*, 181–85 and recently MacDonald, *No Male and Female*, 5–14.
13 Meeks, *Androgyne;* MacDonald, *No Male and Female*, 65–111.

concrete social meaning in this church of legitimating the women's particular conduct in prayer and prophecy. This could be what Paul does not want to evoke.

Paul's long argument for distinct gifts within one body is summarized and strengthened three times by attributing distributed gifts to an act of God: ". . . the spirit distributing to each as it wills"; "God placed the parts, each single one of them, in the body as God wanted"; "God placed these in the church: first apostles, second prophets, third teachers. . . ." In this last case the distinctions become a ranked list ending with tongues and their interpretation and with the instruction, "but seek the greater gifts" (12:11, 18, 28–31).

This extended argument shows that the Corinthians do not already assume that spiritual gifts are distributed differently to each person to make them interdependent, either mutually or hierarchically. They must be taking themselves as "the spiritual" in a comprehensive sense, each of them being filled or led by God's spirit to speak divine mysteries in prophecy, prayer, wisdom, knowledge, revelation, and tongues. Paul's opening thanks to God in this letter, where Paul seeks common ground with them, can be read in this way: "You are rich in him in every way, in each spoken word and all knowledge as Christ's witness is established in you, so that you lack no spiritual gift" (1:5–7). In general Paul's flexibile terminology when speaking of their gifts suggests that Corinth is not used to drawing sharp lines, identifying each person with one gift, or even self-consciously cultivating many different gifts. Without such distinctions the Corinthians would have no basis for thinking of certain persons among themselves as having a spiritual potential that others do not. They probably share the common tradition that every believer receives the one spirit.

This is supported by Paul's earlier complaints that they consider themselves "already filled, already rich, already ruling" and "are puffed up one over the other against each other" (4:10, 6). Wherever each person has the exercise of all gifts, people are bound to be not only more exalted in cumulative spiritual experience but also more prone to contest among themselves for full demonstration of the spirit. Mary Douglas predicts this for what she calls "low grid" societies, where leadership is not ascribed (that is, pre-distributed) but achieved by some people exercising more effectively options that are in principle open to all.[14] It is worth remembering that such a process is not so much threatening to participants, who can always try again tomorrow, as it is to those who see leadership as ascribed and any change as a revolt.

By this point Paul's differentiation of gifts at God's hand has allowed him to introduce a hierarchy of gifts and to call everyone to seek the second highest gift, prophecy. How gifts can be sought if they are already distributed is not at first apparent. This new argument is not consistent with the previous one but

14 Douglas, *Natural Symbols,* 88–90, 102–10, 130–35, 153–59; *Cultural Bias,* 21, 46–54; "Enthusiasm and Heterodoxy."

points in the same direction. If they will not settle for distributed gifts and learn their place, some of them may be drawn away from making much of little by learning to contribute more. Here he can begin where they are: "So you yourselves, since you are zealots of the spirits, seek to build up the church so that you might abound" (14:12).

What did this mean in Corinth, to be "zealous for spiritual things" or "zealots of the spirits" (14:1, 12, 39)? Paul continues to concede their desires in one phrase in order to get them to go his way in the next, giving us some clues of what they want: "Each of you when you gather has a song, a teaching, a revelation, a tongue, an interpretation—let all things you do be constructive" (14:26). They want freedom for each of them to say whatever the spirit speaks in them under each other's mutual stimulation. Paul wants it to be constructive. When Paul says, "You are all able to prophesy in turn so that all may learn and all be encouraged" (14:31), their interest is in all prophesying together, Paul's interest is in speaking in turn and learning. And when Paul in the letter's opening self-defense claims to speak the divine wisdom that they seek, he mirrors their interest in knowing "the depths of God" and "the mind of Christ," which he calls "discerning spiritual things among the spiritual"—a kind of knowing God from within through a communal process (2:10–16). A further indication of their zealousness appears on negative film, so to speak, in Paul's praise of love. Here he interrupts his call for zealousness in prophecy in order to distinguish what he wants from their very assertive zeal: "Love suffers long; love is kind and not zealous; love does not brag or boast; love is not improper, does not seek her own, does not provoke . . .; love bears all things, trusts all things, hopes all things, endures all things" (14:4–7). In contrast, the Corinthian zeal is active, expressive, impatient, provocative.

Paul's extended argument distinguishing prophecy and tongues shows that he cannot assume that these two are distinct in the Corinthian church. But how the Corinthians experience the two and how they are integrated is harder to determine. The verbs he uses throughout this argument when referring to tongues—"speaking," "praying," "singing praises," "blessing," and "thanking"—and his description of tongues as address to God, indicate that this is a language of prayer (14:2, 14–19, 28). His critique of those who "speak with the tongues of humans and of angels" (13:1) suggests that the Corinthians take ecstatic prayer as a language of the heavenly hosts praising God and see themselves in this company. Paul, on the other hand, disparages this speech by associating it with self-development rather than community development, with barbarian speech, with barrenness, immaturity, madness, and perhaps with musical instruments used in pagan religious processions (14:4, 11, 14, 20, 23, 6; 13:1). This indicates some contrary valuation of ecstasy in Corinth. It may be taken as a sign of mature fruitfulness and cohesion in God's spirit.

Corinthian prophecy is harder to characterize, because Paul's critique is more ambiguous. He praises prophecy yet considers inadequate those who claim, "I have prophecy and I know all mysteries and all knowledge" (13:2), if their attitude is more assertive than receptive. He tries to attract these assertive Corinthians away from tongues into prophecy by contrasting the public ridicule that their ecstasy might arouse with the public recognition of God that their prophecy might evoke (14:23–25). This assumes not only that they want to avoid ridicule but also that they value the power to evoke God's presence so that people fall down and worship. Possibly Paul's particular example of an outsider judged and convicted of sin reflects Corinthian practice—earlier he does accuse them of judging outsiders without applying the same judgments to themselves (5:9–13). But more probably this particular judging is Paul's example of prophecy in the service of mission, whereas they, as he often complains, reach out through wisdom and statements of confidence and power (3:3, 18; 4:6–10; 4:18–5:2; 10:12, 15, etc.).

Because Paul says nothing directly about the content of their prophecy, it is helpful to consider what his letter intimates about the presence or absence in Corinth of David Aune's six major forms of early Christian prophecy.[15] The first four forms are unlikely in the Corinthians' prophecies. Oracles of assurance encourage people not to fear in times of lament and persecution. Prescriptive oracles restrict or warn in danger. Salvation oracles and judgment oracles, which often appear together as blessings and curses, are categorical announcements of divine acts to which people are subject without recourse. Aune's fifth type, the legitimation oracle, fits the assertive Corinthians better. This could be a divine self-commendation in the first person, such as "I am the Alpha and the Omega" (Rev 1:7), or Maximilla's "I am chased like a wolf from the sheep. I am not wolf. I am word and spirit and power."[16] Could the Corinthians' "All things are authorized me" (6:12; 10:23) have such a spirit-spoken origin? If not, what Paul calls their "boasts" could take this form (3:21; 4:7; 5:6). The legitimation oracles that commend a third party are called recognition oracles, as in "These are servants of the Most High God" (Acts 16:17), or Paul's "Jesus is Lord" (1 Cor 12:3). Both kinds of legitimation oracles are positive authority claims and would fit particularly well where people are claiming a new identity in God's image and/or making claims on behalf of God's spirit or Christ. Aune's final category, the eschatological theophany oracle, is suggested for Corinth by Paul's calling both their prophecy and their tongues a speaking of "mysteries" (13:2; 14:2), a term he uses as a formula to introduce his own theophany oracles (Rom 11:25–26; 1 Cor 15:51–52). Because he also encourages them to share their revelations (14:6, 26, 30), these oracles could be narratives of their visions, or—more like Paul's "mysteries"—revealings of the present through seeing the future, or they could be immediate revelations of the "depths of God" now given in the spirit (2:6–16).

Still, the question remains concerning how the Corinthians integrate the

15 Aune, *Prophecy*, 317–38, 439–41.
16 Eusebius, *Ecclesiastical History* 5.16, 17.

ecstatic prayer and prophecy that Paul is trying to dissociate from each other. Paul's effort to change the dress of women when "praying and prophesying" (11:5) shows that even he sees these two functions as a pair and as the most visible roles in public worship. It could be a kind of two-way mediation, prophecy from God and prayer from the people. Their voices speaking for the people to God in opening invocations or in responding praise would then be alternating with God's voice speaking through them to the people in prophecy. If they surround their own prophecies with prayer and praises to God, it would indicate that they are not drawn into illusions of grandeur by the spirit's self-affirmation through them. Yet it is important to remember that ecstatic prayer is taken—also by Paul—as inspired by the spirit (12:10–11; Gal 4:6; Rom 8:15–16, 23, 26–27). So the two-way communication is not simply seen as human on one side and divine on the other, but as in both directions a work of the spirit through those who speak.

Most revealing about this two-way spirit communication in Corinth are Paul's regulations of different voices at the end of his argument. First he regulates speaking in tongues, then prophecy. In each case the initial statement calls for two or at most three to speak, indicating that many more people usually take part (14:27, 29). Paul also insists that both speakers in tongues and prophets speak "one by one" or "in turn" (14:27, 31). This means that people do not normally stop speaking when others begin. A further clause underscores the point: "If something is revealed to another person still sitting, let the first speaker be silent" (14:30), conjuring up contrasting pictures of a fight for the floor or of mass simultaneous speech. Paul's earlier descriptions of "the whole church speaking in tongues" and "all prophesying" suggest the latter (14:23–24).

Finally, in each kind of speaking, Paul wants reflection to follow. One person must interpret the tongues—otherwise they should not be spoken— and "the others" who did not prophesy are to discern what was said (14:27–29). This interpretation and discernment are listed earlier as gifts of the spirit (12:10, 30), and since Paul does not explain his meaning, these practices must be known in Corinth—but are clearly not in use in the way that Paul wants. Either the Corinthians have little interest in each other's speech, or they do not consider that secondary reflection on something already spoken is the proper response. Perhaps more in line with what Dautzenberg finds in apocalyptic Judaism and Aune differently at the Greek shrine, they take up each other's visions and oracles and make them the basis of their own inspired speech, but here without limited number or closure.

Paul's regulations can be summarized as follows, using three valuations of conduct—destructive, provisionally acceptable, and constructive. Prophecy in a communal setting, possibly even with overlapping voices, he considers provisionally acceptable; two or three prophesying in turn is constructive; discerned prophecy is highly constructive (14:24–25, 29; 12:10). This high valuation of prophecy reflects its rational nature, but even here preference is given to fewer speakers and more reflection. Speaking in tongues simultaneously Paul considers destructive; when two or three speak in turn it is provisionally acceptable; when one person interprets, or when one person speaks in private, it can be constructive (14:23, 27–28, 2, 18–19). Again preference goes to fewer people speaking and more reflection.

It is clear that Paul wants to move Corinth away from communal and expressive leadership toward more individual and reflective leadership. Tongues have farther to go to become constructive by these canons. Yet he shows, by also regulating prophecy, that he is not favoring one gift over another but expecting the best practice—the most individual and reflective practice—of all gifts. In contrast, the Corinthians prize their communal and expressive practice of all gifts, working by a dynamic of mutual stimulation and response. Their expansive "discerning spiritual things among the spiritual" could not differ more from Paul's effort to clarify meanings, narrow down options, and get decisions—as when he expects them to confirm his spiritual judgment on the man living with his father's wife, and again when he demands their spiritual recognition of these very regulations of speech (5:3–5; 14:37–38).

Paul's regulation of the women's speech follows immediately his regulation of speaking in tongues and his regulation of prophecy. Again Paul begins by naming the group, stating the rule about their speech, giving an example in conditional form, and justifying what he has said (which comes before the rule in the case of speaking in tongues).

The first data here on the women prophesying in Corinth—beyond what is said about all prophets and speakers in tongues—appear when the last things said about prophecy and the silencing of women are juxtaposed. There is a double justification of why the prophets' spirits are subject to them, first due to God's character as God of peace not disruption, and then due to this being the practice in all the churches. Then follows: "Let the women be silent in the churches, for it is not proper for them to speak but to be subject . . ." (14:34). This cannot be an unrelated list of rules that just happens to juxtapose the women who must "be subject" "in the churches" to prophets whose spirits "are subject" to them in order not to violate God's peace and the practice "in all the churches." The implication—particularly because we have been told that women are prophesying (11:5)—is that the women prophets have violated God's peace and the self-control that prophets practice in all the churches. Yet it is not clear whether Paul's decision to demand silence of the women is first triggered by these strong arguments applying to all prophets, or whether the arguments are carefully set here to prepare the way for the silencing of women.

The latter is suggested by the fact that both the arguments from God's peace and church practice have been used earlier in the letter to regulate women. To those separated from non-believing spouses Paul concedes that the brother or sister is not bound if the unbeliever leaves, yet "God has called you to peace" on the chance that the spouse may be converted (7:15–16). Since Paul normally uses "brother" inclusively for all believers, the explicit "sister" here suggests a special appeal to women in Corinth who are not doing their utmost to continue living with non-believing husbands. God's fostering peace in their case means that believers learn to tolerate subjection for the benefit—the possible benefit—of others. God's nature as God of peace rather than disruption/instability/anarchy means to Paul that the prophets are most in tune with God's nature when they are subject to the spirit in themselves or to each other, not when they are moved by the spirit in themselves or move each other. Though the Corinthians would hardly choose Paul's pejorative term, which could even imply sedition, they may well claim the God that Paul slanders as "God of disruption."

Paul appeals to universal church practice only in this letter, in each of four cases concluding and legitimating different arguments for church order. The call to learn from Timothy "my ways in Christ Jesus as I teach them in every church" (4:17–20), is the only one of the four in a context where Paul has not mentioned women; he speaks generally here of "some who are puffed up." Elsewhere he rules that marriage partners should continue as they were when called, "as I commanded in all the churches" (7:17); that women praying and prophesying should not worship uncovered because "we have no such custom, nor do the churches of God" (11:16); and in chaps. 12–14 that the prophets' spirits (and immediately following, the women) be subject "as in all the churches of the saints" (14:33). Though, strictly speaking, universal church practices can hardly have existed at this time, the credibility of Paul's claim depends on certain patterns' being at least usual in the churches he has founded. This means that the Corinthians, and it seems especially the women among them, have adapted from elsewhere or have themselves generated new kinds of participation, sexual life, worship stance, and prophetic speech.

Paul's effort to silence the Corinthian women further characterizes their speech in several ways. They speak regularly in the "churches" or "gatherings." This plural may mean the same group at different times or may signify the various groups in which people gather but can hardly exclude what Paul means by the "whole church" when it gathers (14:34, 23). His conditional clause functions effectively as a concesssion, "If they want to learn anything, let them ask their own men at home," blunting the offense of his blanket silencing without giving anything away. It cannot be used to prove that they want to learn by asking questions. Even their general desire to learn, which makes his concession credible, will not have been taken by them in the same sense as he has just advocated, "You can all prophesy in turn so that all can learn and be encouraged" (14:31). Their chosen learning is not by listening to the few in public or private but by speaking among others who speak.

The best evidence about the women's speaking is that Paul states this rule at the climax of an extended argument dissociating speaking in tongues from prophecy. Since Paul's arguments on one issue, even when inconsistent, always assume the same situation and point in the same direction, this means that the women are part of the situation of spiritual speech that Paul hopes to correct, and that he silences them to move toward a more individually led and reflective worship. Do they then speak only in tongues and without translation? Paul himself says that they prophesy as well as pray when he argues that they should cover their heads (11:5). And if the sharp dissociation of these gifts is an achievement of his argument rather than a reflection of their practice,[17] they cannot be credited with ecstatic speech alone. His effort to silence their voices at this point suggests that they are particularly gifted in what he wants to rule out of public worship. This, however, includes quite a broad range of speech, for example a whole group's praising and prophesying in overlapping voices, all extended sessions of inspired speech, all ecstatic speech not interpreted, apparently also multiple rather than single such interpretations of tongues (14:27–31).

In comparison to Paul's regulations of tongues and prophecy, his silencing of women in the church is far more stringent and offers no constructive speech options. Women's prayer and prophecy in the churches he considers destructive. If only two or three speak in turn, it remains destructive. Even a single woman's voice in interpretation or discernment is not provisionally acceptable. Paul's arguments on prophecy, speaking in tongues, and women's speech have elements in common that can be visualized as in figure 1.

In the case of women Paul has gone beyond his own standards of more individual and reflective leadership. That he does not consider his general restrictions to be already sufficient for the women suggests that he fears that he cannot persuade them to control the number, sequence, and interpretation of speakers; or he rejects the content of their prophecies or their consequent influence over others no matter how circumspectly they act.

This points to one aspect of the women's speech that can be clearly determined, namely, its extraordinary confidence and broad social influence in the churches. It is attested first of all in the culminating position of their being silenced in this argument, not a place for an aside about nuisance interruptions. (An afterthought could only come after his spiritual challenge in 14:47–48.) Second, it is reflected in his arguments to silence them from the law and from shame. These women are not marginal in the community but have reputations for honor and uprightness that they can be challenged to defend. Finally, and most dramatically, it is confirmed in the way Paul ends his argument. In tone this closely parallels the end of the argument for head-covering where he makes a shocked rhetorical challenge, "Judge for yourselves, is it proper . . .?" and then delivers a two-edged cut-off of any further debate, "If anyone wants to make an issue of this, we have no such custom, nor do the churches of God" (11:13, 16).

By now the stakes have been raised by Paul's rule of silence, sharpening

---

17 This is argued convincingly by Engelson, "Glossolalia," and Gillespie, "Prophetic Speech," 81–84.

Paul's Evaluation of Each Level	Social Description		
	Communal speaking	*Orderly sequence of individuals speaking*	*Reflection by a few on previous speaking*
Most Constructive			Others discerning the prophecy (14:29)
Constructive		Two or three prophesying one after another (19:29–33)	One person interpreting the prayers (14:29)
Provisionally Acceptable	Prophesying together (14:24–25)	Two or three praying in tongues one after another (14:27–28)	One woman asking questions at home (14:35)
Destructive	Praying in tongues together (14:23)	Two or three women praying or prophesying one after another (14:34–35)	
Most Destructive	Praying in tongues and prophesying together, women and men (14:34–35)		
Women Prophets' Apparent Evaluation	*Productive*	*Less Productive*	*Least Productive*

Figure 1

both the challenge and the cut-off of debate. The rhetorical questions, "Or did God's word start out from you? or did it reach as far as you people only?" ridicule their claim to function as an original source and destination of God's communication in Christ. This second-person-plural address, and especially the final adjective "only" in the masculine plural or inclusive gender, might suggest that this is directed to all the spiritual whose speaking has been restricted. But in Paul's previous reference to speakers in tongues and prophets he has at key points made direct address to that group: "Will they not say you are raving?" and, "You can all prophesy one by one . . ." (14:23, 31). So Paul's "Or did God's word start out from you? or did it reach as far as you people only" is likely an equally pointed challenge to the women. If so, the inclusive masculine at the end reflects not all the speakers just mentioned but all the people whom the gospel has reached in that geographic location. Paul uses mission language here, pitting his personal credentials from seeing the resurrected Christ and carrying the gospel around the world (2 Cor 10:13–14; Rom 15:19; cf. Acts 16:1 passim) against their strictly local reception and dissemination of God's word. They, on the contrary, see themselves not as receptors of a witness whose agents have come and gone, but as a primary point of Christ's appearance and activity. Such is their confidence.

Their social influence he reflects by constructing a two-jawed vise with which he plans to cut off debate, incorporating all the spiritual in his address without diminishing his focus on the women. First he challenges those who think themselves prophets or spiritual to recognize the things he has written to them as the Lord's command. This is not an acceptance of their credentials as prophets and spiritual, let alone a commitment to accept their decision, witness Paul's earlier use of the same argument challenging what they think of themselves—"If any among you think they are wise . . .," "If any think they know something . . .," "If any think they can win out on this" (3:18; 8:2; 11:16; cf. 10:12). In each case he takes up their claim about themselves and challeges them to prove it to be true by some act of self criticism. In the final challenge to the prophets and spiritual he forces a vote of confidence on his silencing of uninterpreted tongues, simultaneous or extended prophecy, and women in the churches. The women have not only been integral to this argument; they are its turning point. Once they are silenced the debate is over, and the task is to get agreement. By identifying the things he has said as the Lord's command, Paul appeals to his own spiritual experience of Christ (cf. 2 Cor 10:8–9) to challenge them to a like experience in the spirit. The ambiguity rising from the fact that oral tradition about Jesus' words could be spoken of similarly only adds authority to what he says (1 Cor 7:10; 9:14; 11:23–25).

Paul must know that the Corinthians' experience of Christ is not his, since he does not leave this powerful challenge as the last word. The other side of his vise is the very brief and categorical statement, "Whoever does not recognize this is not recognized," or as it more literally reads, "If anyone does not know, he/she is not known." As when he challenges them to gather in the Lord's name to judge the man living with his father's wife, here also he has already pronounced judgment in the spirit (5:3–5). So a spiritual oracle can take a legal form, according to which the human act meets its divine retribution. Once this is done, the tone lightens instantly: "So, my brethern, be zealous to prophesy, and do not forbid speaking in tongues." Yet nothing is forgotten—"but let all things be done decently and in order" (14:39–40).

Paul seems to think that he has persuaded them. The male prophets may well concede under pressure to wait their turn, now that the line is much shorter, and the interpreter should not be lacking when there are men to speak in tongues. But the ammunition Paul has used shows that even the male spirituals will not take easily to his decimation of their strength by silencing the women among them. How much more must Paul be misgauging the women to think that they will demonstrate their status as prophets by agreeing that they can never speak as prophets. This double-bind can only have forced the spirit in them into prophetic speech against the possibility of this being the Lord's command in the spirit, and quite probably also against his earlier restrictions of the style of leadership that they practice. These are speakers not easily to be pressed into the pews to hear a few voices exercise their secondary reflections.

Unfortunately we do not have a report of the session when this letter was read in order to hear the Corinthians "discerning spiritual things among the spiritual." But 2 Corinthians does not suggest a pacified or half silent community. More likely the spiritual are defying or, perhaps worse for Paul, ignoring his challenge to recognize his rulings or not be recognized. Yet when Paul writes again there is some progress. He has apparently learned that a rhetoric that isolates the women and categorically denies the spirit speaking in them will not be effective in persuading the church in Corinth.

What can be learned from 1 Corinthians about the nature of early Christian prophecy is not less important because it cannot answer all our questions about the theological content of this prophecy. We learn first and last that there was more than one practice of prophecy, often in the same place and time. Prophecy thrived in conflict with itself, though its health required that the conflict be kept within broad limits of respect for the spirit wherever it spoke. The primary phenomenon in this place seems to have been the experience of people taken to be divinely inspired within a speaking community. One person's speaking inspired others to speak until voices overlapped and became extended into periods of communal prophecy. People were inspired less by what they heard than by what they spoke in this context where the spirit also was speaking in others. Yet inspired interpretation of others' speech and even secondary discernment of meanings was practiced. There were multiple kinds of inspired speech—perhaps including revelation narratives, proverbial-style words of wisdom, legitimation oracles, and eschatological projections. But particular attention was given to inspired prayer, which could take forms from traditional acclamation to plea and intercession to praise, thanks, song, and blessing. Here ecstatic speech might take up where human language failed.

Speaking in the spirit was not limited to people of any age or ethnic group or condition of servitude or marriage status or sex, though there are signs that single adult women were especially looked to for inspiration. They did not cover their heads when prophesying or speaking in tongues, which demonstrated that they had put on Christ, God's image, as a new identity not male or female. Other parts of this letter can tell more about how prophecy and inspired prayer were shaped as experience, for example, of Jesus' resurrection, God's wisdom, or the new creation in Christ.

Paul's letter is also witness to what was probably a steady struggle by some people to build greater order and reflection into the church's experience of prophetic inspiration. Here interpretation and discernment were emphasized, and attempts were made to limit the number and overlapping of speakers. This was a movement of reflective individuals to increase their control over communities whose leadership was based on prophetic inspiration. There were brief and recurring times of strong resistance. Nonetheless, prophecy was specialized, marginalized, and, in effect, expelled from the church.

James M. Robinson, the editor (Photograph courtesy of the Institute for Antiquity and Christianity)

Interpreting the Kerygma

EARLY CHRISTIAN PROPHECY
ACCORDING TO 1 CORINTHIANS 2:6–16

Thomas W. Gillespie

In his own contribution to the recent spate of monographs on the topic of early Christian prophecy, David Hill asks, "Is the phenomenon of 'prophecy/ prophet' always and necessarily absent when the word προφήτης is not found?" An affirmative answer, he concedes, enjoys the strength of relying upon the sources to "label" their own subject matter. Yet, he warns, "to assume that the phenomenon of prophecy was *always* bound in a one-to-one correlation to the word or word group causes this approach to the material to have limited value."[1]

The present essay argues that 1 Cor 2:6–16 represents one instance where early Christian prophecy is the unlabeled subject matter and that, according to its testimony, the function of such prophecy was the interpretation of the apostolic kerygma.[2] The case for this thesis will be made by demonstrating exegetically: (1) the inherent wisdom character of the kerygma as attested in 1 Cor 1:18–2:5; (2) the material relation between this kerygma and the wisdom revealed by the Spirit according to 2:6–16; and, (3) the identity of this revelatory activity of the Spirit as a function of early Christian prophecy on the basis of the description of the phenomenon provided by the apostle in 1 Corinthians 12–14.

1. Wisdom and Kerygma in 1 Corinthians 1:18–2:5

The literary context of 1 Cor 1:18–2:16 is the first major section of the body of the letter (1:10–4:21). Occasioned by the "divisions" (σχίσματα, 1:10) and "quarrels" (ἔριδες, 1:11) among members of the Corinthian congregation as reported to Paul, the burden of the argument here is the overcoming of the misguided loyalties that are the apparent source of the disruption (1:12).

---

1 Hill, *New Testament Prophecy*, 3. For other treatments of the topic, see also Aune, *Prophecy;* Boring, *Sayings of the Risen Jesus;* Crone, *Early Christian Prophecy;* Dautzenberg, *Urchristliche Prophetie;* Grudem, *Gift of Prophecy;* Müller, *Prophetie und Predigt.*
2 A similar thesis is defended by Dautzenberg, "Botschaft und Bedeutung," 131–61, who argues that 1 Cor 2:6–16 is itself an example of a prophetic revelation of a mystery.

Moreover, these loyalties are implicitly connected to claims of special wisdom. This is evident from Paul's statement that, in his case, Christ did not send him to baptize but to preach the gospel "not in the wisdom of word" (οὐκ ἐν σοφίᾳ λόγου) lest the cross of Christ be emptied [of its power] (1:17). Whatever the precise meaning of this enigmatic phrase may be, it serves to put "wisdom speech" in opposition to "the cross of Christ" and thus provides the theme of 1:18–2:5. In 2:6–16 the apostle reclaims "wisdom speech" by grounding it materially in, and qualifying it as inspired exposition of, the kerygma. At 3:1 the subject of community divisions is resumed.

The argument of 1 Cor 1:18–2:5 is predicated upon a series of categorical antitheses. Two of these may be formulated by the terminological sets of *wisdom/foolishness* (σοφία/μωρία) and *power/weakness* (δύναμις/ἀσθένεια). Curiously, however, the antithetical terms of each set are never juxtaposed in the text. In no statement is wisdom played off against foolishness or power against weakness.[3] Rather, foolishness is opposed to power in 1:18, and wisdom to power (twice) in 2:4, 5. Such formulations convey not a lack of logical precision, but rather the coordinate character of the terms wisdom/ power and foolishness/weakness. Through this coordination, the two logical sets of antitheses are reduced to one. The assumption shared by all parties to the dispute is that wisdom without power is weakness and thus foolishness. Authentic wisdom is thereby characterized by a certain (for the moment unspecified) power. At issue in the text, therefore, is what counts as power/ wisdom, on the one hand, and as weakness/foolishness on the other.

These antithetical sets of terms function in the text within the context of yet another, that set forth in 1:18 between "those who are perishing" and "those who are being saved" (= "those who believe" [1:21] and "those who are called" [1:24]). Here what counts as wisdom/power and foolishness/weakness is assessed differently. The specific test case that Paul addresses is the κήρυγμα (1:21), the apostolic message of "Christ crucified" (1:23; cf. 2:2).

From Paul's perspective this message is characterized by both wisdom and power among "those who are being saved." He, as the paradigmatic believer, recognizes that "the power of God and the wisdom of God" are inherent in "Christ" (1:24)—the one crucified. The precedence of power over wisdom in this formulation is not fortuitous; for it is precisely the divine power at work in the evident weakness of "Christ crucified" that constitutes this event as divine wisdom. Apart from this power, the message of the cross would qualify only as human foolishness.

The nature of this power that establishes the wisdom of the kerygma is stipulated in 1:30. In a somewhat awkward sentence, Paul explains to the church in Corinth that it is "out of [God]" that it has its existence "in Christ, who has been made wisdom to us from God, [that is] righteousness and holiness and redemption."[4] The sense of the text is not that "wisdom" is one of

---

3 An exception is found in 1 Cor 3:19, where "the wisdom of this world" is declared to be "foolishness to God," but this does not invalidate the observation with regard to 1:18–2:5.
4 Fee, *First Corinthians*, 84–87.

four christological appellations. It is rather that the wisdom that characterizes the crucified is constituted as such by the "righteousness and sanctification and redemption" that are equally "to us from God in Christ." For Paul then the power that establishes the authentic wisdom character of the kerygma is soteriological.[5] The "word of the cross" (1:18) counts as wisdom because God is pleased "to save those who believe" by means of the message of this event (1:21). "Christ crucified," as the one who has become to us "righteousness and sanctification and redemption" from God, is "the power of God and the wisdom of God" (1:24).

From the perspective of "those who are perishing," however, the "word of the cross" is a scandal to Jews and foolishness to Greeks (1:22). This is so, Paul explains, because the former require "signs" and the latter (with Gentiles in general) seek "wisdom" (1:23). By *signs* ($\sigma\eta\mu\epsilon\hat{\iota}\alpha$) he means, of course, the Jewish criterion of divine redemptive activity, namely, evidences of power. By such a standard the message of "Christ crucified" is as much an oxymoron as is that of "fried ice."[6] It is scandalous in that it claims power (and thus wisdom) for an event of ultimate weakness (and thus foolishness).

Why Gentiles in general and Greeks in particular pronounce a verdict of foolishness upon the apostolic kerygma is suggested by the evident religious character of the wisdom that they are said to seek. Its soteriological function is implicit in Paul's rhetorical question, "Has not God made foolish the wisdom of the world?" (1:20b).[7] That this is the case is confirmed by the ensuing explanation, "For since in the wisdom of God the world did not know God through wisdom, it pleased God to save those who believe through the foolishness of the kerygma" (1:21). Here the event by which God *"befooled* wisdom"[8] is identified as the event attested in the apostolic message ("Christ crucified").

Hence the salvation of God announced in the kerygma denies to "the wisdom of the world" the knowledge of God that it claims to afford. The clear implication is that the $\sigma o\phi\iota\alpha$ here in view is indeed religious in nature and soteriological in function.

The same point is scored in the subsequent illustration of the correspondence between the apostolic kerygma and the social composition of the Corinthian congregation (1:26–31). Since, at their calling, "not many" were "wise according to the flesh" or "powerful" or "well-born" (1:26), Paul perceives that "God has chosen the foolish things of the world to shame the wise, the weak things of the world to shame the strong, the base and despised things of the world, even things that are not, to nullify the things that are, so that no flesh

---

5 Conzelmann, *1 Corinthians*, 51, observes, "The unity of thought in the whole verse is strictly soteriological."

6 Fee, *First Corinthians*, 75.

7 Conzelmann, *1 Corinthians*, 43, notes that the judgment on "the wisdom of the world" is "passed, in the form of a question, not by reasoning, but by asserting an act of God."

8 Godet, *First Corinthians*, 94, cited by Fee, *First Corinthians*, 72 n. 22.

may boast in the presence of God" (1:29). A wisdom capable of effecting the knowledge of God and thereby occasioning human boasting in the presence of God is clearly religious in nature and redemptive in function.[9]

This being the case, Greeks deem "the word of the cross" as foolishness because their wisdom criterion shares with the Jewish criterion of signs the common assumption that weakness cannot be the medium of wisdom in this religious sense. Both the Jewish requirement of signs and the Greek quest for wisdom function ultimately as criteria of power. Neither permits a perception of wisdom in the apostolic kerygma, because neither is capable of entertaining the possibility of divine power manifesting itself in human weakness. For this reason, it does not occur to "those who are perishing" that "the foolishness of God is wiser than [the wisdom of] humans, and the weakness of God is stronger than [the power of] humans" (1:25).

The conflicting perspectives on what counts as wisdom/power and foolishness/weakness remain at an impasse, however, only so long as the criteria of judgment represented by Jews and Greeks remain in force. That people are not necessarily the prisoners of their assumptions, however, is attested by the Corinthian Christians themselves, who have made the transition from life among "those who are perishing" to life among "those who are being saved." How this occurred is the topic of 2:1–5.

Just as the social composition of the Corinthian church corresponds to "the word of the cross," so also the ministry of the apostle corresponds to his message. Paul reminds the church in Corinth that in his initial proclamation to them of "the mystery of God" (τὸ μυστήριον τοῦ θεοῦ)[10] he did not meet the standards of "excellence of speech or of wisdom" (ὑπεροχὴν λόγου ἢ σοφίας)[11] that they, being at the time among "those who are perishing," had every cultural reason to expect (2:1). On the contrary, he came to them "in weakness" (ἐν ἀσθένεια) and "in fear" (ἐν φόβῳ) and "in much trembling" (ἐν τρόμῳ πολλῷ) (2:3). Moreover, neither his "speech" (λόγος) nor his "message"

---

9 Stuhlmacher, "Hermeneutical Significance," 335–36, notes: "It is easy to understand how, in the syncretistic situation of first-century Corinth the women and men who made their way to the Christian church from the Jewish community, the world of the synagogue, and from the pagan populace of Corinth, understood the teaching presented by Paul, his co-workers and the 'apostles of Christ' (who figure especially in 2 Corinthians and were opposed by Paul, cf. 2 Cor 11:13), as revelatory knowledge which enabled them to ascend to God and praise him in their own strength. (We can see a clear example of what knowledge of revelation meant for people at that time in the Hermetic tractate *Poimandres*.)"

10 The manuscript evidence in favor of reading μυστήριον rather than μαρτύριον ("witness") is impressive although not conclusive, thus accounting for the strong differences of opinion among scholars. Metzger, *Textual Commentary*, 545, argues persuasively that the issue can only be resolved on internal grounds, and that the term μυστήριον is to be preferred on the basis that it "here prepares for its usage in ver. 7." For the contrary view, see Fee, *First Corinthians*, 88 n. 1.

11 Barrett, *1 Corinthians*, 65, observes that the term λόγος "has no uniform English equivalent, but suggests 'speech in rational form,' with the emphasis now on 'speech,' now on 'rational,' and now on 'form.'"

(κήρυγμα)[12] enjoyed "the persuasive [power] of wisdom" (οὐκ ἐν πειθοῖ σοφίας) (2:4a). His apostolic performance, put simply, reflected his decision "not to know anything among [them] except Jesus Christ, and that one crucified" (2:2).

As Paul previously coordinated the terms *speech* (λόγος) and *wisdom* (σοφία) in the phrase "not in wisdom of word" (1:17), so now he relates them under the rubric of "excellence" (ὑπεροχή, 2:1), a term connoting superiority, authority, and thus power. The parallel qualification of wisdom by "persuasive" (πειθώ) in 2:4, with negative reference to the apostle's λόγος and κήρυγμα, further suggests that for Paul wisdom and speech are coordinate terms that together connote the notion of power actualized by their interaction. Given the religious character and redemptive function of the wisdom here under discussion, this power cannot properly be identified with the "excellence" and "persuasiveness" associated with Greek rhetoric. It is more appropriate to infer that the power manifested in and through the interaction of wisdom and speech is considered divine in its origin and redemptive in its purpose. At issue, therefore, is the question of authentic *inspiration*.

Clearly, Paul claims such for his own proclamation. His speech and his message may not evidence the "persuasive [power]" of this alien wisdom, but they do combine "in demonstration of the Spirit and power" (a hendiadys) (2:4b). In the weakness of both his public presence and proclamation, this power (which is the Spirit) is at work. Yet, and this is the paradox, it is demonstrated in and through the weakness of the ministry and message of the apostle. By the proclamation of the kerygma through such evident human weakness, the Spirit convinces hearers of the reality of God's redemptive power at work in the weakness of "Christ crucified." The validity of this claim is confirmed by the incontrovertible fact that the members of the church in Corinth have themselves come to faith through the weakness of Paul's ministry. In this fact lies their assurance that their faith rests "not in human wisdom but in the power of God" (2:5).

The conflict reflected in 1:18–2:5, therefore, is not between the apostolic kerygma and wisdom *per se*. It is between the power/wisdom claimed by the kerygma and that power/wisdom claimed by at least some of the Corinthians. What distinguishes the two versions of Spirit-inspired discourse is the grounding of the apostolic kerygma in "Christ crucified." Its competition in Corinth is either not grounded or no longer grounded in "the cross." Because the power (and thus wisdom) that Paul claims for his message is that of the Spirit (2:4), it is not surprising that his argument should turn in 2:6–16 to the role of the Spirit in his proclamation of "wisdom among the mature."

---

12 The distinction intended here between λόγος and κήρυγμα is difficult to determine. Many commentators read the terms as a differentiation between the content (λόγος= "message") and the act (κήρυγμα = "preaching") of Paul's proclamation. Stendahl, "Kerygma und Kerygmatisch," 715–20, demonstrates clearly that κήρυγμα is a content term in the apostle's vocabulary. Apart from this being a redundancy, λόγος must mean "speech" in this context.

2. The Relation Between 1 Corinthians 1:18–2:5 and 2:6–16

It is important to note that what changes in the transition from 1:18–2:5 to 2:6–16 is not the subject matter itself but the manner in which it is articulated.[13] In 1:18–2:5 the emphasis falls upon the first term in the power/wisdom duality as it is related to the kerygma. At 2:6 the emphasis shifts to the second term. The wisdom implicit in the kerygma of "Christ crucified" now comes to explicit expression in Paul's claim that "we speak wisdom among the mature" (2:6).[14]

Although this wisdom is contrasted to the "human wisdom" of 2:5 by the Greek particle δέ in its adversative sense ("but"), it remains "wisdom" nonetheless. As Gerd Theissen explains, "The term 'wisdom' always contains a cognitive element." It includes knowledge, reflection, even "theory." In the present context it enables people "to understand" (εἰδέναι, 2:12), "to interpret" (συγκρίνειν, 2:13), and "to judge" (ἀνακρίνεσθαι, 2:14, 15). In sum, "All these cognitive verbs indicate a process of understanding, conceiving, and interpreting."[15] Wisdom as such is thus not alien to the apostolic kerygma. The latter is foolishness to "those who are perishing" not because it is unintelligible, but because it all too intelligibly calls for a reversal of the human standard (power) that determines what counts as "wisdom."[16]

13 Stuhlmacher, "Hermeneutical Significance," 330–32, chronicles the remarkable reversal of scholarly opinion on the history-of-religions background of 1 Cor 2:6–16 and the relation of the pericope to its immediate context. In the exegetical line that begins with Bousset and extends through Bultmann to Käsemann and Wilckens, a consensus developed that viewed the thematic shift from "the word of the cross" (1:18–2:5) to "wisdom among the mature" (2:6–16) as a loss of the subject matter intended in 1:18–2:5. Paul loses his grip on the critique of wisdom conducted in the previous section and capitulates in 2:6–16 to the vocabulary and conceptuality of the mystery religions or incipient gnosticism. Stuhlmacher marks the beginning of the reversal of this interpretation with the 1968 publication of *Paul* by Günther Bornkamm (163–64), followed by Wilckens ("Zu 1. Kor. 2:1–16," 513), Theissen (*Psychological Aspects,* 345–94), Sellin ("Das 'Geheimnis' der Weisheit," 69–96), Lang (*Korinther,* 41), Ellis (*Prophecy,* 47–50) and himself ("Hermeneutical Significance," 334). According to the new consensus, Jewish wisdom traditions provide the history-of-religions background to 2:6–16 and allow its material continuity with 1:18–2:5 to be recognized. Also: Schlier ("Kerygma und Sophia," 206–32), Niederwimmer ("Erkennen und Lieben," 75–102), Funk ("Word and Word," 275–305), and O. Betz ("Der gekreuzigte Christus," 195–215).

14 The often noted shift from the first person singular in 2:1–5 to the first person plural in 2:6–16 should not be pressed too hard. Paul often expresses himself by the editorial "we," as Fee, *First Corinthians,* 101 n. 13, correctly observes. Such a shift at this point in the text is warranted by the fact that 2:1–5 refers to the apostle's own ministry at the time of his initial missionary visit to Corinth, a specificity that requires the first person singular. The verbs in 2:6–16 indicate activities more general in scope. This does not rule out the possibility, of course, that the subject of "we speak" (2:6) includes Paul and other preachers who remain unspecified. In any case, λαλοῦμεν ("we speak") in 2:6 resumes κηρύσσομεν ("we preach") in 1:23, as Funk, "Word and Word," 279 n. 12, points out.

15 Theissen, *Psychological Aspects,* 386.

16 Niederwimmer, "Erkennen und Lieben," 85, asks, "Wherein consists the 'foolishness' of the kerygma? Not in the sense that the kerygma is absurd—it is stated in meaningful statements—but in this, that it is paradoxical. It does not fit into the value world of man. It calls for a 'reversal of value.'"

The wisdom that Paul claims to speak "among the mature" is differentiated from "human wisdom" (2:5) and "the wisdom of this age and of the rulers of this age" (2:6) by both its source and its content. As "God's wisdom" (θεοῦ σοφία, 2:7), it belongs to God and thereby has its source in God.[17] For this reason it is qualified as "hidden" (ἡ ἀποκεκρυμμένη, 2:7), meaning unknown and implying unknowable unless made known by God. With regard to content, it is the "wisdom of God [consisting] in a mystery" (θεοῦ σοφίαν ἐν μυστηρίῳ, 2:7).[18] All attempts to interpret μυστήριον in a purely formal sense fail because it is fundamentally a substantive term.[19] Here it picks up the mystery mentioned in 2:1, where it designates the content of apostolic proclamation.[20] The "wisdom of God," accordingly, consists in the mystery of "Christ crucified" as attested in "the word of the cross."

The two relative clauses that qualify the opening statement of 2:7a regarding "God's hidden wisdom" affirm respectively its soteriological and its hidden character. The first designates it as a wisdom "which God fore-ordained before the ages unto our glory" (2:7b), indicating that it is a pre-temporal *Heilsplan* ("salvation plan") that is directed toward an eschatological *Heilsgut* ("salvation blessing"). The second describes it as a wisdom "which none of the rulers of this age knew, for if they had known, they would not have crucified the Lord of Glory" (2:8).[21] This knowledge lack on the part of the rulers implies that "God's wisdom" was "hidden" in the crucifixion of Jesus, here titled "the Lord of Glory" (ὁ κύριος τῆς δόξης).[22] Not only does "God's hidden wisdom" consist in the mystery of "Christ crucified," but it provides that event with its cognitive value. It is precisely this meaning of the cross which the wisdom spoken by Paul among the mature claims to articulate.

The ignorance of "God's hidden wisdom" represented by the rulers is sharply contrasted in 2:9 with the knowledge of this wisdom among believers.

---

17 Fee, *First Corinthians*, 104 n. 26: "The θεοῦ is emphatic, θεοῦ σοφίαν; the genitive is probably possessive in this case, although it may also lean toward source, i.e., wisdom that not only belongs to God, but also comes from God."
18 Bauer, *Lexicon*, 260, lists "consisting in" among the legitimate senses that the Greek preposition ἐν can bear. In agreement is Dautzenberg, "Botschaft und Bedeutung," 142: "We speak wisdom, which is the mystery."
19 Bornkamm, *TDNT*, 4.820: "The mystery is not itself revelation; it is the object of revelation. This belongs constitutively to the term."
20 Funk, "Word and Word," 295.
21 The issue of the intended reference of the phrase τῶν ἀρχόντων τοῦ αἰῶνος τούτου in 2:6 and 8 continues to vex New Testament scholarship, the alternatives being the "historical rulers" responsible for the crucifixion of Jesus and the "demonic powers." Fee, *First Corinthians*, 103–4, contends that the latter possibility "needs finally to be laid to rest since the linguistic evidence, the context, and Pauline theology all argue against it" (citing the decisive linguistic evidence in n. 24). Theissen, *Psychological Aspects*, 369–70, agrees that "civil officials" are meant but argues that these "are not merely the concrete rulers of Palestine, Pilate and Antipas, but earthly rulers in general, in Corinth and Judea." He then astutely observes, however, that these historical rulers "are heightened symbolically to demonic powers" (378).
22 Lang, *Korinther*, 43–44, notes that "'Lord of glory' in Judaism is a divine title (Ethiopic Enoch 22:14; 63:2; and often)."

158 • Thomas W. Gillespie

By an appeal to the testimony of scripture,[23] Paul links his discussion of the wisdom that is hidden (2:6–8) with the ensuing topic of the wisdom that is revealed (2:10–13).[24] Of the possible solutions to the problem created by the anacoluthic character of the citation (caused by the lack of a main verb), that proposed by Bo Judd illuminates the text most convincingly.[25] The four relative clauses that compose the citation itself are viewed as an ellipsis, the reader being invited to supply the unexpressed verb. What verb is warranted, he argues, is suggested by the opposition of vs 9 to vs 8 established by the introductory strong adversative ἀλλά ("but"). Because what is opposed by vs 9 in vs 8 is the ignorance of the rulers (οὐδεὶς ἔγνωκεν, "none knew"), the elliptical sentence may be completed by adding the required counterclaim (ἐγνώκαμεν, "we do know").[26]

What is known is specified by the two relative pronouns (ἅ, "the things") that introduce the four clauses of the citation. Each has as its textual anteced-ent the "hidden wisdom of God" (2:7). The first three clauses ("The things that eye has not seen and ear has not heard and the human heart has not conceived") again point up the hidden nature of God's wisdom, while the fourth ("the things that God has prepared for those who love him") once more underscores the soteriological character of the divine wisdom. Further, ἡτοί-μασεν ὁ θεός ("God has prepared") is coordinate with προώρισεν ὁ θεός ("God has fore-ordained") in 2:7.

This claim to knowledge of "God's hidden wisdom" is valid, Paul explains in 2:10 (reading γάρ rather than δέ), "because to us God has revealed [it] through the Spirit." Stuhlmacher aptly identifies this statement as "the pri-mary hermeneutical thesis of the apostle."[27] That this is the case is confirmed by the turn of the discussion at this point from the character and content of "God's wisdom" to its medium, "God's Spirit" (τὸ πνεῦμα τοῦ θεοῦ, 2:11). The way has been prepared for this shift by the apostle's earlier claim that his speech and kerygma at Corinth were "in demonstration of the Spirit and power" (2:4). From the coordination of authentic wisdom with effective power throughout 1 Cor 1:18–2:5, together with the identification of the Spirit as the agent of such power, it is clear that the Spirit is the implicit coordinate of wisdom throughout 2:6–9. As the Spirit is the agent that effects faith through the kerygma (2:5), so the Spirit is the medium of the wisdom that unfolds the kerygma.

Being the one who "searches all things, even the depths of God" (2:10), the Spirit is privy to "the things of God" (τὰ τοῦ θεοῦ, 2:11). Based, as the latter phrase is, upon its analogy in "the things of a human" (τὰ τοῦ ἀνθρώπου), the

23 The source of the quotation is unknown. Although similar phrases can be found in Isa 64:4; 52:15 (cf. Sir 1:10), the text as cited can be found neither in the Old Testament nor in Jewish apocryphal literature.
24 Barrett, *1 Corinthians*, 72.
25 Judd, "I Corinthians 2.9," 603–9.
26 Judd, "I Corinthians 2.9," 607–8.
27 Stuhlmacher, "Hermeneutical Significance," 337.

neuter plural definite article τά ("the things") denotes something like "the mind" or "the thoughts" of a human and of God respectively. Yet in the context of Paul's argument, the definite article has its antecedent in the indefinite pronoun ἅ ("the things") of 2:9, and thus in "the hidden wisdom of God" of 2:7. Accordingly, the Spirit is enabled to make that wisdom known.

That the Spirit does make "God's wisdom" known to humans is implicit in the giving of the Spirit itself. "We have received not the spirit of the world but the Spirit that is from God," Paul declares, "in order that we may understand the gracious things that have been bestowed upon us by God" (ἵνα εἰδῶμεν τὰ ὑπὸ τοῦ θεοῦ χαρισθέντα ἡμῖν, 2:12). The participial phrase in this clause picks up and interprets ἃ ἡτοίμασεν ὁ θεός ("the things that God has prepared") in 2:9,[28] a phrase which has its own antecedent in ἥν προώρισεν ὁ θεός ("which God fore-ordained") and thus in the θεοῦ σοφία ("God's wisdom") of 2:7. But the ultimate antecedent of "the gracious things bestowed by God" in the context of 1:18–2:16 is located in 1:30, where the apostle specifies the content of the wisdom that Christ has been made to us from God in terms of "righteousness, sanctification, and redemption."[29]

The wisdom that is given and received "through the Spirit" (2:10) is also articulated in human speech by the Spirit. Paul thus avers in 2:13, "the things that we speak [we speak] not in words taught by human wisdom but [in words] taught by the Spirit" (ἃ καὶ λαλοῦμεν οὐκ ἐν διδακτοῖς ἀνθρωπίνης σοφίας λόγοις ἀλλ' ἐν διδακτοῖς πνεύματος). In the opening phrase ἃ καὶ λαλοῦμεν ("what things also we speak"), the relative pronoun refers to τὰ χαρισθέντα ("the things given") in 2:12, and the verb reaffirms the claim made initially in 2:6 and repeated in 2:7. What is new in vs 13 is the transition from knowing to speaking.[30] The participial phrase that concludes 2:13, πνευματικοῖς πνευματικὰ συγκρίνοντες, is ambiguous due to the uncertainty of (1) the gender of πνευματικοῖς (being either masculine or neuter) and (2) the intended sense of the verb. The latter can mean "to compare" (as in 2 Cor 10:12), "to combine" (as in classical Greek), or "to interpret" (as in the LXX often). Although used by Paul in the sense of "to compare" in 2 Cor 10:12, this seems inappropriate in the present context. Given the known influence of the Septuagint upon the apostle, the classical sense may also be discarded. The verb συγκρίνειν ("to interpret") may then be combined with a neuter reading of πνευματικοῖς ("interpreting spiritual things in spiritual words")[31] or with a

28 Barrett, *1 Corinthians*, 75, identifies "the things that God has freely given us" with "the undefinable and undescribable things of verse 9." Cf. Fee, *First Corinthians*, 113; Conzelmann, *1 Corinthians*, 67 n. 108.
29 Stuhlmacher, "Hermeneutical Significance," 338, comments: "What Christians gain with the gift of the Spirit as the power of illumination is insight into the mysteries of revelation, but above all the understanding of the gracious gifts bestowed by God in Christ in the form of justification, sanctification and redemption (cf. 2:12 with 1:30)."
30 Conzelmann, *1 Corinthians*, 67.
31 Thus Barrett, *1 Corinthians*, 76; Conzelmann, *1 Corinthians*, 67, and Fee, *First Corinthians*, 115.

masculine reading of the noun ("interpreting spiritual things to spiritual people").[32]

The forward flow of the argument in 2:6–16, however, favors a masculine reading of πνευματικοῖς. For the apostle immediately proceeds to comment on what he says in vs 13 by contrasting the ψυχικός ("natural person") in vs 14 with the πνευματικός ("spiritual person") in vs 15. The former, it is said, does not receive "the things of the Spirit of God" (τὰ τοῦ πνεύματος θεοῦ), because they are "foolishness" (μωρία) to him. In that the neuter plural article τά ("the things") has its antecedent in the πνευματικά ("spiritual things") of vs 13, it would seem that Paul is here designating the type of person who is unable to benefit from the charismatic activity denoted just previously as "interpreting spiritual things to spiritual people." In contrast to the ψυχικός, the πνευματικός is said in 2:15 to judge "all things" (πάντα=τὰ τοῦ πνεύματος τοῦ θεοῦ, "the things of the Spirit of God," 2:13). This distinction is then applied to the actual Corinthian situation in 3:1–3.

What is interpreted to such "spiritual people" is specified in 2:6–16 by a variety of terms and phrases that have a common reference: "the things of the Spirit of God" (2:14); "what things also we speak" (2:13); "the things that God has given to us" (2:12); "all things" investigated by the Spirit (2:10); "what things eye has not seen and ear has not heard and the human mind has not conceived, what things God has prepared for those who love him" (2:9); "the hidden wisdom of God in a mystery, which God fore-ordained before the ages for our glory, which none of the rulers of this age knew, for if they had known, they would not have crucified the Lord of glory" (2:7). It is this grounding of the wisdom that Paul speaks to the mature in the one crucified that establishes its material connection to the kerygma on the basis of a common subject matter. "We speak wisdom" (2:6, 7, 13) has as its literary and theological antecedent, "We preach Christ crucified . . . the power of God and the wisdom of God" (1:23, 24). The proclamation of this wisdom is thus the interpretation of the apostolic kerygma.[33]

---

32 Kümmel, *An die Korinther,* 13; Robertson and Plummer, *I Corinthians,* 46–48; Stuhlmacher, "Hermeneutical Significance," 338.

33 This conclusion is widely shared. Niederwimmer, "Erkennen und Lieben," 86, holds that the wisdom that Paul affirms in 2:6–16 "is precisely the kerygma" in the sense that it is the "explication of the kerygma." Bornkamm, *Paul,* 163–64, views the argument itself in this passage as an example of the wisdom it advocates, terming it "a very positive exposition of the gospel of the cross." Lang, *Korinther,* 41, sees in "the mysterious wisdom which Paul and his co-workers proclaim among the perfect (2:6) 'a more penetrating interpretation of the word of the cross' (U. Wilckens) which Paul has not yet presented to the Corinthians in this way." The source of Lang's quotation from Wilckens is the latter's 1979 essay ("Zu 1. Kor. 2:16"), in which he reverses his former position, wisdom in 2:6–16 now being understood "as interpretation of the λόγος τοῦ σταυροῦ in direct continuation of the antithetical theme of the previous argument." Stuhlmacher, "Hermeneutical Significance," 334, contends that the discussion in 2:6–16 "has the practical aim of leading the Corinthians . . . into complete insight into the gospel." Conzelmann, *1 Corinthians,* 57, while remaining convinced that the possibility of "a

3. Relevance of 1 Corinthians 12–14

The crucial question in the present argument, of course, is whether the wisdom spoken in "words taught by the Spirit" (2:13) can be identified legitimately as prophetic speech despite the fact that the specific terms προφήτης ("prophet"), προφητεία ("prophecy"), and προφητεύειν ("to prophesy") do not appear in 2:6–16.

A *prima facie* case for such an identification can be made by noting the number of key terms from 2:6–16 that reappear in the apostle's explicit discussion of prophecy in 1 Corinthians 12–14. These include: (1) ἀποκαλύπτειν ("to reveal," 2:10; 14:30); (2) πνευματικοί ("spiritual ones," 2:13; 12:1[?]) and πνευματικός ("spiritual one," 2:15; 14:37); (3) πνεῦμα ("Spirit," 2:10 [twice], 13; 12:4, 7, 8 [twice], 9, 11) and πνεῦμα θεοῦ ("Spirit of God," 2:11, 12, 14; 12:3); (4) σοφία ("wisdom," 2:6 [twice], 7; 12:8); and (5) τέλειοι ("mature," 2:6; 14:20). Such a clustering of common terms in these two passages addressed to the same congregation and focused upon the same topic of speech inspired by the Spirit surely warrants the assumption of a common subject matter identified explicitly in chapter 14 as prophecy.

Funk notes also the terminological correspondence with regard to 1 Cor 2:13. "The choice of λαλοῦμεν in preference to κηρύσσομεν (1:23) or καταγγέλλων is striking," he writes, "and suggests that Paul may have certain charismatic gifts in mind (cf. the characteristic use of λαλεῖν in 1 Cor 12:3, 30; 13:7; 14:2ff.), the profusion of which in Corinth he has already indicated (1:5ff.)." Further, "The language of 2:6f.; 2:12f.; 3:1 especially bring this context to mind."[34] If the verb λαλεῖν ("to speak") does in fact intimate that the apostle has charismatic discourse in mind in 2:6–16, then its use in 14:3, 6, and 29 with reference to speech explicitly labeled as prophecy provides an important clue. The fact that this verb is also used extensively in 1 Corinthians 12–14 with reference to "tongue speaking" (γλῶσσα λαλεῖν, 12:30; 13:1; 14:2, 4, 5, 6, 13, 18, 19, 23, 27, 39) does not detract from but rather enhances the value of this observation. For it can be shown that this phenomenon was identified in the religious milieu of the first century with prophecy, functioning as the legitimating "sign" (σημεῖον, 14:22) of authentic divine inspiration.[35]

Dautzenberg calls attention to the clear correspondence between the speaking of God's hidden wisdom "in a mystery" (ἐν μυστηρίῳ) in 2:7 and the knowing "all mysteries" (τὰ μυστήρια πάντα) that is specifically associated

---

positive, undialectical wisdom" is presented in 2:6–16, concedes that in the apostle's argument here it "cannot be a supplementary factor alongside the word of the cross, but can only be the understanding of this word, which includes in particular the understanding of its foolishness." So conceived, "Wisdom would then be theology as a clarification of the proclamation. . . ."

34 Funk, "Word and Word," 285 n. 42.
35 See Gillespie, "Prophetic Speech," 74–95, esp. 81–82, and the literature cited there.

with having "prophecy" (προφητεία) in 13:2.[36] While his further correlation of συγκρίνειν ("to interpret," 2:13) with διακρίνειν ("to judge" or "to discern," 14:27) is inappropriate,[37] the latter verb is a terminological variant of ἀνακρίνειν ("to judge," 2:15 [twice]) and suggests a possible connection between the discernment of prophetic speech encumbent upon "the other [prophets]" (οἱ ἄλλοι)[38] according to 14:29 and that ability to judge which in 2:15 is attributed to "the spiritual one" (ὁ πνευματικός).

The material issue in 1 Cor 1:18–2:5, as identified above, is that of wisdom speech that claims the power of God. Paul criticizes the discourse venerated among the Corinthians as inspired utterance for having lost its substantive relationship to the kerygma. In 2:6–16 he counters the Corinthian claim by advocating a wisdom that is grounded in the kerygma (2:8), revealed through the Spirit (2:10), and articulated in words taught by the Spirit (2:13). It can be demonstrated that this same issue of what counts as inspired utterance dominates the discussion in 1 Corinthians 12–14.[39]

Whether 1 Corinthians 13 is regarded as an extended digression or as an editorial insertion,[40] it is evident that chapters 12 and 14 represent a literary unity under the superscription περὶ δὲ τῶν πνευματικῶν ("concerning spiritual matters or persons"; 12:1). The gender ambiguity of the genitive plural makes it impossible to determine grammatically whether the intended subject is the masculine πνευματικοί ("spiritual ones") or the neuter πνευματικά ("spiritual things"). The ambiguity is clarified by the immediately succeeding verses (12:2, 3).

36 "Botschaft und Bedeutung," 142–43.
37 "Botschaft und Bedeutung," 141–42. Dautzenberg rightly relates διακρίσεις πνευμάτων ("discernment of spirits," 12:10) to διακρίνειν ("to discern," 14:27) but seeks to interpret both expressions in the sense of συγκρίνειν ("to interpret," 2:13). The argument is stated in full in his *Urchristliche Prophetie*, 122–40. It is refuted by Grudem, *Gift of Prophecy*, 58–60.
38 Exegetical opinion is sharply divided on the question of the proper reference of οἱ ἄλλοι ("the others") in 14:29. Those favoring their identification with "the other prophets" include Dautzenberg, *Urchristliche Prophetie*, 129; Friedrich, *TDNT*, 6.851; Greeven, "Propheten," 6; and, Robertson and Plummer, *I Corinthians*, 322. Among those who hold that the reference is to "the other members of the congregation" are Barrett, *I Corinthians*, 328; Bruce, *Corinthians*, 134; Fee, *First Corinthians*, 694; Grudem, *Gift of Prophecy*, 60–62; and, Kümmel, *An die Korinther*, 74. Given Paul's stipulation that it is "the spiritual one" who alone "judges all things" (2:15) and the fact that the "discernment of spirits" (12:10) is one charism among many that are not universally distributed among church members (12:4–11; cf. 29–31, where it is clear that not all possess all the gifts of the Spirit), it is impossible to identify "the others" in 14:29 with the community at large. At a minimum they belong to the circle of those charismatics who are endowed with the gift of "discernment." Because this gift is closely associated with that of "prophecy" in 12:10, it seems warranted to conclude that "the others" who "discern" prophetic speech in 14:29 are themselves identifiable as prophets.
39 Why the same subject is taken up twice in the same letter may be explained by noting that Paul responds in 1:10–4:21 to an oral report received from Chloe's people (1:11), whereas in 12–14 he is replying to one of several questions addressed to him in a letter from the Corinthian congregation (cf. 12:1 with 7:1, 25; 8:1; 16:1, 12).
40 For a survey of the discussion, see J. T. Sanders, "First Corinthians 13."

The question raised by the Corinthians occasions in response two inter-related allusions.[41] The first (vs 2) is to the pre-Christian experience of the Gentile believers with the religious ecstasy of Hellenistic enthusiasm, "You know that, when you were heathen, how you were caught up to the dumb idols, being carried away."[42] The second (vs 3) refers to their common Christian experience of ostensibly inspired utterance within the assembly and focuses on the issue of authenticity: "For this reason I make known to you that no one speaking in the Spirit of God says, 'Jesus [be] cursed,' and no one is able to say, 'Jesus [is] Lord,' except in the Holy Spirit" (12:3). From the introductory formula διὸ γνωρίζω ὑμῖν ὅτι, which indicates that an authoritative decision is being rendered, it is evident that the issue raised by the Corinthian question is here being identified and addressed.

Given the crisis over what counts as inspired utterance that is reflected in vs 3, the allusion to the ecstatic experiences of the Corinthians in their pagan days in vs 2 serves to call into question the validity of ecstasy as a criterion of authentic inspiration. If in their pagan idolatry they had known ecstatic transports, how can they now rely upon such phenomena as the test of genuine inspiration by the Holy Spirit?

In place of this experiential criterion, Paul establishes the confessional acclamation Κύριος Ἰησοῦς. The authenticity of inspired speech is to be determined not by the authenticating evidences of ecstasy but by its material appropriateness to the church's confession of Jesus. Put simply, the exalted Jesus is the norm of inspired speech here even as the crucified Christ is the norm of inspired discourse in 2:6–16.

The introductory verses thus illuminate the subject matter of chapters 12–14. They show that the central issue is that of determining by means other than ecstatic states the genuineness of utterances claiming the inspiration of the Spirit of God. A masculine reading of τῶν πνευματικῶν in the superscription is thus required. For the pronouncement that no one speaking by the Spirit of God ever says, "Ἀνάθεμα Ἰησοῦς," in response to a Corinthian question about "spiritual things" in general would be "the height of banality."[43] The issue focused in 12:3 is relevant only if the church's question concerns those who style themselves as πνευματικοί and claim to speak for God.

---

41 Maly, "I. Kor 12,1–3," 82, speaks of "zwei ineinandergeschobene Antithesen."
42 Although rendered grammatically difficult by the pleonastic use of ὡς following the introductory ὅτι, the sentence is best understood if the phrase ὡς ἂν ἤγεσθε is taken as a resumption of the clause introduced by ὅτι rather than as a parenthetical statement. The redundancy is necessitated by the development of the sentence too far away from the original conjunction, ὡς having the significance of ὅτι when following a verb of knowing (Bauer, *Lexicon*, 907). The particle ἄν may then either have its ancient iterative sense, denoting repeated action in past time with the imperfect indicative, or be prefixed to ἀγεῖν, having the technical sense of being caught up into the world of pneumatic powers. The translation is based on this second reading.
43 Schmithals, *Gnosticism*, 124 n. 13.

The πνευματικοί are thus identified as those who engage in inspired utterance. That they may be further identified thereby as προφῆται ("prophets") remains to be demonstrated.[44] This may be achieved by noting the structure of the apostle's argument in chapters 12 and 14. Following the introduction (12:1-3), Paul creates a theological context in 12:4-31 within which the primary issue may be addressed in 14:1-40 under the rubrics of "prophecy" and "tongues."

Given the Corinthian predilection to judge inspired speech on the basis of its attendant manifestations of ecstasy, it is clear why Paul: (1) distinguishes "tongues" from prophecy, in defiance of popular opinion,[45] on the ground that the former is unintelligible utterance directed to God while the latter is intelligible speech directed to humans (4:1-5); (2) defines "tongues" as a discrete gift of the Spirit that manifests itself as prayer and praise (14:6-19);[46] and (3) disciplines its use within the assembly (14:26-28). His statement in 14:22 that "tongues are a sign not to believers but to unbelievers" gives a clear indication of the function of this ecstatic speech in Corinth.[47]

With regard to prophecy, in addition to its being designated clearly as utterance effected by the Spirit (12:10) through which revelation is mediated (14:30; cf. 14:6, 26), Paul provides two clues to his understanding of its function and content. The first is given in 14:3, where it is stated that "the one who prophesies speaks edification and exhortation and comfort." When taken together, these three terms "provide the nearest approach in Paul's letters to a definition of the prophetic function."[48] In the formulation, however, the second word (παράκλησις) and the third (παραμυθία) serve to clarify what is intended by the first (οἰκοδομή).[49] The latter is in Paul's usage a *nomen actionis,* which denotes according to Vielhauer the *creatio continua* of the church.[50] This definition of the οἰκοδομή process is intended by Vielhauer to point up the identity of that which calls the Christian community into existence and that which sustains it, namely, the preaching of the gospel. The prophetic function as delineated in 14:3 is not at all inhospitable, therefore, to that continuing interpretation of the kerygma specified in 2:6-16. In fact, the revelations mediated to the community through prophets (14:6, 26, 30) correlate nicely with the earlier discussion in the letter of the "hidden wisdom of

---

44 Hill, "Christian Prophets," 118 n. 32, with reference to Dautzenberg's thesis in "Botschaft und Bedeutung" that 1 Cor 2:6-16 is identifiable as a prophetic revelation of a mystery, observes correctly that the proposal "depends on the virtual identification of πνευματικοί with prophets, and that cannot be assumed without further ado."

45 Bornkamm, *Early Christian Experience,* 38, notes that in "the ordinary Christian understanding" of prophecy, "tongues" was conceived as prophecy at its inspired highest.

46 Aune, *Prophecy,* 199, thinks "that Paul was probably the first to separate glossolalia out as a distinctive category."

47 See Sweet, "A Sign for Unbelievers," 24.

48 Hill, "Christian Prophets," 122-23.

49 Conzelmann, *1 Corinthians,* 234-35.

50 Vielhauer, *Oikodome,* 92.

God" (2:7) that is "revealed through the Spirit" (2:10) and communicated in "words taught by the Spirit" (2:13).

The second clue to the apostle's understanding of prophecy in terms of its function and content is provided in 14:20–25, a subsection that begins with an appeal to the readers to "become mature in thinking" (ταῖς φρεσὶν τέλειοι). Paul here takes up the issue of the negative impact of unintelligible glossolalia upon the "inquirers" (ἰδιῶται) or "unbelievers" (ἄπιστοι) who may be present in the worshipping community (14:23). He contrasts the inevitable results of such a situation with the benefits of prophecy. "But if all prophesy, and some unbeliever or inquirer should enter, he is convicted by all, judged by all; the secrets of his heart are made manifest, and thus falling upon [his] face he will worship God, exclaiming 'God is truly among you!'" (14:24).

Dautzenberg recognizes the implicit connection between the kerygma and prophecy in this scenario but spoils his insight by arguing that it is a completely hypothetical case introduced by Paul in order to focus attention upon the apocalyptic powers of cardiognosis.[51] More acceptable is the conventional view that the text represents the genuine possibility of the presence of unbelievers in early Christian worship, and that Paul focuses upon this likely situation, as Hill puts it, in order "to affirm the missionary function of the word, even of the inspired prophetic word spoken in worship."[52] The point to be scored, of course, is that in order for this to be the case "the missionary function of the word" and "the inspired prophetic word" must both be grounded in the one apostolic kerygma.

The argument of chapter 14 draws to a conclusion with the exhortation, "If anyone thinks he is a prophet or a spiritual one, let him recognize that that which I write to you is a command of the Lord" (14:37). Προφήτης and πνευματικός are linked here by the disjunctive particle ἤ ("or"), indicating that some distinction is intended between the two terms. The problem is that the particle separates either opposites or related and similar terms, "where one can take the place of the other or one supplements the other."[53] How then should the relationship between these two key words be understood in this text?

Proposed solutions range from sharp differentiation[54] to strict synonymity.[55] One mediating proposal relates the two terms as species (προφήτης) to genus (πνευματικός).[56] Such a distinction may be valid for the general range of Pauline usage, but it is evident that in 14:37 the *pneumatikos* represents one who communicates inspired utterance.[57] Given the distinction between prophecy and "tongues" throughout chapter 14, it is tempting to identify προφήτης and πνευματικός as the respective mediators of these two phe-

---

51 "Botschaft und Bedeutung," 138; cf. Dautzenberg, *Urchristliche Prophetie*, 250ff.
52 Hill, "Christian Prophets," 123–24.
53 Bauer, *Lexicon*, 342.
54 Grudem, *Gift of Prophecy*, 160–61.
55 Schmithals, *Gnosticism*, 284.
56 Schweizer, *TDNT*, 6.423; Ellis, *Prophecy*, 25, 29; Conzelmann, *1 Corinthians*, 246.
57 Müller, *Prophetie und Predigt*, 30.

nomena.[58] If so, however, it must be remembered that the differentiation between these phenomena is one made by Paul and not (yet) by the Corinthians. In their view, the πνευματικός is precisely the mediator of the prophetic word that is confirmed by ecstatic speech. In 14:37, therefore, the two terms are closely linked by the apostle in the manner of προφήτης (my word) and πνευματικός (your word). The πνευματικοί mentioned in the superscription to 1 Corinthians 12–14 (12:1) are those in the community who mediate inspired utterances (including that which Paul designates as prophecy in distinction from "tongues" in chapter 14).

The same designation in 2:13, in the context of a discussion of speech inspired by the Spirit, warrants the conclusion that 1 Cor 2:6–16 shares a common subject matter with 12:1–14:40 and that both passages illuminate it mutually. The function of that which Paul designates as prophecy in the latter text thus may be understood as "interpreting spiritual things to spiritual people" on the basis of the former. In the context of 1:18–2:16, of course, "spiritual things" refers to the apostolic kerygma of "Christ crucified . . . the power of God and the wisdom of God" (1:23, 24). The function of early Christian prophecy, at least as advocated by Paul, is the continual creation of the church through the ongoing exposition of the mystery of redemption in Jesus Christ as attested in the kerygma and interpreted through the Spirit.

58 Theissen, *Psychological Aspects,* 274, 332.

Textual Limits
to Redactional Theory
in the Pauline Corpus

Frederik W. Wisse

Since my scholarly association with James Robinson has revolved around work with manuscripts it would seem appropriate that I try to honour him by raising some fundamental questions about the relevance of textual evidence for redactional theories involving early Christian literature, specifically the Pauline corpus. The question of the reliability of the early Christian text is fundamental to the study of this literature. One could say that the search for an accurate and appropriate way to assess the reliability of these texts is the most basic of enduring problems in the study of early Christianity.

Texts are absolutely fundamental in the study of early Christianity. In the absence of archaeological data and the virtual absence of contemporary outside witnesses, our knowledge of the first century of the Christian movement depends wholly on a relatively small and diverse collection of Christian texts. Our dependence on these texts is absolute. It is the only "hard" evidence available to the historian and interpreter. There is no secure viewpoint available to the historian of the early church apart from these texts. Our knowledge of the Hellenistic world and of first-century Judaism is far too limited to offer another vantage point to control the analysis of these writings. At best this knowledge confirms and complements what we can learn from early Christian literature; it does not lessen our dependence on these texts.

This complete dependence on early Christian texts presents a peculiar problem for historical criticism. If the critic questions the reliability of a text— and there may be weighty reasons for this—the result is usually not scholarly gain but loss. If there are reasons to suspect that a text in part or as a whole does not represent what it claims or appears to represent, then its value as basic data is greatly diminished. What appeared to be hard evidence has become soft. One reason for this is that questioning the reliability of an aspect of the text has not normally led to more certainty about the nature of the data but to a frustrating state of uncertainty.

Questioning the reliability of early Christian texts has its starting point in the perception that a text in its received form does not measure up to the expected unity in theology, composition, or style. During the late nineteenth and first half of the twentieth century the most common scholarly way to explain such perceived incongruities in the text was to pose the incorporation of otherwise unknown and unacknowledged sources by the author or interpolations by a later redactor. As the introductory literature to early Christian texts shows, a great variety of such source and redactional theories has been suggested for all but the shortest of the New Testament writings.[1] However, only if the text itself presents unambiguous evidence to substantiate such theories, which is seldom the case,[2] the result is a state of uncertainty and diversity of scholarly opinion. Historians and interpreters can no longer be sure whether a text or parts of it represent the views of the author or of someone else.[3] This means that parts of the already limited direct evidence for early Christianity can be used only with major qualifications.

This risk of undermining the scholarly usefulness of the limited amount of evidence that is available should put a burden on the critic to protect this evidence against arbitrary treatment and unwarranted doubts. In the end, the claim that early Christian studies are a scientific enterprise is not proved by the multitude and complexity of its methods and theories but by the way it treats and accounts for the basic evidence, the texts. Respect for the evidence and findings based on this evidence is essential. This is taken for granted and strictly enforced in the natural sciences. The manipulation of the evidence to make it fit one's theories is considered an unforgivable sin. Any challenges to the reliability of the basic data, or to earlier findings based on this data, have to meet the highest standard of proof or they will be rejected for publication in refereed journals. The reason for this is obvious: If manipulation of the data and inconclusive challenges are tolerated the whole scientific enterprise will soon end in confusion and futility.

The risk is equally great if not greater when the basic data are limited to ancient Christian texts. They fall prey more easily to manipulation and challenge than does evidence in the natural sciences. Their protection should be a primary task of scholarship. Of the various challenges to the reliability of a text, the claim that it includes redactional interpolations is the most prob-

---

1 Since about 1950, there is a marked trend away from source and redactional theories in favour of posing a very specific and complex historical situation that the text is assumed to reflect and that is the cause of the apparent incongruities. A good example of this is offered by the commentaries on the Johannine literature by Raymond E. Brown in contrast to those by Rudolf Bultmann. The historical transparency of early Christian texts that Brown and others assume has recently been questioned from the side of reader-response and narrative criticism (e.g., Kingsbury, "Reflections," 442–60).

2 It lies in the nature of the matter that only very clumsy incorporation of sources and redactional changes can be identified with any degree of certainty. No refinement of method can overcome this problem.

3 An example of this is the case against the authenticity of the Letter to the Colossians, which most critics agree has some weight, but which is far less certain than the inauthenticity of the Pastorals. As a result it can no longer be considered reliable as evidence for Paul or as evidence for deutero-Paulinism.

lematic. Of course, at issue is not the possibility of redactional changes made in early Christian literature. The manuscript evidence gives unquestionable proof of numerous small and at least some larger redactional interventions. The problem is if and when, in the absence of manuscript support, it is legitimate to resolve apparent incongruities in the text by designating part of the text as an interpolation.

The same question could be asked also with reference to challenges involving the authorship and unity of a text, but here the problem is somewhat less urgent. There is substantial agreement in critical New Testament scholarship on the question of authenticity, with the possible exception of Colossians. To be sure, there is much disagreement on the integrity of such writings as the Gospel of John and Paul's letters to the Romans, the Corinthians, and the Philippians, but the consequences are relatively minor, since the authorship is not normally in question. However, claims that parts of a text were added by a later redactor have far more serious consequences.

In essence redactional changes are foreign elements that have been added surreptitiously in order to become an integral part of the text, but that cannot be assumed to represent the views of the author of the text. Not recognizing such foreign elements for what they are could lead to a serious misinterpretation of the views of the author. On the other hand, if a passage is wrongly claimed to be an interpolation this could be even more misleading. Since in this case the attention is focussed on a distinct and usually prominent passage, the consequence is often that an important view or meaning is specifically highlighted as *not* being held by the author of the text. Actually, except in rare cases when the interpolation includes an obvious anachronism, this goes well beyond the evidence. Normally all that can be said about an interpolation is that the author of the text did not actually say this. This has no implication for the question as to whether or not the author would have agreed with the sentiments included in the interpolation. However, as a rule the scholar who proposes the interpolation starts from the premise and wants to conclude that the author could not and would not have said it.

The problematic of interpolations can be clarified by an analogous situation in geology. Just as a piece of literature can be taken to represent the views of its author, so the fossils in a certain sedimentary layer are the basic data from which the paleontologist can reconstruct the life forms that existed during the geological period in which the layer was deposited. Occasionally some fossils are found together with others against expectations. Their presence does not fit the researcher's views of the period in question. Either they represent life forms that were thought to have been extinct during the period of the other fossils, or they may be ones that were thought to be characteristic only of a later period.

There are only two ways to explain this incongruous state of affairs. It is possible that through geological upheaval fossils from different layers have been mixed, thus causing anachronisms in the fossil record. This would be

170 • Frederik W. Wisse

parallel to an interpolation in a piece of literature.⁴ However, in order to resort to such an explanation there would have to be sufficient evidence of an upheaval caused by the faulting, folding, or erosion of layers. In the absence of such indications and with the layer apparently undisturbed, there is no other option for the paleontologist than to adjust his reconstruction of the life forms during the geological period in question. Many such adjustments have been necessary in the sciences. Without them scientific knowledge would stagnate.

To claim that part of the available data is due to a foreign intrusion or interpolation into the normal state of affairs is extremely serious. Obviously it bears the full burden of proof. As in a court of law, the evidence deserves to be judged innocent of being an interpolation until proven guilty. This proof must be able to stand up before the jury of scholarship, which must decide whether "guilt" has been established beyond a reasonable doubt. If there is reasonable doubt about the extraneousness of the accused data then it should not remain any longer under a cloud of suspicion. In that case the verdict must be acquittal in order to protect the innocent. If scholarship does not follow such a "rule of law," serious injustice will be done to much innocent data.⁵

The burden of proof is such that redactional hypotheses can never be a normal or common way to resolve perceived problems of incongruity in the evidence. There are no absolute or constant criteria for congruity whether in geology or literary studies. The limits of congruity are set only by the basic evidence itself. They are defined by the range of ideas and stylistic features that can be found together in one text, or the variety of fossils that can be found in one geological layer. Obviously the extent of this range may differ from layer to layer, from author to author, from text to text. Our expectations of what this range will be is a product of our limited experience and is easily influenced by ideological considerations. Such expectations, however dear to us, must be adjusted to fit the evidence and not vice versa.⁶

Designating a passage in a text as a redactional interpolation can be at best only a last resort and an admission of one's inability to account for the data in any other way. It is always a "violent" resolution akin to removing an offending organ through amputation. To resort to this without sufficient cause and justification is scholarly malpractice. It would be tantamount to manipulating the facts, by denying their relevance, in order to uphold one's theory. Respect for the basic evidence demands that it be taken seriously even if, or rather especially if it does not fit our expectations and hypotheses.

4 The unacknowledged incorporation of a source by an author forms a parallel to the depositing of some older fossils together with those from a later period.
5 More than 10% of the text of the seven undoubted Pauline Epistles—24% of Romans!—has now been put under suspicion of being redactional additions. Of these only Rom 16:25–27 can be said to be an interpolation beyond a reasonable doubt (see also n. 11).
6 Such an adjustment is now being made towards accepting less consistency in compositional unity for the Gospel of John, e.g., by Haenchen, *John 1*, 71–90. However, Haenchen still holds John accountable to a fully coherent theology and resorts to interpolations when the expected coherence is not evident.

In light of this the frequency and ease with which New Testament scholars have resorted to interpolation theories are very hard to excuse. Redactional theories certainly do not deserve the scholarly prestige they have enjoyed in biblical studies during the last hundred years. However, there are signs that the tide is turning. For example, the complex source and redactional theories for the Apocalypse of John that were popular during the first half of the twentieth century are now generally discounted as being unnecessary and indefensible.

In Pauline studies, however, interpolations are still widely seen as an obvious and legitimate technique to resolve perceived theological incongruities. A recent example of this is presented by François Refoulé, who argues that Romans 9–11 cannot belong together with Romans 1–8. He believes that it must originally have been a separate Pauline fragment, or more likely, a piece written by a student of Paul that was added to Romans at a later point to correct Paul's "théses brutales" in Romans 1–8 and Galatians.[7] He does not see any serious obstacles to his thesis in the fact that the manuscript and patristic witness is unanimous on the unity of Romans 1–11, and that the style and vocabulary of Romans 9–11 are unquestionably Pauline.[8] The contradictions he sees are limited to aspects of the history of salvation, and up to now Pauline scholars have not considered such incongruities to be serious. Furthermore, with no hint of an "upheaval" in the text of Romans 1–14, it is baffling how Refoulé can justify such a drastic "solution" as posing the composite nature of the text or even the non-Pauline authorship of Romans 9–11.

Refoulé, however, thinks it easy to justify his rejection of the unity of Romans 1–11; he spends only a few lines on it.[9] He obviously expects that his readers will readily agree that posing a composite text or an interpolation is a legitimate solution to the theological contradictions that one finds in the Pauline corpus. No sign of textual upheaval or manuscript support appears to be required to resort to such drastic surgery. All Refoulé does is refer to the scholarly recognition given to claims for the composite nature of the two letters to the Corinthians, of Philippians, and of 1 Thessalonians; for Romans 16's being a fragment of a letter to the Ephesians; and for interpolations in 1 Cor 14:33b–36 and 2 Cor 6:14–7:1—all of which have left no traces in the manuscript tradition. Apparently the logic of this is that since scholars have suggested interpolations and lack of unity elsewhere in the Pauline corpus, it is legitimate to do so also for Romans 9–11.

---

7 Refoulé, "Unité de l'Epître aux Romains," 219–42. This article also illustrates that in Pauline studies interpolations do not simply function as a way to resolve apparent problems in the text. Modern objections to ideas found in the text often play an insidious, if not decisive role. This has been shown convincingly by Tjitze Baarda for the history of interpretation of 1 Thess 2:13–16 in "Maar de toorn," 15–74. It appears also to be the case for Romans 9–11; 13:1–7; 1 Cor 11:2–16; 14:33b–36; 2 Cor 6:14–7:1; and 1 Thess 5:1–11.

8 He conveniently ignores the carefully argued study by Gamble, Jr., *Textual History*.

9 Refoulé, "Unité de l'Epître aux Romains," 219 and 241.

Of course, such an appeal only has relevance if the arguments for interpolations or lack of unity elsewhere in the letters of Paul are more or less conclusive; for in order to support one hypothesis it does not help to appeal to similar hypotheses that stand equally in need of compelling textual evidence. The fact is that apart from those which have manuscript support, none of the proposed instances of redaction in the Pauline corpus are certain enough, nor do they have broad enough support in critical scholarship, to strengthen the probability of other such instances.

This lack of certainty is sometimes obscured by scholars who wishfully refer to certain redactional theories as if they were facts. This can only be done if one ignores the minimum requirements of proof and the serious challenges that have been put forward in recent years against even the strongest cases.[10] Looking at the arguments for and against the main redactional hypotheses, one can only conclude that matters are at an impasse. Since the burden of proof rests on the arguments for redactional interference, the benefit of the doubt rightfully should go to the integrity of the text. If the case of the prosecution is not able to overcome serious doubts, then the text deserves to be acquitted.

Thus appeals to other instances in which scholars have resorted to a redactional hypothesis cannot offset the lack of textual evidence; the burden of proof remains entirely on Refoulé and others who have proposed redactional theories for the Pauline epistles. Furthermore, this proof will have to be in terms of clear signs of redactional interference in the passage itself or in its manuscript attestation; the modern interpreter's difficulties in reconciling different Pauline statements and theologumena can never be reason enough to pose a redactional intrusion. Our expectations of congruity in Paul's style and theology should be determined by the Pauline text itself and not be imposed on the text.

The prohibitive weight of the burden of proof in arguments for interpolations was frankly admitted by William O. Walker, Jr., in a recent article; he also deserves credit for raising the larger problematic of redactional theory.[11] The issue has obvious urgency for him since he wants to prove that 1 Cor 11:3–16

---

10 Gamble's incisive analysis ("The Redaction of the Pauline Letters") has greatly weakened the arguments for the composite nature of Pauline letters. After a full review of the literature David E. Garland sees no need to reject the unity of Philippians ("Composition and Unity"). Duane F. Watson comes to the same conclusion ("A Rhetorical Analysis of Philippians"). Perhaps the strongest case for an interpolation is in terms of 2 Cor 6:14–7:1, but arguments to the contrary are serious and weighty (e.g., Kümmel, *Introduction*, 287–92; Dahl, "A Fragment and Its Context"; and more fully Thrall, "The Problem of II Cor. VI. 14–VII. 1"). Arguments for another interpolation, 1 Thess 2:13–16, which were accepted by many scholars, have recently been undermined by Hurd ("Paul Ahead of His Time") and Baarda ("Maar de Toorn"). The cases for the other proposed interpolations in the Pauline corpus, Rom 3:24–26; 5:6–7; 9–11; 13:1–7; 1 Cor 11:3–16; 13; 14:33b–36 and 1 Thess 5:1–11, are comparatively weaker.

11 Walker, "The Burden of Proof."

is an interpolation.[12] Indeed, in view of the heavy burden of proof, it would appear that in practice it is virtually impossible to make a convincing case for any interpolation that lacks manuscript support. It is likely that even such sure interpolations as the *pericope adulterae* (John 7:53–8:11) and Mark 16:9–20 could not be proved—and might even have escaped notice!—if it had not been for the textual evidence. Hence it would seem that as a rule the identification of passages as interpolations is beyond proof or disproof, and thus is of no scholarly value. That would mean that we are dealing with nothing more than educated guesses that lead nowhere and needlessly clutter the scholarly literature.[13]

It is clear to Walker that the only way out of such an impasse is lowering the burden of proof for a specific interpolation. He does not, like Refoulé, think it enough to refer simply to those interpolation proposals that have gained a certain standing in New Testament scholarship. However, Walker does believe that if there are otherwise good reasons to assume that the Pauline corpus was extensively interpolated, then this "significantly reduces the weight of the burden of proof attaching to any argument that a particular passage is, in fact, such an interpolation."[14] This kind of argument may look logical but does not stand up to scrutiny. For example, it may well be that statistics leave no doubt that a certain percentage of the population will at some time be involved in criminal action, but this does in no way lighten the burden of proving the guilt of any specific individual. Similarly it can readily be granted that the Pauline corpus suffered at least some redactional intervention, but this does not prejudice the case for or against any specific interpolation.[15]

Although certainty about the reality of redactional changes in the Pauline letters has no obvious bearing on the burden of proof in individual cases, still it will inevitably influence the researcher's attitude towards the text. It is important to know whether redactional intervention was largely limited to small and incidental "improvements" and clarifications or whether we must reckon with major editing, such as the combining of originally independent fragments of letters and the introduction of a considerable number of extensive interpolations with a theological outlook different from that of Paul. In the former case the text can still basically be trusted to provide accurate data about Paul's views and historical situation. However, if the latter is the case the textual data will no longer allow firm conclusions about Paul. Since text and interpolation

---

12 Walker, "I Corinthians." Walker's method and conclusion were rejected by Murphy-O'Connor, "I Corinthians 11:2–16."

13 Though it is unlikely that Refoulé will receive much scholarly support for his redactional theory, he can count on a secure place in any future treatment of the text of Romans.

14 Walker, "The Burden of Proof," 615.

15 This point was made already more than twenty years ago by Kurt Aland, "Glosse," 34. This article is fundamental for any discussion of redactional theory in the study of early Christian literature.

could no longer be distinguished with certainty, the Pauline corpus as a whole would have to be considered soft and untrustworthy evidence.

Consequently one would expect that those who are engaged in Pauline studies would be very reluctant to conclude that the text of Paul has suffered major redaction changes by later hands. Nothing could be more frustrating for a scholar than having to admit that the evidence with which he or she has to work has seriously been tampered with. Curiously enough, Walker appears eager to emphasize the over-all edited character of the Pauline corpus well beyond what the evidence would seem to require. He is far from alone in this and can list striking examples of the same opinion from the writings of Leander E. Keck, Victor P. Furnish, John Knox, and Dennis R. Mac-Donald.[16] No doubt other such testimonies could have been added. What stands out is the confidence and certainty with which major redactional changing of the text of Paul is affirmed.

Much of this confidence is due to the common fallacy according to which somehow the sum is considered more certain than any of its parts. While one swallow "doth not a summer make," ten possible but uncertain sightings would still not make a summer. When discussing the general phenomenon of redaction scholars tend to ignore the basic uncertainty of almost all of the proposed instances. The case for the major editing of the Pauline letters is not proved by simply adding up the redactional hypotheses that have been proposed over the years by various scholars.

These testimonies by fellow scholars form the substance of Walker's literary-critical considerations that are to prove his case. This *opinio communis* is certainly impressive, but in the final analysis it is only multiple attestation to the same circular argument. In the proposals for specific interpolations the general phenomenon of major editing of the Pauline text is taken for granted, while the general phenomenon is thought to have been proved by those same specific cases. With these literary-critical considerations we are stuck in the realm of the possible without ever getting solid footing.

Walker believes that there are also text-critical considerations that indicate that the text of the Pauline letters underwent extensive redactional modification. This will come as a surprise to the textual critic, for the manuscript evidence shows the opposite of what Walker wants to prove. As he knows, the extant Greek and versional manuscripts and early patristic evidence present a remarkably unified text without a hint of major editing. Though there is manuscript evidence for numerous small changes in the text of Paul, there is proof for only one large redactional intervention. At an early point in the history of the transmission there must have circulated a truncated edition of Romans that omitted chapters 15 and 16 and added a concluding doxology (Rom 16:25–27).[17]

16 Walker, "The Burden of Proof," 611–12.
17 For a full discussion of the evidence, see Gamble, *Textual History*. There is also some manuscript evidence for the dislocation of 1 Cor 14:34–35 after vs 40, but this does not

Actually what Walker calls text-critical considerations are in reality his explanations for why the manuscript evidence—the only "hard" data available in the study of early Christian literature!—does *not* support his contention that the text of Paul was extensively interpolated. The only way out for him is to challenge the witness of the manuscript evidence by claiming that it is deceptive. He must discredit the only "eyewitness" by claiming that the unified voice of the extant manuscripts belies the state of the text in the first and second centuries. To do this he resorts to the historian's favorite sleight of hand, the conspiracy theory.[18] He argues that all the interpolations must have been introduced before the beginning of the third century and that the manuscripts that lacked these redactional additions were eliminated by the Catholic leadership.[19]

In order to have a case at all, Walker would have to show first of all that the history of transmission of the Pauline letters during the second century was governed by quite different factors from later centuries, which show no evidence of major editing. Secondly, he has to find clear indications that the Catholic hierarchy near the end of the second century had both the motivation and the means to eliminate manuscripts that lacked the alleged interpolations.[20]

The strongest argument in favour of setting the early history of transmission of the text apart from the later periods is the fact that it took some time for the Pauline corpus to gain full canonical status. This has led to the assumption that Christian scribes would have been very reluctant to tamper with the text of a canonical writing but would have felt free to introduce changes before a text was recognized as apostolic and authoritative. There are, however, good reasons to doubt this assumption. If true, this would mean that those New Testament writings for which the canonical status was long in doubt would have suffered more extensive and more serious textual corruption, but this is not at all the case. They have suffered far fewer scribal alterations than those that enjoyed unquestioned canonical status already at an earlier point. It is only when a text is considered authoritative that its features become problematic if

really help the case of those who want to argue that 1 Cor 14:33b–36 is an interpolation. To be convincing the whole interpolation would have had to be subject to dislocation.

18 Of course, conspiracy theories cannot be permitted in serious historical reconstruction. Rather than accounting for the existing evidence, such hypotheses included a second level hypothesis, the "conspiracy," which explains why the available evidence does not fit. Such hypotheses have no scholarly value, for they are by definition invulnerable to being defeated by the evidence.

19 Walker, "The Burden of Proof," 614. He appeals for support to Bauer (*Orthodoxy and Heresy,* 160–67). In this section Bauer speculates on the possible editing or suppressing of orthodox heresiological literature by heretics. Even if there were clear proof for this— and there is not—it has no obvious relevance for the possibility that early "defective" manuscripts of the Pauline letters were suppressed in the late second century by the orthodox authorities.

20 For a treatment of the same issues applied to the canonical gospels, see my forthcoming contribution, "Nature and Purpose."

they no longer conform to current beliefs, practices, and literary convention. It may be so that in the pre-canonical period scribes were less hesitant to take liberties with the text,[21] but at the same time there would have been less urgency to change or adapt the language and theology of these writings.

Furthermore, if we judge by the interpolations in New Testament writings for which there is textual evidence then it appears that the numbers increase rather than decrease after the second century. Many of them, including the *pericope adulterae,* are not attested before the fourth century.[22] It would appear that the frequency of copying was a much more important factor in the creation of variants and interpolations than was the canonical status of a writing.

These facts speak against the assumption that by the early third century emerging orthodoxy brought an end to a period of considerable redactional freedom by deciding on a "standard" text and by suppressing all manuscripts that deviated. Far beyond the third century the church was in no position to establish and control the biblical text, let alone eliminate rival forms. Though there may have been an attempt at establishing a standard text as early as the fourth century, only beginning with the twelfth century do we have evidence for a large-scale effort. This is Von Soden's group K^r, which shows evidence of careful control. Even at that late date there was no way to prevent the creation of many divergent copies. Only a small number of manuscripts were consistently corrected to conform to the text of K^r or to that of other groups or text-types. There is no evidence for the Byzantine period or an earlier date of efforts to eliminate divergent copies of New Testament manuscripts.[23]

It is too quickly assumed that second century heretics provide clear examples of the liberties that were taken with the text of New Testament writings. Particularly Marcion is mentioned in this regard.[24] However, as far as we know, Marcion did *not* interpolate the text,[25] but rather excised those parts that he believed the Judaizers had succeeded in adding to the true gospel defended by Paul in Galatians. Apparently Marcion assumed that the original gospel had been preserved; it only needed to be purged from contamination. The criteria he used to distinguish between the original gospel and later

21 This is generally assumed by textual critics (e.g., Aland and Aland, *The Text of the New Testament,* 64), but the evidence for this is scant.
22 The most drastic redactional intervention for which there is evidence, the so-called long text of Acts, is likely not earlier than the third century. This is the "Western" text of Acts in its strictest sense, No. 2 in Haenchen's excellent overview (*Acts,* 51–53).
23 The high cost of producing a biblical manuscript makes any interest in eliminating deviant texts improbable. The obvious procedure was to enter correction. Scribes who copied from a corrected manuscript often alerted their readers that a certain reading or sentence was found above the line or in the margin. We do know of concerted efforts in the late fourth and in the fifth century to destroy copies of heretical writings such as those of Origen. In spite of the fact that the number of copies of these writings must have been very limited, the attempt to eliminate them was only partially successful. It appears that as late as the fourth century the Nag Hammadi Codices, with clearly heretical content, could be produced in an "orthodox" Pachomian monastery.
24 E.g., Walker, "The Burden of Proof," 614.
25 Harnack, *Marcion,* 61.

interpolations can still be perceived. Marcion was far from typical for his time, and the closest parallel to him is the modern, scholarly attempt to free the text of Paul from interpolations. Both start from the assumption that the text has suffered extensive corruption. Marcion thought the Judaizing pseudo-apostles were the culprits, while modern critics tend to put the blame on early Catholic scribes who must have shared the theological outlook of the Pastorals.[26] Neither view is historically implausible, but nonetheless the charges have no historical basis. Also in both cases theological, or rather ideological criteria are used to distinguish the genuine text from interpolations.[27]

Also other second-century heretics have been accused of taking liberties with the scriptures, but normally this involves their *interpretation* and not redactional changes. Gnostics were able to manipulate the meaning of the text in such a way that it always supported their views. Concerning the Valentinians, whose use of scripture is best attested, Elaine Pagels concludes:

> While Marcion sought to exclude elements of the texts he considered inauthentic, Valentinus tended instead to accept the full texts available to him, interpreting them esoterically. Valentinus' followers accepted, apparently, the full texts of Paul's own letters; and while they virtually ignored the Pastorals, they willingly included (and, indeed, highly revered) Ephesians, Colossians, and Hebrews as sources of Pauline tradition.[28]

The appeal to a conspiracy theory must face another, perhaps even more serious objection to overcome the obvious lack of textual evidence for extensive redactional changes in the text of Paul. It runs counter to the remarkable tenacity of the shorter form of a text in spite of the overwhelming acceptance of many of the evident interpolations.[29] Kurt Aland has argued and documented this convincingly.[30] He refers to it as the inevitable "ripple effect" caused by a disturbance in the "pool" of the history of transmission. In a more recent publication, Barbara Aland stresses that "major disturbances in the transmission of the New Testament text can always be identified with confidence, even if they occurred during the second century or at its beginning," and, "Every reading ever occurring in the New Testament textual tradition is stubbornly preserved, even if the result is nonsense."[31]

---

26 E.g., MacDonald, *The Legend and the Apostle,* 86.
27 One apparent difference is that the modern critic often adds philological reasons to justify the identification of an interpolation. However, this is little more than a rationalization, since no effort is made to show that other, unquestionably Pauline passages normally can survive such a test, or that clearly non-Pauline passages of a similar type could normally not pass it. Actually it is widely agreed that our present criteria to determine authentic Pauline style and vocabulary are not really satisfactory.
28 Pagels, *The Gnostic Paul,* 163.
29 The acceptance of these interpolations was almost certainly not due to hierarchical decision and enforcement, but to the fact that they commended themselves to almost all copyists and readers. Until the modern period *lectio facilior* was *potior* and not *lectio difficilior* or *lectio brevior!* (The easier reading was more likely the original one, not the more difficult or the shorter reading.)
30 Aland, "Glosse," 35–57.
31 Aland and Aland, *The Text of the New Testament,* 290–91.

Thus the claim of extensive redaction of the Pauline corpus runs counter to all the textual evidence. This lack of evidence cannot be explained away by speculations about an extensively interpolated "standard" text that was imposed by the orthodox leadership late in the second century, or by the successful suppression of all uninterpolated copies. The Church certainly lacked the means and most likely also the will to do this. If indeed the text of the Pauline letters had been subjected to extensive redactional change and adaptation during the second century, the unanimous attestation of a relatively stable and uniform text during the following centuries in both Greek and the versions would have to be considered nothing short of a miracle.

This leaves only one way open for those who would still want to maintain that the text of Paul underwent major editing. They can try to escape where the manuscript evidence cannot reach, the brief period before the "publication" of the letters. However, there is little comfort to be gotten there. To concentrate the redactional activity at this early stage is to attribute what Walter Schmithals rightly calls a *Kompositionspsychose* to the editors of the letters.[32] This would be entirely implausible and unprecedented. The unknown period before publication of the letters may leave room for the imagination but not for scholarly argumentation.

It seems, therefore, appropriate to draw the following conclusions. What sets the scholarly study of early Christian literature apart from the long history of ecclesiastical interpretation is its commitment to stay within the bounds of the evidence. This evidence is the text, which is established on the basis of physical data, a large and varied collection of manuscripts. These manuscripts indicate that the text underwent many minor and some major alterations during the long history of transmission.

The question must be asked whether there are good reasons to suspect that a number of major redactional changes were introduced that left no "ripples" in the extant manuscript attestation. Though the possibility of this cannot be ruled out, we know enough about the history of transmission to make it highly improbable. An important part of the scholarly task is to protect the text against unwarranted challenges to its reliability. Proposals for interpolations must shoulder the full burden of proof. If they cannot present clear and convincing evidence of textual upheaval they are of no scholarly value, and the passages in question should continue to be treated as genuine.

There are no good reasons to doubt that the reliability of the text of the Pauline letters is what it appears to be on the basis of the manuscript evidence. Even if by chance it were not, scholarship is in no position to bring order to the matter. Redactional theory that steps outside the bounds of textual evidence and minimizes the burden of proof is counter-productive and a hindrance to Pauline studies.

---

32 Schmithals,"On the Composition," 272. Gamble has shown that Schmithals's own solution, i.e., to attribute the editing to a single compiler and publisher of the corpus, is also untenable ("The Redaction of The Pauline Letters").

Works Consulted

Achilles Tatius. Trans. S. Gaselee. LCL. London: William Heinemann Ltd; New York: G. P. Putnam's Sons, 1917.

Aland, Kurt, "Glosse, Interpolation, Redaktion und Komposition in der Sicht der neutestamentlichen Textkritik." Pp. 35–57 in *Studien zur Überlieferung des Neuen Testaments und seines Textes.* Arbeiten zur neutestamentlichen Textforschung 2. Berlin: Walter de Gruyter & Co., 1967.

_____, and Barbara Aland, *The Text of the New Testament: An Introduction to the Critical Edition and to the Theory and Practice of Modern Textual Criticism.* Trans. Erroll F. Rhodes. Grand Rapids, MI: William B. Eerdmans Publishing Company; Leiden: E.J. Brill, 1987.

_____, et al., ed., *The Greek New Testament.* Stuttgart: Wuerttemberg Bible Society for the United Bible Societies, 1966.

_____, et al., ed., Nestle-Aland, *Novum Testamentum Graece.* 26th ed. Stuttgart: Deutsche Bibelstiftung, 1979.

Anderson, Graham, *Ancient Fiction. The Novel in the Graeco-Roman World.* London and Sidney: Croom Helm; Totowa, NJ: Barnes and Noble, 1984.

Anderson, Hugh, "Broadening Horizons: The Rejection at Nazareth Pericope of Luke 4:16–30 in the Light of Recent Trends." *Intepretation* 18 (1964): 264–66.

Apuleius, *The Golden Ass. Being the Metamorphoses of Lucius Apuleius.* Trans. W. Adlington, rev. S. Gaselee. LCL. Cambridge, MA: Harvard University Press; London: William Heinemann Ltd., 1977.

Aristotle. Vol. 22: *The "Art" of Rhetoric.* Trans. John Henry Freese. LCL. Cambridge, MA: Harvard University Press; London: William Heinemann Ltd., 1975.

Asmus, V. P., *Antichnaya filosofia.* Moscow: Vysshaya shkola, 1976.

Attridge, Harold A., "Gospel of Thomas." Pp. 355–56 in *Harper's Bible Dictionary.* Ed. Paul J. Achtemeier. San Francisco: Harper & Row, 1985.

Augustine, *De consensu evangelistarum.* PL 34. Paris: Migne, 1887.

Aune, David E., *Prophecy in Early Christianity and the Ancient Mediterranean World.* Grand Rapids, MI: William B. Eerdmans Publishing Company, 1983.

Baarda, Tjitze, "Maar de toorn is over hen gekomen . . . ! 1 Thess. 2:16c." Pp. 15–74 in *Paulus en de andere Joden.* Delft: Meinema, 1987.

Barrett, C. K., *The Holy Spirit and the Gospel Tradition.* New York: Macmillan, 1947.

_____, *The First Epistle to the Corinthians.* London: Adam & Charles Black, 1968.

_____, *A Commentary on The Second Epistle to the Corinthians*. London: Adam and Charles Black, 1973.

_____, *The Gospel According to St. John: An Introduction with Commentary and Notes on the Greek Text*. 2d ed. London: SPCK, 1978.

Barth, Gerhard, "Matthew's Understanding of the Law." Pp. 52–164 in *Tradition and Interpretation in Matthew*. By G. Bornkamm, G. Barth, and H.-J. Held. London: SCM Press; Philadelphia: The Westminster Press, 1963.

Bauer, Walter, *Orthodoxy and Heresy in Earliest Christianity*. Ed. and trans. Robert Kraft and Gerhard Krodel. Philadelphia: Fortress Press, 1971.

_____, *A Greek-English Lexicon of the New Testament and Other Early Christian Literature*. 2d ed. Trans., rev., and aug. William F. Arndt, Wilbur Gingrich, and Frederick W. Danker. Chicago: University of Chicago Press, 1979.

Baur, Ferdinand Christian, *Kritische Untersuchungen über die kanonischen Evangelien, ihr Verhältnis zueinander, ihren Charakter und Ursprung*. Tübingen: Fues, 1847.

Beasley-Murray, G. R., "John 3:3, 5: Baptism, Spirit and the Kingdom." *Expository Times* 97,6 (1986): 167–70.

Benstock, Shari, "At the Margin of Discourse. Footnotes in the Fictional Text." *Proceedings of the Modern Language Association* 98,1 (1983): 204–25.

Beskow, Per, *Strange Tales about Jesus: A Survey of Unfamiliar Gospels*. Philadelphia: Fortress Press, 1983.

Betz, Hans Dieter, *Galatians: A Commentary on Paul's Letter to the Churches in Galatia*. Hermeneia. Philadelphia: Fortress Press, 1979.

_____, *Essays on the Sermon on the Mount*. Philadelphia: Fortress Press, 1985.

_____, "Neues Testament und griechisch-hellenistische Überlieferung," read at the Annual Meeting of S.N.T.S. at Göttingen, 1987.

_____, *Hellenismus und Urchristentum. Gesammelte Aufsätze I*. Tübingen: J.C.B. Mohr (Paul Siebeck), 1990.

_____, "The Problem of Christology in the Sermon on the Mount," to be published in the *Festschrift* for Hendrikus W. Boers.

Betz, Otto, "Der gekreuzigte Christus: Unsere Weisheit und Gerechtigkeit (Der alttestamentliche Hintergrund von 1. Kor 1–2)." Pp. 195–215 in *Tradition and Interpretation in the New Testament*. Ed. Gerald F. Hawthorne with Otto Betz. Grand Rapids, MI: William B. Eerdmans Publishing Co.; Tübingen: J.C.B. Mohr (Paul Siebeck), 1987.

Bjerkelund, Carl J., *Tauta Egeneto. Die Präzisierungssätze im Johannesevangelium*. Tübingen: J.C.B. Mohr (Paul Siebeck), 1987.

Booth, Wayne, *The Rhetoric of Fiction*. Chicago and London: University of Chicago Press, 1961.

Borg, Marcus J., "A Temperate Case for a Non-Eschatological Jesus." *Forum* 2,3 (1986): 81–102.

Boring, M. Eugene, "The Influence of Christian Prophecy on the Johannine Portrayal of the Paraclete and Jesus." *New Testament Studies* 25 (1979): 113–23.

_____, *Sayings of the Risen Jesus: Christian Prophecy in the Synoptic Tradition*. SNTSMS 46. Cambridge and New York: Cambridge University Press, 1982.

Bornkamm, Günther, Gerhard Barth, and Heinz Joachim Held, *Tradition and Interpretation in Matthew*. Trans. and ed. Percy Scott. Philadelphia: The Westminster Press, 1963.

_____, "μυστήριον." *Theological Dictionary of the New Testament* 4 (1967): 802–28.

_____, *Early Christian Experience*. New York and Evanston, IL: Harper & Row, 1969.

_____, *Paul*. Trans. D. M. G. Stalker. New York and Evanston, IL: Harper & Row, 1971=*Paulus*. Stuttgart: W. Kohlammer, 1968.

Bovon, François, *Luc le théologien*. Neuchâtel and Paris: Delachaux et Niestlé, 1978.

Braun, Herbert, *Qumran und das Neue Testament*. Vol. I. Tübingen: J.C.B. Mohr (Paul Siebeck), 1966.

_____, *Spätjüdisch-häretischer und frühchristlicher Radikalismus*. 2d ed. Beiträge zur historischen Theologie 24. Tübingen: J.C.B. Mohr (Paul Siebeck), 1969.

Brown, Raymond E., *The Gospel According to John I–XII* and *The Gospel According to John XIII–XXI*. AB 29, 29A. Garden City, NY: Doubleday & Co., 1966–1970.

_____, "The Relation of 'The Secret Gospel of Mark' to the Fourth Gospel." *Catholic Biblical Quarterly* 36 (1974): 466–85.

_____, *The Birth of the Messiah: A Commentary on the Infancy Narratives in Matthew and Luke*. Garden City, NY: Doubleday & Co., 1977.

Brox, Norbert, *Zeuge und Märtyrer*. Studien zum Alten und Neuen Testament 5. Munich: Kösel Verlag, 1961.

Bruce, F. F., *1 and 2 Corinthians*. London: Oliphants, 1971.

_____, *The "Secret" Gospel of Mark*. Ethel M. Wood Lecture. London: Athlone Press, 1974.

Bultmann, Rudolf, *Theology of the New Testament*. 2 vols. Trans. K. Grobel. New York: Charles Scribner's Sons, 1951–55.

_____, *The History of the Synoptic Tradition*. Trans. and ed. John Marsh (from 2d German ed., 1931). Rev. ed. Oxford: Basil Blackwell, 1963; rev. ed. 1968.

_____, *The Gospel of John: A Commentary*. Trans. G. R. Beasley-Murray, R. W. N. Hoare, and J. K. Riches. Philadelphia: The Westminster Press, 1971.

_____, *Theologie des Neuen Testaments*. 9th ed. Tübingen: J.C.B. Mohr (Paul Siebeck), 1984.

_____, *The Second Letter to the Corinthians*. (Original German Edition [1976] ed. Erich Dinkler.) Minneapolis: Augsburg Publishing House, 1985.

Butts, James R., "Probing the Polling." *Forum* 3,1 (1987): 98–128.

_____, and Ron Cameron, "Sayings of Jesus: Classification by Source and Authenticity." *Forum* 3,2 (1987): 96–116.

Cadbury, Henry J., *The Style and Literary Method of Luke*. HTS 6. Cambridge, MA: Harvard University Press, 1920.

Callan, Terrance, "Prophecy and Ecstasy in Greco-Roman Religion and in 1 Corinthians." *Novum Testamentum* 27 (1985): 125–40.

Cameron, Ron, *The Other Gospels*. Philadelphia: The Westminster Press, 1982.

_____, *Sayings Traditions in the Apocryphon of James*. HTS 34. Philadelphia: Fortress Press, 1984.

_____, "Parable and Interpretation in the Gospel of Thomas." *Forum* 2,2 (1986): 3–40.

Campenhausen, Hans von, *The Formation of the Christian Bible*. Trans. J. A. Baker. Philadelphia: Fortress Press, 1972.

Carlston, Charles E., "Betz on the Sermon on the Mount—A Critique." *Catholic Biblical Quarterly* 50 (1988): 47–57.

Chatman, Seymour, *Story and Discourse. Narrative Structure in Fiction and Film*. Ithaca, NY, and London: Cornell University Press, 1978.

Chevallier, Max-Alain, *Souffle de dieu: Le saint-esprit dans le Nouveau Testament*. Vol.

1: *Ancien Testament, Hellénisme et Judaïsme; La tradition synoptique; L'oeuvre de Luc.* Le pointe théologique 26. Paris: Editions Beauchesne, 1978.

Chrysostom, John, *Homiliae XC in Matthaeum.* PG 57. Paris: Migne, 1862.

Cicero, *Ad C. Herennium. De ratione dicendi (Rhetorica ad Herrenium).* Trans. Harry Caplan. LCL. Cambridge, MA: Harvard University Press; London: William Heinemann Ltd., 1954.

———, *De officiis.* Trans. Walter Miller. LCL. London: William Heinemann; New York: The Macmillan Co., 1913.

Claudii Aeliani Varia Historia. Ed. Rudolph Hercher. Leipzig: B. G. Teubner, 1887.

Clemens Alexandrinus, *Stromata.* PG 8. Paris: Migne, 1891.

Collins, John J., "Cosmos and Salvation: Jewish Wisdom and Apocalyptic in the Hellenistic Age." *History of Religions* 17 (1977): 121–42.

———, *Between Athens and Jerusalem: Jewish Identity in the Hellenistic Diaspora.* New York: Crossroad, 1983.

Conybeare, F. C., "The Testament of Solomon." *Jewish Quarterly Review* 11 (1899): 1–45.

Conzelmann, Hans, *Die Mitte der Zeit.* 2d ed. Beiträge zur historischen Theologie 17. Tübingen: J.C.B. Mohr (Paul Siebeck), 1957.

———, *The Theology of St. Luke.* Trans. and ed. Geoffrey Buswell (from the 2d German ed. [1957]). New York: Harper & Row, 1960.

———, *Die Apostelgeschichte.* Handbuch zum Neuen Testament 7. Tübingen: J.C.B. Mohr (Paul Siebeck), 1963.

———, *1 Corinthians: A Commentary on the First Epistle to the Corinthians.* Trans. James W. Leitch, bibl. and ref. James W. Dunkly, ed. George W. MacRae. Hermeneia. Philadelphia: Fortress Press, 1975.

Crone, T. M., *Early Christian Prophecy: A Study of Its Origin and Function.* Baltimore: St Mary's University Press, 1973.

Crossan, John Dominic, *In Parables: The Challenge of the Historical Jesus.* New York: Harper & Row, 1973.

———, "Mark 12:13–17." *Interpretation* 37 (1983): 397–401.

———, *In Fragments: The Aphorisms of Jesus.* San Francisco: Harper & Row, 1983.

———, *Four Other Gospels: Shadows on the Contours of Canon.* Minneapolis: Winston Press, 1985.

———, *Sayings Parallels. A Workbook for the Jesus Tradition.* Sonoma, CA: Polebridge Press, 1986.

Cullmann, Oscar, *Baptism in the New Testament.* Trans. and ed. J. K. S. Reid. Studies in Biblical Theology 1. London: SCM Press, 1973 (orig. pub., 1950).

Culpepper, R. Alan, *Anatomy of the Fourth Gospel. A Study in Literary Design.* Foundations and Facets. Philadelphia: Fortress Press, 1983.

Dahl, Nils A., "A Fragment and Its Context: 2 Cor. 6:14–7:1." Pp. 62–69 in *Studies in Paul.* By N. A. Dahl. Minneapolis: Augsburg Publishing House, 1977.

Dautzenberg, Gerhard, *Urchristliche Prophetie.* Stuttgart: W. Kohlhammer, 1975.

———, "Botschaft und Bedeutung der urchristlichen Prophetie nach dem ersten Korintherbrief (2:6–16; 12–14)." Pp. 131–61 in *Prophetic Vocation in the New Testament and Today.* Ed. J. Panagopoulos. Leiden: E.J. Brill, 1977.

———, "Zur Stellung der Frauen in den paulinischen Gemeinden." Pp. 182–224 in *Die Frau im Urchristentum.* Ed. G. Dautzenberg, H. Merklein, and K. Mueller. Quaestiones Disputatae 95. Freiburg, Basel, and Vienna: Herder, 1983.

Davies, Stevan L., *The Gospel of Thomas and Christian Wisdom*. New York: The Seabury Press, 1983.

de Wette, Wilhelm Martin Leberecht, *Kurze Erklärung des Evangeliums Matthäi*. Pp. 66–69 in *Kurzgefasstes exegetisches Handbuch zum Neuen Testament*. Vol. 1, Part 1. Leipzig: Hirzel, 1st ed. 1836–38; 4th ed. 1857.

Degenhardt, H.-J., *Lukas—Evangelist der Armen*. Stuttgart: Katholisches Bibelwerk, 1965.

Dijkman, J. H. L., "I Peter: A Later Pastoral Stratum?" *New Testament Studies* 33 (1987): 265–71.

Diogenes Laertius, *Lives of Eminent Philosophers*. 2 vols. Trans. P. D. Hicks. LCL. Cambridge, MA: Harvard University Press; London: William Heinemann Ltd., 1972.

Dodd, C. H., *The Interpretation of the Fourth Gospel*. Cambridge: University Press, 1953.

_____, *Historical Tradition in the Fourth Gospel*. Cambridge: University Press, 1963.

Douglas, Mary, "Social Preconditions of Enthusiasm and Heterodoxy." Pp. 69–80 in *Forms of Symbolic Action*. Ed. R. F. Spencer. Proceedings of the 1969 Annual Spring Meeting of the American Ethnological Society. Seattle: University of Washington Press, 1969.

_____, *Natural Symbols: Explorations in Cosmology*. Harmondsworth, England, and New York: Penguin Books, 1973.

_____, *Cultural Bias*. Royal Anthropological Institute of Great Britain and Ireland, Occasional Paper 35, 1978.

Duke, Paul D., *Irony in the Fourth Gospel*. Atlanta: John Knox Press, 1985.

Dunn, James D. G., *Baptism in the Holy Spirit: A Reexamination of the New Testament Teaching on the Gift of the Spirit in Relation to Pentecostalism Today*. Studies in Biblical Theology 2/15. London: SCM Press, 1970.

_____, "1 Corinthians 15:45—Last Adam, Life-Giving Spirit." Pp. 132–41 in *Christ and Spirit in the New Testament*. Ed. Barnabas Lindars and Stephen S. Smalley. Cambridge: University Press, 1973.

_____, *Jesus and the Spirit*. London: SCM Press, 1975.

Eichhorn, Johann Gottfried, "Ueber die drey ersten Evangelien. Einige Beyträge zu ihrer künftigen kritischen Behandlung." Pp. 761–996 in *Eichhorn's Allgemeine Bibliothek der biblischen Litteratur*. Vol. 5, parts 5 and 6. Leipzig: Weidmann, 1794.

_____, *Einleitung in das Neue Testament*, in *Kritische Schriften*. Vol. 5. Leipzig: Weidmann, 1804.

Elliott, John H., Review of *Authority in Paul and Peter* by Winsome Munro. *Religious Studies Review* 10 (1984): 71.

Ellis, E. Earle, *Prophecy and Hermeneutic in Early Christianity*. Grand Rapids, MI: William B. Eerdmans Publishing Company, 1978.

_____, "The Silenced Wives of Corinth (I Cor. 14:34–5)." Pp. 213–20 in *New Testament Textual Criticism: Its Significance for Exegesis. Essays in Honour of Bruce M. Metzger*. Ed. Eldon Jay Epp and Gordon D. Fee. Oxford: The Clarendon Press, 1981.

Engelson, Nils Ivar Johan, "Glossolalia and Other Forms of Inspired Speech According to I Corinthians 12–14." Ph.D. diss., Yale University, 1970.

Eskenazi, Tamera, *In an Age of Prose. A Literary Approach to Ezra–Nehemiah*. Atlanta: Scholars Press, 1988.

Esler, Philip F., *Community and Gospel in Luke–Acts*. SNTSMS 57. Cambridge and elsewhere: Cambridge University Press, 1987.

Eusebius, *The Ecclesiastical History*. 2 vols. Trans. Kirsopp Lake and J. E. L. Oulton. LCL. London: William Heinemann; New York: G. P. Putnam's Sons, 1926.

Euthymius, *Expositio in Matthaeum*. PG 129. Paris: Migne, 1864.

Ewald, Heinrich, *Die ersten drei Evangelien übersetzt und erklärt*. Göttingen: Dieterich, 1850.

Fallon, Francis T., and Ron Cameron, "The Gospel of Thomas: A Forschungsbericht and Analysis," *Aufstieg und Niedergang der römischen Welt*, Part II, Vol. 25,6 (1988): 4195–54.

Fee, Gordon D., *The First Epistle to the Corinthians*. Grand Rapids, MI: William B. Eerdmans Publishing Company, 1987.

Filson, Floyd V., "Who Was the Beloved Disciple?" *Journal of Biblical Literature* 68 (1949): 83–88.

Fischer, Bonifatius, "Das Neue Testament in lateinischer Sprache: Der gegenwärtige Stand seiner Erforschung und seine Bedeutung für die griechische Textgeschichte." Pp. 1–92 in *Die alten Übersetzungen des Neuen Testaments, die Kirchenväterzitate und Lektionare*. Ed. Kurt Aland. Berlin and New York: Walter de Gruyter & Co., 1972.

Fitzmyer, Joseph A., *The Gospel According to Luke I–IX* and *The Gospel According to Luke X–XXIV*. AB 28, 28A. Garden City, NY: Doubleday & Co., 1981–85.

Flemington, W. R., *The New Testament Doctrine of Baptism*. London: S.P.C.K., 1948.

Foerster, Werner, "κύριος, κτλ.: E. κύριος in the New Testament." *Theological Dictionary of the New Testament* 3 (1965): 1086–98.

Fortna, Robert T., *The Gospel of Signs*. SNTSMS 11. London and New York: Cambridge University Press, 1970.

Frede, Josef, *Altlateinische Paulus–Handschriften*. Vetus Latina 4. Freiburg: Herder, 1964.

Friedrich, Gerhard, "προφήτης." *Theological Dictionary of the New Testament* 6 (1968): 828–61.

Fuller, Reginald H., *The Formation of the Resurrection Narratives*. First Fortress Press Edition. Philadelphia: Fortress Press, 1980 (orig. pub. 1971).

Funk, Robert W., *The Poetics of Biblical Narrative*. Foundations & Facets. Sonoma, CA: Polebridge Press, 1988.

———, "Word and Word in I Corinthians 2:6–16." Pp. 275–305 in *Language, Hermeneutic, and Word of God*. By Robert W. Funk. New York, Evanston, IL, and London: Harper & Row, 1966.

Gamble, Harry, Jr., "The Redaction of the Pauline Letters and the Formation of the Pauline Corpus." *Journal of Biblical Literature* 94 (1975): 403–18.

———, *The Textual History of the Letter to the Romans. A Study in Textual and Literary Criticism*. Studies and Documents 42. Grand Rapids, MI: William B. Eerdmans Publishing Company, 1977.

Garland, David E., "The Composition and Unity of Philippians. Some Neglected Literary Factors." *Novum Testamentum* 27 (1985): 141–73.

Garvie, A. E., *The Beloved Disciple. Studies of the Fourth Gospel*. London: Hodder and Stoughton, 1922.

Genette, Gérard, *Narrative Discourse. An Essay in Method.* Trans. J. E. Lewin. Ithaca, NY: Cornell University Press, 1980.

Georgi, Dieter, *Die Geschichte der Kollekte des Paulus für Jerusalem.* Theologische Forschung 38. Hamburg–Bergstedt: H. Reich, 1965.

_____, *The Opponents of Paul in Second Corinthians: A Study of Religious Propaganda in Late Antiquity.* Philadelphia: Fortress Press; Edinburgh: T. & T. Clark, 1986 [translated from German (1964), with Epilogue added].

Gewalt, Dietfried, "Neutestamentliche Exegese und Soziologie." *Evangelische Theologie* 31 (1971): 87–99.

Gillespie, Thomas W., "A Pattern of Prophetic Speech in First Corinthians." *Journal of Biblical Literature* 97 (1978): 74–95.

Goguel, Maurice, *Au seuil de l'Evangile: Jean-Baptiste.* Paris: Payot, 1928.

Grant, Robert M., and David Noel Freedman, *The Secret Sayings of Jesus.* Garden City, NY: Doubleday & Co., 1960.

Greene, Graham, *The Power and the Glory.* New York: Viking Press, 1961.

Greeven, Heinrich, "Propheten, Lehrer, Vorsteher bei Paulus: Zur Frage der 'Ämter' im Urchristentum." *Zeitschrift für die Neutestamentliche Wissenschaft* 44 (1952–53): 3–15.

Grudem, Wayne A., *The Gift of Prophecy in 1 Corinthians.* Washington, DC: University Press of America, Inc., 1982.

Grundmann, Walter, *Die Frage der ältesten Gestalt und des ursprünglichen Sinnes der Bergrede Jesu.* Weimar: Verlag der Deutschen Christen, 1939.

_____, *Jesus der Galiläer und das Judentum.* Leipzig: Wigand, 1940.

Gundry, Robert H., *Matthew. A Commentary on His Literary and Theological Art.* Grand Rapids, MI: William B. Eerdmans Publishing Company, 1982.

Gunkel, Herman, *The Influence of the Holy Spirit: The Popular View of the Apostolic Age and the Teaching of the Apostle Paul.* Trans. and ed. Roy A. Harrisville and Philip A. Quanbeck II. Philadelphia: Fortress Press, 1979=*Die Wirkungen des heiligen Geistes nach der populären Anschauung der apostolischen Zeit und der Lehre des Apostels Paulus* (orig. pub., 1888).

Hägg, Thomas, *The Novel in Antiquity.* Berkeley and Los Angeles: University of California Press, 1983.

Haenchen, Ernst, "Literatur zum Thomasevangelium." *Theologische Rundschau* 27 (1961–62): 147–78, 306–38.

_____, *The Acts of the Apostles: A Commentary.* Trans. and ed. R. McL. Wilson. Philadelphia: The Westminster Press, 1971.

_____, *John 1: A Commentary on the Gospel of John, Chapters 1–6.* Ed. and trans. Robert W. Funk and Ulrich Busse. Hermeneia. Philadelphia: Fortress Press, 1984.

Harnack, Adolf, *Sprüche und Reden Jesu. Die zweite Quelle des Matthäus und Lukas.* Vol. 2 of *Beiträge zur Einleitung in das Neue Testament.* Leipzig: J. C. Hinrichs, 1907.

_____, *The Sayings of Jesus.* London: Williams and Norgate; New York: G. P. Putnam's Sons, 1908.

_____, *Marcion: Das Evangelium vom fremden Gott.* TU 45. 2d ed. Leipzig: J. C. Hinrichs, 1924.

_____, *Das Wesen des Christentums.* Leipzig: J. C. Hinrichs, 1900. Reprint ed. with an introduction by Rudolf Bultmann. Stuttgart: Ehrenfried Klotz Verlag, 1950.

Hauschild, W.-D., "Christentum und Eigentum." *Zeitschrift für evangelische Ethik* 16 (1976): 34–49.

Hedrick, Charles W., "The Treasure Parable in Matthew and Thomas." *Forum* 2,2 (1986): 41–56.

———, "Narrator and Story in the Gospel of Mark: *Hermeneia* and *Paradosis*." *Perspectives in Religious Studies* 14,3 (1987): 239–58.

———, Review of Gilbert Van Belle, *Les parenthèses dans l'Evangile de Jean*. *Journal of Biblical Literature* 106 (1987): 719–21.

Heinrici, Carl Friedrich Georg, *Die Bergpredigt (Matth. 5–7. Luk. 6, 20–49) quellenkritisch und begriffsgeschichtlich untersucht*. Parts 2 and 3 of his *Beiträge zur Geschichte und Erklärung des Neuen Testaments*. Leipzig: Dürr, 1900, 1905.

Hengel, Martin, *Eigentum und Reichtum in der frühen Kirche*. Stuttgart: Calwer Verlag, 1973.

Herder, Johann Gottfried, *Erläuterungen zum Neuen Testament aus einer neueröffneten Morgenländischen Quelle*. Riga: Hartknoch, 1775.

Hill, David, "Christian Prophets as Teachers or Instructors in the Church." Pp. 108–30 in *Prophetic Vocation in the New Testament and Today*. Ed. J. Panagopoulos. Leiden: E.J. Brill, 1977.

———, *New Testament Prophecy*. Atlanta: John Knox Press, 1979.

Hoffman, Paul, Review of *Q. Die Spruchquelle der Evangelisten*, by Siegfried Schulz. *Biblische Zeitschrift* NF 19 (1975): 104–15.

———, "Die Anfänge der Theologie in der Logienquelle," Pp. 134–52 in *Gestalt und Anspruch des Neuen Testaments*. Ed. Josef Schreiner. Würzburg: Echter Verlag, 1969.

———, *Studien zur Theologie der Logienquelle*. 2d ed. Neutestamentliche Abhandlungen, NF 8. Münster: Aschendorff, 1975.

Holtzmann, Heinrich Julius, *Die synoptischen Evangelien, ihr Ursprung und geschichtlicher Charakter*. Leipzig: Engelmann, 1863.

Hommel, Hildebrecht, "Herrenworte im Lichte sokratischer Überlieferung." *Zeitschrift für die Neutestamentliche Wissenschaft* 57 (1966): 1–23. Repr. as pp. 51–74 in his *Sebasmata: Studien zur antiken Religionsgeschichte und zum frühen Christentum*. Vol. 2. WUNT 32. Tübingen: J.C.B. Mohr (Paul Siebeck), 1984.

Hooke, S. H., "The Spirit Was Not Yet." *New Testament Studies* 9 (1962–63): 372–80.

Horn, F.-W., *Glauben und Handeln in der Theologie des Lukas*. Göttinger theologische Arbeiten 26. Göttingen: Vandenhoeck & Ruprecht, 1983.

Horsley, Richard A., "Paul and the *Pneumatikoi*: First Corinthians Investigated in Terms of the Conflict between Two Different Religious Mentalities." Ph.D. diss., Harvard University, 1970.

———, "How Can Some of You Say That There Is No Resurrection of the Dead? Spiritual Elitism in Corinth." *Novum Testamentum* 20 (1978): 203–31.

———, "Ethics and Exegesis: 'Love Your Enemies' and the Doctrine of Non-violence." *Journal of the American Academy of Religion* 54 (1986): 3–31.

———, *Jesus and the Spiral of Violence*. San Francisco: Harper & Row, 1987.

Hurd, John C., "Paul Ahead of His Time: 1 Thess. 2:13–16." Pp. 21–36 in *Anti-Judaism in Early Christianity*. Vol. 1. Ed. P. Richardson and D. Granskou. Waterloo: Wilfrid Laurier University Press, 1986.

Iamblichi De vita Pythagorica liber. Ed. Augustus Nauck. Amsterdam: Adolf M. Hakkert, 1884.

Jacobson, Arland D. "Wisdom Christology in Q." Ph.D. diss., Claremont Graduate School, 1978.

Jaffee, M. S., *Mishnah's Theology of Tithing: A Study of Tractate Maaserot.* Brown Judaic Studies 19. Chico, CA: Scholars Press, 1981.

Jeremias, Joachim, *New Testament Theology: The Proclamation of Jesus.* Trans. and ed. John Bowden. New York: Charles Scribner's Sons, 1971.

Johnson, L. T., *The Literary Function of Possessions in Luke-Acts.* SBL Dissertation Series 39. Missoula, MT: Scholars Press, 1977.

———, *Sharing Possessions.* Overtures to Biblical Theology 9. Philadelphia: Fortress Press, 1981.

Judd, Bo, "The Enigmatic *ALLA* in I Corinthians 2.9." *New Testament Studies* 31 (1988): 603–11.

Judge, E. A., *The Social Pattern of the Christian Groups in the First Century.* London: S.P.C.K., 1960.

Kahl, Brigitte, *Armenevangelium und Heidenevangelium.* Berlin: Evangelische Verlagsanstalt, 1987.

Karris, R. J., "Poor and Rich: The Lukan Sitz im Leben." Pp. 112–25 in *Perspectives on Luke-Acts.* Ed. C. H. Talbert. Special Studies Series 5. Edinburgh: T. & T. Clark, 1978.

Keck, L. E., "The Poor among the Saints in Jewish Christianity and Qumran." *Zeitschrift für die Neutestamentliche Wissenschaft* 57 (1966): 54–78.

Kelber, Werner H., *The Oral and the Written Gospel: The Hermeneutics of Speaking and Writing in the Synoptic Tradition, Mark, Paul, and Q.* Philadelphia: Fortress Press, 1983.

King, Karen, "Kingdom in the Gospel of Thomas." *Forum* 3,1 (1987): 48–97.

Kingsbury, Jack D., "Reflections on 'the Reader' of Matthew's Gospel." *New Testament Studies* 34 (1988): 442–60.

Kippenberg, H.-G., *Religion und Klassenbildung im antiken Judäa.* Studien zur Umwelt des Neuen Testaments 14. Göttingen: Vandenhoeck & Ruprecht, 1978.

Klauck, H.-J., "Gütergemeinschaft in der klassischen Antike." *Revue de Qumran* 11 (41) (1982): 47–79.

———, "Die Armut der Jünger in der Sicht des Lukas." *Claretianum* 26 (1986): 4–47.

Kloppenborg, John S., "Tradition and Redaction in the Synoptic Sayings Source." *Catholic Biblical Quarterly* 46 (1984): 34–62.

———, "Symbolic Eschatology and the Apocalypticism of Q," *Harvard Theological Review* 80 (1987): 287–306.

———, *The Formation of Q. Trajectories in Ancient Wisdom Collections.* Studies in Antiquity and Christianity 1. Philadelphia: Fortress Press, 1987.

———, *Q Parallels: Synopsis, Critical Notes, & Concordance.* Foundations and Facets Reference Series. Sonoma, CA: Polebridge Press, 1988.

———, "'Easter Faith' and the Sayings Gospel Q." In *Reconsidering Christian Beginnings: The Challenge of the Apocryphal Jesus.* Ed. Ron Cameron. Semeia (Forthcoming).

Klostermann, Erich, ed., *Origenes Werke.* Vol. 10: *Matthäuserklärung.* GCS 40. Leipzig: J. C. Hinrichs, 1935.

Koester, Helmut. *Synoptische Überlieferung bei den Apostolischen Vätern.* TU 65. Berlin: Akademie-Verlag, 1957.

———, Review of Ulrich Wilckens, *Weisheit und Torheit. Gnomon* 33 (1961): 590–95.

_____, "One Jesus and Four Primitive Gospels." Pp. 158–204 in *Trajectories through Early Christianity*. By James M. Robinson and Helmut Koester. Philadelphia: Fortress Press, 1971.

_____, "GNOMAI DIAPHOROI: The Origin and Nature of Diversification in the History of Early Christianity." Pp. 114–57 in *Trajectories through Early Christianity*. By James M. Robinson and Helmut Koester. Philadelphia: Fortress Press, 1971.

_____, "La tradition apostolique et les origines du gnosticisme," *Revue de théologie et de philosophie* 119 (1978): 1–16.

_____, "Gnostic Writings as Witnesses for the Development of the Sayings Tradition." Pp. 238–56 in *The Rediscovery of Gnosticism*. Vol. 1: *The School of Valentinus*. Ed. Bentley Layton. Studies in the History of Religions 41. Leiden: E.J. Brill, 1980.

_____, *Introduction to the New Testament*. Vol. 2: *History and Literature of Early Christianity*. Philadelphia: Fortress Press, 1982.

_____, "History and Development of Mark's Gospel (From Mark to *Secret Mark* and 'Canonical' Mark)." Pp. 35–57 in *Colloquy on New Testament Studies*. Ed. Bruce C. Corley. Macon, GA: Mercer University Press, 1983.

_____, "Überlieferung und Geschichte der frühchristlichen Evangelienliteratur." *Aufstieg und Niedergang der römischen Welt*, Part II, Vol. 25,2 (1984): 1463–1542.

_____"Gnostic Sayings and Controversy Traditions in John 8:12–59." Pp. 97–110 in *Nag Hammadi, Gnosticism, and Early Christianity*. Ed. Charles W. Hedrick and Robert Hodgson, Jr. Peabody, MA: Hendrickson, 1986.

Kümmel, Werner Georg, *Introduction to the New Testament*. 17th ed. Trans. Howard C. Kee. Nashville, TN: Abingdon Press, 1975.

_____, *An Die Korinther I.II*. See Lietzmann.

Lake, Kirsopp, "Note IX. The Holy Spirit." Pp. 96–111 in *The Beginnings of Christianity, Part I: The Acts of the Apostles*. Ed. F. J. Foakes Jackson and Kirsopp Lake. Vol. V: *Additional Notes to the Commentary*. Ed. Kirsopp Lake and Henry J. Cadbury. London: Macmillan, 1933.

Lang, Friedrich, *Die Briefe an die Korinther*. Göttingen: Vandenhoeck & Ruprecht, 1986.

Laufen, Rudolf, *Die Doppelüberlieferung der Logienquelle und des Markusevangeliums*. Bonner Biblische Beiträge 54. Bonn: Peter Hanstein, 1980.

Lausberg, Heinrich, *Handbuch der literarischen Rhetorik: Eine Grundlegung der Literaturwissenschaft*. Munich: M. Hueber, 1960.

Layton, Bentley. "The Sources, Date and Transmission of Didache 1.3b–2.1." *Harvard Theological Review* 61 (1968): 343–83.

Lietzmann, Hans, *An die Korinther I. II*. Handbuch zum Neuen Testament 9. 4th ed. expanded by W. G. Kümmel. Tübingen: J.C.B. Mohr (Paul Siebeck), 1949.

Lightfoot, John, *Horae Hebraicae et Talmudicae, impensae in Evangelium S. Matthaei*. Cambridge: Field and Story, 1658.

Lightfoot, R. H., *St. John's Gospel: A Commentary*. Ed. C. F. Evans. Oxford: Clarendon Press, 1956.

Lohfink, Gerhard, "Jesus und die Ehescheidung: Zur Gattung und Sprachintention von Mt. 5, 32." Pp. 207–17 in *Biblische Randbemerkungen: Schülerfestschrift für Rudolf Schnackenburg*. Ed. Helmut Merklein and J. Lange. Würzburg: Echter Verlag, 1974.

Lohse, Eduard, ed., *Die Texte aus Qumran: Hebräisch und deutsch mit masoretischer Punktation; Übersetzung, Einführung und Anmerkungen.* Darmstadt: Wissenschftliche Buchgesellschaft, 1964.

———, "Das Evangelium für die Armen." *Zeitschrift für die Neutestamentliche Wissenschaft* 72 (1981): 51–64.

Lucian, *De morte Peregrini.* Pp. 1–51 in *Lucian.* Vol. 5. Trans. A. M. Harmon. LCL. Cambridge, MA: Harvard University Press; London: William Heinemann Ltd., 1936.

Luz, Ulrich, "Die wiederentdeckte Logienquelle," *Evangelische Theologie* 33 (1973): 527–33.

Lührmann, Dieter, *Die Redaktion der Logienquelle.* WMANT 33. Neukirchen-Vluyn: Neukirchener Verlag, 1969.

Maccoby, Hyam, "The Washing of Cups." *Journal for the Study of the New Testament* 14 (1982): 3–15.

MacDonald, Dennis Ronald, *The Legend and the Apostle: The Battle for Paul in Story and Canon.* Philadelphia: The Westminster Press, 1983.

———, *There Is No Male and Female: The Fate of a Dominical Saying in Paul and Gnosticism.* Harvard Dissertations in Religion 20. Philadelphia: Fortress Press, 1987.

Mack, Burton L., "The Kingdom Sayings in Mark." *Forum* 3,1 (1987): 3–47.

———, *A Myth of Innocence: Mark and Christian Origins.* Philadelphia: Fortress Press, 1988.

———, "The Kingdom That Didn't Come: A Social History of the Q Tradents." Pp. 608–35 in *Society of Biblical Literature 1988 Seminar Papers.* Ed. David J. Lull. Atlanta: Scholars Press, 1988.

———, and Vernon K. Robbins, *Patterns of Persuasion in the Gospels.* Sonoma, CA: Polebridge Press, forthcoming.

Mahnke, Hermann, *Die Versuchungsgeschichte im Rahmen der synoptischen Evangelien.* Beiträge zur biblischen Exegese und Theologie 9. Frankfurt: Peter Lang, 1978.

Maly, Karl, "I. Kor 12, 1–3, eine Regel zur Unterscheidung der Geister?" *Biblische Zeitschrift* 10 (1966): 82–95.

Mansfield, M. Robert, *Spirit and Gospel in Mark.* Peabody, MA: Hendrickson, 1987.

Manson, T. W., *The Sayings of Jesus.* London: SCM Press, 1949.

Martyn, J. Louis, *The Gospel of John in Christian History.* New York, Ramsey, Toronto: Paulist Press, 1979.

Mánek, Jindřich, "On the Mount—on the Plain (Mt V, 1—Lk VI, 17)." *Novum Testamentum* 9 (1967): 124–31.

McNeile, A. H., *The Gospel According to Matthew.* London: Macmillan & Co., 1915.

Mealand, D. L., "Community of Goods and Utopian Allusions in Acts II–IV." *Journal of Theological Studies* 78 (1977): 96–99.

Meeks, Wayne A., "Image of the Androgyne: Some Uses of a Symbol in Earliest Christianity." *History of Religions* 13 (1974): 165–208.

———, *The First Urban Christians.* New Haven and London: Yale University Press, 1983.

Metzger, Bruce M., *A Textual Commentary on the Greek New Testament. A Companion Volume to the United Bible Societies Greek New Testament.* 3d ed. London and New York: United Bible Societies, 1971.

_____, *The Early Versions of the New Testament: Their Origins, Transmission and Limitations.* Oxford: The Clarendon Press, 1977.

Meyer, Marvin, "The Youth in the *Secret Gospel of Mark.*" In *Reconsidering Christian Beginnings: The Challenge of the Apocryphal Jesus.* Ed. Ron Cameron. *Semeia.* (Forthcoming).

Meyer, Paul D., "The Community of Q." Ph.D. diss., University of Iowa, 1967.

Meyer, Rudolf, *Der Prophet aus Galiläa: Studie zum Jesusbild der drei ersten Evangelien.* Darmstadt: Wissenschaftliche Buchgesellschaft, 1970 (orig. pub., 1940).

Michel, H.-J., *Die Abschiedsrede des Paulus an die Kirche Apg 20, 17–38.* Studien zum Alten und Neuen Testament 35. Munich: Kösel, 1973.

Molnár, Amedeo, "L'évolution de la théologie Hussite." *Revue d'Histoire et de philosophie religieuses* 43 (1963): 113–71.

Montefiore, Hugh, "A Comparison of the Parables of the Gospel of Thomas and of the Synoptic Gospels." Pp. 11–39 in *Thomas and the Evangelists.* Ed. H. E. W. Turner and H. Montefiore. London: SCM Press, 1962.

Müller, Ulrich B., *Prophetie und Predigt im Neuen Testament.* Gütersloh: Gerd Mohn, 1975.

Munro, Winsome, *Authority in Paul and Peter: The Identificaion of a Pastoral Stratum in the Pauline Corpus and I Peter.* Cambridge and New York: Cambridge University Press, 1983.

Murphy-O'Connor, Jerome, "The Non-Pauline Character of I Corinthians 11:2–16?" *Journal of Biblical Literature* 95 (1976): 615–21.

Nestle. See Aland.

Neusner, Jacob, *Rabbinic Traditions about the Pharisees before 70.* 3 vols. Leiden: E.J. Brill, 1971.

_____, *Eliezer ben Hyrcanus: The Tradition and the Man.* 2 vols. SJLA 3–4. Leiden: E.J. Brill, 1973.

_____, "'First Cleanse the Inside.' The 'Halakic' Background of a Controversy-Saying." *New Testament Studies* 22 (1976): 486–95.

New, Silva, "Note XI. The Name, Baptism, and the Laying on of Hands." Pp. 134–40 in *The Beginnings of Christianity,* Part I: *The Acts of the Apostles.* Ed. F. J. Foakes Jackson and Kirsopp Lake. Vol. V: *Additional Notes to the Commentary.* Ed. Kirsopp Lake and Henry J. Cadbury. London: Macmillan, 1933.

Newmann, Louis E., *The Sanctity of the Seventh Year: A Study of Mishnah Tractate Shebiit.* Brown Judaic Studies 44. Chico, CA: Scholars Press, 1983.

Nicander, *Alexipharmaca.* Pp. 94–137 in *Nicander: The Poems and Poetical Fragments.* Ed. and trans. A. S. F. Gow and A. F. Scholfield. Cambridge: The University Press, 1953.

Niederwimmer, Kurt, "Erkennen und Lieben: Gedanken zum Verhältnis von Gnosis und Agape im ersten Korintherbrief." *Kerygma und Dogma* 11 (1965): 75–102.

Nolland, John, "Classical and Rabbinic Parallels to 'Physician, Heal Yourself' (Luke 4:23)." *Novum Testamentum* 21 (1979): 193–209.

O'Rourke, John J., "Asides in the Gospel of John." *Novum Testamentum* 21 (1979): 210–19.

Ovid, *Metamorphoses.* 6 vols. Trans. Frank Justus Miller. 2d ed. Rev. G. P. Goold. LCL. Cambridge, MA: Harvard University Press; London: William Heinemann Ltd., 1984.

Pagels, Elaine H., *The Gnostic Paul. Gnostic Exegesis of the Pauline Letters*. Philadelphia: Fortress Press, 1975.

Panagopoulos, J., *Prophetic Vocation in the New Testament and Today*. Supplements to Novum Testamentum 45. Leiden: E.J. Brill, 1977.

Parrott, Douglas M., "Eugnostos and the Sophia of Jesus Christ." In *The Nag Hammadi Library in English*. 3d rev. ed. Ed. James M. Robinson. San Francisco: Harper & Row, 1988.

Patterson, Stephen J., "The Gospel of Thomas within the Development of Early Christianity," Ph.D. diss., Claremont Graduate School, 1988.

Pearson, Birger A., *The Pneumatikos-Psychikos Terminology in 1 Corinthians: A Study in the Theology of the Corinthian Opponents of Paul and Its Relation to Gnosticism*. SBLDS 12. Missoula, MT: Society of Biblical Literature, 1973.

Perdue, Leo G. "The Wisdom Sayings of Jesus." *Forum* 2,3 (1986): 3–35.

Perelman, Chaim, and L. Olbrechts-Tyteca, *The New Rhetoric: A Treatise on Argumentation*. Notre Dame, IN: University of Notre Dame Press, 1969.

Perrin, Norman, *Rediscovering the Teaching of Jesus*. London: SCM Press, 1967.

Perry, Ben Edwin, *The Ancient Romances. A Literary-Historical Account of Their Origins*. Sather Classical Lectures 37. Berkeley and Los Angeles: University of California Press, 1967.

Petronius. Trans. Michael Heseltine; Seneca, *Apocolocyntosis*. Trans. W. H. D. Rouse. LCL. Cambridge, MA: Harvard University Press; London: William Heinemann Ltd., 1951.

Pilgrim, Walter E., *Good News to the Poor: Wealth and Poverty in Luke–Acts*. Minneapolis, MN: Augsburg Publishing House, 1981.

Plato, *Phaedrus*. Pp. 412–579 in *Plato*. Vol. 1. Trans. Harold North Fowler. LCL. Cambridge, MA: Harvard University Press; London: William Heinemann Ltd., 1982.

———, *The Republic*. 2 vols. Trans. Paul Shorey. LCL. London: William Heinemann Ltd.; New York: G. P. Putnam's Sons, 1930.

Plutarch, *Coniugalia praecepta*. Pp. 138–46 in *Plutarch's Moralia*. Vol. 2. Trans. Frank Cole Babbitt. LCL. London: William Heinemann Ltd.; New York: G. P. Putnam's Sons, 1928.

———, *Moralia*. 14 vols. Trans. Frank Cole Babbit, et al. LCL. London: William Heinemann Ltd.; New York: G. P. Putnam's Sons, 1928ff.

Pöhlmann, Robert von, *Geschichte der sozialen Frage und des Sozialismus in der antiken Welt*. Munich: C. H. Beck, 1925.

Polag, Athanasius, *Die Christologie der Logienquelle*. WMANT 45. Neukirchen-Vluyn: Neukirchener Verlag, 1977.

———, *Fragmenta Q: Textheft zur Logienquelle Q*. Neukirchen-Vluyn: Neukirchener Verlag, 1979.

Polybius, *The Histories*. 6 vols. Trans. W. R. Paton, et al. LCL. London: William Heinemann; New York: G. P. Putnam's Sons, 1922ff.

Popkes, Wiard, "Gemeinschaft." *Reallexikon für Antike und Christentum* 9 (1976): 1100–1145.

Przybylski, Benno, *Righteousness in Matthew and His World of Thought*. SNTSMS 41. Cambridge: Cambridge University Press, 1980.

Quesnell, Quentin, "The Mar Saba Clementine: A Question of Evidence." *Catholic Biblical Quarterly* 37 (1975): 48–67.

_____, "A Reply to Morton Smith." *Catholic Biblical Quarterly* 38 (1976): 200–203.

Quintilian, *Institutio Oratio.* 4 vols. Trans. H. E. Butler. LCL. London: William Heinemann; New York: G. P. Putnam's Sons, 1920–22.

Quispel, Gilles, "The Gospel of Thomas and the New Testament." *Vigiliae Christianae* 11 (1957): 189–207.

_____, "L'Evangile selon Thomas et le Diatessearon." *Vigiliae Christianae* 13 (1959): 87–117.

Ranke, E., *Codex Fuldensis.* Marburg and Leipzig: N. G. Elwert, 1865.

Refoulé, François, "Unité de l'Epître aux Romains et histoire du salut." *Revue des sciences philosophiques et théologiques* 71 (1987): 219–42.

Reiling, J., *Hermas and Christian Prophecy: A Study of the Eleventh Mandate.* Leiden: E.J. Brill, 1973.

Rese, Martin, "Das Lukas-Evangelium: Ein Forschungsbericht." *Aufstieg und Niedergang der römischen Welt,* Part II, Vol. 25, 3 (1985): 2258–2328.

Rimmon-Kenan, Shlomith, *Narrative Fiction. Contemporary Poetics.* London and New York: Methuen Press, 1983.

Robbins, Vernon K., *Jesus the Teacher. A Socio-rhetorical Interpretation of Mark.* Philadelphia: Fortress Press, 1984.

_____, "Pronouncement Stories from a Rhetorical Perspective." *Forum* 4,2 (1988): 3–32.

Robertson, Archibald, and Alfred Plummer, *A Critical and Exegetical Commentary on the First Epistle of St Paul to the Corinthians.* Edinburgh: T. & T. Clark, 1953.

Robinson, James M., *The Problem of History in Mark.* Studies in Biblical Theology 21. London: SCM Press, 1957.

_____, "Basic Shifts in German Theology." *Interpretation* 16 (1962): 76–97.

_____, "LOGOI SOPHON: Zur Gattung der Spruchquelle Q." Pp. 77–96 in *Zeit und Geschichte. Dankesgabe an Rudolf Bultmann.* Ed. Erich Dinkler. Tübingen: J.C.B. Mohr (Paul Siebeck), 1964.

_____, "Kerygma and History in the New Testament." Pp. 114–50 in *The Bible in Modern Scholarship.* Ed. J. Philip Hyatt. Nashville, TN: Abingdon Press, 1965; reprinted as pp. 20–70 in *Trajectories through Early Christianity.* By James M. Robinson and Helmut Koester. Philadelphia: Fortress Press, 1971.

_____, and Helmut Koester, *Trajectories Through Early Christianity.* Philadelphia: Fortress Press, 1971.

_____, "LOGOI SOPHON: On the Gattung of Q." Pp. 71–113 in *Trajectories through Early Christianity.* By James M. Robinson and Helmut Koester. Philadelphia: Fortress Press, 1971.

_____, "Jesus as Sophos and Sophia: Wisdom Tradition and the Gospels." Pp. 1–16 in *Aspects of Wisdom in Judaism and Early Christianity.* Ed. Robert L. Wilken. Notre Dame, IN, and London: Notre Dame University Press, 1975.

_____, "Jesus—From Easter to Valentinus (Or to the Apostles' Creed)." *Journal of Biblical Literature* 101 (1982): 5–37.

_____, "The Sayings of Jesus: Q." *Drew Gateway* 54,1 (1983): 26–38.

_____, "Judaism, Hellenism, Christianity: Jesus' Followers in Galilee until 70 CE." *Archivio de Filosofia* 53 (1985): 241–50.

_____, "On Bridging the Gulf from Q to the Gospel of Thomas." Pp. 127–75 in *Nag Hammadi, Gnosticism, and Early Christianity.* Ed. Charles W. Hedrick and Robert Hodgson, Jr. Peabody, MA: Hendrickson, 1986.

———, "Very Goddess and Very Man." Pp. 111–22 in *Encountering Jesus: A Debate on Christology*. Ed. Stephen T. Davis. Atlanta: John Knox Press, 1988.

Rudolf, Kurt, "Gnosis und Gnostizismus: Ein Forschungsbericht." *Theologische Rundschau* 34 (1969): 121–75, 181–231, 358–61.

Sanders, E. P., "The Covenant as a Soteriological Category and the Nature of Salvation in Palestinian and Hellenistic Judaism." Pp. 11–44 in *Jews, Greeks and Christians. Studies in Honor of W. D. Davies*. SJLA 21. Ed. R. G. Hamerton-Kelly and R. Scroggs. Leiden: E.J. Brill, 1976.

———, *Paul and Palestinian Judaism: A Comparison of Patterns of Religion*. Philadelphia: Fortress Press; London: SCM Press, 1977.

Sanders, Jack T., "First Corinthians 13: Its Interpretation Since the First World War." *Interpretation* 20 (1966): 159–87.

Sato, Migaku, *Q und Prophetie. Studien zur Gattungs- und Traditionsgeschichte der Quelle Q*. WUNT 2/29. Tübingen: J.C.B. Mohr [Paul Siebeck], 1988.

Schelkle, Karl Hermann, "Israel und Kirche im Anfang." *Theologische Quartalschrift* 163 (1983): 86–95.

Schenk, Wolfgang, *Synopse zur Redenquelle der Evangelien*. Düsseldorf: Patmos Verlag, 1981.

———, *Die Sprache des Matthäus: Die Text-Konstituenten in ihren makro- und mikrostrukturellen Relationen*. Göttingen: Vandenhoeck & Ruprecht, 1987.

Schenke, Hans-Martin, "The Mystery of the Gospel of Mark." *The Second Century* 4 (1984): 65–82.

———, "The Function and Background of the Beloved Disciple in the Gospel of John." Pp. 111–25 in *Nag Hammadi, Gnosticism, and Early Christianity*. Ed. Charles W. Hedrick and Robert Hodgson, Jr. Peabody, MA: Hendrickson, 1986.

Schlier, Heinrich, "Kerygma und Sophia: Zur neutestamentlichen Grundlage des Dogmas." Pp. 206–32 in *Der Zeit der Kirche*. Freiburg: Herder, 1958.

Schlosser, Jacques, *Le Règne de Dieu dans les dits de Jésus*. EBib. Paris: J. Gabalda et Cie., 1980.

Schmithals, Walter, *Gnosticism in Corinth: An Investigation of the Letters to the Corinthians*. Trans. John E. Steely. Nashville, TN, and New York: Abingdon Press, 1971.

———, "On the Composition and Earliest Collection of the Major Epistles of Paul." Pp. 239–74 in *Paul and the Gnostics*. By Walter Schmithals. Trans. John E. Steely. Nashville, TN: Abingdon Press, 1972.

———, *Einleitung in die drei ersten Evangelien*. Berlin and New York: Walter de Gruyter & Co., 1985.

Schnelle, Udo, "Jesus, ein Jude aus Galiläa." *Biblische Zeitschrift* 32 (1988): 107–13.

Schottroff, Luise, and Wolfgang Stegemann, *Jesus von Nazareth—Hoffnung der Armen*. Urban Taschenbücher 639. Stuttgart: Kohlammer, 1978.

Schöttgen, Johann Christian, *Horae Hebraicae et Talmudicae in universum Novum Testamentum*. 2 vols. Dresden and Leipzig: Hekel, 1733–42.

Schrage, Wolfgang, *Das Verhältnis des Thomas-Evangeliums zur synoptischen Tradition und zu den koptischen Evangelienübersetzungen*. BZNW 30. Berlin: Alfred Töpelmann, 1964.

Schroeder, H.-H., "Haben Jesu Worte über Armut und Reichtum Folgen für das soziale Verhalten?" Pp. 397–409 in *Studien zum Text und zur Ethik des Neuen*

194 • *Works Consulted*

Testaments: Festschrift für H. Greeven. Berlin and New York: Walter de Gruyter & Co., 1986.

Schulz, Siegfried, "Die Bedeutung des Markus für die Theologiegeschichte des Urchristentums." *Studia Evangelica* 2 (1964): 138–39.

———, *Q: Die Spruchquelle der Evangelisten.* Zurich: Theologischer Verlag, 1972.

Schweizer, Eduard, "πνεῦμα, πνευματικός." *Theological Dictionary of the New Testament* 6 (1968): 396–451.

———, *The Holy Spirit.* Trans. and ed. Reginald H. and Ilse Fuller. Philadelphia: Fortress Press, 1980= *Heiliger Geist.* Stuttgart: Kreuz Verlag, 1978.

———, "Jesus Christus I. Neues Testament." *Theologische Realenzyklopädie* 16 (1987): 671–726.

Scobie, Charles H. H., *John the Baptist.* Philadelphia: Fortress Press, 1964.

Scott, Bernard Brandon, "Essaying the Rock: The Authenticity of the Jesus Parable Tradition." *Forum* 2,1 (1986): 3–53.

Scott, Ernest F., *The Spirit in the New Testament.* New York: George H. Doran, 1923.

Sellin, G., "Das 'Geheimnis' der Weisheit und das Rätsel der 'Christuspartei' (zu I. Kor 1–4)." *Zeitschrift für die Neutestamentliche Wissenschaft* 73 (1982): 69–96.

Seneca, *Ad Lucilium epistulae morales.* 3 vols. Trans. Richard M. Gummere. LCL. London: William Heinemann; New York: G. P. Putnam's Sons, 1925ff.

Sheeley, Steven M., "Narrative Asides in Luke-Acts." Ph.D. diss., Southern Baptist Theological Seminary, 1986.

Sieber, John Harold, "A Redactional Analysis of the Synoptic Gospels with Regard to the Question of the Sources of the Gospel of Thomas." Ph.D. diss., Claremont Graduate School, 1966.

Siegert, Folker, *Argumentation bei Paulus gezeigt an Röm 9–11.* WUNT 34. Tübingen: J. C. B. Mohr (Paul Siebeck), 1985.

Smith, Morton, "Monasteries and Their Manuscripts." *Archaeology* 13 (1960): 172–77.

———, *Clement of Alexandria and a Secret Gospel of Mark.* Cambridge, MA: Harvard University Press, 1973.

———, *The Secret Gospel: The Discovery and Interpretation of the Secret Gospel According to Mark.* New York: Harper & Row, 1973.

———, "On the Authenticity of the Mar Saba Letter of Clement." *Catholic Biblical Quarterly* 38 (1976): 196–99.

———, "Clement of Alexandria and Secret Mark: The Score at the End of the First Decade." *Harvard Theological Review* 75 (1982): 449–61.

———, "Regarding *Secret Mark:* A Response by Morton Smith to the Account by Per Beskow." *Journal of Biblical Literature* 103 (1984): 624.

Stanton, Graham N., Review of *Essays on the Sermon on the Mount,* by Hans Dieter Betz. *Journal of Theological Studies* 37 (1986): 521–23.

———, "The Origin and Purpose of Matthew's Sermon on the Mount." Pp. 181–92 in *Tradition and Interpretation in the New Testament. Essays in Honor of E. Earle Ellis for His 60th Birthday.* Ed. Gerald F. Hawthorne with Otto Betz. Grand Rapids, MI: William B. Eerdmans Publishing Company, 1987.

Stauffer, Ethelbert, "Jesus, Geschichte und Verkündigung." *Aufstieg und Niedergang der römischen Welt,* Part II, Vol. 25,1 (1982): 3–130.

Stählin, Otto, ed., *Clemens Alexandrinus.* Vol. 4/1: *Register.* 2d ed. Ursula Treu. GCS. Berlin: Akademie-Verlag, 1980.

Stendahl, Krister, "Kerygma und Kerygmatisch: Von zweideutigen Ausdrücken der

Predigt der Urkirche—und unserer." *Theologische Literaturzeitung* 77 (1952): 715–20.

———, *The School of St. Matthew and Its Use of the Old Testament*. 2d ed. Philadelphia: Fortress Press, 1968.

Stier, Rudolf, *Die Reden des Herrn Jesu*. 6 vols. Barmen: Langewiesche, 1843–47.

Strauss, David Friedrich, *Das Leben Jesu, kritisch bearbeitet*. 2 vols. Tübingen: Osiander, 1835–36.

Streeter, B. H., *The Four Gospels*. London: Macmillan & Co., 1924.

Stronstad, Roger, *The Charismatic Theology of St. Luke*. Peabody, MA: Hendrickson, 1984.

Stuhlmacher, Peter, "The Hermeneutical Significance of 1 Cor 2:6–16." Pp. 328–47 in *Tradition and Interpretation in the New Testament*. Ed. Gerald F. Hawthorne with Otto Betz. Grand Rapids, MI: William B. Eerdmans Publishing Company; Tübingen: J.C.B. Mohr (Paul Siebeck), 1987.

Sweet, J. P. M., "A Sign for Unbelievers: Paul's Attitude to Glossolalia." *New Testament Studies* 13 (1967): 240–57.

Talbert, Charles H., *Luke and the Gnostics*. Nashville, TN: Abingdon Press, 1966.

Talley, Thomas, "Liturgical Time in the Ancient Church: The State of Research." *Studia Liturgica* 14 (1982): 34–51.

Tannehill, Robert C., "The 'Focal Instance' as a Form of New Testament Speech: A Study of Matthew 5:39b–42." *Journal of Religion* 50 (1970): 372–85.

———, *The Sword of His Mouth*. Semeia Supplements 1. Philadelphia: Fortress Press, 1975.

Tenney, Merrill C., "The Footnotes of John's Gospel." *Bibliotheca Sacra* 117 (1960): 350–64.

Theissen, Gerd, *Soziologie der Jesusbewegung*. Theologische Existenz heute 194. Munich: Kaiser Verlag, 1977.

———, "Die soziologische Auswertung religiöser Überlieferungen." Pp. 35–54 in *Studien zur Soziologie des Urchristentums*. By Gerd Theissen. 2d ed. WUNT 19. Tübingen: J.C.B. Mohr (Paul Siebeck), 1983.

———, "Theoretische Probleme religionsgeschichtlicher Forschung und die Analyse des Urchristentums." Pp. 55–78 in *Studien zur Soziologie des Urchristentums* (see above).

———, "Wanderradikalismus." Pp. 79–105 in *Studien zur Soziologie des Urchristentums* (see above).

———, *Psychological Aspects of Pauline Theology*. Trans. John P. Galvin. Philadelphia: Fortress Press, 1987.

Theophrastus, *Enquiry into Plants*. 2 vols. Trans. Arthur Hort. LCL. London: William Heinemann; New York: G. P. Putnam's Sons, 1916.

Theophylactus, *Enarratio in Evangelium S. Matthaei*. PG 123. Paris: Migne, 1864.

Tholuck, August, *Die Bergrede Christi*. 5th ed. Gotha: Perthes, 1872.

Thrall, Margaret E., "The Problem of II Cor. VI. 14–VII. 1 in Some Recent Discussion." *New Testament Studies* 24 (1978): 132–48.

Throckmorton, Burton H., ed., *Gospel Parallels: A Synopsis of the First Three Gospels*. 4th ed. Nashville, TN, and Camden, NJ: Thomas Nelson, 1979.

Thucydides. 4 vols. Trans. Charles Forster Smith. LCL. Cambridge, MA: Harvard University Press; London: William Heinemann Ltd., 1956.

Trilling, Wolfgang, "Die Täufertradition bei Matthäus." *Biblische Zeitschrift* NF 3 (1959): 271–89.

Tuckett, Christopher M., *Nag Hammadi and the Gospel Tradition.* Edinburgh: T. & T. Clark, 1986.

Uro, Risto, *Sheep among the Wolves: A Study on the Mission Instructions of Q.* Annales Academiae Scientiarum Fennicae, Dissertationes Humanarum Litterarum 47. Helsinki: Suomalainen Tiedeakatemia, 1987.

Vaage, Leif, "The Woes in Q (and Matthew and Luke): Deciphering the Rhetoric of Criticism." Pp. 582–607 in *Society of Biblical Literature 1988 Seminar Papers.* Ed. David J. Lull. Atlanta: Scholars Press, 1988.

Van Belle, Gilbert, *Les parenthèses dans l'Evangile de Jean. Aperçu historique et classification du texte grec de Jean.* Studiorum novi testamenti auxilia 11. Leuven: Peeters/University Press, 1985.

Van der Horst, Pieter W., ed. and trans., *The Sentences of Pseudo-Phocylides.* Studia in Veteris Testamenti Pseudepigrapha 4. Leiden: E.J. Brill, 1978.

Vermes, Geza, *The Dead Sea Scrolls in English.* Rev. ed. Baltimore, MD: Penguin, 1968.

———, *Jesus the Jew: A Historian's Reading of the Gospels.* Philadelphia: Fortress Press, 1981 (orig. pub., 1973).

Vielhauer, Phillip, *Oikodome: Das Bild vom Bau in der christlichen Literatur vom Neuen Testament bis Clemens Alexandrinus.* Karlsruhe-Durlach: Gebr. Tron, 1940.

Voss, Isaac, ed., *Epistulae genuinae S. Ignatii Martyris.* Amsterdam: Blaeu, 1646.

Walker, William O., Jr., "I Corinthians 11:2–16 and Paul's Views Regarding Women." *Journal of Biblical Literature* 94 (1975): 94–110.

———, "The 'Theology of Woman's Place' and the 'Paulinist' Tradition." *Semeia* 28 (1983): 101–12.

———, "The Burden of Proof in Identifying Interpolations in the Pauline Letters." *New Testament Studies* 33 (1987): 610–18.

Watson, Duane F., "A Rhetorical Analysis of Philippians and Its Implications for the Unity Question." *Novum Testamentum* 30 (1988): 57–88.

Wead, David W., *The Literary Devices in John's Gospel.* Theologische Dissertationen 4. Basel: Friedrich Reinhart Kommission, 1979.

Weiss, Bernhard, "Die Redestücke des apostolischen Matthäus. Mit besonderer Berücksichtigung von 'Dr. H. J. Holtzmann, die synoptischen Evangelien, ihr Ursprung und geschichtlicher Charakter. Leipzig 1863.'" *Jahrbücher für deutsche Theologie* 9 (1864): 49–140.

———, *Das Matthäusevangelium und seine Lucas-Parallelen.* Halle: Buchhandlung des Waisenhauses, 1876.

Weiss, Johannes, *Die Predigt Jesu vom Reiche Gottes.* Göttingen: Vandenhoeck und Ruprecht, 1892; 3d ed., 1964.

———, review of C. F. G. Heinrici, *Die Bergpredigt. Theologische Rundschau* 4 (1901): 153–55.

Weisse, Christian Hermann, *Die evangelische Geschichte, kritisch und philosophisch bearbeitet.* 2 vols. Leipzig: Breitkopf and Härtel, 1838.

Wellhausen, Julius, *Das Evangelium Lucae übersetzt und erklärt.* Berlin: Reimer, 1904.

———, *Das Evangelium Matthaei übersetzt und erklärt.* Berlin: Reimer, 1904; 2d ed., 1914.

_____, *Einleitung in die drei ersten Evangelien*. Berlin: Reimer, 1905; 2d ed., 1911.

_____, *Evangelienkommentare*. Mit einer Einleitung von Martin Hengel. Berlin: Walter de Gruyter & Co., 1987.

Wernle, Paul, *Die synoptische Frage*. Freiburg, Leipzig, and Tübingen: J.C.B. Mohr (Paul Siebeck), 1899.

Wilckens, Ulrich, "Zu 1. Kor. 2:1–16." Pp. 501–37 in *Theologia Crucis—Signum*. Ed. C. Andreson and G. Klein. Tübingen: J.C.B. Mohr (Paul Siebeck), 1979.

Wild, Robert A., "The Encounter between Pharisaic and Christian Judaism: Some Early Evidence." *Novum Testamentum* 27 (1985): 113–17.

Wink, Walter. "Neither Passivity nor Violence: Jesus' Third Way." Pp. 210–24 in *Society of Biblical Literature 1988 Seminar Papers*. Ed. David J. Lull. Atlanta: Scholars Press, 1988.

Wisse, Frederik, "The Nature and Purpose of Redactional Changes in Early Christian Texts: The Canonical Gospels." In *Gospel Traditions in the Second Century*. Ed. William L. Petersen. Studies in Christianity and Judaism in Antiquity. Notre Dame, IN: Notre Dame University Press, 1989.

Wolff, Christian, *Der erste Brief des Paulus an die Korinther*. Vol. 2. Berlin: Evangelische Verlagsanstalt, 1982.

Worsley, Peter, *The Trumpet Shall Sound: A Study of "Cargo" Cults in Melanesia*. 2d, augmented ed. New York: Schocken Books, 1968.

Wrege, Hans-Theo, *Die Überlieferungsgeschichte der Bergpredigt*. WUNT 9. Tübingen: J.C.B. Mohr (Paul Siebeck), 1968.

Wuellner, Wilhelm, "Narrative Criticism and the Lazarus Story," read at the Annual Meeting of S.N.T.S. at Rome, 1981.

_____, "The Whispering Wizard of the Fourth Gospel. Response to Culpepper's Approach to the Narrator in John." Unpublished paper.

Zeller, Dieter, "Die Versuchungen Jesu in der Logienquelle." *Trierer Theologische Zeitschrift* 89 (1980): 61–73.

_____, *Kommentar zur Logienquelle*. Stuttgarter kleiner Kommentar, Neues Testament 21. Stuttgart: Verlag Katholisches Bibelwerk, 1984.

Index of Ancient Literature

Old Testament

New Testament

Old Testament Pseudepigrapha

Dead Sea Scrolls

Rabbinic Literature

Nag Hammadi Tractates and Related Literature

Patristic Literature

Hellenistic and Classical Literature

Index of Modern Authors

Index of Subjects

Abraham, 85
acclamation, 163
adultery, 45
Akiba, 42
allegorical interpretation, 134
almsgiving, 112, 113, 115
Andrew (disciple), 100, 101
apocalyptic, apocalypticism, 5–17, 72, 106, 111, 124, 134
Apollos, 52
apostle, apostolic, 111, 116, 136, 153–66
apostrophe (rhetorical device), 75, 76
apothegm, 54
Aramaic language, 21, 22, 25, 27, 28, 31, 33
aretalogy, 104
ascetics, 113
aside (rhetorical device), 74, 75, 76, 77–81, 82, 89, 93
authority (scriptural), 137, 138

baptism, 12, 13, 14, 52, 84, 122, 124–33, 139
    Spirit baptism, 124, 125, 126, 128
beatitudes, 108, 113, 114
Beloved Disciple (Johannine), 94, 99–105
Bodmer Papyri, 94
Byzantine period, 176

canon, 135, 137, 175
cargo cults, 72
Carpocratians, Carpocrates, 95, 96, 110
catchword connections, 66
charismatic, charismatics, 123, 161, 162, 165
chria, chriae, 47, 49
Christ, 52, 136, 139, 145, 148, 152–66
Christian origins, 3, 4, 5, 6, 7, 17, 35
christology, 3, 5, 17, 25, 32, 153
Clement of Alexandria, 95, 96, 97
conspiracy theory, 175, 177
Corinth, Corinthians, 134–66
covenant, 36, 47
cross (of Christ), 152–66

crucifixion, 53, 119, 120, 126, 133
Cynics, 9, 12

diatribe, 91
disciples of Jesus, 20, 23, 26, 34, 113, 114, 116, 119–33
divorce, 37, 44, 45

Easter, 4, 5, 6, 10, 12, 17, 109, 111, 114
ecstasy (religious), 141, 143, 146, 163, 164, 166
Eliezer b. Hyrcanus, 42
Elijah, 129
Epiphanes, 110
eschatology, 49, 59, 60, 72, 73, 106, 107, 108, 111, 112, 113, 125
Essenes, 107, 109, 110, 123, 134
ethics, 37, 38, 40, 41, 43, 47, 48

false teachers (early Christian), 116, 117
folly, 151–66
form criticism, 66, 68, 69, 131

Gentiles, 47
geology, 169
gloss (textual), glossator, 43, 46, 47
Gnosticism, gnostic, 3, 4, 8, 11, 50, 51, 52, 64–73, 96, 102, 103, 137, 177
God, 40, 41, 45, 140, 141, 143, 144, 145, 147, 153–66
gospel traditions, 3, 4, 119, 129, 133
Greek language, 22, 25, 27, 28, 31, 33, 156, 158, 159, 160
Greeks (Gentiles), 153, 154, 163

halakah, 36, 37, 38, 46
Hanina ben Dosa, 123
head covering, 137, 139, 145, 146
Heilsgeschichte, 45
Hellenism, 107, 110, 137, 167
Hellenistic Judaism, 45, 47

212